LIBERAL JUDAISM

Books by Eugene B. Borowitz

A Layman's Introduction
to Religious Existentialism

A New Jewish Theology in the Making

How Can a Jew Speak of Faith Today?

Choosing a Sex Ethic

The Mask Jews Wear

Reform Judaism Today

Understanding Judaism

Contemporary Christologies,
a Jewish Response

Choices in Modern Jewish Thought

Liberal Judaism

LIBERAL JUDAISM

·BY·

EUGENE B. BOROWITZ

UNION OF AMERICAN HEBREW CONGREGATIONS

NEW YORK ◆ NEW YORK

Library of Congress Cataloging in Publication Data

Borowitz, Eugene B.
  Liberal Judaism.

  1. Reform Judaism.   I. Title.
BM197.B66   1984   296.8'346   83–17997
ISBN 0–8074–0264–8

Book design by Victoria Hartman

*For
Drucy and Phil
and Zoey Rose*

CONTENTS

FOREWORD
ABOUT LIBERAL JUDAISM

I have written this book for the person who knows something about liberal Judaism and now wants to learn more about its religious ideas. That goal involves two tasks. One is historical. I therefore present a quick overview of the central attitudes of the Bible and Talmud toward significant Jewish beliefs and, where relevant, of their later development. I have given greater attention to the second task, understanding some modern efforts to explain Jewish belief. Our thinkers have created several intellectual options to give credence to our religious tradition. Delving into their ideas challenges our old ways of thinking about Judaism, not the least because contemporary philosophers often disagree with one another. I see this pluralism as a sign of our spiritual vitality. I trust that the stimulation of confronting these differing views will enable you to grow as a person and in devotion to Judaism.

The theories of Jewish belief described here are mostly not identified with one or another of our American non-Orthodox religious movements. They are part of the intellectual give-and-take of all of them—sometimes even including Orthodoxy. I use the term "liberal" Judaism as an inclusive way of referring to this pluralistic sector of our contemporary Jewish world of ideas. When, as in Part Three, *The Bible and Tradition,* the differences between the movements are associated with specific conceptual issues, I name the groups involved.

In my descriptions of classic Jewish belief and modern Jewish thought, I have tried to reflect the mainstream of contemporary scholarship. Where the interpretation or theorizing is my own, I indicate that by using the first person singular. For the sake of brevity and clarity, a great deal of qualifying data and detail was omitted. In partial compensation, citations are included from a broad variety of the sources in which the ideas were historically developed. The English renderings represent my interpretation of the meaning of the texts.

The individual chapters and the four parts themselves were designed to be read independently of one another. That way you can directly pursue what interests you. However, a systematic development underlies the work as a whole so that, read in order, its various sections complement and strengthen one another.

In preparing this manuscript, I sought the guidance of its intended readers. District Three of the National Federation of Temple Sisterhoods graciously devoted a spring course at the New York School of the HUC-JIR to reading and responding to an early draft of some chapters from Parts One and Two of the book. Some time later, thanks to an invitation from the Adult Education chairperson of the synagogue to which I belong, I had the benefit of the reactions of some of my neighbors to a few chapters from Part Four. I am deeply grateful to all those who participated in these sessions, particularly those who reacted in writing to the material. I learned much from their criticism. They also taught me a great deal about overcoming the distance that separates professors and intelligent, devoted laypeople. Their partnership should be kept in mind whenever my pages truly communicate.

Over the years I have had many fruitful discussions concerning human nature with my wife, Estelle, who is a psychoanalyst in private practice and on the faculty of the Center for Modern Psychoanalytic Studies. She is, however, not to be held responsible for the numerous psychological comments I have made all through this book.

I also appreciate the help of the professionals who sought to aid me in improving this book, in the first instance, the various readers of the CCAR-UAHC Commission on Jewish Education, beginning with its director, Rabbi Daniel B. Syme, and including Rabbis Morton Bauman, Jordan Pearlson, M. Robert Syme, Leonard Schoolman, David Katz, Kenneth Roseman, and Patrice Heller.

I was saved from several scholarly errors and usefully forced to rethink some of my judgments by the careful, critical comments of Rabbi Bernard Zlotowitz and therefore I am particularly indebted to him. Steven Schnur and Josette Knight of the UAHC Publications Department kindly lent their expertise to smooth out the flow of the text and free it of stylistic contradictions.

This work has occupied me on and off for several years. It will always have a special place in my heart, in part for the reason given in the Afterword. I therefore repeat in joy the words of the Psalmist:

לֹא־אָמוּת כִּי־אֶחְיֶה וַאֲסַפֵּר מַעֲשֵׂי יָהּ
אוֹדְךָ כִּי עֲנִיתָנִי וַתְּהִי־לִי לִישׁוּעָה

> I shall not die but live
> > and proclaim Adonai's deeds.
> I praise You, for You answered me
> > and have become my deliverance. (118:17,21)

The New York School   *Eugene B. Borowitz*
Hebrew Union College-
Jewish Institute of Religion

ABBREVIATIONS

A.Z.	Avodah Zarah	Mak.	Makkot
Ber.	Berachot	Mal.	Malachi
B.B.	Bava Batra	Matt.	Matthew
B.K.	Bava Kama	Mech.	Mechilta
B.M.	Bava Metzia	Men.	Menachot
Chul.	Chullin	Ned.	Nedarim
Deut.	Deuteronomy	Neh.	Nehemiah
Deut. R.	Deuteronomy Rabbah	Num.	Numbers
		Num. R.	Numbers Rabbah
Eccles. R.	Ecclesiastes Rabbah	Oh.	Ohalot
		P. Av.	Pirke Avot
Er.	Eruvin	Pe.	Peah
Exod.	Exodus	Pes.	Pesachim
Exod. R.	Exodus Rabbah	Prov.	Proverbs
Ezek.	Ezekiel	Ps.	Psalms
Gen.	Genesis	R.	Rabbi
Gen. R.	Genesis Rabbah	Sam.	Samuel
Git.	Gittin	San.	Sanhedrin
Hab.	Habakkuk	Shab.	Shabbat
Judg.	Judges	Shev.	Shevuot
Ket.	Ketuvot	Sot.	Sotah
Kid.	Kiddushin	Suk.	Sukot
Lam. R.	Lamentations Rabbah	Taan.	Taanit
		Tan.	Tanchuma
Lev.	Leviticus	Tos.	Tosefta
Lev. R.	Leviticus Rabbah	Y.	Yerushalmi
Macc.	Maccabees	Yev.	Yevamot

IN BEGINNING

ETERNAL TRUTHS
IN CHANGING FORMS

Some years ago at a friend's apartment, another guest, hearing I was a rabbi, started to talk to me about God. He asked me to help him regain his belief. I tried to explain some of our modern reasons for having faith, but the more he understood what I was saying the more disturbed he became. Finally, in exasperation he exclaimed, "No, no! That's not the God I want. If I can't have an old man, with a beard like my grandfather's, sitting on a throne in heaven, I don't want any God at all!" I was startled at the comment for I knew him to be a person of high intelligence and I was not a little relieved to see him smiling. What he had said suddenly came to him as a powerful self-revelation. Then our conversation could begin in earnest.

Since that experience, I have encountered similar attitudes many times. People who are not upset to learn that Jewish practices evolved over the years may become quite anxious when they hear that the same is true of our way of speaking about God. Here, as in many other religious areas, some psychological as well as intellectual probing will be helpful.

In our doubting, modern world, many of us display an ironic ambivalence about belief in God. Emotionally, we connect having faith with some of the most pleasant experiences of our childhood. We felt warm and comforted knowing there was a God in the universe who watched over people and guided their destinies. For all that God commanded and judged us, sometimes making us feel guilty, our faith set firm standards for our lives and thereby gave us a feeling of worth and security.

3

To lose that close, dear, concerned God is to lose much that is certain and significant in our lives. But to hold on to that God seems to keep religion on the level of our childhood imagination, an attitude we can reinforce by taking literally the Bible and prayer book terms for God. In other aspects of our lives we are quite sophisticated: we know babies aren't brought by storks. Faith in God, however, seems an infantile notion, one utterly inconsistent with our mature sense of reality. Nature runs largely on its own, history moves in random ways, and good people are not always rewarded. We would like to believe in a parent-like God, yet that is the God education and experience will not let us accept. The infant in us yearns for the comforting God of childhood and resists modern Jewish views of God for they are not as cozy as the faith we yearn for. And the adult in us doubts that any God worth worshiping can be part of our demystified world outlook.

The Major Intellectual Argument for Permanence: God Is One

The psychological basis for denying that our religious beliefs should change with time can be supported by two good intellectual arguments. If there is but one God then there ought to be one religious truth, not a series of shifting ideas. Then, too, if nothing is permanent in Judaism, not even our ideas about God, we cannot know whether we today are being true to Judaism. Modern Jewish thinkers have been troubled by these issues but I believe they have responded to them effectively. Let me deal with the first of these problems here. I shall return to the other at the end of this chapter.

Logically, one cannot deny that if there is but one God in the universe then there can be but one truth. But we must now ask, "Who among us is intelligent enough to know that truth fully?"

A person would have to be as great and wise as God to know God truly. Some philosophers have claimed that the human mind had such infinite capacity, but Jewish teaching, for all its intellectuality, has been far more humble. The Jewish attitude in this regard is captured in the Torah's repeated comment, "No one can see My [God's] face and live." The God of Judaism is so great that human reasoning cannot reach the one, full, unchanging truth about the universe. We should never confuse what God is as *God* knows it with what *people* can know or say about God.

Traditional Judaism (as well as Christianity and Islam) therefore relied heavily on what God "told" them. (We'll discuss the problem of God "telling" things to people in chapter 2, "How Does God Speak to People?" of Part Three, *The Bible and Tradition.*)

Theologians term what God has "said" to humankind God's revelation. That is, to begin with, God has a truth we do not have. But, what was hidden to us, God then makes known to us; God reveals it to us. For traditional Judaism, God's revelation is the Torah. Through its books and their interpretation, our teachers said, God tells us how to act, individually and as a people. The Torah says very little about what God is and makes no claim to reveal fully what God is like. Rather, again and again, whether indirectly, by calling God Creator or King, or directly, by long poems about God's majesty, as in the latter part of Isaiah (ch. 40 and following) or in Job (chs. 38–41), it reminds us how little of God we can understand.

This sense of the distance between humankind and God is, in my opinion, the factor that accounts for traditional Judaism's relatively open attitude (as compared, say, to traditional Christianity) to the creation of fresh notions of God. The Midrash, for example, contains astonishingly diverse images which the rabbis used in referring to God. This suggests to me that, since our teachers believed we cannot fully describe God, they would not prohibit speculation about God as long as it did not contradict what the Torah directed us to do.

The Consequences of Affirming a Liberal View of Revelation

As we shall see in detail later, liberal Jews have a different view of revelation. We place very much more weight than our tradition did on the human role in creating religion. We are also much less certain about exactly what God has revealed to us. Thus, we also have a more positive appreciation of change in religious ideas. In this book, I shall be explaining belief from this liberal perspective, that is, what we can believe if we start largely from human religious experience rather than from God's direct revelation.

I think it is quite difficult for us today to appreciate how revolutionary liberal Jewish thinkers were when they proclaimed that Judaism had always changed with the times and still needed to do so. We can hardly imagine what it might be like to conceive of the world in relatively static terms. In fashion or government or lifestyle, things seem only to hold still momentarily before proceeding with further transformation. Nature itself seems one vast process: mountains thrust up or erode, coastlines recede, deserts expand, and our very globe occasionally shakes from the grinding movement of the great terrestrial plates. We take for granted Darwin's, Marx's, and Einstein's views of reality as constantly in motion. None of them had yet written when the liberals, early in the nineteenth century, proclaimed their notion of religion as substantially a human creation, one that therefore continually adapted itself to new knowledge and circumstances.

Almost everything I will be saying in these pages rests on the liberal conception of Judaism as a dynamic process of human spiritual discovery. I therefore want to explain this premise with some care. I can do so most easily, I believe, if I retell one of the classic stories of the early days of the movement to liberalize Judaism. Characteristically, it centers on an issue of Jewish practice—always dearer to Jews than philosophical matters—but it has a definite relation to our question about the legitimacy of changing Jewish views of God.

In 1823 the traditionalist leaders of the Berlin Jewish community persuaded the Prussian government to close the private liberal synagogue of Jacob Herz Beer. They charged that he had changed the practice of Judaism for he had introduced the custom of weekly sermons at the services. Preaching—and doing so in German—was condemned by the traditionalists as a departure from Jewish practice (and privately as aping gentile practices). The Prussian authorities were opposed to all changes in religion. They feared that the liberal spirit might then be applied to the political realm and stir up demands for changes in government.

The matter might have ended there except for the courage and persistence of one of the synagogue's preachers, Leopold Zunz. He not only had the classic Jewish training of the *yeshivah,* but he was one of the early modern Jews to gain a doctorate from a university (Halle). Zunz decided to investigate Judaism's attitude toward sermons as if it were another academic topic in humanistic scholarship—in itself, a daring notion. The resulting research revolutionized Jewish study and became a model for all subsequent modern Jewish investigations of Judaism.

Unlike the method used in traditional Jewish scholarship, Zunz began by making a critical survey of the relevant source material. Audaciously, he no longer took for granted what a given work said about its authorship or what tradition had said about it. Rather, he set about determining the time and place of its actual origin by meticulously examining its linguistic usage and historical references. He then put the sources in chronological order and related what they said to what was known of the general history of the time—overthrowing the old idea that Jewish truth was self-contained and unchanging. As a result, he was now able to give a proper academic account of the history of Jewish preaching.

No one had ever taken a philological-literary-historical approach to Jewish sources before, and the results were startling. Any reader not biased against modernity could now easily see that, over the centuries, Jews had preached sermons until oppressive governments prevented them from doing so. What seemed so un-Jewish in 1823 had long before been a significant part of Jewish practice. The right to preach had been taken away from the Jewish community by those who wanted Judaism to die. Historically analyzed, this hardly seemed like the sort of precedent Jews should continue passionately to defend.

From Zunz's time on, whenever a critical, chronological study has been made of almost any Jewish practice—services, name-giving, Bar Mitzvah, the wearing of *yarmulkes* or *kipot*—one sees a dynamic process of adjustment and innovation at work. Judaism has not stood still. It would have petrified had it done so. Change has been the means of Jewish survival.

Religious Ideas too Have Changed with Time

Jewish beliefs are no exception to this rule. When we investigate them by Zunz's method, refined and extended to be sure, we see religious evolution at work. The evidence incontrovertibly demonstrates that, depending on the cultural situation, Jews often changed the way they talked about their faith. Even Jewish descriptions of God have regularly altered with time. I shall shortly sketch in the highlights of that development. I would first like to show you how the liberals have reinterpreted the classic Jewish caution about "no one" being able to "see God's face."

For all their appreciation of humankind's creative powers, liberal Jewish theologians do not assert that we can know the full truth about God. The record of their own creativity proves them right. In the last century and a half, what one generation visualized as a proper perspective about God has often appeared inadequate to another. We shall soon take a look at the philosophies of God formulated by Hermann Cohen, Leo Baeck, Martin Buber, Mordecai Kaplan, and Abraham Heschel. They gave us five widely admired yet distinct approaches to thinking about God —and they appeared in less than one hundred years.

Perhaps our basic premise should be that we won't believe what we don't understand. Then, as long as our understanding of God is adequate to our other knowledge and experience, it should not change. It might have to, though, for few of us are so self-confident about what we know as to declare that we have nothing more to learn. And we would consider it a moral duty, if our sense of ultimate reality expanded or deepened, or if we found a better way to describe it, to integrate that new knowledge into our concepts of God and Judaism.

We liberals do not want our understanding of Divinity to stand still while the rest of us keeps growing. Not every intellectual fad or social fashion has deep religious significance. Obviously, much of what the Jewish tradition has said about God remains compellingly true. I would further argue that most of us are not highly creative thinkers. Nonetheless, some of us have fresh ideas that may help others in our time and perhaps later. Liberal Judaism is hospitable to such development. While not denigrating what remains true, it glories in our efforts to refurbish or restate the truth, for it believes such innovation is the sign of a living religiosity.

Note how this reverses traditional Judaism's attitude toward the Torah (and thus illustrates how religious ideas change). Because "no one can see God's face," our teachers gave absolute credence to the books and interpretations they believed came to them from God as revelation. Liberal theologians believe people are as much responsible for the Torah and tradition as is God. But now, because "no one can see God's face," we cannot accept any human description of God as absolute. Even those given us by our spiritual geniuses, our prophets and lawgivers, our rabbis and ethical teachers, our philosophers and mystics, are subject to revision. Anything we humans say about God is subject to improvement. Apparently, the Jewish people unconsciously followed this rule for, as we now study our history, we see definite shifts in the way Jews over the ages have understood God.

Biblical Insights into God's Reality

Strictly speaking, the Bible doesn't give us "ideas" or "concepts" of God. God is depicted in many different ways in the Bible, and modern biblical scholars agree that they cannot all be reduced to a single, intellectual "concept of God." The Bible writers simply did not think in an abstract, philosophical way. They generally express their religious sensibilities in stories or poems. It would be best, I think, if we spoke of the Bible's *images* of God (as long as we don't confuse literary "images" with idols!).

At times in the Bible God is described in very human, even physical terms. We read in Genesis 3:8 of God taking a walk in the Garden of Eden when the day began to cool down—almost as if God, like people, needed relief from the hot mid-eastern afternoon. A quite startling image is given in Exodus 33:20–23 when Moses asks to see God's full glory. The account has God replying, "You can't see My face because no one could stand that. . . . But there's a place near Me where you can stand on a rocky cliff. When My glory goes by there, I'll put you in a small cave which I'll cover with My hand until I've passed by. Then I'll take away My hand and you can see My back. But no human being can see My face." (I shall return to this story in a later chapter.)

I must also postpone a discussion of these anthropomorphisms, the expressions describing God in human form, as having hands, a face, a back, and such. Here I want only to point out that other passages give us a radically different impression of God. Predominantly the Bible writers stress that God is incomparably greater than any idol and that any attempt to identify a specific object with God is wrong, even sinful. The second of the Ten Commandments makes that categorically clear. "You must not have any gods beside Me. That means you must not make a god of any piece of sculpture or any sort of figure of anything that's in the sky, on the earth, or in the waters below the earth." (Exod. 20:3–4)

The authors of the Bible regularly tell us that God is altogether greater than we are. Thus, when Solomon dedicates his magnificent Temple he can be reported to say, "Will God really live in a house on earth? The heavens, even the heavens above all other heavens cannot contain God, how much less this house I have built for God." (1 Kings 8:27) And the "Second" Isaiah (who wrote chapters 40 and following in that book) argues repeatedly that God is unique and, therefore, cannot adequately be described by anything else we know. "To whom will you liken Me or who will you say is My equal, and compare to Me, that we may be called alike? . . . I am God. There is none else. I am God. There is no one like Me." (Isaiah 46:5,9)

The Rabbis and the Hellenistic Jews
Created New Images of God

Rabbinic literature, by which we mean the Talmud and Midrash, produced in the first five centuries of the Common Era (c.e.),* preserves much of the Bible's style of using physical terms to talk about God, but self-consciously treats it as a symbolic way of referring to God. The rabbis (the teachers mentioned in the Talmud and Midrash) often speak of God acting like a human being. They can say God "prays" and "studies" as a good Jew should, or "cries" or "rejoices" as befits a concerned parent. Many times, they carefully note that it is "as if" God did such things, or that this is all "in a manner of speaking." Rabbi Ishmael had a rule, "The Torah speaks the language of ordinary people." (Ber. 31b) It is indicative of the rabbinic attitude toward the Bible's descriptions of God; they use a down-to-earth approach so that we may understand something about God, not because that is what God is truly like.

The rabbis also did not hesitate to coin their own ways of speaking about God. Some are quite human, such as "Our Father," "Our King," while others point to God's nature, "The Merciful One," "He who spoke and the world was," or, simply, "The Power." They could even call God, "The Place," as spatial

*I shall follow the accepted notations of modern Jewish historians: c.e.=Common Era and b.c.e.=Before the Common Era.

as that sounds, and say that "God is the place of the world but the world is not God's place." (Gen. R. 68:9) They also utilized spiritual terms, calling God, "The Holy One" (to which one normally adds, "Blessed be He"). The rabbinic imagination is so bold and daring in depicting God that one cannot guess what is likely to be said about God when one turns to a fresh page of rabbinic literature.

When Jews learned about Greek philosophy, they were led to speak about God in a far more abstract fashion. The earliest Jewish philosopher of whom we have any substantial account is Philo. He lived in Alexandria, Egypt, during the first half of the first century C.E.

Philo based his conception of God on the Hellenistic idea of spirit, a notion which was radically contrasted with matter, the stuff of which things as we know them are made. In ordinary life, spirit is always involved in matter. Thus, people have a body and a soul. For Philo, God is Pure Spirit and, therefore, unlike anything we usually encounter.

Philo's theory would seem to separate God utterly from the world, a concept contrary to the Bible's view that God is involved with people. Philo proposed a solution to this gap between reason and tradition. He suggested that God's very first creation was not heaven and earth but reason or intelligence. This, then, provides the order which turns chaos into cosmos. He termed this very first creation the *logos,* a Greek word we know from "logic," the right way to think. The *logos* is, so to speak, the bridge between the Pure Spirit, God, and humankind whose spirits are embedded in matter. People's minds are, thus, their chief means of making contact with and understanding God. This became the basic idea through which, in later generations, philosophy found an important place in religious thinking. This fusion of philosophy and faith was particularly important to early Christianity, and the church preserved Philo's writings which Jews have only become reacquainted with in recent times.

Medieval Philosophers and Mystics Had Their Own Unique God-Ideas

Philosophy became a living concern in the Jewish community only in later centuries with the Moslem discovery and revival of

Greek philosophy. The most famous exemplar of the fusion of Arabic philosophic notions with Jewish thought was Moses Maimonides (1135–1204 C.E.).

Maimonides recognized that the recovery of Aristotle's thought required a radical rethinking of many of the conclusions of religious philosophy before his time. In the course of carrying out the restructuring of philosophy, Maimonides argued that an unbridgeable gap always remained between the most comprehensive ideas people could conceive and what God actually was. Fortunately, besides what we knew from revelation, the Torah, we can see God's effect upon creation and thus have some proper notions about God. God, so to speak, thinks the ideas which order the universe and which our intellect grasps. Insofar as people learn to think on this level of divine intellectuality, they participate in God's eternal reality. Maimonides leaves us with the impression, then, that God, as best we are able to express it, is Pure Thought.

There were probably always more Jewish mystics than Jewish philosophers. In fact, we can trace Jewish mysticism further back than we can trace Jewish philosophy, for we find evidence of mystical thought among the early rabbis. Such early glimpses as we get of the mystic notions of God seem quite strange by contrast to even the broad range of thinking permitted in the Talmud. They are so fragmented that we generally do not know quite how to understand them. One of the most notorious early mystic documents about God is the book, *Shiur Komah, The Dimensions of God's Stature,* which gives the precise measurement of each part of God's mystical "body"!

The classic work of Jewish mysticism is the *Zohar* which was written in Spain about 1275 C.E. by Moses de Leon, though ascribed, as was the custom, to an earlier time. It intimates that God should be understood in two absolutely different ways. Both of these constitute the one God of Judaism "even as the coal and the flame make up the fire." On the one hand, God is *En Sof,* Without Limit, so pure and exalted that nothing at all can properly be said about God. On the other hand, God may be understood as ten coordinated centers of power, *Sefirot.* All the biblical and talmudic images for God can then be connected with the divine capacity which functions in one or another of the ten *Sefirot.* No simile which had ever been applied to God in the Bible or Talmud is too physical or gross for the mystics; they simply connect it with one of the *Sefirot*. They talked about God as a river, a tree, a garden, or even a physical body, complete with masculine and feminine sexual organs, whose inner harmony might therefore be described in terms of sexual intercourse.

In the Modern Age Truth Is Dynamic, Not Static

When Jews entered the modern world and encountered its science and philosophy, our thinkers propounded new notions of God. Much of this book deals with these ideas so I will not extend this survey further. I only wanted to present some notion of the range of thinking about God that has been going on in the several thousand years of Jewish history. The data clearly demonstrates that, despite an agreement that idols are never God, and that God is one, Jews have had many different ideas about how best to think about God.

I would like to take this liberal attitude one step further. We are convinced that what keeps Judaism or any world view alive is its ability to grow and adapt. We would be worried if, over many years, Judaism did not change.

This positive attitude toward new ideas should not be identified with the kind of insecurity which demands that every fresh cultural ripple requires a revision of our belief. Many a highly ballyhooed intellectual breakthrough barely lasts beyond a single publishing season. Self-respect properly demands that modern ideas should be questioned and, when appropriate, rejected. With all that, we moderns feel we cannot claim to know permanent truth, that is, truth that *is* true, *was* true, and always *will be* true as we know it now.

Traditional Judaism regularly asserted that it possessed an unchanging truth. The rabbis could not imagine that our Patriarch Abraham did not keep *kosher* centuries before the Torah says the laws of *kashrut* were given on Mt. Sinai to Moses. (Yoma 28b) Some of the Midrash masters ingeniously proved that Adam, who lived long before Abraham and thus was not a Jew, had set aside tithes and recited the talmudic blessings over the fruits of the Garden of Eden. (Gen. R. 16:5) These teachers had a sense of reality far more fixed than ours. For us, truth is, and always has been, something dynamic, a process of finding more adequate understanding rather than something we could ever fully express or realize.

Can We Be Good Jews if Our Ideas about God Keep Changing?

If you agree with this liberal view of our human situation, you will understand why we do not agonize over whether this open religious quest of ours will keep us authentic Jews. We are doing in our time what our Jewish forebears did in their time, though we seem to be far more self-conscious about the changes we make in Judaism. Surely we would not be better Jews by ignoring the moral and intellectual challenges of modernity. Rather, because we seek to give proper place to the human role in religion, we emphasize intellectual honesty and spiritual integrity as the great motives for contemporary religious change.

I believe these considerations apply to the very topic we are discussing. By utilizing some modern ideas we can better understand how a tradition remains true to itself while evolving through history. Much modern philosophy concentrates on the language we use to express what we think. In religion, many thinkers believe there is a gap between what we can put into words and what we experience. That prompts me to suggest that what has changed for Jews over the years is their language about God, not their underlying belief. I find some evidence for this in the fact that Jews, despite the many different terms and names they have used for God over the centuries, have always felt they were talking about the same God. They had almost no difficulty distinguishing the beliefs of Jews from those of Gentiles.

There is no way to prove the hypothesis that we have shared a pre-verbal experience, but I find much in the history of Jewish thought that lends support to it. Jews have argued over many things but rarely indeed over other Jews' ways of talking about God. By contrast, a good deal of early Christian history centers on controversies over the proper doctrine of God (as related to the concept of the Christ, to be sure). Judaism knows nothing like that. Jews never evolved an institution to rule on people's proper belief in God though the rabbis and their courts took vigorous action when questions of religious practice were involved.

Jews seem to have taken a rather historical view of demonstrating the value or lack of value of a given way of talking about God. Ideas were permitted to come into the community with some freedom. If our people found them worthy, it tried to live by them. If the ideas survived over generations or centuries, they became a living part of our tradition. Most new ways of talking about God simply came and went. They did not pass the test of life our community subjected them to.

I should like to think that pattern still holds true. If so, we cannot know now, as our predecessors could not know in earlier centuries, which contemporary language for describing God will be accepted and carried on by the Jewish people as an authentic addition to our tradition. All we can be asked to do today is to be honest to the God we know as part of our people's ongoing religious experience. That certainly includes being true to our own intellects and spirits and therefore trying to express our spiritual insights in the most compelling language of our time and place.

The Difference between Knowing God and Having an Idea of God

A historical comment about concepts of God and Jewish authenticity is also in order. Only in modern times did thinkers identify *the idea* of one God as the essence of Judaism. Like all intellectual formulations, it grew up in a given setting and it too is not immune to the law of change. Specifically, that theory came into being within the context of nineteenth-century German philosophy. It stressed the importance of ideas above all other possible factors in philosophy, such as sense perception, imagination, or matter. The philosophers who worked in this fashion are still called the German "idea-lists."

Jews emerging into Western society in the nineteenth century quickly adopted this style of thinking and used it to show the virtues of Judaism. They argued that, at heart, Judaism was not law but an *idea,* the concept of one God, or, as they preferred to call it, ethical monotheism.

In the brilliant formulation of Hermann Cohen, late in the nineteenth century, this conception became widely accepted among liberal Jews; in various forms, it still has many advocates. For Cohen, Jewish practice might change but not the Jewish idea of God. Cohen knew, of course, that over the centuries our Jewish ways of talking about God have varied widely. He dismissed this as mere history for he did not feel that what had happened among people was nearly as significant as true ideas. In his highly elaborated technical philosophy, he felt that he had isolated the essential Jewish idea behind all the many historical shifts of thinking: ethical monotheism.

Few contemporary thinkers accept Cohen's judgment of history or philosophy. They regard his notion that a specific idea of God has been the permanent basis of Judaism as a typical nineteenth-century idealistic theory which twentieth-century intellectuality has outgrown. To put it more personally: Our thinking and our spiritual experience have led us to fresh "ideas" of God and, in seeking new ways of talking about God, we are doing today what Cohen did in his time. What we see as the essence of Judaism is not one specific formulation of what God means to us but our continuing relation to the one God whose greatness continually beggars our grandest words and ideas.

I admit that there are risks in seeking to be so open and honest with ourselves about what we can now believe and say about God. But, as long as our religious search is carried out with spirits open to who God is and what God means to us, as long as our quest for better ways of talking about God is pursued as part of the Jewish people, with high regard for what our tradition has said about God and what our people continues to affirm today, I think we may be confident that ours will be an authentic Jewish approach to the age-old subject of belief in God.

PART

· I ·

THE JEWISH PEOPLE

Part One: The Jewish People

·1·

WHAT SORT OF GROUP
ARE THE JEWS?

Ask Americans about the Jews and they are almost certain to tell you, "The Jews are a religious group." Their answer is clearly correct, yet, the more one thinks about it, the less certain one becomes.

Much data demonstrates the contrary. Only a bit more than half the Jews in the United States belong to synagogues. In the largest cities the overwhelming majority of Jews remain unaffiliated. Those who do associate with a religious institution rarely do so for spiritual reasons. They speak instead of their children's needs for Jewish identification or their sense of community responsibility. The State of Israel far more effectively summons Jewish pride and energy than do the Torah and its commandments. Though the Israeli Declaration of Independence calls *Medinat Yisrael* a "Jewish State," more than a quarter of its citizens are Moslem and Christian Arabs. Legally, it is a secular nation. It is not ruled by its clergy, the rabbinate, but by officials whose religion is, in principle, their private affair. Jewish religious political parties do participate in Israeli politics but they garner only about 10 percent of Israeli votes. (Because of Israeli coalition politics, they exercise much more power than their size would indicate.) Most Israelis do not identify with the religious parties for they consider themselves Jews for secular and not religious reasons. They feel bound to other Jews by a common land, language, history, destiny, and much else.

Something of that may be felt in the strong ties American Jews

19

have with Israelis and Jews in other countries. We know we share the same past and we are particularly conscious of our joint history of suffering. We know we have a common lot, one that makes the trials and triumphs of Jews in one corner of the world affect Jews everywhere. We have our own languages, foods, and family styles—though here we divide into two great cultural streams, the Sephardim, roughly the Jews from Mediterranean countries, and the Ashkenazim, roughly those from more northern European lands. In almost every individual country, we develop intimate, barely describable yet effective expressions and signals of our Jewishness. We have our special ways of eating, of drinking, of handling class status; we have familiar jokes, patterns of gossip, and reference signals that connect us with other Jews. Against all scientific evidence we often find these subtle signs enable us to detect in an unfamiliar crowd who else is a "member of the tribe."

Almost none of what I have described is normally considered part of a religion yet it comprises much of the reality of American Jewish lives. This anomaly lies behind the perennial modern question about the nature of the Jews.

What Does the Bible Teach Us about Our Group?

The problem of Jewish identity arose in relatively recent times as a brief historical survey of the issue makes clear.

The roots of the modern difficulty may be traced back to the Bible. No book can match its status in Western spiritual life, yet the Bible itself has no word for "religion." Its authors use a term from everyday legal affairs, *berit,* covenant or contract, to describe the relationship between God and humankind. Many of their concerns hardly seem religious. The books of Joshua, Judges, Samuel, and Kings are largely about kings and politics, wars and social structure. The Book of Proverbs conveys wisdom about getting along in society; Ruth tells a pleasant love story; Ecclesiastes pessimistically tells us nothing much matters.

When the biblical writers talk about the Jews as a whole they often describe them in much the same way they do the Ammonites or the Edomites or other groups they knew. They consider the Jews (more accurately, the Hebrews) one of the many "nations" of the ancient Near East. These folk groups had their own tongues—all classified today as Semitic languages. They had their own territory, history, myths, and traditions, as well as a distinctive way of life. Mostly, they were independent monarchies but conquest might make them subject to a foreign power. They also had their own religions, the Moabites worshiping *Molech,* the Ammonites *Chemosh,* and the Cannaanites various of the *baalim.*

Like the other peoples, the Hebrews' God was the source of their society's legal system. But their God was not merely culturally distinctive but qualitatively different from the gods of the other Near Eastern peoples. The Jews had no idols for their God and no mythology about their God's activities. Rather, they daringly insisted that their invisible God was the one and only God of the universe. This exclusive sovereignty gave great power and scope to what they perceived to be God's primary demands, that all human beings be just and merciful with one another. As a result the Hebrews' system of law and folk life had a unique quality.

Thus, already in the Bible, the Jews are similar to everyone else, yet also different. This experience of being like yet unlike other peoples created the problem Jews have had explaining themselves adequately to others. And the puzzled and sometimes hostile reactions of Gentiles (literally, "the nations") toward the Jews have made the issue of the nature of the Jewish group a trying and sensitive one.

A Hellenistic Description of Jewish Identity

Roman times provide our first records of efforts to describe the Jews in the terms of another culture. About 40 C.E., the philosopher Philo was part of a delegation of Alexandrian Jews who went to Rome to petition the Emperor Gaius for help against the local anti-semites. Philo wrote a book about this experience which seems as much addressed to the cultured, Greek-reading non-Jews of his time as to his own community. He speaks to them about the Jews in terms of the social structures they know, namely, the city-state. (Rome had expanded and become an empire.) He writes that he told Gaius: "Jerusalem is my native city and it is the metropolis not merely of the country of Judaea alone but also of many other places. For it has, from time to time, sent out colonies into the nearby districts of Egypt, Phoenicia, and Syria . . . into the greater part of Asia Minor as far as Bithynia and

the farthest bounds of Pontus. It has done the same in Europe
. . . and not only are the continents full of Jewish colonies but also
all the most celebrated islands. . . . Hence, if my native land is
. . . entitled to share in your favor, it is not one city only that would
then be benefited by you but ten thousands of them in every
region of the habitable world.''

Philo speaks in what we would call "national" terms. Though
apparently born in and devoted to Alexandria in Egypt he identifies himself as a "native" of Jerusalem. That is to say, Jerusalem
is his "Rome." It would never occur to Philo that speaking about
himself and other Jews this way might make Gaius accuse him of
dual loyalties. Rather the emperor and other Gentiles could not
have understood Philo had he used any other terms.

Roman imperial law officially recognized a certain nationality
called "Judaeans," rather than Jerusalemites (citizens and "colo-
nists" of that city). They were nationals of the Roman province
Judaea. The statutes treat them like any other subject nation of
the empire—but not entirely so. The laws make specific provision
for the fact that the Judaeans have an odd religion about which
they are quite obdurate. To enable them to observe its commandments, the regulations make unique exceptions for them. For
example, their poor might receive cash instead of the oil which
was part of the government dole, for the Judaeans considered
Roman oil religiously tainted.

Incidentally, "Judaean" is the root term for most European
words denoting our people. In German we are *Juden,* the "J"
being pronounced as an English "Y." (That yields the name of
the language *Juedisch,* which we know as Yiddish.) In English, the
"d" dropped out and "J" was given its usual English pronunciation, giving us the word "Jews." In 1948, when the third Jewish
commonwealth was founded, many people expected it to be
named Judea as a matter of continuity. David Ben-Gurion rea-
soned differently. He wanted the new state to be identified with
all Jews today—the people of Israel—rather than with its political
ancestry. He therefore insisted it be called the State of Israel.

Josephus Characterizes His People

Another Jewish writer of Roman times made a somewhat different effort at Jewish self-explanation. Josephus, the son of a highly

placed Judaean family, was the general in charge of the Jewish defense of the Galilee during the Jewish rebellion against Rome, 67–70 C.E. Having betrayed his people and gone over to the Roman side, he received a pension from the empire and spent the rest of his life on a small estate north of Rome writing books about Jewish history for Roman readers.

In one volume Josephus set aside his role as a chronicler and defended his people against the charges made by a vicious Alexandrian anti-semite named Apion. In the course of his discussion he boasts of his people's distinctive way of life. This he attributes to Moses, whom he calls "the most ancient of the legislators recorded anywhere" and the wisest. Other lawgivers gave "instruction in words" or stressed "exercises in practice. . . . Our legislator very carefully joined these two methods of instruction together. . . . Beginning with the earliest infancy and the partaking of food, he left nothing, not even of the smallest consequence, to be done at the pleasure and caprice of the persons themselves, but made fixed laws and rules. He did not suffer the pretext of ignorance to be valid . . . but ordained that people should stop their activities and assemble together to hear the Law and be perfectly instructed in it . . . every week. . . . And it is this very thing that principally creates such wonderful oneness of mind among us. Because we have one and the same religious belief and have no difference from one another in our way of living and our manners, we have the most excellent agreement in our human character."

Josephus's description is more "religious" than is Philo's, yet it is unmistakably cast in "national" terms. As Solon gave law to the Greeks, so Moses made the Judaeans a proper nation with their own law code.

In Roman times nationality and religion were always closely identified. To proclaim that you were from a given province was a good indication of what your practices and beliefs were likely to be. This certainly held true of the Judaeans. They were distinguished from all other nations by their worship of an invisible God and their absolute denial of all other claims to divinity. Judaean law was at one and the same time what we would call national and religious.

The Atrophy of Jewish Nationality in Medieval Times

The national definition of the Jews could not easily survive the crushing of the two rebellions against Rome and the steady diminution of the Judaean community. The Jews had no government of their own; most of the nation lived elsewhere than in the homeland. The Temple in Jerusalem no longer existed as a center to which world Jewry could come on pilgrimage or to which they could send annual tribute. Hebrew had become a language for scholars, the average Judaean speaking Aramaic, a cognate tongue; most Diaspora Jews used the language of the country where they lived.

One might plausibly argue that after a few centuries the Jews stopped being the Judaean nation and became the Jewish religion. But that does not satisfactorily describe the reality of medieval Jewish existence. The Jewish "religion" remained, so to speak, uncommonly national. Regardless of their daily tongue, Jews daily prayed in Hebrew. The grace after meals and the synagogue liturgy kept Jerusalem and the Land of Israel a living memory and celebrated the hope for a return there under a Davidic king. The religious calendar itself had a geographic orientation. Thus, today, Jews in Milwaukee, Montreal, and Boston, facing a snowy March, may not feel much like celebrating the coming of spring when Passover falls. But they will do so at the traditional date in accord with the change of seasons in the Land of Israel. The situation is even more dramatic on the other side of the equator. In Melbourne and Rio de Janeiro, Sukot falls in the local spring and not in the autumn when a harvest festival is appropriate. Jews in these countries ignore their own climate and observe religious practices which are geared to their old national home.

External as well as internal factors kept the Jews more than a spiritual association. Modern Jewish historians like Simon Dubnow and Salo Baron have shown that Christian and Moslem treatments of the Jews helped preserve certain aspects of Jewish nationality. In the Middle Ages, Jews gained the right to reside in a locality by being part of a Jewish community formally enfranchised by the ruler. They could not participate in the general social institutions since these operated on the basis of religious oaths which the Jews could not conscientiously swear. The Jews, therefore, operated their own law courts according to their own legal system. Their community leaders were responsible for collecting the taxes which the ruler specially imposed on the Jews. The leaders also had the duty and power to enforce community discipline on Jews who disturbed the peace of Jews or Gentiles. With some exaggeration, the old comment on medieval Jewry is correct: the Jews were as good a state within the regular state.

After 1500 C.E., we can trace the development of officially segregated Jewish quarters in western European towns, the ghettos, and, in due course, of the eastern European shtetl, its cultural but not physical analogue. Responding to this enforced isolation, the Jews produced a rich folk life and group self-consciousness which far transcended what we would normally include under the rubric "religion."

A Revolution in Status Exacerbates the Problem

The abnormal social situation of the Jews was radically changed by the process Jewish historians call the Emancipation. As the nineteenth century began, a new mood affected much of Europe. Years of Protestant-Catholic warfare had exhausted many nations and disgusted thoughtful people. The French Revolution proclaimed the radical idea that nations should be purely secular, concerned only with the political loyalty of their subjects. Religion should be left to the sphere of citizens' individual, private preference. With nations no longer Christian (though, as in England, they retained an established church), it was possible to conceive of Jews being citizens and having the same political rights everyone else had. Prejudice and social conservatism aside, a pressing intellectual question now arose—one not without its anti-semitic overtones. Could the Jews fit into the society created by this new division between political nationhood and religion? Specifically, were the Jews members of a religious group, as Catholics and Protestants were, or were they a nationality of their own and thus unable to give full political loyalty to the countries in which they resided?

In 1807, Napoleon, in his grand style, summoned a Great Sanhedrin of French Jews to give him a formal statement of the Jewish religion's teaching about the Jews' relation to France. The Sanhedrin responded in terms which set a pattern for all other

Jewries who received civil equality. "We declare that the divine law . . . contains political as well as religious commands, that the religious ones are by their nature absolute and independent of circumstances and time but that this does not hold true of the political commandments, that is, those which relate to the government of the people of Israel in Palestine when it had its own kings, priests, and magistrates, that these are no longer applicable since Israel no longer is a nation. . . . Thus, by virtue of the right vested in us by our ancient tradition and our sacred laws . . . we hereby religiously enjoin on all obedience to the state in all matters civil and political." Wherever Jews have been granted full citizenship in this modern fashion, they have regularly identified themselves to their neighbors as adherents of a religion.*

With the inception of the politics of modernity, religion and nationality were sundered from one another, making it far more difficult to adequately describe the Jews as a group. The French Sanhedrin took place some years before the first signs of a movement to reform Jewish religious practice, but both are part of one historic development. The fateful step was taken when Jews decided to participate in the new free social situation. To do so meant identifying themselves as a religious group. Religious reforms naturally had to result. The Jewish commitment to general society implied changing the forms of Jewish observance so that they might reflect Western style and bring Judaism the benefits of Western cultural achievements. Thus, early in its history, German Reform Judaism, which pioneered the new relationship between Jews and general culture, unequivocally gave up all interest in Jewish nationality.

In the United States, Reform Judaism had by the end of the nineteenth century established itself as the leading religious group in the community. In 1885, a group of Reform rabbis issued a manifesto called the Pittsburgh Platform. On the topic of social adaptation they said, "We recognize in the Mosaic legislation a system of training the Jewish people for its mission during its national life in Palestine, and today we accept as binding only the moral laws and maintain only such ceremonies as elevate and sanctify our lives, but reject all such as are not adapted to the views and habits of modern civilization." A later paragraph con-

*See the additional discussion in Part Four, *Living as a Jew*, chapter 4, "What Are Our Duties to Humanity?"

cludes, "We consider ourselves no longer a nation but a religious community and, therefore, expect neither a return to Palestine, nor a sacrificial worship under the administration of the sons of Aaron, nor the restoration of any of the laws concerning the Jewish state."

A Religion with More than Religious Concerns

The identity of the Jews seemed to have been settled, but it wasn't. The Reformers of the late nineteenth century knew that the term religion didn't fully define the Jewish group. In America, to be a religion implies being a church. That, in the Protestant sense, implies adherence to a creed or confession. One "joins the church" not merely by filling out a form or paying a certain fee, as one does in secular organizations, but by acknowledging that one shares the church's faith. Conversely, members who deny its truth can be tried for heresy and, if convicted, expelled from the faith. To call American Jews a religion appeared to identify them as a group essentially united by a common belief. Though Judaism centered around the affirmation of ethical monotheism, most Jews, except for the most radical reformers, rejected the notion that Jewish identity was a matter of religious ideas.

The Central Conference of American Rabbis' debate on intermarriage in 1904 indicates the difficulty the Reformers had defining Judaism solely as a religion. If the Jews are a "church" whose creed is ethical monotheism, why should a Jew not marry a non-Jewish ethical monotheist, say a Unitarian or other liberal Christian believer? No one in 1904 seriously explained what made Judaism more than a religion and thus made the intermarriage of monotheists unacceptable. Nonetheless, the Reform rabbis' association overwhelmingly voted its opposition to its members performing a wedding ceremony between a Jew and a non-Jew.

Subsequent events helped prove how inadequate the term "religion" was to describe the Jewish community. East European immigrants brought their *folk-oriented* Jewish life-style with them to this continent. Then Hitler came and persecuted Jews for *racial* reasons. The State of Israel, *secular* as it is, ultimately became the chief focus of modern Jewish loyalty. In the face of these developments, the American Jewish community was no longer content to identify itself as merely another of the Western world's churches.

The Temptation of the Concept of Race

At one point early in the twentieth century, thinkers began to use a new term to describe groups: race. The concept seemed to fulfill the hopes of those who sought to apply the methods of science to the realm of human behavior. The new discipline of psychology had begun to explain individual behavior but group distinctiveness proved more difficult to handle. Some scientists then suggested applying to human beings the zoological method of classifying animals by their physical characteristics. They thereby hoped to find measurable ways of distinguishing human types. Large groups could be identified by skin color and then divided into subspecies by head shape, hair structure, and other quantifiable characteristics. With the chemistry of life still poorly understood, it was thought that the features of each given human subspecies were transmitted through one's blood.

As soon as the theory was carefully tested it proved faulty. Physical anthropologists showed conclusively that there are no pure races and that, in any mathematically distinctive sense, it is unlikely that there ever were any. Racial subspecies are even more imprecise notions, more the creations of our need to classify than of any consistent data. At best, racial terms are useful as a shorthand explanation of the long and tedious development of humankind.

The concept of race survived the negative data because the early scientists used it to explain differences in group behavior. As against the sociologists—whose discipline was just forming—the racialists attributed social variation to biological causes. The sociologists argued that group behavior was a creative corporate phenomenon of its own. They soon demonstrated that all groups, based on their time, place, circumstance, and leadership, naturally create their own unique, rich, integrated way of life.

The racial thinkers, identifying cultural differences with peoples' physical reality, gave an apparently unchangeable, scientific basis to differences in culture and style. Before the notion of race had been elaborated, one could not easily explain why certain groups were hateful, though they adapted to overcome the criticisms one had made of them. Now their loathesomeness could be attributed to their very physical stuff. They had "bad blood," "inferior genes." And nothing they could do would ever change that. *You* were biologically good but *they* were doomed by their very birth.

The Holocaust resulted from applying this pseudoscience to the Jews. For the Nazis, race replaced religion as the ostensible justification of anti-semitism. The horrifying consequence of this substitution was that the Jews could find no way to appease their persecutors. In the medieval persecutions, the victims could always convert and save their lives. But if one's "blood" is faulty, nothing one can do would remove one's taint. The Nazis took that one demonic step further by insisting that the Jewish race was a biological danger to humankind. Like many cancers, the best treatment was radical surgery. The Holocaust thus had a "scientific" basis. Prejudice, seeking a justification as always, had found it in race. No wonder the concept troubles many people.

During the first quarter of the twentieth century Jewish authors often spoke of Jewish blood. Kaufmann Kohler, the leading Reform Jewish theologian of the period, attributed Jewish cohesion not only to our affirmation of ethical monotheism but to our common blood. He considered us the chosen people in that our chief "racial" characteristic was a predisposition to ethical spirituality. Franz Rosenzweig in Germany, for all his pioneering of an existentialist understanding of Jewishness, linked the individual Jew to all the children of Israel by Jewish blood. A similar usage is found in the writings of Martin Buber before 1923 when he evolved his theory of the "I-thou" relationship.

In addition to the appalling overtones of the word "race" since the Holocaust, there is no scientific basis for applying the term to the Jews. No study has ever shown that most Jews worldwide share any physical characteristics. In some studies Jews tend to be more like the people among whom they live than like most other Jews. Informally, one only needs to watch the passing crowds from a Tel Aviv cafe table to be struck by the physical variety among Jews. Even with sociobiology promising to show us some new links between genetic makeup and group behavior, no data exists to demonstrate that Jewish cultural distinctiveness is essentially biologically based.

Despite this preponderance of negative arguments, one occasionally still comes across a Jewish thinker who utilizes the notion of a characteristic Jewish biology. Some rabbis still speak of a more than cultural Jewish "genius for religion." I recall hearing the eminent British literary critic George Steiner speculate that someone, someday, might discover a special Jewish variety of DNA.

Are the Jews, then, a Nationality?

A much happier product of the turn of the century thinkers was Zionism. The Zionists contended that the Jews were a nation and they should assert their distinctive identity by devoting themselves to their folk culture. Theodor Herzl gave Zionism intellectual credence, though arousing intense opposition, when he defined Jewish existence in political terms. His ideas could not be ignored once he created the World Zionist Organization to work publicly on the agenda of Jewish nationalism.

Herzl announced his program in a pamphlet provocatively entitled *The Jewish State*. His revolutionary understanding of the Jewish people may be gauged from these excerpts from its introduction: "I consider the Jewish question [anti-semitism] neither a social nor a religious one, though it occasionally takes these and other forms. It is a national question. To solve it we must first make it an international political problem to be discussed and resolved by the civilized nations of the world in council. We are a people—*one* people. . . . The distinctive nationality of the Jews neither can, will, nor must die. It cannot, because its external enemies keep it distinct. It does not wish to as it has proved during two thousand years of awesome suffering. It need not as I, a descendant of numberless Jews who refused to despair, am trying to prove in this pamphlet."

Herzl's political definition of Jewish identity, and that of the preceding and later Zionists, needs to be understood in the context of the emergence of European nationalism in the nineteenth century and the special circumstances of Jewish life. The Italians under Mazzini and the Germans under Bismarck had unified large states by leading groups with a common language and culture to independent political sovereignty. The Poles, the Irish, the Czechs, and other European peoples then began to dream of uniting their national groups into states of their own.

The Jews of western Europe and America felt threatened by the notion of the Jews as a separate nationality. It seemed to contradict the primary loyalty to their countries which was the condition of their being granted citizenship. The Jews in eastern Europe were more receptive to the idea that Jewishness was primarily a matter of nationality. Their countries were composed of many national groups whose right to promote their distinctive way of life was taken for granted. Moreover, considering the Jews a national group gave an internal political advantage to the modernists. It invalidated the leadership of the traditional rabbinate which adamantly opposed innovations in Jewish life or accommodations to modernity. If the Jews were fundamentally a secular group, individuals might choose how they would live as Jews. Those who wished to be religious, even in a pre-modern fashion, would be free to do so, while a similar liberty would be granted to those who wanted to recast Jewish culture in contemporary terms.

The Zionist theoreticians believed founding a Jewish state would end anti-semitism by providing a haven for "unwanted" Jews and clearly defining the nature of the Jewish people. Positively, they hoped to create an authentic Jewish culture, the first since Judaean days which did not adulterate Jewish ideals by aping the values of the gentile nations among whom the Jews had been dispersed.

The State of Israel, Yes; Classic Zionism, No

The rest of the history many of us have lived through. Until Hitler, only a few hundred thousand Jews responded to the Zionist call for immigration to Palestine. After World War II, their numbers were expanded by all the refugees who could gain permission to enter the land or be smuggled in despite the British effort to limit immigration. Then in 1948, against the advice of world leaders, and in the face of an imminent Arab attack, the State of Israel was established. Since that day, the Jewish population of the State of Israel has grown to well over three million and its problems and accomplishments have increasingly occupied the center of world Jewry's attention. Today, when people everywhere think of Jews, they immediately connect them with the State of Israel. Shall we then say that the classic Zionist theory, that the Jews today are a nation, has been proved correct?

Most American Jews, for all their devotion to the State of Israel, do not think so. For one thing the term "nation" carries the wrong connotations to most Americans. By contrast to its benign European implications, based on countries composed of several nationalities, its usage in the United States has always seemed to carry political implications. North American Jews have no formal political connection with the State of Israel though they identify with and work for its interests. Our national duties and responsibilities are unequivocally given only to our countries of citizenship. More important, for all our disbelief and nonobservance, we American Jews think of the long history of Jewish tradition as primarily religious. Until a century ago, no knowledgeable Jew had ever asserted that we were essentially a secular people among whom religion had once been highly significant.

For all its positive consequences, classic Zionism seems as false an interpretation of Jewish identity as was the classic Reform Jewish notion that the Jews are only a religion. Indeed, I would argue that the notion of Jewish nationalism is the mirror-image error of asserting that the Jews are a religious group. When modern political reality split nationality from religion the Jews were no longer able to maintain their unity of folk and faith. To identify themselves to their neighbors, Jews had to choose one or the other term as faulty as it might be. In western Europe and America, the Jews overwhelmingly spoke of themselves as a religion, thus losing much of the national side of historic Judaism. In eastern Europe, most Zionists rejected the religious definition. They proclaimed the Jews to be a nation like all other secular nations, thus denying the centrality of God and Torah in Jewish existence over the millennia.

Zionist Theory and Israeli Reality

Most Israelis still think and talk in terms of the secularism of classic Zionist theory—to the consternation of the American Jews who take the religious interpretation of Jewish life for granted. Numerous problems in communication arise from the lack of understanding on both sides. At the same time there are signs that some Israeli secularists recognize that their ideology has cut them off from an aspect of Judaism that has much to offer. Human existence in our time has become so problematic for everyone that it presses spiritual questions upon us. In Western civilization this has fostered a fascination with mysticism, cults, and evangelical religion. Among Israelis it surfaces in the occasional religious motifs utilized by poets or in the quest by some kibbutzim to introduce acceptable forms of Jewish tradition.

The religious dimension of life—as distinct from the observance of traditional Jewish law—can hardly be avoided in the State of Israel. With the Bible treasured as the great national saga, one must be acquainted with its central figure, God. Though the calendar has been secularized, Yom Kippur, an observance with no national overtones, remains the year's most awesome day. The Israelis are surely hindered in this area by their perception of the options open to them. If they did not believe they had to choose between a democratic, secular socialism and a European-oriented, unadaptive Orthodoxy, they might be more open to the possibility of Jewish religiosity. And were Israeli energies not substantially drained by the awesome struggle for economic and political well-being, the quest for a proper Israeli spirituality might lead to results of value to all Jews.

The basis for such a development is already visible. Two Israeli court cases have demonstrated the limitations of defining the Jews as a secular group. In 1962 the Israeli Supreme Court heard the plea of Daniel Rufeisen. He had been denied permission to immigrate to the State of Israel under the Law of Return which guarantees that right to all Jews. The ruling was made because he had converted to Christianity and this, the officials indicated, excluded him from the special category of Jewish immigration. (His conversion had taken place while he was hiding from the Nazis in a convent; he later became a Catholic lay brother.)

Brother Daniel argued that though he had changed his religion he was still a member of the Jewish nation. He was thus entitled to be treated as a Jew under Israeli law which is secular. By a 4 to 1 decision the court rejected Brother Daniel's plea. The majority acknowledged that he remained a Jew in some theoretical sense. However, most Jews feel that one who has converted has defected from the community and they ruled in this spirit.

In 1968 an Israeli naval officer, Binyamin Shalit, appeared before the court with a similar case. He sought to force the government to register his children by his unconverted, non-Jewish wife, as Jews by nationality but not by religion. (Both terms are used in the official Population Registry and on identity cards to allow various Israeli groups, like the Druze, to properly identify themselves.) The full complement of judges sat on this case. They decided 5 to 4 that, against religious law but in accord with the common secular Israeli understanding, the Shalit children should be registered as Jews but without religion. The decision caused such a furor that a new procedure was worked out for all future cases. No distinction between Jewish nationality and religion would be allowed. One who registered as a Jewish national would also be registered as a Jew by religion.

The results of the Brother Daniel and Shalit cases resulted in this complex summary by a contemporary commentator: For the State of Israel a Jew is a person born of a Jewish mother or having converted to Judaism, not being a person affiliated to some other religion. I suggest that this is a significant though limited admission by the Israelis that religion is a necessary constituent of Jewish identity.

Shall We Define Ourselves as a Hybrid?

Apparently, the only adequate way of characterizing the Jews today will be to combine aspects of religion and nationality. Those words do not easily fit with one another in American usage. Fortunately, the times have now provided us with a term which eases our problem from the "national" side. We can say with little fear of misunderstanding that the Jews are "an ethnic group."

Belonging to an ethnic group means that one shares a special culture, generally related to the country one's family came from. Maintaining one's distinctive ethnic style is consonant if not positively desirable in contemporary American nationalism. The Italians, the Irish, the Chinese, or the blacks are all entitled and perhaps encouraged to maintain their unique way of life so as to enhance our country's cultural pluralism. A generation or two back, preserving one's foreignness seemed un-American. These days the melting pot theory of Americanism, which demands that everyone assimilate to Episcopalian or Puritan standards, sounds repressive and undemocratic. Jews find it relatively easy, then, to be understood when they say they are an ethnic group, though one which has its own distinctive religion. (Ironically, the acceptable term "ethnic" derives from the Greek word *ethnos* which means "nation.")

To call the Jews a combination of a religious and an ethnic group still leaves room for some confusion. It does not make clear the special relationship between our peoplehood and our religion.

A comparison with the Armenians is illuminating. Both ethnic groups come from the Near East. Both have substantial diasporas and boast communities abroad that are uncommonly loyal to their traditions. Much of Armenian culture centers on religious practice. The Armenians have also known vicious persecution, by the Turks, and went through a holocaust of their own in their homeland before and during World War I.

What the Contrast with the Armenians Discloses

The similarities between Armenians and Jews are quite striking. So is one major difference between them—their connection to their religion. Though the Armenians are Christians of their own special sort, they are not the only Christians in the world. A precious culture would be lost if there were no Armenians to carry on and elaborate the Armenian way of being a Christian. But Christianity as a whole does not depend on the survival of the Armenians. The same cannot be said of the Jews. They have a religion which is theirs alone in all the world. If there are no Jews there is no Judaism. To anyone who holds that Judaism possesses a qualitatively significant religious truth, the end of the Jewish people would mean the disappearance of its unique spiritual insight.

Ethnicity and religion interact in Judaism in quite special ways. Historically, Jews invested their ethnicity with unusual significance because they believed in the uniqueness of their religion. Even today, when religious belief is difficult for many, I would argue that, in an authentic Jewish life, religion validates peoplehood rather than the other way around, though the two cannot be separated one from another.

Our odd situation is best seen in the two ways in which one becomes a Jew. Obtaining Israeli citizenship, living on the land, speaking Hebrew, and participating actively in Israeli culture do not yet make one a Jew. The State of Israel has more than a million Moslem and Christian citizens who do all that. Rather, one is normally born a Jew, wherever that happens to take place.

While circumcision is a commandment for males and naming ceremonies are accepted practices for all children today, neither "makes one" a Jew. Biology does that for us as for all ethnic groups. So someone is a Dane not by believing in Denmark but by being born into a Dánish family. Less commonly, people "become" Jews, regardless of their birth, by the act of conversion, a religious process. By study, will, decision, and acceptance one is as much a Jew as anyone whose Jewishness came biologically. Jewish law is quite firm on the full status of converts to Judaism. Any Jew who has qualms about converts is not reacting out of genuine Jewish values but from plain prejudice. Note too that, once someone has converted, their children are *born* Jewish.

The Jews, then, are a religion but they are not a "church"; in our religion, the community has the structure of an ethnic group. But, unlike other ethnic groups, we Jews have a unique religion which we alone affirm. There are not many such religio-ethnic groups in the world but, for example, the Sikhs of India are very much like us. I suppose that if there were more groups like the Jews and the Sikhs the English language would invent a term for them. Until then, we will have to insist that our richly complicated character is badly conveyed by simple words like religion, race, or nation. For the time being we shall have to make do with awkward hybrid coinages and say the Jews are a religio-ethnic group.

·2·

HOW DID JUDAISM BEGIN ?

Intellectuals cannot leave simple questions alone. When someone asks me how Judaism started I suspect that they really are interested in two separate issues: how did the Jewish people begin? and, how did monotheism, the unique Jewish belief, arise?

Having already surrendered to my proclivity to complicate matters, let me continue. Where did the term "Judaism" come from? Classic Jewish literature knows no such word. Not until modern times, did Jewish authors begin to discuss their "ism." I shall therefore say something later about the circumstances in which the term arose and the peculiar effect it can exercise on our self-understanding.

Asking about Judaism raises all these problems because the coming of modernity created special problems for categorizing our community and its traditions. For the last two centuries, Western civilization has made a sharp distinction between ethnic groups and religions. When people ask about Judaism, they may want to hear either about a certain group of people or about a religious faith and practice. Much of this book deals with the difficulties created by this perception: that we are *either* a folk *or* a faith.

The Traditional Account of Hebrew Origins

We begin with the question about our start as a people. The Torah tells us the Jews began with Abraham. To be precise, the Bible calls Abraham's descendants "the Hebrews." Academic

37

usage reserves the term "Jews" until Roman times when it refers to all those who called the province of Judaea their homeland.

Despite the Torah's primary interest in the Jews, the first chapter of Genesis does not begin the story of Abraham. Apparently, he and his people must be understood against the background of universal human origins. The first eleven chapters of Genesis recount what preceded him.

God, in creating the cosmos, fashioned Adam and Eve so that they could be commanded. God told them to procreate, to manage the world and tend the Garden of Eden, but not to eat from the trees of knowledge and life. Startlingly unlike other creatures, these humans were free to obey or disobey God's word. They chose to transgress one of the commands and were banished from the garden. Their children and their children's children for several generations were similarly disobedient until "the earth was full of violence." (Gen. 6:11)

Because humankind had become so perverse, the Torah says God brought a flood that drowned everyone but a single righteous man, Noah, and his family. Within generations a proliferated humankind sought to build a tower which would reach into the heavens, God's dwelling place, thus usurping God's status and challenging God's rule. God then punished these willful creatures by dividing them into separate nationalities speaking separate languages, thus thwarting their scheme to make their unity a means to divinity.

To understand Abraham's appearance we must be sensitive to the predicament which, according to the Torah, God now faces. How can God get free people to be good? To punish them fully for their evil would mean wiping them out, frustrating God's purposes in creation. Starting all over again with the seed of one righteous person would not likely be more effective than it was in Noah's case. God therefore tries another tactic. God "comes to" a certain man, Abram, later Abraham, a resident of Ur in Chaldea, and proposes to create a new people through his descendants. Abraham and his progeny are to be especially loyal to God, observing commandments not given to the rest of humankind. In turn, God promises to make them a populous nation, giving them a land of their own and guarding them throughout history. While the Genesis texts do not say so explicitly, the stories imply that as a result of the Abrahamites' service all the world will come freely to serve God.

Though Abraham survives several tests of his faith, for which God rewards him, he has only one son, Isaac, with his wife, Sarah. For this, as for so much else, the Torah gives no reason; it merely recounts the facts it knows. Isaac, in turn, does no more by way of propagating the Jewish people. But his son, Jacob, sires the twelve boys who initiate the tribes that create the Hebrew people. Their descendants called themselves the family of the father of their nation, namely, "the children of Jacob," or, more commonly, by his other name "the children of Israel." This familiar phrase should be taken literally. The Jews are one family, one which includes their converts. This sense of themselves united their communities though they scattered through the world and their practice diverged over the ages.

In sum, the Torah knows precisely how the Jewish people began: God brought them into being about twenty generations after creation to fulfill the divine purpose in creating the universe.

How Would a Modern Historian Tell the Story?

Liberal Jews do not find this sort of answer satisfactory. It ascribes all significant action to God and gives little credit to human initiative. We moderns feel much more certain about how people act than about how God effects history. For us the Bible itself is as much the result of human creativity as of God's revelation.* Its account of Jewish origins will likely tell us much more about its authors' beliefs than about what "really" happened. An adequate answer to our question, then, must be given in terms of modern history, not traditional theology—though history and theology cannot ultimately be kept separate.

Contemporary scholarship only partially satisfies our curiosity about the historical antecedents of our people. It can find almost no direct, reliable data on this topic. The historians must, then, work by drawing parallels from the history of other Near Eastern peoples or by trying to tease out the historical substrata of the Torah's tales of the patriarchs. Their results are, therefore, highly speculative.

*On this topic see Part Three, *The Bible and Tradition.*

The archeological data offers an example typical of our difficulties. For all the help that various discoveries have given us regarding later Jewish history, particularly the period of the Kingdoms of Israel and Judah, they give no hard evidence concerning the first Jews many centuries before. The earliest unambiguous archeological reference to our people has been dated about 1225 B.C.E. (Scholars estimate the approximate date of Abraham as about 2000 B.C.E.) The stele of Merneptah, an Egyptian pharaoh, preserves a poem proclaiming the king's many important victories. In the course of listing the many peoples he has conquered, the poem boasts, "Israel is laid waste. His people no longer exists." Our first, nonbiblical data concerning the Jews proclaims their destruction, so far back does the problem of Jewish survival go!

At one time archeologists thought that they might have a good answer to the problem of Jewish origins. Documents discovered in a number of sites that date back to the third millennium B.C.E. refer to a group called the Habiru. The name reads like a Semitic variation of the word "Hebrews." The texts describe the group as unusually mobile, perhaps nomad-like. As a result, a number of scholars declared the Habiru to be the forerunners of the Hebrews.

The consensus of scholarly opinion today considers the Habiru hypothesis most unlikely. The linguistic similarities which appear so close in English are dubious from what we know of the variations of the dialects. Indeed, the English transliteration of the name as "Habiru" may reflect a biblical bias on the part of the investigators. More important, the Habiru seem to constitute a social class, something like a group of respected migrant workers, one of whose specialties was soldiering. They do not at all seem a family-based ethnic group as the earliest Hebrews were. Finally, the data about the Habiru continues down to about the time when the Jews were already a distinct people, making the evolution of the one group into the other most unlikely.

We Do Not Know Much and Are Unlikely to Learn More

The lack of direct archeological data leaves us largely with the Bible as the raw material for our historical account of Jewish origins. Liberal historians try to read the tales of the patriarchal period in terms of what is known of the surrounding peoples and of the way history in general proceeds. Scholars differ as to the credence they place in the historicity of the patriarchs or given incidents of their lives. Some decades back, there was much debunking of these biblical accounts. These days the scholarly community treats them with much more respect, largely because many of their details now seem quite plausible as a result of archeological finds from other peoples in this area.

All our evidence appears to indicate that various familial-linguistic-ethnic groups came into being in the Near East about the time of Abraham. Over the centuries some groups increased in numbers, acquiring national identity of the kind we are familiar with from the Bible's references to peoples like the Edomites or Amalekites. But we cannot say much more than that with reasonable certainty. Thus, though Egyptian historical records are relatively detailed, they tell us nothing about the rise of a Hebrew nation, ten destructive plagues, or the exodus of a former slave-people from their land. Some scholars argue that only part of the Hebrew tribes were in Egypt, namely the so-called Joseph tribes, Ephraim and Manasseh. The exodus of so small a group would not have troubled the Egyptians enough to be noted in their histories. The events, however, might have had religious significance for all the other Hebrew tribes, eventually being adopted by them as the story which told of the birth of their nation.

The Torah's portrayal of the journey through the wilderness adds little to what we can say with historical accuracy. The books which tell of the Hebrews' entry into the Land of Israel and their subsequent history there become increasingly reliable as they leave the period of Hebrew beginnings. That is about all we "really" know.

Many people are unhappy with this misty picture. They would like to know clearly and unambiguously where the Jews came from. Every new archeological find arouses their hope that they will finally get the answer they seek. In recent decades the excavations at Tel el Amarna and at Mari especially have expanded our understanding of Semitic languages and ideas. Though the documents found there have enabled us to read the Torah tales with a somewhat altered perspective, they did not solve the riddle of the Hebrews' origins.

Considerable excitement has recently been generated among

biblical scholars by the discovery of over 15,000 tablets at the Syrian site of Ebla. These, we have been told, promise to shed new light on the period of Abraham. Unfortunately no substantial number of texts has thus far been published and thereby submitted to general academic scrutiny. That has not prevented popularizers from making sensational proclamations that these documents provide us with the earliest traces of Jewish history. But a number of biblical scholars have given me the impression that new texts, these or others, are most unlikely to revolutionize our understanding of the ancient Near East. We have had many such discoveries over the past century. They mesh with one another well enough to give us a good, broad-scale impression of the civilizations in the area. In the future, we can realistically expect to gain new understandings of detail rather than radical revisions of perspective. The great exception to that rule would be our finding Hebrew documents of the patriarchal period for they would be a thousand years or so earlier than anything we now possess. Without such direct data our relatively nebulous picture of the origins of the Jewish people will remain unchanged.

The Origins of Monotheism Are Not Much Clearer

We cannot be much more precise as to when the Hebrews' belief in one God emerged. Again, let us begin with the Torah's version. It continually emphasizes God's deeds. God makes a Covenant* with Abraham. God renews the Covenant with Isaac and Jacob, preserves Jacob's family despite their strife, and, most spectacularly, takes the Hebrews out of Egypt, splitting the Sea of Reeds for them but drowning their pursuers. God then personally speaks Ten "Words" (Hebrew, *dibrot*) to the entire people encamped at the foot of Mount Sinai. The Torah, in Abraham Heschel's telling title, knows a "God in search of man."

Our liberal dissatisfaction with an answer that speaks essentially of God's feats appears most charmingly in our frequent elevation of a midrash about Abraham to the status of a Bible tale. In rabbinic literature (Gen. R. 38:13) we read that Abraham was the son of an idol merchant. One day he realizes that statues are

*To distinguish between God's covenant with all humankind—on which see chapter 3 of this unit—and God's Covenant with the people of Israel—also discussed in chapter 3— I capitalize when the latter usage is involved.

unworthy of worship. He smashes all but the largest one, in whose hand he places a club. When his father upbraids him for the carnage, he puts the blame on the remaining idol. His father then ridicules the notion that an idol could have caused the damage, allowing Abraham to retort that his incredulity testifies to the futility of all idol worship. Abraham thus brings his father to belief in the one God.

Liberal Jews have told this tale so often that many among us believe it is in the Book of Genesis. They would like it to be for it replaces an active God as the source of Jewish monotheism with human discovery. For liberals, appeals to human reason or experience rather than divine revelation make religion believable.

When we ask modern historians to explain how the Hebrew idea of one God "really" began, we get little beyond informed imagination. Archeology provides us almost no relevant information in this regard. The one possible exception illustrates the problems we encounter seeking to draw parallels to Hebrew belief.

Late in the nineteenth century, Egyptologists discovered texts recounting the religious reforms of Amenhotep IV, who reigned briefly in the fourteenth century B.C.E. He broke with traditional Egyptian polytheism and worshiped Aton, the solar disc, as the sole god of the universe, changing his own name to Ikhnaton. Scholars suggested that Moses, whom the Bible pictures as raised by pharaoh's daughter, might have learned the idea of one God from what was still remembered of Ikhnaton. This hypothesis seemed finally to remove Hebrew monotheism from the realm of the supernatural and show it to be only another human discovery. Sigmund Freud added to the popularity of this theory when he utilized it in one of his last books, *Moses and Monotheism*—one generally conceded to be his poorest mature creation.

For some time now most academicians have found little in Ikhnaton's faith which parallels that of Moses (insofar as we adjudge him to have been a pure monotheist). Ikhnaton was an idolater though he worshiped the sun disc exclusively. His religion was limited to himself and his family. His courtiers worshiped him as god; the common people remained unaware of his religious revolution. He moved from Egypt's royal city to a new capital to effectuate his religious innovations. After his reign of a few years, the city was abandoned and the court returned to its customary site. The likelihood of Moses' having learned about monotheism from one of Ikhnaton's courtiers seems quite remote. This hypothesis takes as factual Moses' upbringing by pharaoh's daughter, a concept which many scholars consider a typical folk elaboration of a hero legend.

Logically, too, the theory is unsatisfactory. Had Moses gained the germ of monotheism from Ikhnaton that would settle nothing. It would only push back our question from a Hebrew to an Egyptian source. We should then ask, Where did Ikhnaton get his idea of monotheism?

Faith in One God Comes Suddenly

In such straits we are tempted to construct a theory of religious evolution. We try tracing a natural growth in human spirituality from fetishism and animism to polytheism and thence to monotheism. This suggests that Ikhnaton, and other proto-monotheists around the world, simply moved on from many gods to a supreme god to the one God. The smoothness and simplicity of this process make it a most appealing explanation. Unfortunately, the evidence uncovered in studying the history of human religions does not bear it out. Polytheism does not naturally lead on to monotheism. It didn't do so among the Hebrews' neighbors even after the Hebrews became monotheists. Nor did belief in one God quickly become common among other peoples despite the centuries the Hebrews lived among them. Where something recognizably like monotheism does appear, it does so unexpectedly, as a break with the past.

Some theoreticians seek to ease our difficulty by suggesting that Moses and the early Hebrew prophets were not so much monotheists as henotheists. That is, they retained the belief in other gods but asserted that their God was supreme, at least in their country, perhaps in the universe as a whole. A number of biblical verses seem to reflect this sort of faith. The best known hint of Hebrew henotheism occurs in that portion of the Song of the Sea used at Jewish services, the *Mi Chamochah*. The praise offered God literally translates as, "Who is like You, *Adonai*, among the gods [*elim*]?" Whoever first said that apparently believed that many gods exist though *Adonai* is incomparably the greatest one of all. Other scholars see such texts as only a literary usage, which testifies more to the Semitic way of expressing religious sentiments than to the nature of the Hebrews' faith in God.

The problem of the origins of Hebrew monotheism generates far more academic controversy than the thorny question of the beginnings of the Jewish people. The problems involved in investigating the historical development of faith in God are overwhelming. Once we agree that many of the Torah's accounts present us more with legend than with history, how shall we read them so as to extract what the Hebrews "really" believed? We cannot easily draw parallels to Hebrew religious development from other peoples. The reason is simple: The spiritual history of ancient humanity knows nothing like the God of the Hebrew Bible. Only the Hebrews arrived at a fully monotheistic faith. Whatever explanation we seek to give for the origins of Hebrew monotheism, it must concentrate on that which has no parallels among nearby or distant peoples. Thus, identifying the early Hebrews as henotheists still does not clarify how they ultimately broke through to the critical insight: There is only one God in the universe.

These difficulties surfaced some years ago in a controversy over a thesis put forward by the greatest American Semiticist of the time, Ephraim Speiser. While writing a commentary to Genesis, Speiser confronted the problem of what moved Abraham to his exceptional faith. Despite his incomparable knowledge of ancient Near Eastern civilization and his feel for the dynamics of history, Speiser insisted Abraham could not be accounted for in the usual historical terms. Speiser instead proposed to attribute Abraham's religious breakthrough to something like personal genius. Speiser specifically did not argue theologically; he did not appeal to divine revelation. He only remarked that some human beings vault so far beyond others of their era that we simply cannot understand how they did so—and Abraham was one such case. For all its humanism, Speiser's view deeply troubled other scholars. They felt that he had abandoned proper historical explanation and resorted to what they considered the murkiness of quasi-religious or mystical reasoning.

Personally, I do not see why secular humanists cannot argue that some people have quite extraordinary talent. In science, it seems the simplest way to explain path-breaking theoreticians like Galileo, Newton, and Einstein. In our earliest records of

Greek philosophy, the pre-Socratics hardly prepare us for the breathtaking accomplishment of Plato and then, with another radical shift, Aristotle—after whom come centuries filled with thinkers of only modest interest to us. Why should not Abraham be considered another of such unexpected geniuses?

History Does Not Proceed by Our Needs

The theory that the times themselves produce the person may often be true but it should not be taken as a rule by which to diminish the uniqueness of a genius. In our own time the field of subatomic physics has sought a new model to harmonize the welter of presently discordant data—but the need has not produced the theoretician. The same is true in religion. Already in the early 1950s, the historian of world civilization, Arnold Toynbee, suggested that our desperate spiritual condition made the times ripe for the creation of a new religion. He thought the best way of filling the void in the human soul would be a faith that bridged the chasm between the oriental and occidental views of reality. Despite a steady parade of visionaries claiming to have such a truth and despite an ever more desperate spiritual state, the new salvation apparently has not appeared. Needing a religious genius does not necessarily produce one. When one has appeared to change our perspective radically, we should acknowledge the exceptional accomplishment. We might then say about the origins of Judaism, "Abraham [Moses, if you prefer to move the explanation up some centuries] was a religious genius whose unique sensitivity gave birth to Hebrew monotheism."

To be fair, we should add a social dimension to this line of argument; in this case, the Jewish people. A founder requires believers and those who continue the faith. There have been many individual religious geniuses among humankind, if we can judge from the fragments of their teachings. Their doctrine did not survive the ages because no group of adherents cherished it so much that they carried it through history. Abraham's unique understanding of God became the passionate faith of a community which has lived by it over the centuries, deepening and extending it as they did so. The Bible leaves us with no illusions about the Hebrews' willingness to accept monotheism. The prophetic writings amply attest to their continual desire for idols and "whoring after strange gods."

These accounts of the Hebrews' backsliding are so human—
which is to say that we recognize ourselves in them—that we can
hardly doubt them. They describe the way we would expect people to behave when challenged by a radical doctrine.

The tales of Hebrew recalcitrance convey only half the story.
The Bible knows not only idol worship but return to God. Regardless of episodes of unfaithfulness, the Covenant relationship
held. Through the prophets' leadership, the Hebrews overcame
their desire to be like all other peoples and made loyalty to
Abraham's God the basis of their folk existence. A nation shaped
its character in terms of one man's insight. This corporate response must be recognized as the needed counterpart of an individual's breakthrough, if the vision is to survive the centuries. If
you will, the "genius" of the Jewish people in accepting the odd
religion of their founder is as much part of the origins of Judaism
as is Abraham's own genius.

Liberal Religious Theories of the Origins of Monotheism

The theories given above are humanistic, that is, they assume
that what "really" happened must be explained only in terms of
what people did. We can account for the beginnings of our faith
somewhat differently, if we believe there is a God and that God
and people can "communicate" (in some non-Orthodox fashion,
to be sure*). Our sense of what "really" happened will then make
some room for our relationship with God. A rationalist thinker,
like Hermann Cohen, would interpret what I have called "genius" as breaking through intellectually to a rational idea of God
and ethics. For Mordecai Kaplan it would mean attaining the
insight that the Jewish people's surging will to live was a response
to nature's support of human self-realization. A semi-rationalist
like Leo Baeck would say that the essence of Judaism was first
grasped when one of our forebears not only conceived of ethical
monotheism but linked it firmly to a consciousness of the mystery
which grounds human existence.

In a way, we may call such theologies varieties of religious
humanism. While they affirm that God is real, God remains relatively passive in the spiritual life. Humankind takes the center of
the religious stage and human search and discovery account for
religious insight. The "genius" comes, as it does in every other

*See Part Three, *The Bible and Tradition*, chapter 2, "How Does God Speak to People?"

field, by a daring break with past assumptions so that we may for the first time truly appreciate what has previously been present but unperceived.

A decisive shift in understanding religion develops in the thought of such nonrationalist thinkers as Martin Buber, Franz Rosenzweig, and Abraham Heschel. They insist our account of the origins of Jewish belief must not limit God to a passive role in human spiritual discovery. Buber and Rosenzweig are loath to say just what God does or how God does it. Each uses a symbol taken from human relationships to point to God's part of human religious discovery. Buber speaks of God's "being present," while Rosenzweig preferred to speak of God's "love." In neither case does God give specific commands or dictate documents. Yet, these thinkers suggest that, if we knew God were truly with us, we would be inspired and know we could not live as we had before. Something like that—which we can know from our own religious experience, as paltry as it may be—happened in the generative encounters between God and Abraham (and Moses) and the people of Israel. Even as they can happen to us, so they "really" took place then. Buber and Rosenzweig deny that a secular history can ever do justice to the reality of the Jewish people's religious experiences.

Abraham Heschel's thought provides an existentialist reinterpretation of traditional Jewish theories of our origins. He held that critical modern conceptions of what transpired in the biblical period say more about our modern self-assertion and denial of God than they do about what "really" happened. Religion results not from human discovery but from God's search for people who will listen, today as in the past. And the Bible accurately, though in human terms, records what God has revealed to us: that God called Abraham to a special Covenant and thus began the Jewish faith.

What Do We Mean when We Say "Judaism"?

The term "Judaism" came into common use only in the nineteenth century. My *Webster Unabridged Dictionary* defines an "ism" as a "distinctive doctrine, cause, theory, or system." Thus, in politics we readily speak of fascism, communism, capitalism, or socialism. Applied to a religion, the suffix "ism" emphasizes its intellectual content. In the relatively rational climate of the nineteenth century high value was placed on the *ideas* of a religious tradition. This usage was particularly congenial to Protestant groups who emphasized the doctrines necessary for a faith that truly saved one. Terms like Protestantism and Catholicism set the model for calling all the world's religions "isms."

Perhaps such terminology does not distort the nature of Buddhism, many of whose groups speak of themselves primarily as a philosophy of life. But it can give us inappropriate cues when we seek to understand other religions, such as Mohammedanism and Hinduism. Moslems object to the use of the term "Mohammedanism" to describe their faith: it does not center on Mohammed, even though he was the last and greatest of the prophets; he did not create their faith, God revealed it in the Koran. Moslem spirituality is not essentially a "doctrine . . . , theory, or system" but a reverent acknowledgment of the majesty and providence of the one, incomparable God. Therefore, Moslems call their religion "Islam," the acceptance of God's rule—and the word also refers to the widespread community of believers, the "nation" of Islam.

The term "Hinduism," too, was not created by Indian religious usage. Western scholars coined it to provide a name to include the many religions found in India. All the efforts to find a common intellectual pattern—an "ism"—in these Hindu faiths have ended in frustration. Major philosophical systems proliferate in Hindu religious history, but some of these substantially contradict one another. Not to recognize the diversity of Indian religion would be to miss one of its chief characteristics.

In the case of Islam and Hinduism (we do not have a better term for Hindu religion as a whole), the designation "ism" has had unfortunate consequences. We westerners come to these faiths expecting them to have the creedal emphasis of modern Protestantism and to be of interest primarily for their theological ideas. This is quite misleading. In both Islam and Hinduism, the groups that bear the faiths—"the nation of Islam" and the people of India—are as important to their spiritual consciousness as are their central doctrines. Certainly in the case of Hindu religions, the traditions, tales, and observances occupy a far greater place in the lives of most believers than do the philosophies or religious ideas.

The Virtues and Defects of a New Name

The nineteenth-century pioneers of modern Jewish life welcomed the term "Judaism" for it effectively explained their status to the general society. It unambiguously proclaimed the Jews were a religion, a status which entitled them to remain a separate group. It also defined the Jewish difference in terms of beliefs and ideas, thus refuting any charge that the Jews could not give full political loyalty to their new nations. Moreover, this self-identification allowed Jews to argue that the essence of their "ism," ethics and monotheism, was far more acceptable to a modern mind than was Christianity to which Jews were being urged to convert.

This intellectual approach to Judaism came to a climax in the pre-World War I system propounded by the German theoretician Hermann Cohen. He identified the "ism" of the Jews with his conception of "rational religion." In his neo-Kantian philosophy he had proved that a modern mind required a concept of God as the basis of a mature world view. Its major consequence was an activist ethics. And, Cohen taught, the Jewish people were the pre-philosophic discoverers and historical teachers of the rational concept of ethical monotheism to humankind.

Since World War II, rational philosophy has increasingly lost whatever confidence American Jews once had in it. Our ethnicity has again become a central component of our Jewish consciousness. Jewish faith involves the Jewish people far more than it does Jewish philosophy; our piety characteristically expresses itself more in doing deeds than in thinking about the universe with an integrated world view. Yet for some people the term "Judaism" still implies that we mainly espouse a "distinctive doctrine, cause, theory, or system." To call us an "ism" may unconsciously cause us to omit or derogate the ethnic component of being a Jew. When understood with such connotations, the coinage is most misleading, for it wrongly separates our ideas of God and ethics from our simultaneous commitment to the people of Israel and its Torah tradition.

This intellectualizing usage of "Judaism" so disturbed Mordecai Kaplan that he made a new definition of the term the focal point of his philosophy. Kaplan equated Judaism with Jewish culture, what in the language of the 1930s he denominated our "civilization." By calling Judaism the full-scale civilization of the Jewish people, Kaplan indicated that a healthy Jewish life must include a rounded folk culture, art, music, dance, literature and not merely a doctrine of ethical monotheism. As American Jews have increasingly reclaimed their ethnicity, Kaplan's ideas have had a great appeal to many.

Critics of Kaplan have charged that identifying Judaism with our ethnic culture secularizes it too much. Kaplan has agreed that his formulation can easily be misunderstood. He had no intention of dispensing with the centrality of religion in Jewish culture. He suggests he would have expressed his full intentions more clearly had he said Judaism was our "religious civilization." This concession does not remedy the flaw which Jews like me see in Kaplan's humanism.* What Kaplan means by religion is something like positively responding to life. Those of us who consider God real and independent of us therefore require a more God-inclusive term than civilization to label our people's relationship to God.

I would be happiest if I could avoid the term "Judaism" when I am asked my religion. Instead I would like to respond, "I follow the Torah in a modern way." I think that would identify me in a more authentic Jewish fashion than implying that I merely hold to the Jews' "ism" or participate in Jewish folk culture. I would hope that people would hear in the word Torah my relation to God as part of the people of Israel, elaborated by its prophets and later teachers, and still being creatively developed by Jews in our community today. However, I am afraid most people will find my Torah-centered answer rather strange, so I shall go on using the word "Judaism." But I do not mean by it any relatively intellectualized or secular notion of what it means to be a believing Jew.

*To see how Kaplan redefines God in terms of human experience, consult chapters 2 and 3 of Part Two, *The God We Affirm.*

·3·

ARE THE JEWS CHOSEN?

Jewish tradition affirms that God chose the Jews. This notion arouses such passionate dissent today that we had better carefully delineate what it meant before considering its modern reinterpretations.

In the Bible, choosing has an unequivocal meaning; of several possibilities one is selected. The biblical authors utilize the same word for God's interest in Israel that they use to denote people's choosing a champion to fight for them or an animal to sacrifice. God identified the Hebrews with God's own purposes in creation. Thus, before giving them the Torah at Mt. Sinai, God is reported to say, "If you will obey Me faithfully and keep My Covenant you shall be My treasured possession among all the peoples." (Exod. 19:5) God might have done this with any other people but God didn't. So the Bible authors say simply, God chose the Jews.

This distinction between the Jews and other peoples creates a paradoxical biblical view of humankind. The biblical writers earnestly believe in the essential equality of all human beings before God. In Adam and Eve they have one father and one mother; despite all apparent differences they are, then, literally, one family. The authors of the Bible also assert that God separated one group from among all other groups of humans and brought them into a unique relationship with God. That is, God divided humanity, theologically, into Jews and "the nations," literally, Gentiles —a word so disturbing to many modern Jews that they regularly substitute for it the euphemism "non-Jews."

52

Affirming the Paradox and Seeking to Justify It

Jewish law and practice made the people of Israel's chosenness a steady theme in Jewish living. The *siddur,* the traditional prayer book, precedes the recitation of the *Shema* with: "You have chosen us from all peoples and nations and associated us with Your great name. . . ." Before every reading from the Torah scroll, one thanks God ". . . who has chosen us from among all peoples. . . ."

During the centuries Jews lived among idolaters; daily experience corroborated their sense of a unique relationship with God. By belief and practice, they obviously differed from all other peoples. When Christianity and Islam spread monotheism to "the nations," the Jews still had little difficulty distinguishing themselves from their neighbors. Christian trinitarianism and iconography reminded the Jews of paganism, and the tones of Moslem and Christian lives, particularly their maltreatment of the Jews, made the differences between the faiths plain. Until modern times and still to some Jews today, Jewish devotion and difference were justified by the belief that God chose the Jews "from among all peoples" and brought them into an unparalleled Covenant.

Occasionally a classic Jewish text reveals an author confronting the paradox of affirming God's universal dominion simultaneously with God's choice of the Hebrews. Another verse preceding the Bible's account of the giving of the Ten Commandments states the tension flatly, "Indeed all the earth is Mine but you shall be My kingdom of priests and holy nation." (Exod. 19:5–6) This logical difficulty can lead to efforts at explanation: "You are a people consecrated to *Adonai,* your God. Of all the peoples on earth *Adonai,* your God, chose you to be His treasured people. It is not because you are the most populous people that *Adonai* set His heart on you and chose you—indeed, you are the smallest of peoples—but because *Adonai* loved you and kept the oath He made to your fathers. . . ." (Deut. 7:6–8)

In talmudic literature we find similar occasional attempts at justifying God's choice of the Jews. One argument, attested above, points to the great merits of the patriarchs which won an eternal Covenant for their descendants. (Scholars today read this as retrojection, that is, a subtle way of reproving their contemporaries, whose sinful behavior the rabbis considered the reason for

the destruction of the Second Temple.) More commonly, however, the rabbis considered the ancient Hebrews worthier than
any other nation to receive the Torah. Apparently their Greco-
Roman neighbors chided them for claiming they had a unique
status with God. They responded by alleging that God had tried
to choose other peoples, all of whom withdrew from God as soon
as they heard about the heavy responsibilities that would devolve
upon them. The Jews alone willingly accepted the Covenant declaring, "We will do and obey." (Exod. 24:7; Mech. Yitro 5)

Again the social circumstances need to be considered. The
Jews lived by standards different from those of the pagan masses.
While the Jews might be sinners by the Torah's demanding standards, the rabbis considered them incomparably more faithful to
the many obligations God had laid upon them than the Gentiles
were to the lesser demands God had made of them.

I put off until now discussing the purpose of being chosen
because I wanted us first to face candidly the way chosenness
troublingly creates two categories of humanity. To dodge that
issue by quickly identifying chosenness with special responsibility
seems to me overly defensive. We have good reason to be sensitive about misinterpretations of our faith, considering how often
it has been maliciously and irrationally attacked. That does not
excuse us from facing the problems generated by our traditional
beliefs. I now hasten to round out my discussion of chosenness
by identifying its content: The Jews were chosen to live by God's
law and guidance. Jewish tradition inextricably identifies choice
and the receiving of the Torah. The twin notions occur in all the
texts cited above. Thus the blessing before reading from the
Torah scroll specifies, ". . . who has chosen us from among all
peoples and given us His Torah." While Torah includes far more
than commandments, to be chosen to receive the Torah means
selection for a life of unique responsibility to God.

Most people do not think of a heavier burden of duty when they
long to be singled out from everyone else. Rather, we hope to
have our desires fulfilled and our joys enhanced. For us, chosenness implies greater personal satisfaction. But the Jews were chosen to serve God through a life of special duty, not to receive an
abundance of privilege or power.

Is God still Involved with Gentiles?

The choice of the Jewish people to receive the Torah does not negate God's intimate relationship with the rest of humankind. Rather the Torah itself provides an unequivocal statement of the Jewish theology of Gentiles. After the flood God made a covenant with Noah, the progenitor of all succeeding human beings.* Noah offered sacrifices to God when he left the ark. In response, God made Noah certain promises and gave him new laws—the classic pattern of covenant-making. God vowed that there would be no more exterminating floods. After each rain God's "bow" will become visible in the heaven as a sign that the divine promise is being kept. God also grants Noah permission to stop being a vegetarian, as Adam and his descendants were. Noah may eat meat, with the condition that he must not do so "with its life in it, which is the blood in it." (Gen. 8:20–9:17)

In a way, we may say that all humanity has its "Torah," its duties to God under the covenant of Noah. Nothing in the accounts of Abraham's Covenant with God or his progeny's renewal of it abrogates or mitigates the covenant with the children of Noah. God's relations with humankind continue to be based on the expectation that they will live up to their continuing responsibilities to God—as the story of Sodom and Gomorrah shows.

The rabbis utilize the Noachide covenant to help them reconcile God's choice of the Jews with God's continuing involvement with all people. We can grasp their reasoning most readily through what I playfully call "theological mathematics."

The rabbis read the Genesis account of the covenant with Noah to yield seven commandments binding upon him and his descendants, i.e., humanity. All people must (1) not blaspheme God's name, (2) not worship idols, (3) not murder, (4) not steal, (5) not commit sexual sins, (6) not eat a limb cut from a living animal, and (7) establish courts of justice. Incidentally, all the provisions of the Noachide covenant were also binding upon the Jews for they remained part of humankind's basic relationship with God.

The rabbis drew a number of logical, but perhaps surprising, inferences from their theory of the Gentiles' covenant. For exam-

---

*For a discussion of how "true" such stories are, see chapter 3, "How True Is the Bible?" of Part Three, *The Bible and Tradition*.

ple, they affirmed that people do not need to be Jewish to know God. Members of every group already have a relationship with God. As a result, the rabbis did not consider it essential to convert non-Jews to Judaism as if, somehow, without Jewish help, they could not have a proper religion. Though the rabbis welcomed sincere converts and did make some efforts to bring people to Judaism, they knew that the Torah did not command or even suggest proselytizing. Gentiles who fulfilled the Noachide covenant had done what God demanded and would be rewarded.for it in the world-to-come. A dictum of R. Joshua's, much cited in modern discussions of Judaism's attitude toward non-Jews, summarizes this attitude pithily: the righteous among the nations have a share in the life of the world-to-come. (Tos. San. 13:2) So to speak, Jews believe Gentiles can be "saved" without becoming Jews, but by observing the seven Noachide commandments.

Now to our "mathematics" lesson. According to R. Simlai, the Jews were given 613 laws to follow, in the Hebrew notation, the *"taryag mitsvot."* (He did not explain how he came to this number and no one else has been able to figure out its basis. See Mak. 23b.) For rabbinic Judaism generally, this became the accepted total of the number of the commandments specified in the Torah. (As with the Noachide laws, these were substantially elaborated through the traditions and the interpretive processes of the Oral Torah.) The numerical implications of chosenness for the rabbis can now be stated. If the Gentiles have seven commandments and the Jews have 613 commandments, chosenness involves undertaking to observe 606 more commandments than the rest of humanity.

Can Chosenness Imply Superiority?

Affirming the Gentile's continuing relationship with God and stressing the Jew's greater obligations do not resolve the problems raised by the doctrine of the chosen people. We must consider its implication, an invidious judgment of the non-Jew's nearness to God. The Gentile's distance, when contrasted to the Jew's intimacy, can become the basis of Jewish chauvinism, particularly in times of persecution or threat.

The special status of the Jews with God is amply attested by the images the prophets use to describe the relationship. We hear of

Israel as God's wife or first-born son, relations which do not preclude God's loving others but which give this beloved one special preference. Under conditions of social trauma this can easily be converted into an assertion of the superiority of Jews and the inferiority of Gentiles. Considering how abominably the world has treated Jews over the centuries, the Jewish use of chosenness to demean the persecutor and exalt the sufferers has been modest indeed. The occasional text brimming with prejudice should be taken as a cry of anguish rather than a statement of belief.

I can recall only three significant Jewish thinkers who predicated the superiority of Jews over Gentiles. Yehudah Halevi (c. 1075–1141) considered the Jews a special genus of the species human beings, for they alone were capable of prophecy. A somewhat similar doctrine, applied to spirituality generally, surfaces in the writings of Judah Loew (c. 1525–1609), the Maharal of Prague. Shneur Zalman (1747–1812), the founder of Chabad, Lubavitch Chasidism, makes Jewish superiority a major premise of his central theoretical work, *Tanya.* Utilizing medieval terminology for aspects of the self, he describes Gentiles as having only animalistic souls and thus limited religious capacities. Jews have fully spiritual souls, enabling them to reach the greatest heights of service to God. This doctrine of the "Alter Rebbe" remains part of the teaching of Lubavitch Chasidism today.

The rest of Jewish tradition rarely equated chosenness with innate superiority. Having Torah doesn't change the human nature of Jews; it merely endows its possessors with heavier responsibility.

Chosenness also never involves a suspension of God's justice. The Jews, by virtue of their nearness to God, may not ask to be indulged when they sin. The prophets sternly reminded their contemporaries that God could not be induced to pamper them and allow them some special measure of iniquity because they had a Covenant with God. To the contrary, the first of the writing prophets, Amos, made God's purposes unmistakable: "Hear this word which *Adonai* spoke against you, O Children of Israel. . . . You only have I known of all the families of the earth. Therefore I will punish you for your sins." (3:2)

To be fair, we must add that the Jews might claim special merit when they observed the commandments. Having obeyed God more fully than anyone else, they felt themselves entitled to God's special favor in this world and the next. With all that, the resounding note in the Jewish literature dealing with chosenness is not reward but obligation. Covenant means that God demands more of Jews than of other people and punishes them more stringently than others.

Is the Jewish People God's Suffering Servant?

Are the Jews, then, chosen to suffer?

In classic Christianity, suffering plays a unique role in the service of God. The Christian Scriptures depict Jesus' crucifixion in terms of images found in Isaiah 53. That chapter speaks at length of God's servant. This term occurs in a number of other places in this portion of the Book of Isaiah (it is often identified with the Jewish people, e.g., Isaiah 44:1–2). The Christian writers understood Isaiah to say that the servant undergoes suffering for the sake of other people. Jesus therefore accepted a humiliating, painful death, out of his love of humanity, to atone for its sins before God. Ever since, Christians have considered suffering a significant means of demonstrating one's devotion to God. They have also assumed that Jews read Isaiah 53 the way Christians do. This line of reasoning reaches the perverse conclusion that, if the Jews are God's chosen, they are destined for special suffering. Indeed, Jews should welcome all such torment as an opportunity to serve God. The contemporary Jewish thinker Richard Rubenstein recalls how this teaching launched him on his death-of-God theology of Judaism. A German pastor who had helped Jews in the Nazi era nonetheless told Rubenstein that because the Jews were God's chosen people they ought to accept their suffering in the Holocaust as the necessary concomitant of their historic role.

Jews reject the Christian interpretation of the virtues of suffering. No Jewish symbol is remotely like a crucifix. A Jew serves God by doing commandments, and Jews ought to be as healthy as possible so that they can fulfill the heavy responsibility of sanctifying daily life. At the same time, we do not see that being in pain makes one especially dear to God. Jewish teachers have discouraged ascetic practices such as monasticism or celibacy. Most people have enough suffering in their lives. They do not need to seek more. Instead, Jews have been taught to do good and avoid imposing suffering. Should it come, they should seek to avoid it whenever possible and bear it in faith when they cannot do so. Then, too, they ought to learn from it whatever it can teach us. But the sages of Judaism knew that not all suffering makes us more spiritual. Often, despite our greatest efforts, it breaks us as people, destroying even our capacity to serve God.

Jews did not commonly apply the suffering servant poem of Isaiah 53 to their people until the massacres that befell their communities as the First Crusade moved through them. From then on some Jewish teachers spoke of persecution as a necessary accompaniment of chosenness. The so-called German Chasidim (thirteenth century) even undertook special bodily rigors as a means of purifying the soul, a practice which influenced a small number of Jewish mystics in succeeding centuries. Most Jewish teachers, knowing the long record of Jewish persecution, remained unimpressed by the religious value of suffering. The popular attitude toward it is encapsulated in the bitter Yiddish crack, "You chose us from among all peoples? So why did You have to pick on us?"

Modern Jews recognize that their people's uncommon belief and practice made them an easy target for personal hostility. Then too those who disliked the standards the Bible demanded of them could displace on us their anger against their religious teachers or parents. In any case and no matter what interpretation we give of chosenness, we are certain that it does not mean God set us aside to provide a scapegoat on which human viciousness could vent itself. We earnestly appeal to all who believe in suffering as a particularly meritorious way of achieving intimacy with God to apply that doctrine only to themselves and not impose it on the Jewish people. After the Holocaust we do not see how anyone can dare suggest to Jews that they need to suffer more for God's sake.

Reinterpreting Chosenness in the Context of Democracy

With the Emancipation, the doctrine of the chosen people came under special strain. The modern mind found it making too great a claim for God and having too little appreciation of the non-Jew's spirituality.

On the theological level, the notion of God choosing seems

irredeemably prescientific. It makes God a continual intruder into
nature and history. Specifically, chosenness depicts God as taking
the Hebrews out of Egypt, leading them to Sinai, personally
speaking the Ten Commandments, and then giving the rest of the
Torah to Moses. Science makes such a description of history
unbelievable. We see events occurring largely in terms of natural
patterns rather than as the result of unpredictable divine incur-
sions. We find God working through the natural order rather
than interrupting it. For most liberals, God's "doing" something
means an inner, personal, human experience which then produces a new human perspective or action. Any people can feel
chosen or choose to serve God, but that God, at one point in
history, selected the Jews from among all the nations can hardly
find a place in our modern world view.

The doctrine also troubles us because our intellectuality demands universalism and denies all particular claims to qualitative
uniqueness. Thus, science shows the unities behind all natural
behavior, including the human—what we once called the "laws of
nature." So, too, ethics insists that limiting duty or responsibility
to any one group rather than the whole of humankind is inherently immoral. In such a purview, chosenness can most easily be
explained as another instance of ethnic self-glorification, or the
projection of our group's will to survive, or our compensating
reaction to others' prejudices against us. We can understand why
Jews once asserted that God had chosen them, but we find that
doctrine difficult to affirm today.

Contemporary Jews also do not feel as different from Gentiles
as did the Jews of biblical and rabbinic times. Then Jews lived
surrounded by idol-worshipers. Today, Jews are clearly not the
only people who believe in the one God and have significant
ethical concerns. With the continuing modernization of Protestantism and Catholicism, and the secularization of American life,
we find ourselves living very much as our neighbors do. The more
we get to know people, the better we see that we want much of
what they want and are troubled by many of the same problems
that agonize them. We know increasingly, as no generation of
earlier times, that humankind is truly one. We speak different
languages, have distinctive customs, rally to separate political
slogans, and are often fearful and hostile to others. Yet, under-
neath the surface differentiation, we are the same. We Jews, of all

peoples, cannot turn our backs on this sense of human solidarity, for one of its earliest triumphs was our emancipation. Then, how can Jews today assert that God has given them a unique status among humankind?

This argument must be extended to acknowledge the ways in which other peoples, through their own religions, truly serve our —and their—God. Most Jews today have some positive appreciation of religions other than their own. They are appalled to hear that many halachic authorities still consider Christianity a form of idol-worship. Though much still separates Judaism from Christianity and Islam, the gap between the modernized forms of these faiths has narrowed substantially since medieval times. For religious or for other reasons then, the traditional concept of the Jews as God's chosen people has received a vigorous reworking in modern times.

Shall We Extirpate Chosenness from Our Teaching?

Mordecai Kaplan has taken the most radical approach to the doctrine of the chosen people. He insists that this Jewish tenet defies reinterpretation and must be abandoned. Its views of God and of humanity are equally intolerable. They cannot be adapted to our social situation with its scientific ethos. No modern, rationally minded person could accept a religion which has a supernaturalistic, choosing God. Moreover, chosenness implies that one group is closer to God than any other. This leads to the temptation of seeking to impose its faith on others, the "beneficent" persecution which recurred with great frequency in the history of religion. Jews who have suffered greatly at the hands of those who claimed a superior religion should be particularly sensitive to the need to make human equality central to contemporary belief. They should forthrightly give up their particularistic religious doctrine, chosenness, in the hope that other groups will follow their lead.

Besides, Kaplan reminds us, we no longer need to assert God's having chosen us in order to validate the Jewish way of life. Ethnic groups naturally produce and cherish their culture and Jews have good reason to rejoice in their rich and humane civilization. If we wish, we may say that our people wants to dedicate its ethnic self-expression to the highest possible human standards. We can then claim a special Jewish "vocation," as long as we remember that all peoples should do so and our ethnic purpose in no way sets us off from others.

Most Jewish thinkers have taken a less revolutionary stand. Some propose, instead, to say that we are a "chosen" people as, in some sense, all people are. That is, all groups demonstrate some distinctive way of living which is their unique contribution to the development of humankind. One might then argue that the Jews have shown a special gift for ethical religion but this would not be extended as a claim for Jewish superiority. Rather one would see this as but one instance of the process by which all ethnic groups have expressed their distinctive originality.

In many cases, group accomplishment has been spectacular. The Greeks exhibited an extraordinary sense of form and beauty. The Roman engineers, administrators, and warriors set an incomparably high standard for succeeding Western civilization. The Spaniards created a unique fusion of Moslem and Christian cultures. The Scandinavians pioneered modern social planning. If we knew more about other peoples, particularly of Africa, Asia, and South America, we would soon see that each folk has elaborated some unique aspect of human existence.

Why some groups should make widely accepted contributions may be ascribed to chance or, perhaps the same thing, attributed to the natural order of things. Not every organist is a Bach or every writer a Melville. Variation rules and no special act of God is required to explain how a people became different or why it should seek to remain so. That the Hebrews demonstrated a gift for religion has made them of special interest to the Western world. It does not indicate that they are qualitatively different from other groups. We can give up chosenness and the invidiousness implicit in it without denying the special contribution our people has made to history. Doing so will be but another example of our people's ethical devotion.

With no people better than another, this democratization of chosenness might imply that its adherents have no specific sense of Jewish loyalty. As a consequence, some writers supplement this theory with a strong argument for the exceptional human accomplishment of the Jews and hence the desirability of keeping the Jewish people alive. They point to the tenacity with which the Jews have asserted and lived up to a commitment to high human excellence. As a result, this people has made extraordinary contributions to civilization, whether considered from the aspect of number, quality, or continuity. Thus, in recent generations, Jewry has spawned a host of notable writers, painters, musicians, scientists, and academicians. No ethnic group comes remotely close to its record at producing Nobel Prize winners. With such a record of accomplishment, this people deserves the love and loyalty of those who have the good fortune to be born into it.

Chosenness as More than a Human Matter

To religious thinkers such as Leo Baeck, the views of Kaplan and other democratizers, while commendable for their emphasis on humankind, demonstrate a dogmatic secularism; they omit God. This takes liberalism to an unfortunate extreme. Baeck denies that to claim God has a role in Israel's distinctiveness requires us to affirm a supernatural, activist doctrine of chosenness. Instead we can speak of what we know more certainly, that humanity constantly seeks God and the good life. Chosenness arises from the human refusal to be satisfied with the gods of nature. The spiritual quest presses on until people finally find the one God of the universe and freely accept God's ethical demands as the basis of their personal and social existence.

All peoples might have done this; most never got beyond idolatry or nature worship. On rare occasions, we now know, some communities found what scholars call a "high god," a belief which is close to monotheism if not already there. When such peoples do not turn from God and God's demands but freely choose to accept God's rule as the basis of their existence, we may apply to them Israel Zangwill's dictum (meant originally for the Jews), "A chosen people is a choosing people."

This universalizing—that all peoples may choose—again raises the question of Jewish particularism; is there anything special about the Jews? We often ask that because we want to know if we ought to dedicate ourselves to the special effort it takes to keep Judaism alive.

For all his universal religious faith, Leo Baeck insisted the Jews had a unique historic role. Any people could have chosen to make its consciousness of God the pivot of its group existence. As a matter of historic fact, he argued, other peoples did not choose to do so. The ethical monotheism developed among the Jews has no true parallel in the other great religions of the world. Baeck rejects the claims of Buddhism and Christianity to be Judaism's spiritual equals. The Asian faith he judges to be insufficiently ethical, in Baeck's activist, Kantian understanding of ethics. Christianity, he accuses of being inadequately monotheistic and only secondarily ethical, since it emphasizes faith over all.

Baeck then went one step further and made an assertion for which nothing in his thought had prepared us. He declared that, over the centuries, the concept of ethical monotheism has become so identified with the Jewish people that the two can no longer be separated. If the Jews do not survive, neither will ethical monotheism. The true consciousness of the one God would then die out among humankind. In this assertion, the universal and particular are linked together for all time.

But Baeck's formulation has troubled many Jewish thinkers. How can a universal idea, essentially the ethical monotheism of neo-Kantian philosophy, be made the unique possession of a particular people, the Jews? Surely ideas can become known by anyone. In fact, there are many ethical monotheists other than Jews. Moreover, how does identification with a concept, even over centuries, establish a necessary and unbreakable connection between an idea and a people? I join in Baeck's faith in the worthwhileness of Jewish survival but I do not find that he has explained my faith in our people in a way I can accept.

Reinterpreting Chosenness from Nonrational Perspectives

Baeck realized Judaism had to include more than the rationalist's exclusive reliance on humanity if it were to function as a religion. Despite his appreciation of the mystery which surrounds existence, he could not clarify in what sense God might be said to be particularly involved with the Jews. For more direct answers to the modern issue of chosenness we must turn to the nonrationalist thinkers Martin Buber and Abraham Heschel.

In Buber's thought God is understood by analogy to our most intimate human relationships, deep friendship or love. The biblical authors regularly refer to love when they wish to symbolize the special chosenness between God and the people of Israel. One might love anyone and we probably do love many people—that is the universal truth of love. If we are fortunate, we have a great love, one distinct from all others by the way it summons us to be ourselves most fully. We cannot adequately explain why we love just this person so dearly. Often, we sheepishly admit, we can see a great disparity between what we once said we sought in a beloved and the person we now actually love—that is the particular truth of love. Apparently, *thought* operates best in abstraction and generality. By contrast, we find *life*'s deepest truth in particular people, places, and times. Authentic Jewish faith, Buber teaches, will give priority to life over thought; we will find and honor the universal only as we respond to the challenge of the everyday particulars.

With regard to chosenness, Buber reminds us that all rich relationships are reciprocal. What pain we feel when we have unrequited love. We reach out to someone in true openness and discover that, consciously or unconsciously, they will not make themselves available to us. What joy we experience then when we present ourselves in love to someone else and they come forth to meet us, reciprocating our affection. At such moments we know that, had the other not personally reached out to us, our love would have been frustrated and our relationship could not have come into being. Love is the giving of the self in which you choose me and I choose you.

So it is, says Buber, with God. Human beings have searched for God through history and occasionally had the experience that God had "been there" with them. As a result, Buber believes there are many instances of true religion in human history. To that extent, he is a universalist.

But only once in human history did an ethnic group confront God and bind itself to God *as a group* for all of history. Buber reads the Torah as the very human account of the courtship, wedding, and marriage—complete with quarrels and reconciliations—of God and the people of Israel. It took centuries for the relationship to mature. As a result of all that the partners had been through in settling the land, creating and dividing the kingdom, enduring the Babylonian Exile, and returning to their homeland, the two may be said to have created a lasting, permanent relationship, the Covenant.

Other national groups had true religions. None ever transformed its ethnic life as Israel did so that the boundary between ethnicity and religion all but disappeared. Historically and qualitatively, the people of Israel's relationship with God is unique. Buber says we cannot explain why history worked out this way but he reminds us that human life characteristically manifests just such particularity. Moreover, because two participants must create every genuine relationship, we may say that God as well as the Jews made the Covenant. That is, had God not been present to the Jews in their spiritual quest, had God not again and again given the Divine Presence to this people, the Covenant could not have come to be and endured. In this sense, for Buber, God chose —and chooses—the Jewish people.

Heschel: The Tradition Is Wiser than We Are

Buber's thought has drawn criticism from both sides of the theological spectrum. Despite its apparent spirituality, Abraham Heschel finds it humanistically presumptuous while the rationalists criticize it for its fuzzy-mindedness in drawing analogies to God from human relationships.

Heschel's response flows logically from his faith in God as the premise which precedes all human reasoning. For him, God cannot properly be understood as the result of human religious striving but only as the absolutely initial reality which validates our spiritual sensitivity and aspiration. He finds it ridiculous to speak of people choosing God. Are not our capacities to search for and bind ourselves to God an incredible mystery which can be solved only by recognizing them as gifts of God?

Secularization has made our vision of God so small and our pride in human power so grandiose that we cannot conceive of God choosing one people. When we regain a radical wonder before the grandeur of the God who makes everything possible —including our questions about particularity—then we can accept the Torah's incontrovertible historic declaration: God's revelation came fully to the people of Israel and to no other. Though the Hebrew Bible has now become the possession of many other peoples, it remains a Jewish book, written in the Hebrew language, telling of the people of Israel's history, and structuring Jewish lives today as it has during millennia of unbroken allegiance.

Jews should not hesitate to welcome every sign that other peoples are coming to know and serve God. That does not preclude them from recognizing themselves, today as in the past, as God's special people in origin, continuity, and goal. For Jews are still called upon to remain faithful to God and testify that God's ultimate rule will one day become real on earth when the Messiah comes. Chosenness does not require much explanation when it arises in the context of an overwhelming appreciation of God's greatness and the spiritual reality of thousands of years of Jewish existence under the Covenant.

Heschel returns us to the world of traditional Judaism with its primary attention to what God has done to make Israel unique. Recognizing that some Jews might convert this absolute assertion of chosenness into tribalism, Heschel balanced his particularism by two universalistic emphases. First, he had a flaming sense of ethical responsibility. The Jewish liberals had been right when they explicated the doctrine of Jewish responsibility to all people, which they found imbedded in the prophets and much else of Jewish teaching. Heschel insisted that the Covenant mandated a concern for all humanity and that, wherever human values were seriously at stake, Jewish interests were necessarily involved.

Second, Heschel had a high appreciation of the truth to be found in other religions. He found no incompatibility between asserting the uniqueness of the Jews' relationship with God and acknowledging that other faiths genuinely knew and served God. Emphasizing revelation as he did, Heschel felt a special spiritual kinship with those religions which took Hebrew Scriptures seriously.

In a way most uncommon for an academic thinker, Heschel lived out his vision of chosenness as he faced the great issues of American and Jewish life. In the civil rights and anti-Vietnam War movements of the 1960s, he was largely associated with Christian clergy and liberal rabbis. In his early protests on behalf of Russian Jewry, he stood side-by-side with a number of traditionally oriented rabbis. No one remotely approaching his stature saw the organic interrelationship of these causes. Most Jews remained fixated on either universal or particular goals. For all the traditional flavor of his theology, Abraham Heschel was too sophisticated and modern a thinker to be content with a doctrine of chosenness that he recognized as only half of Judaism. By insisting on both realms of Jewish responsibility, Abraham Heschel became American Jewry's outstanding exemplar of the fusion of particular Jewish devotion and universal human involvement.

·4·

WHAT DO WE EXPECT
IN THE MESSIANIC AGE ?

Thorleif Boman, in a provocative book, has argued that the Hebrews had a radically different sense of time than did the Greeks. Biblical thought, he contended, was linear. It moved from a beginning to an end, from creation, through history, to the coming of the Messiah. Greek thinkers, he alleged, had a cyclical view of time. For them, history repeated itself endlessly after long intervals. Subsequent scholarship has disparaged Boman's thesis. Many Greek writers did not think of time as repetitive but refer to the mythological notion that a Golden Age awaits humankind in some distant future. What remains of Boman's study is his insight that Hebrew messianism, and not merely its monotheism, distinguishes its faith from even its most enlightened Mediterranean neighbors.

With some exaggeration, we may say that Judaism's messianic belief makes it unique among world religions. Believing Jews look forward devoutly to an end to history as we know it. In that "world-to-come," all the ills of contemporary existence will be remedied and human life will be perfected in the full acceptance of God's rule.

Judaism bequeathed to its daughter religions the faith that life has a goal. Christianity centers on messianism far more so than does Judaism. Jesus of Nazareth is called the "Christ," a Greek word equivalent to the Hebrew term "Messiah," and his Christhood becomes the pivot of Christian life. Jews, by contrast, build their lives on the Torah, of which the messianic hope is one feature. Moslems insist that Mohammed was not a messiah but a prophet, though the last and greatest one. Like the Jews they await a great day of judgment and a resolution of human history. The various Moslem sects disagree, however, whether there will be a specific figure to inaugurate this era.

Most Asian religions have a different attitude to history. Universal redemptive tones are rarely sounded in Hinduism, Buddhism, or the Taoist and Confucian traditions. For most Asian religious teachers, history is relatively unimportant, or essentially static, or endlessly cyclical until one finds a way to transcend it. The "redemption" to which one aspires in these faiths is release from the process of history. One commonly gains this liberation by determined individual meditation or wholehearted ritual practice.

Internally, Jewish messianism animated Jewish piety and empowered Jewish survival over many difficult centuries. In their extremity, the believing martyrs of the Holocaust sang *Ani Maamin,* a song about the coming of the Messiah. Its text is an abridgement of the twelfth of Maimonides's thirteen principles of Jewish belief. "I believe with perfect faith in the coming of the Messiah and even though he tarries, with all that, I daily await his coming." How can one hope to understand Judaism without insight into so stubborn a faith?

The Problems in Being Objective about Messianism

A major difficulty prevents our gaining an undistorted view of this central Jewish aspiration. Christian belief developed out of the Jewish messianic hope and in the process transformed that faith in terms of its particular religious experience. Today, despite decades of secularization, one can hardly discuss messianism without hearing the Christian overtones which surround that doctrine. For example, consider the English words, "salvation" and "redemption." When we use them to translate the Hebrew *yeshuah* and *geulah,* we bring words heavily laden with christology into whatever is said. One needs to be on guard, then, against reading back into Judaism notions which are inauthentic to it.

The topic is also complicated by the long history of polemics between Jews and Christians. For a while, as the American appreciation of religious pluralism grew, the antipathy which animated the discussions seemed to have been largely overcome. More recently, as evangelical Christian groups have pressed their claim that Jesus fulfilled the Hebrew Bible's messianic texts, passionate arguments have become more common.

We cannot circumvent that problem by appealing to academic historians for an objective view. Scholars have not reached any well-accepted consensus in this area. The origin and earliest development of the people of Israel's messianic faith remain obscure. Such data as we have is scanty and difficult to interpret. Much of what later Jewish (or Christian) generations saw as messianic prophecies seems to critical-minded academics today the backward projection of a later belief. The interpretations testify more to the personal commitments of those who made them than to a commonly available standard of judgment. Prudence therefore demands that we not try to reconstruct the beginnings of the Jewish faith in the Messiah. We shall have to content ourselves with an overview of the messianic traditions of Judaism. We will begin by analyzing some major motifs which the rabbis saw in the Bible.

A Messianic King and/or a Messianic Era

Some prophecies in the Bible look forward to the coming of an ideal king. Thus, Isaiah, allowing for poetic exaggeration, seems to look beyond political ideals to a qualitatively unique age. Here are some pertinent excerpts from that vision:

A sprout will come forth from the trunk of Jesse [King
    David's father]
And a shoot will rise up from his roots.
The spirit of *Adonai* will fill him,
A spirit of wisdom and understanding,
A spirit of counsel and might,
A spirit of knowledge and faith in *Adonai*. . . .
With righteousness he will judge the poor
And bring justice to the little people of the land. . . .
The wolf will live with the lamb,
The leopard lie down with the kid. . . .
No one will hurt or destroy
In all My holy mountain,

For the earth shall be full of knowledge of *Adonai*
As the sea is full of water. (11:1–9)

This passage is richly symbolic. We would like to know what to expect and how it will come about. Instead, the poet speaks of plants, animals, and water. The symbols being "alive," we have little problem understanding what he is driving at: justice, peace, and general well-being. But we cannot tell whether Isaiah meant it as a practical, soon-to-come expectation or an abstract, far-distant dream. Did he look forward to a reasonably benevolent king or did he anticipate God's wondrous transformation of the natural order through a specially inspired king? Simply put, we do not know how "messianic" this passage was to the prophet.

In the biblical references to the coming ideal king, he is never called the Messiah, *mashiach* in Hebrew. (True to its cultural context, the monarchical Messiah tradition is masculine, awaiting a king, not a queen.) The word *"mashiach"* derives from a common Hebrew root meaning to anoint with oil. When priests and kings were installed in office, the Bible calls for them to be touched with oil. Hence anyone serving in such a special role, such as the priest accompanying the Israelite army, can be called "an anointed one," a *mashiach.* In the old English transliteration system (by way of the Latin), this became "messiah." By rabbinic times, the general term, *"mashiach,"* had also acquired a specific meaning. It referred to the perfect king who, with God's help, would bring history to its fulfillment.

Some passages in the Bible which envision the ideal future do not mention a king. They refer only to what God will do in those extraordinary days. Perhaps the most famous of all the messianic passages is of this sort. Oddly enough it appears in almost identical form in Micah 4 and Isaiah 2, with the Micah version continuing a bit further:

This is what will happen at "the end of days" [the future? some day?]
The mountain of *Adonai*'s House will be raised up.
It will be higher than any hill.
Peoples will come to it in streams.
Nations will go around saying,
"Come, let's go up to *Adonai*'s mountain,
To the House of the God of Jacob.

He will teach us of His ways
And we will walk in His paths." . . .
They will beat their swords into plow blades,
Their spears into tree pruners.
No nation will raise a sword against another nation.
They won't even study war any more.
People will sit under their vines and fig trees
And no one will make them afraid. (Micah 4:1–4)

Here, the encompassing well-being is associated with the coming of one religion for all humankind. "For Torah will go forth from Zion and *Adonai*'s word from Jerusalem." (Micah 4:2) All people will see the truth of Judaism and live it. The result is messianic peace. Though a King Messiah is not mentioned here, the passage contains, characteristically, both national and religious elements (see above, chapter 1).

"The Day of the Lord," Judgment and Resurrection

Two other major motifs need to be considered. Various prophets warn the people of a coming day of judgment. Thus, Joel says:

[In those days]
I will show wonders in the heaven and on the earth,
Blood and fire and pillars of smoke.
The sun shall be turned into darkness
And the moon into blood
Before the coming of the great and terrible day of *Adonai*.
But it will come to pass that whoever calls on *Adonai*'s
    name will be saved
For in Mount Zion and in Jerusalem there will be those that
    escape. (3:3–5)

On the judgment day those who have been faithful to God will be rewarded and evildoers will be punished.

By the time of the Book of Daniel, "the end of days" is associated with a great cosmic transformation. In Daniel, too, we can see the other significant idea associated with the coming of the Messiah. Judgment will be passed not only on the living but on the revived dead as well. The righteous among them will be rewarded with everlasting, ideal life. (12:2–3) For the rabbis this meant the bodily resurrection of the dead and this teaching became a major feature of Jewish messianism.*

I will venture one bit of speculation about biblical messianism. I would not be at all surprised if another generation of scholars discovers that much of the rabbinic belief is already to be found in the Bible. To me it seems the natural religious outgrowth of biblical faith in God. The human will to do evil prevents God's rule from being effective on earth. People, having been created free enough to accept or rebel against God's rule, regularly spurn God's commands. But, though people are free, the biblical authors affirm that God's rule will not be ultimately frustrated. God will not infringe on human freedom; yet God's beneficent dominion, not humankind's errant will, determines the outcome of history. God's kingship will therefore ultimately be manifest in human lives.

How God finally gets the recalcitrant human will to accept freely God's sovereignty is never made fully clear. Some biblical and rabbinic authors emphasize the Messiah's wisdom and piety. Others cherish the possibility that all Israel might one day become observant. A number daringly assert that the Messiah will come only to a thoroughly impious generation, their faithlessness provoking a loving God to action. Some envision God beneficially filling all humankind with knowledge of the Lord. Whatever the method, it seems "logical" to me that if God is the supreme ruler of the universe then one day God's kingdom must be realized on earth among people.

Coalescing the Rabbinic Views on the Messianic Times

In rabbinic literature, a full-scale messianic belief is evident, but the opinions concerning it are imprecise, variegated, and occasionally inconsistent. However, much of it can be brought together in a scheme depicting the end of days as a drama with a prelude and four acts.

The time preceding the coming of the Messiah is the worst of times. It abounds with natural catastrophes and extreme social upheaval, "the [birth] pangs of the Messiah." In every period of Jewish disaster this doctrine has given rise to the hope that God

*On the Jewish view of life after death, see Part Two, *The God We Affirm*, Chapter 5, "Is There Life after Death?"

might soon send deliverance. On the basis of Malachi 3:23 it is also commonly believed that Elijah will first come to announce the Messiah's advent.

As the first act begins the Messiah's immediate task is military, to defeat the enemies who have been attacking the people of Israel, symbolically, the kings Gog and Magog (based on Ezek. 38:2). He restores in Jerusalem the rule of the Davidic dynasty, of which he is a descendant. He brings back Jewish exiles from all over the world to his Jewish kingdom where they will live in peace and happiness. And he institutes a universal, ideal social order. This period, "the days of the Messiah," seems so this-worldly and historical that the rabbis can speculate just how many years this period of messianic rule will last.

With this first act of the end-of-days drama in mind we can understand the dictum of the early third-century Babylonian teacher Samuel, "The only difference between our world and that of the days of the Messiah is that then the people of Israel will no longer be subject to the oppressive rule of other nations." (Ber. 34b) In line with the naturalism of this stage of the messianic era the rabbis do not consider the Messiah an angelic or divine being. Though he succeeds because of God's special help, he is only another inspired human being like a biblical judge or king.

Thus far, the world remains very much as we know it, only greatly improved. As the other acts ensue we move away from the natural order to which we are accustomed. Our vision becomes increasingly dim and we are less certain of what the rabbis en-vision. They admit their own limits in this regard. Trusting God more fully than most modern Jews do, they maintained an abid-ing faith in the messianic transformation of existence without having a detailed picture of what to expect.

In the second act—some time after the messianic rule begins —the dead are resurrected. The graves open and the corpses, healed, purified, and perfected, receive their souls back, thereby coming to life.*

The third act, the judgment day, is distinguished by its corpo-rate aspect, the judgment of the nations. Though each individual soul had received evaluation and subsequent atoning punishment immediately after death, a climactic judgment also now decides

---

*This notion is discussed in some detail in chapter 5 of Part Two, *The God We Affirm.*

each person's eternal fate. The rabbis generally affirm that "each Jew has a share in the life of the world-to-come." Some rabbis except certain notorious sinners, and the wholesale acceptance usually involves some additional punishment being imposed at this stage.

More dramatically, the various historical peoples appear before God to learn their ultimate fate. The people of Israel is declared the only nation faithful to God. It receives public vindication for its stubborn, iconoclastic observance of the Torah. By contrast, most rabbis assert that "the nations" will be adjudged sinful, not the least for oppressing the people of Israel. They will then be destroyed, though, as Rabbi Joshua says, "there are righteous individuals among the nations who share in the life of the world-to-come." (Tos. San. 13:2) Later Jewish thinkers echoed this view that, despite humankind's pervasive wickedness, one does not need to be Jewish to share in the ultimate redemption.

With act four, the stage, which has been growing dimmer and more indistinct, reaches the point of bare visibility. After the judgment and purifying punishment comes the great reward of existence, entrance into the *atid lavo,* the "future-to-come" (also called the *olam haba,* the "world-to-come"—a term which likewise refers to the state of the individual immediately after death).

The rabbis do not discuss what this afterlife consists of, what one does then, or why it is so blissful. Except for stray speculations, they tell us little about it. God, having graciously given the Torah to the people of Israel, the proper human concern is studying and living by its guidance, not fantasizing about life in the future-to-come. Because of that emphasis, traditional Judaism may properly be called a this-worldly religion. It has, as we have seen, a strong other-worldly commitment and a rich doctrine of "last things." But it bids its adherents devote their lives to the spiritual challenges of everyday existence rather than concentrate on what is likely to happen to us in the world-to-come.

Limiting Messianic Speculation

Permit me a brief digression. I want to speculate about the reasons for the paucity of apocalyptic literature in rabbinic Judaism. The latter chapters of the biblical books of Zechariah and Daniel are filled with extraordinary visions of things to come.

There and in some post-biblical Jewish books preserved in the Apocrypha and Pseudepigrapha, the authors dream of God's climactic entry into history to bring it to its close. Such literature is called apocalyptic, a Greek word for "uncovering" (the last things). Apparently, as messianism developed, apocalyptic visionaries increased in the Jewish community.

The rabbis took another direction in their study and writing. There are apocalyptic passages in rabbinic literature but they are not long or detailed. No classic rabbinic book is devoted to apocalyptic visions. The rabbis forbade Jews from speculating when the end of history might come. They likewise banned the apocalyptic books from the Jewish community insofar as it would accept their guidance. The Christians considered these writings a bridge from the Hebrew Bible to the Christian Scriptures and found foreshadowings of the coming of the Messiah in some of them. Had it not been for Christianity, the Apocrypha and Pseudepigrapha would have been lost to later Jewish tradition.

Perhaps the rabbis objected to the content of these forbidden works for apocalyptic forecasts are wildly imaginative and often expressed in bizarre images. By contrast to such dreamlike fantasies, the Torah, God's instruction for human existence now, is clear, definite, and practical. I am suggesting that rabbinic literature makes law, not apocalyptic vision, central because Jewish faith is dominated by the Torah God has given, not the Messiah God will yet bring. Revelation rather than redemption pervades the immediate Jewish sense of relation to God. Yet since we possess the former we confidently await the latter.

A historical event is most important for the subsequent development of Jewish attitudes toward the Messiah. In 133 C.E. Simon Bar Kochba (probably Bar Kosba) led a Jewish rebellion against Rome. The Temple having been destroyed by the Romans in 70 C.E. and the ensuing years having been harsh ones, many Jews felt it was time for God to send the Messiah. Rabbi Akiba, a leading figure then, proclaimed Bar Kochba to be the promised "son of David." But Bar Kochba was defeated and Jews suffered terribly as a result. One Roman source says that Jewish slaves were so plentiful that their price was less than that of good cattle. The spiritual disillusionment must also have been crushing. Any national hopes for a restoration of Jewish sovereignty, any religious dreams of rebuilding the Temple were ended, at least for the time being.

Messianic figures arose all through subsequent Jewish history, but because of Bar Kochba Jewish hope was regularly balanced with Jewish skepticism about any particular person's claim. Not until 1665 and the Shabbetai Zevi movement did a large sector of world Jewry again believe the Messiah had arrived, only to be bitterly disillusioned once more. This post-Bar Kochba realism seems echoed in a number of surprisingly negative rabbinic statements about the coming of the Messiah. Perhaps the most well-known of these is attributed to Rabban Yohanan ben Zakkai who is reported to have said, "If you have a plant in your hand and someone comes and says the Messiah has arrived, plant the plant." (A.d.R.N. B 31) Since he lived during the first rebellion against Rome, 67–70 c.e., many scholars assume his name was attached to this statement because of his importance.

The Jewish Denial that Jesus Was the Messiah

Christians have made messianic claims for Jesus of Nazareth though he made none directly himself. I have delayed considering them until after discussing Bar Kochba, though Jesus lived a century earlier, because I believe the later event makes the Jewish expectations unambiguous. The Jews understood the Bible to promise a Messiah who would be an ideal king, one who would reestablish Jewish rule in the Holy Land, gather in the Jewish exiles, and inaugurate a perfect society, starting humankind toward the life of the world-to-come. Since Jesus didn't do that he was not the Messiah. The issue was—and is—as simple as that.

This immediate, practical sense of what the Messiah should do continued throughout Jewish history. In the eighteenth century, the chasidic *rebbe* of Vitebsk, Menahem Mendel, immigrated to Jerusalem. One day a man went up to the Mount of Olives and began blowing a *shofar.* People thought the Messiah had arrived and someone came running to Menahem Mendel with the good news. He went to the window and saw the Jerusalemites going about their business in the usual way. He said simply, "The Messiah hasn't come," and returned to his study and prayer.

The Messiah is supposed to bring the world complete justice, peace, and well-being. Neither Jesus, nor Bar Kochba, nor Shabbetai Zevi, nor anyone else has done that. The world is not yet redeemed; therefore, the Messiah has not yet arrived. Surely our generation of Jews knows that; we still feel the effects of the

Holocaust. Should someone tell you that the Messiah has appeared, may I urge you not to start studying the relevant biblical texts, as valuable as that might be; instead go to the window and see what is going on in the world. You should quickly be able to see whether the Jewish hopes for our people and for all humanity have been fulfilled.

Christian theologians have an interesting response to this Jewish refutation of their claims. They admit that the world remains radically unredeemed but they argue that the Messiah will have a Second Coming. The first one, nearly two thousand years ago, announced his reality and the forgiveness of sins for believers. The next one will inaugurate the fullness of God's rule so all can see it. Evangelical Christians believe the Second Coming is imminent and prove it by citing biblical verses allegedly pointing to current events.

Jews do not find the idea of a Second Coming in the Bible or in rabbinic literature. Jews have thought it odd that God would have to send the Messiah once merely to demonstrate the truth of messianism and God's forgiveness. The prophets had already spoken at length of God's redemptive purposes. Christian thinkers then rejoin that Jesus also came to show how faulty the Jewish vision of the Messiah had been. Instead of the King Messiah the Jews awaited, Jesus disclosed that the Messiah would be a Suffering Servant.

At this point the discussion cannot go much further. Jews are told that Jesus came to fulfill Judaism's unique religious idea but did so in such a way as utterly to transform it. He therefore cannot be invalidated as the Messiah by not fulfilling the false Jewish expectations. Since such reasoning empowered much Christian persecution of Jews until recent years, it is difficult not to respond emotionally. Suffice it to say that we Jews believe we will know the Messiah when we see "him." Our long, historic expectation stemmed from our unique sense of God, was given utterance in our Scriptures, and has been kept alive in unbroken continuity among us for millennia. We do not see that anyone else is in a better position to explain so central a doctrine in our prophets. We might be more inclined to give Christian claims some credence had we seen Christians through the ages behave as models of a redeemed humanity. Looking through the window of history we have found them in as much need of saving as the rest of humankind. If anything, their social failings are especially discrediting of their doctrine for they claim to be uniquely free of human sinfulness and freshly inspired by their faith to bring the world to a realm of love and peace.

Disputing What the Prophets Said

While arguing the proper meaning of the relevant biblical texts generally leads nowhere, we also cannot entirely avoid a brief look at some of the disputes. We can begin by acknowledging that many of the Gospel stories depict Jesus fulfilling prophecies of Hebrew Scriptures. Most liberal scholars, Christian as well as Jewish, ascribe that to their having been written with this purpose in mind. That is, the Christian Scriptures authors were not simply setting down the facts they had. Rather, their accounts of Jesus are pious biographies, the result of their religious response to him and the traditions about him. They tell us about the Jesus they believed in, not the one an openminded non-believer would have described. Believing that Jesus was the Messiah and that he had fulfilled the promise of Hebrew prophecy, they naturally shaped their stories about him to show the many prophecies he had fulfilled. To many scholarly eyes, the Gospel accounts seem written to convince people he was the Messiah, and they adduce texts and occurrences for that purpose. Though this tendency makes many arguments superfluous, Jews see important differences between what the prophets and the Christian Scriptures say. Let us consider two famous cases.

The Gospels describe Jesus as coming of a virgin birth. Mary, rather than being impregnated by her husband Joseph, had conceived Jesus by a direct, miraculous act of God. This is supposed to fulfill the prophecy which Isaiah made (7:14) that God would send the people of Israel a sign through the birth of a child. The Septuagint, the Greek translation widely used in those days, describes the mother with a word which can be understood as either a virgin or a young woman. But the Hebrew text says *almah,* which means young woman and not virgin. Today most liberal scholars will agree that the proper translation of Isaiah 7:14 is that a young woman will conceive and give birth. The major modern Protestant translation of the Bible, the Revised Standard Version, says "young woman" and has in a footnote to Isaiah 7:13 (the numbering being different), "Or virgin." Here the Christian Scriptures account of Jesus' birth fulfills a prophecy that Jews insist isn't even in the Bible.

The other classic case is Isaiah 53, a long poem about God's servant and his many sufferings. Christian theologians consider it the model for many of the things Jesus is reported to have done. It does not mention serving God as a good king, ruling the people of Israel or the world. Consequently this text becomes basic to the contention that, in his first coming, Jesus inaugurated a new understanding of the Messiah's role. Setting to one side the broader question of the relation of the servant of God to the Messiah, Jews insist that Jesus does not fulfill the prophecy of Isaiah 53. True, the Gospel tales reflect some of the references in this poem but there are many important discrepancies between what Isaiah (the Second) said and what we are told about Jesus.

Discounting the poetic exaggeration, the text plainly says (v.2) that the servant was ugly: "He had no form or handsomeness that we would want to look at him, no beauty that we should take delight in him." Jesus is not described that way in the Christian Scriptures. In verse 3, we hear that the servant is "acquainted with disease" and verse 7 twice says that he "opened not his mouth" though oppressed. The Gospels do not mention Jesus being ill but in the course of his crucifixion they say Jesus uttered the seven "last words" (statements) which still provide the basis for much Good Friday preaching.

Christians have also used verses 11–12 as the basis for their theory of vicarious atonement. Jesus by his suffering despite his innocence took on himself the punishment due humanity for its sins. He thereby reconciled God with humankind for all time to come. Jews do not find that idea in Isaiah 53. Moreover, we consider unduly harsh the concept of a God who does not accept each person's repentance. That, instead, God responds to an innocent person's suffering—Jesus' crucifixion and death—as atoning compensation for the guilty seems to us utterly unethical and thus unbelievable.

Obviously, what constitutes "fulfilling" the prophecies is highly subjective. These days the major Christian theologians make their case for the Christ by discussing his spiritually complete personhood. In general, only the fundamentalists still seek to prove to Jews Jesus' messiah-ship by citing the many biblical verses he fulfilled. Mostly, there is little one can discuss with them. If you bring a liberal, historical-critical attitude to the texts they cannot understand you. Besides, they don't care what you say. They have the truth and are certain it will be to your benefit to share it, too. Some even believe that a special merit comes with converting Jews to Christianity. No matter how many verses you show are inapplicable to Jesus, they have dozens more to support their case—and, since their faith revolves around the Bible, they generally know it better than you do. Though they cite endless verses with ingenious messianic interpretations, thoughtful Jews will still give major consideration to the condition of our world. It has not changed much since the days of Jesus or Bar Kochba. Until sinfulness ceases and well-being prevails, Jews know the Messiah has not come.

Modernity Mandated a Thoroughgoing Reinterpretation of Messianism

The Emancipation of the Jews in the nineteenth century persuaded the early Reformers that the Jewish hope for the Messiah needed reconsideration. (Interestingly enough, secularized Jews later shared in this attitude.) Some German Reform Jews determined on a decisive change in Jewish belief. In 1841, in a prayer book created for use in the Hamburg Temple, all the traditional prayers for the coming of the Messiah were replaced with aspirations for a Messianic Age.

The religious liberals had three arguments for their innovation. First, they felt that praying for a King Messiah would hurt their chances of gaining full citizenship. The anticipated Son of David was to reestablish Jewish political rule and bring the exiles of his people back to their homeland. If they prayed for such national restoration could the Jews be genuinely loyal to the countries in which they lived? Should citizenship be granted to people of such divided loyalties? The traditional Messiah-idea, by blocking the full emancipation of the Jews, seemed an impediment to Jewish survival.

Second, messianism had become highly miraculous. The modern temper, increasingly impressed with science's accomplishments, found such an attitude toward history utterly unacceptable. Who could believe that one person, by some special powers of leadership, would reestablish a Jewish state, bring back all the Jews, establish an ideal social order, revolutionize international relations, and inaugurate a time leading to a resurrection of the dead and God's judgment day? Moreover, over the ages, the Jewish imagination had attached a host of legends to the coming of the Messiah. One of my favorites is one of the oldest. In the Talmud we hear that in the messianic time each grape would yield thirty kegs of wine! (Ket. 111 b)

Third, the liberals felt they had a much more realistic theory of messianism: democracy. Here they followed their principle that traditional Judaism had given too great emphasis to God's acts and that modern religiosity ought to focus on humanity's powers. Instead of God sending an ideal king, they foresaw all humankind working together and by social reconstruction producing a perfected world. In place of people being relatively passive, performing their religious duties but relying on God to redeem history, they would become activists, applying their reason and conscience to effect their salvation.

The instruments of this messianism were available and effective. Democracy endowed citizens with power. Education gave them information. Research provided them with understanding. The spread of culture sensitized their souls. Practically, one could see great social progress as the nineteenth century moved forward. Much of the poverty, the intolerance, and the social neglect of previous centuries was being overcome. Even Jews were receiving rights. In their Emancipation they had the living experience of society's messianic progress.

Most Reform Jews found these arguments convincing. They therefore gave up the belief in a Messiah and substituted for it a belief in the coming of a Messianic Age. Though no other Jewish groups openly adopted this stance, the traditional personal language for the Messiah soon became highly symbolic for almost all modernized Jews.

The liberals uncovered many places in Jewish literature where the human side of the covenant relationship with God is stressed. They often cited these as the Jewish basis of their new messianism. One of their favorite Torah texts was Exodus 14:15. The Jews, fleeing Egypt, found their escape blocked by the Sea of Reeds and the Egyptian army about to overtake them. Moses then prayed to God for help. But the text has God chiding him, "Why are you crying out to Me? Speak to the children of Israel and let them go forward." Here the Torah itself seems to validate human initiative rather than reliance on religious rites.

I enjoy a similar sort of tale told about Menaham Mendel, the chasidic *rebbe* of Kosov. When he was asked why the Messiah tarried so, he quoted King Saul's question to his courtiers, "Why hasn't the son of Jesse [David] come to the banquet yesterday or today?" The *rebbe* then added, "The reason is that we are no different today from what we were yesterday." Much chasidic teaching stresses human change as the key to bringing the Messiah. However, chasidic activism, unlike that of the liberal Jews, was directed inward, to personal spiritual transformation. The liberal's messianism was oriented to society and its improvement through politics and education. They had a substantially different sense of human power than did the unemancipated pietists of eastern Europe. Their optimistic view of human nature forms the foundation of their concept of the Messianic Age. It motivated Jews to unparalleled involvement and accomplishment in humanitarian affairs wherever they received equal rights.

The Messianic Faith of Jewish Secularists

Secularized Jews may have given up God and ritual but they created their own versions of messianism. For them, modernity made religion unbelievable. Marx's analysis of society with its revelations about power and class interests were widely influential among searching Jews. As one of the most underprivileged and oppressed sectors of society, they found the Marxist revolution appealing as a realistic means of achieving the messianic goal. They also became strongly anticlerical for they had learned from Marx that the ruling class fostered religion to keep the impoverished from actively exercising their power. Besides, modern science had convinced them that religion was superstition if not wholly false and delusive.

Marxism was also anti-nationalist. The exploiters used national loyalty as a means of keeping the proletariat from recognizing and working for their worldwide class interests. As a result, the fervent Jewish Marxists were even more universalistic than the Reform Jews who, at least, sought ways to perpetuate their Jewish identity. The passionate un-Jewish Marxism of Jews seemed so powered by self-hate that new groups arose seeking to blend Jewish particularity and Marxist universalism while not surrendering to religion or nationalism. The most notable of these movements was the Yiddishist folk-socialism which was so significant a feature of immigrant Jewish life in the United States. For all their ethnic devotion, these Yiddishists remained resolutely anti-Zionist until the Hitler period and the establishment of the State of Israel.

Zionism, too, should be considered a secularized messianism. Though it rejected the miraculous and affirmed social activism, it disagreed with the liberals' and Marxists' evaluation of nationalism. The Zionist theoreticians denied that Jews would ever get full equality outside a country of their own. What the law could be brought to give them, anti-semitism would take away. At the same time, the social adaptation expected of all citizens would rob Diaspora Jews of the opportunity to produce a distinctive Jewish culture. Authentic Jewish existence required cultural self-determination. That could realistically come about only when the Jews had power in their own society on their own home soil.

A decade or so before Herzl, Leo Pinsker captured this idea in the title of his Zionist appeal to his people, *Auto-Emancipation.* Traditional messianism had the right goal but the wrong means. Pious reliance on God would not reestablish the Jewish state and gather in the exiles. Instead, Zionism politicized the old faith and transferred power to the Jewish people itself. The Orthodox rabbinate recognized the revolutionary implications of this interpretation of Judaism. They overwhelmingly opposed early Zionism as heretical where the Reform Jews objected to it for fostering political ambiguity. With the passage of time, compromise and accommodation grew. A substantial number of Orthodox leaders accepted the value of having a Jewish state, albeit a secular one. Some traditional Jews, those associated with Agudat Israel and various of the chasidic sects, still maintain an uneasy involvement in the State of Israel. They do not wish to appear to validate its secular definition of Jewish existence.

Zionist messianism eventually expanded to include various forms of Marxist idealism in its nationalism. Socialist Zionism long dominated the World Zionist movement and is largely responsible for the Israelis' development of a highly ramified welfare state. In the early years of the state's existence, David Ben-

Gurion often spoke of the State of Israel's messianic role in helping the world reach an ideal standard of international relations. With daily survival a major Israeli concern in recent years, no succeeding Israeli leader has sounded that grand note. For the time being, Zionist messianism has effectively been reduced to the practice of decent nationalism.

· Little is left of other secular messianisms today. The Marxists' claim that they would transform humanity has not survived a half century of Russian brutality and the totalitarianism of most other Marxist governments. Yiddishist socialism has suffered from the loss of those whose mother-tongue was Yiddish and the growing middle class and right-wing interests of the immigrants' children. Diaspora Zionism amounts to little more than political action and heartfelt prayers that the State of Israel may survive. Intellectually, too, liberals retain little of their old confidence that humankind can perfect itself. For Jews, after the Holocaust, to base their faith in our ultimate destiny on the innate goodness of humanity seems ludicrous.

Some liberal thinkers now suggest that the collapse of humanistic optimism makes the doctrine of the Messianic Age itself needful of reinterpretation. Steven Schwarzschild has argued that the miraculousness of traditional messianism demands no more faith than expecting human beings as we know them to be their own Messiah. He and other philosophers have argued that modern Jews should return to the traditional symbol of their faith, the personal Messiah.

For myself, I do not see how the liberal notion of a Messianic Age can be freed from its corollary faith in the perfectibility of humankind by human effort. However, I do not have such trust in us alone. I prefer, then, to return to our use of the term "Messiah." In doing so, I emphasize the Messiah's humanity. I thereby hope to avoid the passivity inculcated by the older teaching and to stress the duty each person has to help bring the Kingdom of God.

Revitalizing the image of the Messiah makes more place in liberal belief for acknowledging God's role in transforming history. In the older liberal rhetoric of "our partnership with God" in bringing the Messianic Age, God was often little more than a euphemism for human self-reliance and social action. Being more modest in our self-estimate today, I think we are ready to acknowledge our need for God's help in finally redeeming this sinful world. Accepting God as a true partner does not require us to surrender the sense of healthy self-reliance we identify with personal maturity. Rather, an able but not omnipotent human- kind, acting as co-creator with God of the ideal society, reflects the classic Covenant relationship between God and the people of Israel. The accents may be modern and the tone is surely more activist. But with this understanding I believe we are entitled to say, as previous generations did, that we too are working and waiting for the coming of the Messiah.

·5·

WHAT DOES THE STATE OF ISRAEL MEAN TO JEWS?

Nothing moves Jews more deeply these days than the trials and the triumphs of the State of Israel. Such close identification might be explained as ethnic pride or simple admiration for the Israelis' high human accomplishment. But the Jewish concern for the State of Israel goes far deeper than that. Often unconsciously, sometimes consciously, Jews consider it their people's definitive response to the Holocaust—and they therefore treat it with a measure of awe and numinous respect.

Hitler's barbarity radically challenged the Jewish will to live. Six million Jews had been murdered, one third of our people. They had been the great exemplars of our tradition, the leaders of our folk life, the standard of authentic Jewish continuity. As our biological heartland, they were the source of the immigrants who for generations populated Jewish communities in Western nations. When World War II ended in 1945, Jewish leadership had to be assumed by the relatively assimilated Jews of the United States and England, those isolated Jews in Russia, and the comparatively small and weak settlement of Jews in Palestine.

In those dark days, one could not easily make a case for the importance of Jewish survival. To answer religiously and say God wanted us to remain Jews made one ask why God let us die so mercilessly and in such unprecedented numbers. To assert we had a mission to spread ethical monotheism suggested the retort that other monotheists should now take up this service to their perennially ungrateful fellow-humans. To proclaim the naturalness of ethnic loyalty made little sense in the face of the unnaturalness of Jewish persecution. After Hitler, no one could make an easy case for continuing Jewish existence. Whatever the head suggested, the weary Jewish bones and the dejected Jewish heart quickly rejected. It made no sense for the Jews to go on being Jews—or, so it seemed in our black hours.

The Positive Turn after the Holocaust

Looking back now, I wonder what would have happened to world Jewry if the survivors had turned away from the Jewish people. In the concentration camps some became walking corpses. They were called "Musselmen" (perhaps out of some bizarre connection with the Moslem teaching of the acceptance of fate). They went through their daily routines without feeling, without thought, and without will. They had withdrawn from life. Why did the Musselman syndrome not characterize the survivors' Jewishness? Having suffered more cruelly than any Jews—than any people?—in history, they had to face the continued callousness of the Western world and their memory of the previous unconcern of most of their fellow-Jews. Their anguish had gained them nothing—not social advantage or human insight or spiritual clarity. If anything, they were a nuisance to the world, a judgment upon other Jews and, whenever they thought back, a torment to themselves. They had every right to give up on Judaism and reject life itself.

That they did not do so must, in some measure, be ascribed to the help which they received from the Zionists for nationalist reasons, and from the more assimilated Jews for humanitarian reasons. We should not underestimate the accomplishments of world Jewry in the late 1940s. But they were only splendid examples of *tsedakah*, the Jewish responsibility to other Jews. They would have been useless had the survivors not themselves had the will to build new lives.

What the survivors did was awesome. They refused to die or languish or disappear—though some took those courses. They turned back to life. They found new places to live and ways to make a living there. They married and had children. They took up all the trivial concerns that occupy people who have never lived intimately with depravity and death. But, unwelcome in their old homes and unwanted elsewhere, they left Europe, mostly for the United States or Palestine.

The record of those who came to North America is impressive in its own right. Hardly any aspect of American Jewish life today does not have some survivors playing a leading role in it. The story of their refusal to be defeated and their many subsequent triumphs deserves fuller telling.

One might discount something of the survivors' stirring achievement in America by linking it to a period of unparalleled economic expansion in the United States. Nothing of the sort occurred in Palestine. To the contrary, rarely in the existence of the State of Israel has there been a time free of military, economic, or social pressures—generally combined to exacerbate one another.

When the concentration camps were liberated the British refused to allow survivors into Palestine. Later, they withdrew from the country without having prepared successor governments. Seven Arab nations immediately moved into the power vacuum and attacked the newly-proclaimed Jewish state. Jewish existence in the Jewish homeland seemed doomed—but the Israeli War of Independence was won and once again the improbable had occurred in Jewish history.

What the Israelis Have Accomplished

Even after the victory there were difficulties in every area. Consider the problem of political inexperience. There had been no Jewish state for about two thousand years. While Jews had maintained various aspects of self-rule, a vast distance separates operating your own legal system and collecting community taxes from successfully running a modern democratic nation. Most new states organized in recent decades have not yet achieved a significant degree of efficiency—and they began with the unity of a people which had long lived together with the same culture on the same soil.

The European Jews who were smuggled into Palestine in the mid-1940s and those who immigrated there in large numbers once the State of Israel was established were relative strangers to one another. They differed by language, by national style, and by degree of modernization. They did not know Hebrew, the language of the Israelis, though it was not totally strange to them; they were unaccustomed to the Mediterranean climate and the life-style it created.

The refugees from Arab countries found the State of Israel far more European than the culture they were accustomed to. They maintained traditional Judaism with great respect, yet they discovered most Israelis were thoroughly secular. These Mediterranean Jews had been socially degraded for so long they found it difficult to take up the opportunities for self-rule and self-improvement that the Jewish state held open to them.

These diverse Jews crowding into the Land of Israel hardly seemed like a nation. Many people doubted that an enduring state could be created out of their mood: aversion for the countries they would not return to and hope that they might will a new life into being.

The first Israelis had almost no natural resources with which to work. The Land of Israel possessed no significant deposits of oil, iron, coal, or other valuable materials. The geography did not provide great natural harbors, and the terrain did not lend itself to lumbering. Much of the country's arable land had eroded and reforestation on a grand scale had to take place to restore some ecological balance. Even water, whether as rainfall or streams, was in short supply and threatened the hopes for expanded population and intensive agriculture.

What is more, the immigrants had not been farmers, construction workers, or common laborers in any great numbers. For centuries Jews had been prohibited from owning or working the land. When they were finally granted entry into the industrial economy it was often in the jobs no one wanted or in the fields that were too risky for prudent people to invest in. An abnormally high proportion of European Jews had used higher education to move into sales, managerial, entrepreneurial, or professional roles. To alter this skewed Jewish economic profile, the Zionists were determined to take on the full range of occupations which kept a nation alive, particularly farming. The nascent State of Israel faced severe economic difficulty. The European refugees were too bourgeois for its deliberately ramified economy and the Arabian Jewish refugees were unattuned to its emphasis on personal initiative.

Jewish Statecraft and Military Prowess

For any Jews since 70 C.E. to build a state would have been an extraordinary feat. For these Jews, largely survivors and refugees, it was an utterly heroic undertaking—one they carried through successfully. The State of Israel *works*—a judgment that cannot easily be made of many recently created governments (including ones based on far greater natural and national resources than the Israelis had). Indeed, except for the Israelis' heavy burden of defense expenditure, we are told that their inflation and balance-of-payments problems would be under reasonable control.

The great Jewish pride in the creation of the State of Israel may only partially rest on these mundane accomplishments, but they should also not be forgotten.

A word too must be said about the Israelis as soldiers. Jews in recent centuries have had little experience in most of the skills needed to operate a modern society but least of all in maintaining an army and conducting warfare. Long before the Holocaust, some Zionists had argued that political power could not be detached from the willingness of Jews to fight. The Jewish self-defense movement in Eastern Europe began after the Kishinev pogrom of 1904 when some Jews consciously broke with the traditional Jewish strategy for survival, reliance on the rulers and bribery. When the Arab riots of 1929 broke out in Palestine and relations between the two peoples degenerated, the importance of Jewish military self-reliance became clear.

After the Holocaust, Jews could not be content to trust their future to the good will of the great nations or to the moral power of non-violent resistance. Jews would never again go quietly, *en masse,* to their own destruction. The attack of the Arab neighbors on the newborn State of Israel tested that Jewish resolve to fight if need be—and in three succeeding wars and countless skirmishes Jewish valor demonstrated itself convincingly. Ever since, physical courage has been a part of Jewish pride in a way it had not been since Bible times.

To that must be added the admiration of Jews around the world for the intelligence and discipline with which the Israelis have fought. Their high competence at these recently acquired yet incredibly complex and changing skills has astonished most observers. In a generation's time, the perennial victims became a people of might. But they have not become militaristic, esteeming generals above civilians, and subordinating democracy to the totalitarian needs of an army. To the contrary, the deep humanity of its citizen-soldiery has generally been extraordinarily impressive. Despite attacks from terrorists and threats from their neighbors the Israelis have not surrendered their Jewish sense of human value.

All this has been a major cause of world Jewry's pride in the State of Israel.

Accomplishing the Dreams of Generations

The State of Israel, by its very existence, refutes many of the charges anti-semites have made against Jews. Almost nothing Jews have accomplished in the Diaspora could still the slurs that Jews are cowards, radicals, capitalists, parasites, and the like. The State of Israel rebuts such charges in a massive, public way that even Jew-haters cannot easily ignore. It conclusively demonstrates that, given a chance, the Jews are not different from most other people, though in some areas their achievement is quite exceptional. No small measure of Jewish pride in the State of Israel comes from its vindication of our worth despite the slander of our enemies. Israeli normalcy has not brought anti-semitism to an end as the early Zionists hoped it would. It has, in large part, shown Jew-hatred to be an irrational hatred seizing on any pretext that might support it.

Positively, the dedication of the Israelis to high social goals, regardless of the intense pressures under which they live, has given new scope to Jewish values. Diaspora Jews long had to limit their community idealism to giving charity or self-help groups. With the advent of democracy they could expand their horizons to join in the general efforts at social betterment. But only in the State of Israel do Jews control an entire society. For them alone, Jewish ethics has a full-scale political dimension, one lived out through their taxes and the government's budget. Through a moderate socialism they have tried to overcome the social inequities associated with capitalism, and despite massive military needs and development outlays they have built a welfare state that impressively serves all its citizens.

Through all the turmoil of its history, the State of Israel has also remained fully democratic. The press is free, criticism of the government abounds, and diverse political parties function and compete. In 1977 when Menahem Begin's Likud party won the right to form a new government, the Labor party, which had ruled the state since its founding, immediately and peacefully transferred power to its longtime opposition group. Not many nations founded since World War II have had or maintained such effective democracy.

One other Zionist hope has also largely been realized—the creation of a modern Jewish culture. The vitality of the Hebrew language shows this most vividly. The very complaints of the purists concerning its degeneration testify to its living quality. A language used in bars and bedrooms and warehouses will naturally refuse to follow the rules of academicians. Daily the Israelis create their own sort of Hebrew, a cultural achievement as significant as is their authors' steady output of novels, poetry, and short stories of high international distinction. With fewer Jews by far than the United States, the State of Israel has become the world center of Jewish publishing and Jewish research. Appropriately enough, it possesses the world's greatest Judaica museums and libraries. Its promise of continued Jewish creativity has no parallel, particularly should genuine peace come to the region.

What Is More Important than People?

With all of this, the greatest accomplishment of the State of Israel is the Israelis themselves. No such Jews have existed for centuries, perhaps, ever. At their best, they have a natural organic Jewishness unknown to Diaspora Jews. They do not feel the need to explain themselves as Jews to anyone for they know who they are, Israelis. They speak the Jewish people's ancient tongue and live on its ancestral soil. Their personal continuity with the Jewish past covers millennia. Having come through so often against all expectation, they are highly self-confident, a trait which, when they are at their worst, becomes arrogance and conceit. But just this sense that they can overcome all obstacles has allowed them again and again to do what most people said could not be done.

Most impressively, despite a hard-bitten realism, they remain idealists. Many endured the foulest treatment ever inflicted upon one group of people by another. Their country has been treated with an international cynicism few imagined possible in our time. Their morale has been shaken as leaders have proved venal, and affluence has undermined the virtues cherished by the early settlers. They have no saints in whom to trust, no fresh revelation to resolve the unparalleled complexities of their lives. Economically, politically, historically, their state seems unlikely to survive. Instead of despairing, they manage to live with hope, if expressed only as a grim determination not to be ground down. The Israeli proverb says, *"en bererah,"* there is no choice—that is, of course, if one continues to be a loyal member of this perennially stiff-necked, idealistic people. Then one sees no self-respecting Jewish alternative except to face up as best as one can to the suffering inflicted by wars and reservist call-ups, by a horrendous inflation, by the threat of one's neighbors' unending hostility, all the while creating a caring, humane society. There is no alternative if one is determined to be a Jew in one's homeland and there live out the possibilities inherent in the history of the Jewish people.

I want to distinguish what I have written from what the public relations departments of the State of Israel or various Jewish organizations present to Jewish readers. For some years now, most Israelis have been so disgusted with the empty rhetoric designed to improve their national morale that their slang term for it is *tsiyonut,* Zionism. The only heroics I want to call to your attention are those of the average, overburdened, hard-working, troubled Israeli one meets when one visits one's relatives in the State of Israel or has a chance conversation with someone there. We find just these ordinary Israelis to be, on the whole, extraordinary human beings. What they have done, what they yet hope to do despite all they have experienced and realistically fear, is inspiring. I am convinced that is why American Jews returning from their visits to the State of Israel feel so proud and invigorated as Jews. When one probes for the ground of this emotion, one discovers one cannot explain it as admiration for national building or exposure to one's biblical roots. The living power of corporate Jewish energy is impressive. But it moves us so deeply because it reflects the everyday devotion of most Israelis.

Some critics have suggested that we overreact, thus saying more about our guilt at the emptiness of our own Jewish existence than about the reality of Israeli lives. I will not deny that many American Jews support the State of Israel out of an unconscious desire to have its citizens vicariously fulfill their Jewish responsibilities. But that should not be allowed to offset what in fact the Israelis have accomplished: they have created a new and admirable sort of Jew. And having done so by a radical assertion of the Jewish will-to-live, one can also see them as the clearest demonstration of the human spirit's indomitable power.

The State of Israel sums up and expresses all our hopes for humanity and all our love of Jewish tradition and the Jewish people. Threats to its survival, therefore, transcend political issues. They assault our most significant evidence that human goodness need not be defeated in history. They attack the most visible and compelling instance of the Jewish people's continuing dedication to the central values of the Jewish tradition. The destruction of the State of Israel would be a shattering blow to the hope by which Jews have survived the ages and worked for the coming of universal justice and peace. Nothing else gives Jews such pride in their people and summons them so to Jewish responsibility.

Facing What Divides Us

With all that, the ties between American Jews and the State of Israel have their limits. Most simply put, our bonds are not political but only ethnic, in the special sense in which Jewish ethnicity is inseparable from Jewish religion. Since this distinction generates much controversy in the Jewish community, it requires careful examination.

One matter seems easily agreed to. American Jews owe political allegiance only to the country of their citizenship. As long as we do not change our national status we pay required taxes only to the United States or Canada; our funds given to the State of Israel are philanthropy or investment. Here we pledge our lives for the defense of our country; there we may become so concerned for the Israelis' survival that we volunteer to assist in their fight. Here we vote and exercise such political power as we have; there we may not appropriately become involved in the political process. *The Star-Spangled Banner* or *Hail Canada* is our national anthem; *Hatikvah,* for all that an effort was once made to have it become the chief song of the Jewish people, is the anthem of a foreign country. It, like the Israeli flag, must be treated with the protocol established by our country's laws.

Short as this list is, it has already brought us to the brink of several major arguments about our relation to the State of Israel. Almost all of these hinge on the question of the obligations of ethnicity and how these relate to nationalism and religion.

To begin with the least emotional issue, how high a priority shall we assign to knowing the Hebrew language? Obviously, any Jew who believes that the Jews are a people will want expertise in its classic tongue, Hebrew. No true Francophile would be satisfied to know French culture only in translation, and the French overseas could not long consider their descendants French if they did not speak the mother tongue, as the Quebecois loudly testify. Can there be an ethnically significant Diaspora Judaism then without a serious commitment to the Hebrew language? Were Americans less determinedly monolingual, a pervasive Hebraism might soon characterize us—but, despite our love of the State of Israel, little progress has been made in this regard.

This issue becomes practical the minute one must plan supplemental Jewish education programs where little time is available. The Menorah Curriculum of Conservative Judaism reflects this dilemma. The program disturbed many Conservative educators who consider the Hebrew language critical to Jewish life yet also want to give their students a rounded Jewish education. The Menorah Curriculum insisted that, even with six hours of instruction a week, a school had to choose between giving its students some good grasp of the Hebrew language *or* of Jewish history *or* of synagogue skills. The old hope of doing them all had proved untenable.

The choices in adult education are equally agonizing: Should a cultured Diaspora Jew first acquire a working knowledge of classical or modern Hebrew? Israeli educators consider our ethnic loyalties substantially national and want us to concentrate on modern Hebrew and contemporary Israeli literature. Most American Jews think of their people in a more traditional fashion. They wish they could know the Hebrew of the Bible and prayer book—or, assuming that one can be religious in any language, they refuse to give the language the time and attention its learning would require.

We Seem to Be Searching for Different Things

This linguistic problem points to a greater difficulty American Jews have, one in relation to Israeli culture generally. Americans look to Israeli writers and artists to express the contemporary Jewish spirit and thereby enrich our impoverished American Jewish life. They hope that our revived national homeland will be, in Ahad Haam's famous phrase, our "spiritual center." But note that, for all their lip service to this ideal, American Jews refuse to learn Hebrew well. Then when they read modern Hebrew literature in translation—the novels of Amos Oz or the poetry of Amichai quickly come to mind—they do not find their Jewish interests satisfied. The Israeli authors, sure of their Jewishness, pay little direct attention to it. They tend to address universal human questions—as seen, of course, through the lens of Israeli existence. The Americans, secure in their humanness, seek a Jewish culture that will confirm their particular ethnic identity. Israeli culture, ideologists to the contrary, appears unlikely to meet their needs.

From the Israeli side, the issue of ethnic self-definition comes to a head in the question of *aliyah,* immigration. If the Jews are a national group, say the Israelis, loyal Jews should return and live in the national home. Jews might have once been justified if they had personal reasons for hesitating to do so. Today, with a viable State of Israel, no good Jewish reason exists for not making *aliyah.* Only personal convenience or other such selfish considerations, they insist, will keep loyal Jews from fulfilling this central ethnic obligation. Besides, for military and economic reasons, the Jewish state has no greater need than more Jews. Anyone seriously committed to the survival of the State of Israel should consider it a primary duty to immigrate there speedily. Classic Zionism has always considered *aliyah* the primary Jewish responsibility. This has regularly embarrassed American Zionists at World Zionist meetings for they have had to join in fervent calls for immigration when they knew their members, out of a different sense of ethnic duty, would not respond to them.

For one moment it seemed as if this problem might be surmounted. When the United Nations voted its infamous resolution equating Zionism with racism, many American Jews quickly identified themselves in public as Zionists. Some international Zionist leaders thought this might then lead them on to the great nationalist duty, *aliyah.* That did not happen then as it has not happened in the past. For most American Jews, Zionism means a vigorous support of the State of Israel but not personal immigration. They identify closely with the State of Israel but, for all their ethnicity, they do not wish to live there.

In this regard an instructive argument divided the two communities. Jewish emigrants from Russia have been given their exit visas on the legal grounds of repatriation to their national territory, the State of Israel. As the outflow of Jews proceeded, a high proportion of Russian émigrés reaching Rome or Vienna, the transfer points, refused to go on to the State of Israel and asked instead to immigrate to the United States or other countries. Officials of the Jewish Agency, the international body for immigration to the State of Israel, acting with the support or by the prodding of the Israeli government, appealed to the international Jewish charities, asking them to reduce radically their assistance to such Russian "drop outs," as the Israelis termed them. Their political and ideological reasons for wanting American Jews to enforce *aliyah* on the Russian Jews were obvious. But, for the first time since its founding, a major demand of the State of Israel was rejected by organized American Jewry. Despite their devotion to the State of Israel, the American Jewish commitment to help Jews go wherever they wanted to go overrode Israeli needs and Zionist doctrine.

American Jewish ethnicity is less nationalistic and more religio-cultural than that of the Israelis. The most authentic Jews most Americans have known were the East European immigrants who came to these shores steeped in a European Jewish culture. Though the land they lived on had been Poland and the language they spoke was Yiddish, there could be no question of their genuine Jewishness. Like them, Jews had for centuries carried on Jewish existence under the most varied circumstances, certain that they lived as Jews.

In their own way, American Jews repeat this historical pattern. Though they suffer with the problems of being Jewish in the Diaspora and worry about their future, they believe their geographical situation does not preclude their being true Jews. Their ethnicity has a cosmopolitan quality to it. At their best, they believe living by Torah, not land or language, determines the authenticity of one's Jewish existence. While living on the Land of Israel and speaking Hebrew would surely enhance one's efforts to order one's life by Torah, one can be faithful to the Torah anywhere.

Politics, the Critical Area

The relations between the two communities became most troublesome when ethnic responsibilities appeared to carry over into the realm of political action. The State of Israel, often isolated on the international scene, depends upon the United States for political support, as well as military and economic aid. American Jewry has played an important role in winning and preserving American backing for the Israelis. Israeli officials could never admit to using American Jewry as a lobbying group with the United States government; that would be unconscionable as interference in the internal affairs of another nation. The classic blunder in that regard was Ambassador Yitzhak Rabin's advice to American Jews in 1972 to vote for Richard Nixon in the presidential election. The leaders of American Jewish organizations do not need much political guidance from Jerusalem. Their hearts are attuned to Israeli needs and they know American Jews are determined not to relive their passivity during the Holocaust. They therefore prefer to err, if at all, on the side of Jewish vigilance. Particularly since the 1967 Six Day War, the Israelis and the American Jewish community have had a common political goal: to frustrate the plans of the Israelis' enemies and promote the survival of the State of Israel. For a people that prides itself on its independence of thought and the contentiousness of its members, American Jews have displayed an extraordinary community discipline in this regard.

In the mid-1970s, however, a significant change took place. A small but not insignificant number of American Jews became critical of the Israeli political posture, what they perceived as its relative stiffness at giving or receiving signals of a desire to make peace. This minority among American Jews felt so keenly about the issues involved that they broke the solid public front the community had previously displayed on behalf of the State of Israel. When the "doves" organized and later communicated their dissenting views to the press and the government, a bitter protest broke out against them. A new question now had been placed on the Jewish community agenda: When, where, and on what grounds may American Jews properly criticize the State of Israel?

The overwhelming majority of American Jews adamantly opposed any public criticism of Israeli government policy. They had various reasons for this stand. Some insisted American Jewish life could not provide us with as good a basis as the Israelis had for judging what was best for the Jewish people or the Jewish state. These Jews believed American Jews should acknowledge the centrality of the State of Israel in world Jewish affairs and gratefully accept its leadership. This may be called the nationalist approach to Jewish political action, though not all who espoused it would call themselves Jewish nationalists.

A more sizable group, including some prominent Israeli officials (whether out of conviction or the need to appear democratic), agreed that criticism was not only acceptable but even desirable. They, then, quickly added that in the present political situation it should not be offered. Their prudential arguments ranged over a wide spectrum. Since the Israelis would have to bear the consequences, they alone should make the decisions. Since this was a matter of national security and military affairs, civilians had no place in it. Since the survival of the State of Israel was at issue, all difference of opinion should be put aside. In any case, they insisted, the Jewish community had its internal channels for making dissent known to the Israelis. Why should any well-intentioned person take the minority case to the outside world where hostile people could use it for their own harmful ends?

Most of those espousing these positions did not deny the rights of Diaspora Jews to judge and comment on Israeli stands. They agreed that if the State of Israel is to be a Jewish state, then every Jew has a stake in it. Its ethnic centrality makes it worthy of the support and subject to the judgment of all members of the folk. To put it bluntly, they acknowledged that the Israeli state might properly be criticized by Diaspora Jews if it were not being "truly Jewish." (We take for granted the reverse criticism, that of the Diaspora by the Israelis.)

Let us take a theoretical example. Totalitarian, military governments are a commonplace among young nations facing crises—but a Jewish dictatorship seems a contradiction in terms. Though we cannot define the Jewish ethos, most Jews would be aroused if they felt the State of Israel violated it. Granting that, these critics of the "doves" believed nothing in the political situation of the mid-1970s validated "going public" with complaints about the State of Israel. If they admitted there were any problems in Israeli policy, they argued that survival or security demanded keeping quiet about them.

The dissenters found these arguments, and particularly the intense community pressures which accompanied them, an effort to deny in practice the democracy which had been affirmed in theory. As they saw it, the majority considered no time, either then or previously, an appropriate one for serious criticism of Israeli policy. They denied that critics in the community had adequate channels of communication with the Israelis. Organizational access was controlled by the government itself or by those whose leadership in America substantially derived from staying on good terms with Israeli leaders. Little searching disagreement with Israeli stands could move through such conduits.

I have raised these sensitive issues only to point to the major unresolved problem in the relationship between the Israelis and Diaspora Jews. It presses particularly hard on American Jews because the Israelis expect them to lobby for the State of Israel. No one denies that the State of Israel has unequalled significance for Diaspora Jews. When should they insist upon their right to define for themselves what is "good for the Jews"—as is in the case of Russian émigrés? And when should they accept Jerusalem's definition of it despite such serious doubts as they might have—as most American Jews did in the mid-1970s? Theoretically put: Is Jewish ethnicity primarily national, so that the Jewish state is the final arbiter of Jewish duty, or does Jewish ethnicity contain within itself a qualitative or spiritual principle in the name of which everything Jewish, including a Jewish state, must be brought into judgment?

In my opinion, most liberal Jews want to maintain something of both positions. They believe that Jews ought not to live by the relatively cynical, a-moral standards of much of contemporary civilization. Yet they know that political reality will occasionally require Israeli governments to subordinate high human standards to the proper demands of power. And they are particularly concerned not to do anything which might hurt the State of Israel.

I share in this dilemma. Why then did I become a "dove" on

Israeli matters? Because, after much soul-searching, I felt that I and others like me could not through internal Jewish community channels adequately convey our moral anguish at certain Israeli government policies. My religious faith, even as it cannot be separated from my Jewish ethnicity, will not survive quarantine from my politics. Applying spiritual values to power realities is agonizingly difficult. Refusing to face that challenge is as un-Jewish today as it was already in biblical times. And I became convinced that, despite the most scrupulous concern for Jewish survival and Israeli security, there are occasions when open, public dissent from given Israeli policies is warranted and, depending on the action of American Jewish leaders, perhaps demanded.

I pray we shall be so blessed that no further issues of practical consequence will arise between the State of Israel and Diaspora Jewry. But it seems unlikely that so quiet a political era will soon come about. If so, then the two Jewries urgently need to learn how those who share an intense love can accept and give criticism, thereby strengthening their relationship and making it properly mature.

·6·

WHY DO JEWS
HAVE TO BE DIFFERENT?

Let me be explicit about the premise underlying this chapter: Judaism teaches, indeed emphasizes, the equality of all human beings. Not all religions proclaim so universal a faith. Ordinary observation discloses that people are quite different from one another. One must transcend the facts to insist that all human beings share the same nature and value. Judaism had that vision as far back as its earliest documents. The Adam and Eve "myths"* categorically declare that all people have a common ancestry, that humankind is one family. Nothing in the Bible's account of the origins of the Hebrews supports the notion that, by virtue of their birth, some people are better in God's eyes than others. For all that the biblical authors were appalled at humanity's sinfulness, for all that they felt the Hebrews were uniquely ready to acknowledge God and do God's will, they never denied the ultimate worth of every individual.

The rabbis perpetuated this doctrine though their intimate, unhappy experience with the Romans intensified their spiritual despair of the "nations." The Mishnah texts dealing with capital punishment say, "Man was created through a single creature to teach you that whoever destroys a single Jewish soul (some texts: 'a single soul') is considered by the Torah as though he had destroyed a whole world and whoever preserves a single Jewish soul (some texts: 'a single soul') is considered by the Torah as if

*On this usage, see Part Three, *The Bible and Tradition*, chapter 3, "How True Is the Bible?"

103

he had preserved a whole world. Another reason man was created singly was for the sake of peace among men, so that people might not say to one another, 'My progenitor was greater than yours.' . . . Another reason he was created singly was to proclaim God's greatness. When a man strikes many coins from one mold, they all come out identical. Though the Holy One, blessed be He, made every man in the mold of the first man, not one of them is identical to his fellowman. Therefore, every single soul is obliged to say, 'For my sake the world was created'." (San. 4:5)

This commitment to human equality continues through historic Jewish teaching. It gives special poignancy, particularly today, to the Jewish desire to remain separate from the rest of humankind.

The Beginnings of Jewish Separatism

Already in biblical times, Jewish law separated the Jews from other peoples; or, as they would have put it, God had commanded them to live distinctively. This inner drive toward differentiation was early matched, in a rather perverse way, by other peoples' prejudice toward the Jews. These two motives for Jewish separateness intermingled and mutually reinforced one another for most of the past two thousand years. Anti-semitism justified the Jewish desire to stay apart, while Jewish separatism gave Gentiles a pretext to claim that Jews could not participate in the general social life. Despite the mixed historic reality, I shall analyze the internal and external factors separately because I wish to concentrate on the Jewish conception of distinctiveness rather than on the history or theory of anti-semitism.

Classic Judaism forthrightly declared: God wants the Jews to be unlike other peoples. God even brought the Hebrew nation into being in a unique way so they might carry out a special task in history. Normal nationhood arose, according to biblical anthropology, from the descendants of Noah's sons, Shem, Ham, and Japheth. After they had settled in Shinar and built a tower to reach into heaven, God punished them by splitting their family up into language-nationality groups. (Gen. 11) By contrast, God came to Abram of Ur and said that in reward for his special loyalty God would make his seed a mighty nation. (Gen. 12) The Torah indicates that God fulfilled this promise in the Hebrew population explosion in Egypt. When God subsequently gave them the

Torah, by which they were to live, the essence of their relationship is stated succinctly: "If you will carefully obey what I say and keep My Covenant, then you shall be my treasured possession among all the peoples though all the earth is Mine. You shall be My priestly kingdom and holy people." (Exod. 19:5–6) This statement encapsulates the Bible's understanding of the Jews as a chosen people (above, chapter 3) and we now need to explore its consequences for Jewish separateness.

From a modern point of view, it seems natural for a group to evolve and maintain a distinctive identity. We even have a science devoted to social creativity, cultural anthropology. Reading the Bible one quickly gets a sense of the rich cultural diversity of the ancient Near East. Thus, to mention only two of many peoples, the Moabites and Ammonites had their own languages, their own celebrations, and their own heroes. We would be excited but not surprised if an archeologist discovered a Moabite or Ammonite national saga, telling of their peoples' history, thanking their gods, and praising their nations' glories. Sociologically, we have no difficulty comprehending why the Hebrews wanted to be different. They grew up with the stories of Abraham and Sarah, of Moses and the Exodus, and they lived the distinctive life ordained by the Torah and elaborated by their folk. They would therefore "naturally" want to continue their people's individual way of life.

The authors of the Bible do not think in terms of a group's cultural self-consciousness. They explain significant matters religiously and relate Jewish difference to belief, in their case, to a unique faith in God. All other nations worship idols. The Hebrews alone worship the one God, who cannot properly be symbolized by anything in creation. Yehezkel Kaufmann, the great Israeli Bible scholar, went so far as to argue in his eight-volume study, *A History of Israelite Faith,* that the fight against idolatry is the central theme of the Bible. In any case, the biblical sense of difference from "the nations" stems from a consciousness of holding a distinctive, true faith—the only true faith in the world. If the Jews were not different they would be idolaters and the only real God would have no representative in history. For God's sake, for the truth's sake, the Jews had to remain apart from other peoples. The prophet Micah summarizes this aspect of biblical religion in the words, "Though all the nations walk each in the names of its gods, we will walk in the name of *Adonai,* our God, forever and ever." (4:5)

The Commandments Create Fences around the Jews

A major purpose of the laws of the Torah is to keep the Jews apart from other peoples. For example, the so-called Holiness Code explicitly prohibits certain sex acts in order to separate the Hebrews from their neighbors. "You shall not do the sort of things done by the Egyptians among whom you lived and you shall not do the sorts of things done in the land of Canaan, whither I am bringing you. You shall not follow their laws. My ordinances shall you do and My statutes you shall keep to walk therein. I am *Adonai,* your God." (Lev. 18: 3–4 and see what follows thereon.) The laws of keeping *kosher* are introduced in the Book of Deuteronomy this way: "You are the children of *Adonai,* your God. Do not gash yourselves or shave the front of your heads for your dead, for you are a people consecrated to *Adonai,* your God. *Adonai,* your God, chose you from among all other peoples on earth to be His treasured people. You must not eat any abhorrent animal. . . ." (Deut. 14: 1–3) Many other laws of the Torah, such as those for the Sabbath, do not say that they are designed to distinguish the Jews from other nations. Nonetheless, it seems apparent to modern scholars, as to many a traditional commentator, that this was one of their primary functions.

The law most directly designed to prevent Jewish assimilation is that against marriage with Gentiles. The original regulation proscribed marriage with the seven nations inhabiting Canaan. "Do not intermarry with them. Do not give your daughters to their sons or take their daughters for your sons, for they will turn your children away from Me to worship other gods. . . ." (Deut. 7:3–4) The connection between separatism and the struggle against idolatry could not be plainer. Ezra followed this strategy when he sought to rebuild Jewish life among the descendants of those who had returned to Jerusalem after the Babylonian Exile, 586–534 B.C.E. He had the Jewish males give up their foreign wives and promise that they and their children would not intermarry. (Ezra 9:5–10:44) Apparently he understood the Torah's law as being applicable to all heathen nations (as did the Talmud, in a later time). Since then, marriage within the community has been a major Jewish value and one of the most effective means of maintaining Jewish distinctiveness.

To Be Holy Implies Being Separate

All of these laws are connected with the biblical perception of *kedushah,* holiness. The word *"kadosh"* apparently points to God's special "character," as when God's heavenly retinue proclaims with a triple emphasis unparalleled in the Bible that *Adonai* of hosts is "holy, holy, holy." (Isaiah 6:3) Because of its identification with God, *kedushah* defies simple definition. Scholars agree, however, that one of its important facets is being exceptional or out of the ordinary. Something sacred may then be understood as that which is set apart from the profane.

A familiar instance of the sacred as that which is separate is the Bible—in Hebrew, *Kitvei Kodesh,* Holy Scriptures. In some respects, it is quite ordinary. Its writings follow the grammar and syntax of the Semitic languages of the time. Indeed, we often turn to them for help when we have trouble with the meaning of obscure biblical words or expressions. Its laws, histories, poems, and proverbs follow the forms common to the ancient Near East. Jewish tradition called these books holy because it recognized them as related to God and, hence, quite extraordinary. As a result, we do not treat the Bible as we do other books. Jewish law requires us to say a blessing before reading from it and has special rules for its careful treatment and preservation.

The same pattern of taking the ordinary and treating it exceptionally produces a "holy day." Nothing astronomical distinguishes the Sabbath from other days of the week. Through God's command fulfilled in human action, each seventh day becomes different from all other days. Jewish law prescribes ceremonies to set the day aside and celebrate its special quality. One does so with a cup of wine, popularly called the *kiddush,* the "sanctified," though the *day* is thereby made sacred and *not* the wine, which itself receives no special religious status. By this act of blessing and drinking, one becomes, as Rabbi Hamnuna nicely puts it, a "partner with God in the work of creating." (Shab. 119b)

A telling instance of holiness as being set aside—though one not often recognized as such—is Jewish marriage. The Hebrew term for it, taken from the act of betrothal, is *"kiddushin,"* literally, "the sanctifying." That has given rise to a good deal of sermonizing on the sacred quality of life expected of a Jewish husband and wife. Though the rabbis advocate a spiritual tone to the relationship between husband and wife, they included little in the process of *kiddushin* itself which points the couple toward the sacred. Many of the parts of a Jewish wedding are legalistic. They constitute the formal procedures by which a man legitimately "sets aside" a woman to be his wife. (In rabbinic law only the male has such agency.) To be sure, a wedding is so significant a Jewish event that its proper celebration involves blessings and festivity in the presence of the community. Surely, marriage is spiritual in modeling the people of Israel's Covenant with God. But one will not be inaccurate in describing *kiddushin* as primarily the acts of consecration by which a man and woman set apart their relations with one another from those between them and any other people.

Leviticus 19:2, which epitomizes all the holiness chapters of that book, says, "You shall be holy for I, *Adonai,* your God, am holy." This verse should be understood in its negative as well as its positive sense. As God is other than the world, so the Hebrews, to be specially God-like, must live in conscious separation from other peoples. For the Torah, holiness differentiates, though not to the point of self-isolation. Many of the Torah's laws seek to create this sanctifying separateness.

The Jews of post-biblical times consciously thought of themselves as different from other peoples so as to serve the one God of the universe. The First Book of Maccabees, apparently written in Hebrew toward the end of the second century B.C.E., provides clear-cut testimony to this effect. The author, utilizing the dramatic style common to Greek histories written then, puts a stirring defense of separatism into the mouth of Mattathias. As he spurns Antiochus's command to worship an idol and thus rebels against the Syrian king, he says, "Though all the heathens in the king's dominions obey him and forsake each of them the religion of their fathers and choose instead to follow his commandments, yet I and my sons and my brothers will live in accordance with the Covenant of our fathers. God forbid that we should abandon the Torah and our other laws. We will not listen to the message of the king. We will not depart from our religion to the right side or to the left." (1 Macc. 2:19–22)

Many people believe Chanukah celebrates a triumph in a struggle for religious freedom. They often forget that the Maccabees fought for the right to be different. Considering how many American Jews face December conflicted between self-respect and their desire to celebrate Christmas, the full message of Chanukah comes each year at an opportune time and with not a little irony.

The Beginnings of Anti-semitism

In the Greco-Roman era we get our first good idea of how "the nations" reacted to the Jews and their unusual ways. Over two centuries before Christianity began, an Egyptian priest named Manetho wrote a scurrilous "history" of the Jews. Among other things, he charged that Moses was a renegade Egyptian priest who had led the Jews, a group of lepers, out of Egypt. His calumnies were preserved and elaborated by Apion, the first-century c.e. Alexandrian anti-semite, in response to whom Josephus wrote the first book of Jewish anti-defamation.* Apion charged, among other slanders, that until the time of Antiochus the Jews had kept an ass's head in the Temple holy of holies as the true object of their supposedly imageless worship. Worse, Apion "revealed" that each year the Jews kidnapped a Greek, fattened him in their temple, and ritually murdered him while cursing all Greeks.

This vile material should not be taken as the normal gentile reaction to Jews in the centuries before the rise of Christianity. But it was also not uncommon or without social acceptance. Apion was esteemed by important Roman writers, a number of whom repeated his lies. He was also one of the Alexandrian delegation which went to the Emperor Gaius Caligula to protest the prominence of Jews in Alexandria. (Philo was in the opposing Jewish delegation and wrote a book about that experience.**) Apion's anti-semitism among that of others demonstrates that Christianity did not invent Jew-hate but only redirected and, in its own way, strengthened it.

Negative and external though it be, anti-semitism cannot be ignored in any discussion of Jewish separateness. It has been a major historical factor in keeping the Jews at a distance from other peoples. Even should Jews reject their religious or ethnic reasons for remaining a distinct people, that would not guarantee that they could easily integrate with general humanity. Gentile

*I have given a brief citation from the Josephus work on p. 23.
**I have also given a brief citation from Philo's work on pp. 21 and 22.

hatred might still keep them from assimilating. We must pause for a moment, then, and seek to understand the roots of anti-semitism, a phenomenon I emphasize, which was already well established in pre-Christian days.

Sociologists regularly discover that groups have a human boundary beyond which feelings of kinship, friendliness, or neutrality are replaced by wariness, suspicion, and hostility. Groups vary widely in their attitudes toward the outsider, but fear of the stranger occurs so commonly that it has been given a name, xenophobia.

Why groups should demonstrate this phenomenon is not clear. Somehow it seems easier to identify one's community negatively, by dissociation from others or by antagonism to them than by a positive, inner bond. Were that corporate isolation all that motivated group hatred, education would largely eliminate it. Make the stranger known and less fearsome and the xenophobia would vanish. To a limited extent, that therapy works. In a democratic context, with great social pressure to accept others as equals, day-to-day contact with the feared stranger often neutralizes one's prejudice. Yehuda Bauer, the eminent Israeli historian of the Holocaust, has noted that in most countries under Nazi rule, until Jews were isolated from their gentile neighbors, they received significant help from them, relatively speaking.

The Scapegoat: An Explanation for Irrational Hatred

We must delve further, for prejudice regularly persists despite education. Some surveys indicate that the best-educated join the least-educated as the most anti-semitic Americans. Social scientists suggest that the persistence of prejudice can best be explained by the scapegoat theory—a name, surprisingly enough, taken from a Jewish ritual model. In the Day of Atonement liturgy described in the Torah, two goats were sacrificed in the Temple. The high priest brought the first atonement goat to the altar in the usual ritual fashion. He treated the other goat in ways without precedent in the Torah. First he confessed "all the iniquities and transgressions of the Israelites, whatever their sins were, putting them on the head of the goat. Then it shall be sent off to the wilderness with someone. Thus the goat will carry on him all their iniquities to an inaccessible region and the goat shall be set free there in the wilderness." (Lev. 16: 21–22) The Mishnah, centuries later, recounts the practice of running the goat over a wilderness cliff so that it was killed in a fall to the ground below. (Yoma 6:6)

The message cannot be misread. Psychologically, people find it easier to load their problems on someone else than bear them personally. When one is angry with a powerful person or institution, particularly one considered to be beyond criticism, one gets great relief by displacing one's feelings on an object our society permits or encourages us to hate. We utilize a(n) (e)scape goat. They may be within the community, e.g., the retarded, the handicapped, or the oddly shaped. If they are outsiders of one kind or another, blacks, Jews, or Catholics, we may be permitted to be more violent. Every frustrated human drive can be channeled into prejudice. When we resent not getting the money, the power, the social status we yearn for, we vent our anger by hating or hurting our society's scapegoat(s).

From this social-psychological point of view, people will be prejudiced as long as human nature and social patterns remain the same. Optimistically, much can be done to satisfy basic human needs, to contain our frustrations, and morally redirect our hostility. Realistically, prejudice, even when quiescent, remains dangerously potent, quickly available to provide us with a new victim when our situation worsens. As Albert Camus noted at the end of his classic novel, *The Plague,* the germs may no longer be visible or active but, though hidden, they are as alive and as destructive as ever.

We cannot tell whether the Jews were only one of many scapegoats in pre-Christian Alexandria or singled out for particular animosity. They were clearly not the Roman Empire's major target of hatred. Christianity abetted and intensified classic anti-semitism when it became the dominant religion of the Western World. It made the Jews the chief scapegoat of European civilization.

The Religious Dimensions of Jew-hate

Extraordinary emotions became attached to this Christian-sponsored hatred of Jews, because Christianity taught that the Jews "had killed God." That is, they bore the responsibility for the crucifixion of Jesus—"His blood be upon us and our children." (Matt. 27:25) Having caused the death of one of the persons of the Trinity, the Jews obviously hated the absolutely good and identified with the absolutely bad. It was right, even holy, to despise them.

Over the centuries, anti-semitism became the accepted European attitude, one which had the weight of history and numbers behind it. Fortunately, Christian anti-semitism did not include a duty to exterminate the Jews but set limits to their maltreatment. Christian teaching asserted that when the Christ returned his ultimate triumph would be the conversion of the Jews. Hence the people of Israel needed to remain alive for his second coming. In the interim, the church only required that Jews be degraded to show the consequences of rejecting God's offer of salvation. Not infrequently, in the Middle Ages, when local clergy or nobility were overly harsh, the Jews appealed to the pope or other high church officials and succeeded in having their persecution eased.

Islam likewise spread prejudice against the Jews. Not having a deicide tradition, its attitude differed from that of the European Christians. Early Moslem teaching made a distinction between conquered peoples who had a religion of revelation, a "people of a book," and those whose faith had another base. The latter faced the choice of conversion or death. The former could exist under Moslem rule but only in second-class fashion. From the early centuries of Moslem expansion on, the book-peoples were expected to make their religious presence as unostentatious as possible and to conduct themselves personally so as to show their social inferiority to Moslems.

Christendom did not introduce formal regulation for Jewish degradation until some centuries later than Islam did. We may conveniently consider the First Crusade a turning point in European Christian practices toward Jews. What had been prejudice marked by occasional violence for about a thousand years now gave way to active persecution, including massacre, riot, expulsion, and forced conversion. Thus, the Fourth Lateran Council, 1215 c.e., demanded that Jews wear a special badge, among other regulations for their degradation. In 1516, Venice established the first formal ghetto, a walled-in Jewish residential area.

How Deep Does Anti-semitism Go?

Scholars like Leon Poliakov, Malcolm Hay, and Edward Flannery have published such notable studies of the history of anti-semitism that I forebear from discussing it further. However, I want to return once again to the question of its basis. Anti-semitism carries so complex and eerie an emotional quality that scholars have puzzled over it. This tone hardly seems explained by the Marxian notion of class manipulation or other contemporary varieties of scapegoating. Without understanding anti-semitism's unique virulence as best we can, we are unlikely to comprehend how Hitler could make it seem reasonable to murder 6,000,000 European Jews. To call it deeply irrational hides as much as it reveals, though it specifies why we must utilize deep-seated therapy and strong social controls to deal with it, rather than merely education and goodwill.

The psychoanalytic theory concerning its source demands serious consideration. Christianity imposed biblical morality on the pagan nations of Europe. Unconsciously, the psychoanalysts claim, all people hate denying their instinctual drives and those who make them behave morally. They cannot directly express their unconscious but fierce resentment, for one must love the parent/church/God who imposed the standards. But, in their very name, a rich hatred is permitted, one against the Jews, the people who gave the world the Bible and the Christ. Anti-semitism arises because the Jews bear the repressed hostilities of all those who, against their unconscious desires, must now be civilized. Thus, even when religion no longer plays a significant role in many peoples' lives, the Jews will still be hated fanatically because the irrational source of anti-semitism, the rebellion against morality, still functions.

The Irresistible Appeal of the New Freedom

Those of us who live after the Holocaust find it difficult to appreciate how intoxicating the Emancipation was to the Jews of the ghetto. To try to appreciate their attitude we must keep in mind the long centuries of persecution and hate which preceded the grant of social and political equality. True, the slogans of the Emancipation became reality only slowly and grudgingly, against the stubborn resistance of important segments of the population, and secular anti-semitism soon replaced the religious variety. All this appeared to be only cultural lag to Jews who remembered the degradation in which their parents or grandparents had lived. Each year brought new evidence of progress. The ghetto was abolished and new areas of opportunity that Jews had hardly dared to dream of were continually opening to them. Democracy seemed to be marching forward irresistibly to a day of international plenty and peace. Today we mock such hopes as wildly unrealistic but we speak out of our hard-won social realism as the newly emancipated Jews spoke out of their optimistic situation. They had anticipated living amid an institutionalized, irrational hatred; when they saw it fall away, they were exhilarated at their gains and blind to everything but their opportunities.

A sizable number of the Jews who modernized—others did not have the opportunity or the desire to accept emancipation—thought it logical to give up Judaism and adopt the majority life-style. There seemed little reason to remain a separate people. They did not believe that God "wanted" anything and considered it perverse for Jews to reject active involvement in society now that it finally welcomed them. Their newly accessible neighbors were not heathens, but, at their best, the bearers of a great civilization. The newcomers felt they had much to learn from them, as evidenced by the way they flooded the universities and devoted themselves to becoming cultured.

A minority of Jews suggested that their coreligionists give up everything distinctive about Jewish life and become indistinguishable from their neighbors. These assimilationists, as they were called, pursued their goal in two ways. Early in the nineteenth century, full integration into the society seemed possible only through conversion to Christianity. Thousands of western European Jews took this step to end being outsiders, Heinrich Heine being the most famous example.

Most Jews, despite their passion for modernity, found even a *pro forma* conversion incompatible with their sense of self-respect. They rather chose to assimilate in a secular way, by substituting culture for religion. In theory, the arts were concerned only with humanistic values. They had no place for anything so mean and narrow as prejudice. Jews avidly embraced literature, music, and art as an escape from the confines of religion. Before long, most modern European nations had an unusually high proportion of Jews involved in their cultural activities. This strategy became ever more appealing as Western civilization secularized and Christianity no longer provided the basic structure for its cultural activity.

Being Modern and Jewish—But How Separate?

The overwhelming majority of Jews have not wanted to give up being Jewish though they were desperately eager to be at home in Western civilization. After fifteen centuries of segregation and persecution, the possibility of their families being able to live with full human dignity made social adaptation their overriding concern. But not their only one, for they also wanted to maintain their Jewishness. In their rush to secure the necessary social and economic base for their new lives, most Jews gave little thought to just how distinctively Jewish they ought to remain. To this day, what constitutes the proper blend of modernity and Jewishness, of social integration and separation, remains the major problem of Jewish life.

The first great positive response to the Emancipation was the liberalization of Jewish religious life by Reform Jews and, in due course, by Conservative and modern Orthodox Jews. (The non-modern Orthodox shun contemporary culture as inimical to an authentic Jewish life, often citing the failures of the adaptive strategy as a justification for their self-isolation.) The liberals contended that change had always been the means to Jewish survival. The radically altered social circumstance of modern Jewish life now mandated new forms of Jewish self-expression. If Judaism could be clothed in a contemporary esthetic and understood in terms of modern intellectuality, Jews would choose to remain religiously different while participating fully in the society.

This inner relaxation of the walls separating Jew from Gentile seemed justified by the obvious fact that Jews no longer lived among idolaters. Christians (and Moslems) worshiped the same God that Jews did and most of their personal and social ideals came from the teachings of the Hebrew Bible. Jews surely did not need to stand aloof from people with whom one shared such fundamental concerns. The Reform Jews, who pioneered the adjustment of Judaism to its emancipated situation, followed this reasoning as far as their desire not to assimilate fully would let them. In the Pittsburgh Platform of 1885, a group of Reform rabbis declared, ". . . today we accept as binding only such ceremonies as elevate and sanctify our lives, but reject all such as are not adapted to the views and habits of modern civilization." They optimistically saw "in the modern era of universal culture of heart and intellect the approach of the realization of Israel's great Messianic hope for the establishment of the kingdom of truth, justice, and peace among all men." Perhaps the ultimate symbol of their desire to participate in Western culture was their practice of baring their heads at services. They risked dissociating themselves from the rest of the Jewish people in the hope of creating a form of Jewish observance which would be comfortable for thoroughly modernized Jews.

Jewish Identity Gets a Higher Priority

The centrifugal drive to integrate Jewish life into Western society has been a major factor in American Jewish history. Not until after World War II did a countervailing centripetal force make itself clearly evident. Following the Israeli Six Day War of 1967 and the simultaneous loss of simple faith in America solving all of humankind's ills, we could no longer make Western culture our supreme concern. The civilization in which we once took such pride appears hollow. We are more apt to encounter cynicism than optimism when we discuss social goals. We cannot any longer identify the universal standard to which our Jewish heritage ought to adapt. Suddenly, holding on to the perennial values of Judaism, not neglecting it for universal culture, seems the best means of assuring our and our children's high humanity.

From the vantage of this renewed particularism a little analysis makes plain why Jews have always been overrepresented among the idealists seeking to overcome all human differences. On the surface that cause seemed a simple secularization of the Jewish messianic vision. But it also served an important modern Jewish self-interest. One humanity would mean no anti-semitism, a condition most Jews would dearly love to reach. But to care only about humankind while ignoring one's people's own right to a distinctive existence is self-hating to the point of self-destruction.

Democracy cannot require assimilation. People are entitled to their dignity regardless of their color, creed, or ethnic style. How can they have worth if we demand they give up their heritage and live only like us? Cultural pluralism, not the melting pot, properly defines Americanism; healthy group self-respect is the moral basis of our contemporary surge of ethnic self-concern. Practically, too, most peoples and religions will continue on their separate ways for a long time to come. The unification of humankind will come through peoples learning to live together, not by their insisting that other groups assimilate to their standard. To give up our separate Jewish existence in the hope of creating a model of the new, undifferentiated humanity is too suicidal to be called a worthy ideal.

Moreover, the world has no intention of allowing us to give up our distinctive identity. Anti-semitism may be nowhere as virulent as it was centuries ago, but it has not died. Hitler should have taught us what demonic power latent Jew-hate still retains. Hardly a year goes by in the United States without some public expression of anti-semitism that a decade or so ago would have been utterly unacceptable. The Jews remain one of the great scapegoats of Western civilization. Third World politicians, whose countries have never had a substantial Jewish population, regularly defame Zionism and the State of Israel and, thereby, the Jewish people. The behavior of the members of the United Nations has exploded whatever delusions we once had about a parliament of nations finally bringing rationality into international politics.

Restating the Case for Jewish Distinctiveness

Now that Americans speak more easily of group interests, Jewish thinkers have found greater acceptability for their arguments for Jewish separatism.

At the simplest, some of our theoreticians argue, as Mordecai Kaplan does, that people naturally want to remain somewhat apart from others. By contrast, conscious assimilation is abnormal and unhealthy. Moreover, living out one's humanity as a Jew adds a special tone to existence, one which may be unspecifiable, but which we would like to benefit from and perpetuate. It infuses one's life with a color and liveliness which contrast favorably with the drabness or tawdriness of many American lives. Were our ethnicity reinforced by the rich rewards which come from Jewish knowledge and community involvement, our devotion to Jewish living would become stronger.

The argument from the values of ethnicity has been extended by other thinkers who speak of a unique approach to life embedded in the Jewish heritage. At its heart, Judaism values intelligence, spurns violence, idealizes justice, encourages industry, mandates loving families, and motivates working for social betterment. More, our people has built a way of life which has, with some limits, successfully transmitted our ideals from one generation to the next. For all our lack of Jewish devotion today, we still have an extraordinary record of human accomplishment. We continue to produce not only a disproportionately large number of thinkers, writers, and scientists but of decent human beings as well. A people with so rare and valuable an ethos, so effectively expressed in real life, deserves to be perpetuated. To continue its uncommon achievement, it must remain somewhat separate from the people among whom it lives and whose civilization it wishes to share.

Religious Arguments for Jewish Separatism

With most Jews thinking of themselves as "not very religious," these ethnic, secular arguments come most easily to mind in Jewish discussions of separatism. But the times have challenged the old, accepted agnosticism of our community. An increasing number of Jews are discovering that they do not "believe nothing."* For such new Jewish searchers, the Jewish distinctiveness of the Jewish people ultimately derives from its continuing response to God, as difficult as that is to acknowledge or talk about.

Most of our rationalist religious philosophers, such as Hermann Cohen, contend that we must remain separate to preserve the distinctive Jewish concept of God. Christianity, even in its modern restatements of the doctrine of the Trinity, obscures the nature and implications of monotheism as Jews understand it. Furthermore, by making faith in the Christ rather than good deeds primary, it diverts people from the ethical activism Jews believe to be the essence of God's service. Islam, though admira-

*I develop this theme in some detail in chapters 2, 3, and 4 of Part Two, *The God We Affirm.*

bly strict about monotheism, seems to Jewish eyes too modest ethically in giving priority to only five duties. Then, too, because Islam stresses God's rulership, Moslems are more given to accept what happens than to change the world.

Our nonrationalist thinkers do not believe we can validate Jewish distinctiveness by claiming we have unique religious concepts. They prefer to make their case from inner experience, in this case the confirmation we often get when we are engaged with our community in a Jewish act. Sometimes, when we give *tsedakah,* or study, or pray, we realize at some level of our being, far deeper than nostalgia or group emotion, that our people still truly serves God. Our particular Jewish way of being religious keeps us close to God. At our best, then, we continue to be a *goy kadosh,* a holy people. Our society has become so empty of holiness that Judaism is too precious not to be maintained in appropriate individuality.

Martin Buber took that religious certainty one step further and pointed out that Judaism's fusion of ethnicity and religion is unique in world religions. It combines the individual and the social in a harmony no other faith has known. Most religions pay too little attention to the social, political, and historical dimensions of being a fulfilled human being, while most ethnic groups live—often ignominiously—by the idol of the tribe. The vision of authentic human community surfaces in Judaism alone, Buber contends. And our prophets applied it to reality in their matchless interplay of national and religious responsibilities. To surrender this Jewish difference from others would be to lose a true and precious form of human spirituality.

The struggle of the contemporary Jewish community with this question of separateness appears most poignantly in its conflict over intermarriage. If most Jews were more concerned with ethnic and religious loyalty rather than social adaptation, marriage with non-Jews would be rare. If most Jews also had no interest in remaining a distinct community, they would not be troubled by this problem. Some decades back, intermarriage was relatively uncommon; for those involved it was an act of assimilation. Today, more than a third of all marriages involving a Jew are intermarriages—though many are the second marriage for the Jewish partner. Despite the startling increase in the number of Jews "marrying out," they largely claim they want to continue being Jewish and expect to raise their children as Jews. Some Reform rabbis have given an equally surprising reason for performing intermarriages for such Jews: they hope to save these positively-oriented families for the Jewish people. Perhaps the gentile spouse will eventually convert or, lacking that, the involvement of the children in Jewish education will validate the next generation's Jewishness and continue the Jewish people. Note the irony. The commitment to Jewish separatism runs so deep among us these days that performing an intermarriage is justified in terms of it.

The great issue raised by the Emancipation has not been resolved. To the extent that Jews continue to affirm their ethnicity and their religion they must maintain a measure of distance from the society. But, despite almost two centuries of experience, we have reached no consensus as to where exactly the balance between integration and separatism should be set or just what forms it should most appropriately take.

·7·

WHO IS A GOOD JEW?

Jews of earlier times seem never to have asked how one might define a "good" Jew. Occasionally, for sermonic reasons, the rabbis asked questions like, "Which is the most inclusive statement in the Torah?" (Gen. R. 24:7) Typically, they then give two answers. Ben Azzai said, "It is, 'This book is about all the children of Adam'." (Gen. 5:1) Rabbi Akiba said, "It is, 'You shall love your neighbor as yourself'." (Lev. 19:18)

One passage of the Talmud (Mak. 23b–24a) presents a delightful number game about the essence of Jewish duty. The first move presents the opinion of Rabbi Simlai that the Torah contains 613 commandments. Immediately we hear that King David "reduced" them to eleven enumerated in Psalm 15: "one who walks uprightly, and does righteousness, and speaks truth in his heart, who has no slander on his tongue, and does no evil to his fellow, and doesn't pass on gossip about his neighbor, who despises vile people but honors those who fear God, who may lose by his oath but won't renege, who does not lend money at interest, who won't take a bribe against the innocent." There then follows the suggestion that Isaiah reduced them to six commandments: "one who walks in righteousness, and speaks uprightly, who despises gain gotten by oppression, who refuses to take bribes, who will not listen to murderous talk, and refuses to look complacently on evil." (33:15) The challenge being clear, other suggestions quickly follow. Micah reduced them to three, "Do justice, love mercy, and walk humbly before God." (6:8) Isaiah reduced them even further to two, "Keep justice and do righteousness." (56:1) But Amos reduced them to one, "Seek Me and live!" (5:4) Rabbi

121

Nahman ben Isaac found this too inclusive for an epitome and suggested instead, "The righteous shall live by his faith." (Hab. 2:4)

I suppose our forebears did not seriously ask how one might define a "good" Jew because they felt the answer was self-evident: a "good" Jew is one who follows the Torah. I think we can be a bit more precise than that—and, to begin with, somewhat more comforting! Since no Jew can be sinless, being a "good"* Jew cannot mean being perfect. Exactly how much observance and how little sin constitute a good Jew varied somewhat with time and situation. Already in biblical days some Jews were so full of good deeds and piety that special terms were coined to describe them. They were *chasidim* or *tsadikim,* the "pious" and the "righteous" of their community. Their opposite number were simply called "the wicked" or "evil doers." Between these extremes one found the mass of the community, what we would term the ordinary, that is, the good-if-not-saintly Jews. Growing up, one quickly learned how to pick up the cues indicating who was in each group. For centuries a living mix of objective law and informal folk judgment set reasonably precise standards for evaluating Jewish conduct. With community opinion a major factor in personal self-esteem, these criteria had a major effect on the lives of most Jews.

The Loss of Authority and Certainty

A minority of American Jews live essentially among their fellow believers and uphold traditional Judaism. For them, the old standards for the good Jew remain in effect. Unlike them most Jews lost their theological certainty and community insularity when they modernized. They base their lives on the possibility of changing Jewish tradition even as they partially continue it. Despite debate and experimentation, we have no consensus as to how one can be fully modern and authentically Jewish. Ideologically, we range from those who identify Judaism with a purely universal ethics and culture to those particularists who insist that everything truly human is already found in the Torah. Practically, our ways of being Jewish vary exquisitely. Hardly an intellectual

---

*I shall now cease using the quotation marks for the word "good" but please remember that I think the usage is often rather odd as I hope the chapter explains.

or social movement surfaces in American culture which does not speedily generate a Jewish counterpart. Advocates of setting biblical texts to rock rhythms, of fostering zero population growth, or accepting homosexuality as an alternate life option, all claim good Jewish warrant. Amid this welter of opinion and practice, people ask, "Who is a good Jew?"

In due course I shall give my answer to this question. Before I do so I want to share my sense of the numerous difficulties in the way of responding. Our Jewish problem is not unique. Western civilization itself can no longer specify clear standards for "good" human behavior. Having liberated ourselves from many of the social constraints which once impeded individual growth and humane relationships, we now cannot easily define proper limits for our personal freedom. Those once reliable arbiters, conscience, reason, science, and common sense, no longer yield a compelling, universal content. And change sweeps over us relentlessly. As soon as we have made some tolerable adjustment to the latest insight into human nature and social relations, a new cultural spasm occurs and we must again adapt. Were our social rhythm less dynamic, we might work out in practice what we cannot easily delineate in ideas. As it is we can no longer specify who is a good person and thus modern Jews are doubly troubled by its sibling issue, "Who is a good Jew?"

Jews also face a critical problem of communal authority. Who among us today has the right to tell other Jews what they ought to do? Some generations back we would have looked to the rabbis and sages to define our obligations. But as Jews accepted the need to change Jewish practice in ways their leaders thought were improper—e.g., the use of the vernacular in prayer or attendance at a university—the old authority of the rabbinate effectively ended for them. Various groups of rabbis have tried to find ways to guide their community's transition. The nineteenth-century German rabbinical conferences and the continuing efforts of the various American rabbinical associations failed to stem our anarchy. They could not succeed, I suggest, because modernity had made individualism central to contemporary Jewish life.

Being True to Self and to One's People

In pre-Emancipation times Jews thought of themselves primarily as members of a certain community. They had little alternative to doing so, for their personal legal status derived from that of their group. For Jews to be allowed to live in a given town or area, their community had to be granted official permission, generally by means of a corporate charter. An individual Jew had rights there only if recognized by the local Jewish community. In turn, the *kehillah* had responsibility for individual Jewish behavior. It collected general taxes for the ruler and policed Jewish observance of the local law of the land. It also determined what Jews might stay within its bounds. What the rabbinate could not enforce as a matter of spiritual discipline, the community regulated for everyone's political well-being. In such a time, being a Jew may have seemed more a social matter than an individual one.

The Emancipation drastically changed this situation. In modern France or the United States, only individuals, not communities, were enfranchised. As the United States Declaration of Independence puts it, ". . . All men are created equal and they are endowed by their Creator with certain unalienable rights." In such states, persons are detached from their groups and operate as citizens independently of them. People may wish to maintain certain private associations—religions being the most honorable case—but these are entirely voluntary as far as the state is concerned.

When Jews received equal rights as individuals, the Jewish community lost its political authority. In the Western, democratic world, Jews associate with one another on a volunteer basis. They may feel bound to one another by ethnic, emotional, and religious ties and thus often willing to accept the community's "discipline." In the end, whatever they do, they do as a matter of choice. Politically, they cannot be forced to do what they do not want to do. This being the case and unbelief being so widespread, I marvel that so many modern Jews have chosen to participate in Jewish life as much as they have done. Such "authority" as can now be exercised in the Jewish community operates essentially in terms of arousing or guiding the individual's will to live as a Jew. And with the emphasis our culture continues to place on thinking for oneself, the appeal to conscience must remain the basic premise of Jewish calls for duty.

What I propose to say about being a good Jew therefore comes with no special claims to "authority." Like other modern Jewish teachers I can only hope to persuade. Since my ideas have grown out of many years of intensive Jewish study, practice, experience, and thought you may find them cogent. They deserve to be considered as more than mere opinion but they are propounded as a lot less than a creed.

Have We Ulterior Motives in Wanting to Set Standards?

I must also caution you that I do not propose to fulfill two expectations often implicit in the request for a definition, namely that the criterion will enable us to shame or to minimize.

In the former instance, I do not want to say whom I consider a good Jew so as to be able to derive or exclude Jews who do not meet my standards. With neither the Torah nor the state able to coerce involvement, people often hope a definition of the good Jew which features their favorite Jewish cause will accomplish by guilt what they cannot do by persuasion. They administer the classic 39 lashes of Jewish punishment with the phrase, "How can you call yourself a good Jew if you don't. . . ."

I am against such strategies. Shaming is almost always unethical and it rarely motivates performance the way its perpetrators hope it will. Equally important, I consider it a special sin after the Holocaust for one group of Jews to attack another group and read it out of the community. In Emil Fackenheim's famous formulation, that would be doing Hitler's work for him. We have lost enough Jews in our time; we must not voluntarily add to their number. This rule sometimes stretches my patience to the breaking point but I consider it a fundamental premise of contemporary Jewish existence. Its widespread acceptance by Jews of varying and intense commitments has been one of the most positive features of contemporary Jewish life. Thus you now know a critical aspect of my answer: Being a good Jew starts with loving, or trying to love, all other Jews.

My answer comes with a second qualification. Many people want to know what constitutes a good Jew so that they can find out how little they need do and still maintain community respectability. I do not consider this concern entirely negative. Many of us do not wish to assimilate completely and yet we are also unhappy with only sporadically undertaking this or that Jewish duty. We want to be better Jews than our fellows who do little or nothing about their Jewish identity. At the same time, we are not "Orthodox" and don't want to be burdened by the "whole" law. We are willing to fit a reasonable amount of Jewish obligation into our already overscheduled lives. How much must we do to be considered loyal Jews? In this context, the term "good Jew" serves to have us enunciate our minimum acceptable standards.

Perhaps I should accept the question in this positive light and so respond to it. The rabbis of the Talmud often defined the minimum needed to carry out certain Jewish observances: One says a blessing only when one's piece of bread has at least the bulk of an olive, and any cup which can contain the volume of an egg will do for the four cups of wine we should drink at the Passover *seder*. There might be some advantage today in setting minimum levels of obligation. Once we made plain the least that everyone should do, perhaps a sizable proportion of the community would actually accept that as their Jewish duty. But I fear the losses would be greater than the gains.

Minimal standards are insidious. They quickly usurp our ideal. We come to accept them as a significant achievement and not a minimum. They make us forgetful of what more we might be doing and probably ought to be trying to do. Worse, human nature being what it is, we find it difficult not to press on and ask how much of our minimal standards are *really* important. Trading down soon compromises all the good inherent in our initial request for a reasonable definition of our duties.

The Level between the Impractical Ideal and the Conveniently Easy

I therefore want to say a word about the level of commitment necessary to be a good Jew. Let me begin by drawing an analogy to being a good cook or a good tennis player. To acquire some proficiency at either skill requires learning, practice, and not a little devotion. Depending on the circles in which one moves, there's quite a difference between a passable and a good cook or tennis player. Being an expert lies far beyond that, and most of us will quickly admit that we do not aspire to reach that level. For us, just being good at cooking or tennis demands so much commitment that we lament not having more time or ability to become what we would like to be.

In a somewhat similar way, being a Jew means to be involved with an unusual, worldwide people, one with a long history full of rich, cultural accomplishment. The Jewish heritage encapsulates the human wisdom this folk has gained in many civilizations, climes, political orders, and human circumstances. It gives unusually profound guidance as to how people and societies should conduct their affairs. Indeed, it projects a messianic outcome to human striving which not only speaks of the future but motivates steadfast devotion to duty now.

Now to my analogy: A good Jew would know and use the Jewish heritage as a good cook would be at home with spices or a good tennis player would utilize a repertoire of strokes and strategy. Obviously, to be a "good" anything will demand much of us. But, since being a Jew has such great communal and historical overtones, being a good Jew cannot be a casual or superficial matter.

We have not yet mentioned religion. It stands at the center of Jewish tradition. How then can we be satisfied to identify a good Jew only minimally? A religion which makes no serious claims upon its adherents should not itself be taken seriously. To say God is one and no other gods are acceptable surely must mean that one's religion ought to set the basic framework of one's life. Being a good Jew cannot be merely participating in another pastime or leisure activity.

Note carefully, please, that I do not identify "being religious" with "being Orthodox." I am a liberal Jew because, affirming the rights of conscience, I emphasize the difference between being serious and being punctilious (though obviously there are Orthodox Jews who are both). Acknowledging the spiritual value of individualism, I think the commitment one brings to one's Jewishness is, in our time, more important than the number of traditionally required deeds one performs—though Jewish commitment necessarily expresses itself in doing Jewish deeds.

Liberal religion does not specify and multiply commandments; that does not make it a minimal religion. For such as me, Jewish belief needs to be central to one's existence not something tacked on to it, the heart of what one *is,* not merely some habits one still maintains. For me, one must be a Jew *in everything one does.* Often this will be in traditional forms, at other times it will follow newly created patterns, but at all times one is seeking to be true to one's self as a Jew. My "serious" Jew may not be Orthodox but such a Jew could also not be content to ask how little one can do and still retain one's Jewish integrity.

We Must Begin with the Question of Belief

In setting before you my sense of a good Jew I shall follow a recent statement made by the Central Conference of American Rabbis (CCAR). While it speaks about Reform Judaism, the document, as I interpret it, goes beyond denominational boundaries and summarizes well what many informed Jews are thinking.

The CCAR Centenary Perspective commends itself to me, among other reasons, because of its balance between Jewish beliefs and obligations. It treats each area in three sections. I find it characteristically Jewish that those on duty are much longer and more detailed than those on faith. That follows Rabbi Eleazar ben Azariah's dictum, "One whose works are more abundant than his wisdom is like a tree whose branches are few but whose roots are many. Even if all the winds in the world come and blow against it, that tree will not be uprooted." (P. Av. 3:17) Most modern Jews want to continue our tradition's ancient emphasis on action. We may not be as certain as previous generations were about the details of proper Jewish living but we know that we shall judge the good Jew more by practice than by thinking, feelings, or mental states.

That doesn't mean beliefs can be considered irrelevant to Judaism or that any set of values should be as acceptable to Jews as any other. Should one know—as some today assert—that life has no meaning and human nature merely extends the traits of the higher primates, one will not long consistently concern oneself with others as with oneself. We can no longer assume everyone begins from the same ethical premises, that every rational, cultured person hears the address of a universal, commanding moral law. When we had such optimism we could ignore the question of belief and turn to the political work which would bring the Messianic Age. Then we were confident that knowing one's duty was independent of having a faith.

Practically that still holds true for many people. They see no need to inquire into what they believe and are quite happy to go on working for good causes despite the many setbacks they have suffered. But they no longer get the support they used to count on from other enlightened people in our society. Many rational, sophisticated people do not consider pleasure a secondary value or social good a primary one. Instead, hedonism abounds and self-interest has become a highly regarded form of ethics. Our culture's permissiveness, powered by our affluence, makes it practical for people to live by the most diverse standards—or, one is sometimes tempted to say, by none. Obviously what one *believes* about human nature and social obligation will profoundly affect how one feels one ought to live. And, more profoundly, what one takes to be the ultimate quality of reality will set the context for our existence. I believe that to be the case for all modern people; how much the more will it be true of Jews who have historically been committed to lives of high excellence. Therefore, to arrive at some recognizable sense of Jewish duty, we must begin with a statement of our Jewish belief.

Must a Good Jew Believe in God?

My first assertion is probably the most controversial one I shall make: I consider nothing more fundamental to being a good Jew than belief in God. Many people can accept that positive formulation but will react strongly to its negative version: one who does not have some sort of faith in God is not a good Jew. I think I understand the emotions my premise arouses. Shall we indeed say that Israelis who have risked their lives for their people but are atheists are not good Jews? Shall we demean the Jewish status of many who, though unbelievers, have worked devotedly to up-build Jewish life here and overseas? By what right do I assert that such people are not good Jews? Surely there are other views of a good Jew which do not involve believing in God or, if they do, do not make it the basis of everything else in Jewish life.

Perhaps now you can understand why I took so much time in this chapter to get around to giving my answer. I hoped that by carefully delineating the context of my response I would make it somewhat easier to accept what I had to say, particularly here. Perhaps a brief recapitulation will help.

Most Jews are born Jewish and no definition of a good Jew can take that away from them—or should try to, in this post-Holocaust era. Since the Emancipation there has been substantial disagreement among us about what constitutes a good Jew. With our religious and communal authority largely replaced by the insistence of modern Jews on thinking for themselves, no one can easily claim the authority to overrule competing views. Having studied and thought about Judaism for many years, I hope that my views about "Who is a good Jew?" will be of some interest and benefit to you. I may be wrong and there are many people who disagree with me. Nonetheless, I do not know a differing view which reflects better the truth of Jewish history as read through the lens of modernity.

For me, being a Jew is fundamentally a religious matter, one which derives from the ongoing validity of the people of Israel's historic relationship with God, the Covenant. The classic Jewish books, the Bible and the Talmud, testify to this assertion for they center about God and the service due God. Until a hundred or so years ago, it did not seriously occur to many people that one could be a good Jew without believing in God. If anything, belief in God was so much a part of Jewish life that one did not need to talk much about it. Though often unspoken, everything else in Jewish life depended on it. Thus, the weight of Jewish history, tradition, and practice connects believing in God with being a good Jew and opposing theories must bear the burden of demonstrating their Jewish authenticity.

I also find that the passage of time has lessened the once nearly universal opposition to this notion that a good Jew believes in God. Since the 1940s ended, we no longer consider atheism great sophistication. Even the agnosticism which allowed us to dispense with God because we trusted culture wholeheartedly increasingly shows its obsolescence. A spiritual shift has begun among serious Jews in our community and this minority can now speak of God in ways that would have made us uncomfortable some years back. With our new appreciation of pluralism, we have also gained greater appreciation of the extraordinary openness with which Judaism has allowed people to talk of God. "My" good Jew believes in God but not necessarily in my view of God. We have numerous differing interpretations of what God might mean to a contemporary Jew, as Part Two of this work indicates. I am saying that we Jews have been and remain fundamentally a religion, not that we are very dogmatic about it.

In my opinion our tradition wisely recognized that God transcends anything we might delineate; it therefore remains hospitable to a great variety of ways of talking about God. If anything, our modern propensity for seeking creative alternatives has amplified the traditional possibilities of talking sensibly about God. To me, we should accept any view which teaches us about a God real enough to set the structure and standards of the universe and thereby capable of authorizing our living a life of Torah amid the Jewish people.

I do not believe that, despite the Holocaust's challenge to our faith, good Jews now know God is dead. Despite its entrenched skepticism, most of our community recognizes that it would be a curious result indeed if we now made Hitler rather than Moses the most important teacher in our history. With all that we do not understand and cannot believe, we must affirm some things with ultimate significance. Our very protest against the Nazis and their kind rests on a radical denial of the neutrality of the universe. To oppose nazidom and its equivalent is not a whim or a cultural quirk but an affirmation that a transcendent standard of goodness applies to all people. In our permissive, relativistic, value-free time, such moral passion arises as a matter of faith. Becoming sensitive to this elemental depth of our devotion to human value awakens us, often to our own surprise, to our own personal contact with what our tradition called God.

Without some such primal faith, the strenuous demands of Jewish duty and loyalty are quixotic. With it, they bear compelling power. My good Jews know that they must live as Jews because, despite their doubts, they somehow "know" God "wants" them to do so. And—as my quotation marks show—that does not mean all their questions have been answered. It only means that in their confused and stammering response to God they begin to find and work out their Jewish authenticity. In their modern way, they are responding to the most awe-inspiring event of modern Jewish times. That, as Eliezer Berkovits, the modern Orthodox theologian, reminds us, was not the death of God at Auschwitz but the way some Jews there and elsewhere maintained and lived by their faith. With a sacred right to protest and question, a good Jew, to me, affirms the reality of God, however understood. Such Jews base their lives on God and do the same for the people of Israel and its way of life.

We Are More than a Religious Group

We will find it much easier to speak of our beliefs about the Jewish people. Indeed, nothing has so aroused the emotions of Jews in our time as has the very folk itself, especially as exemplified by its greatest contemporary accomplishment, the State of Israel. For all my insistence that God and religion are primary to a good Jew, I also wish to assert that though Christians are a church the Jews are not. We are an ethnic group.

Socially, the Jews derive from one of the tribal entities we know from the history of the ancient Near East, peoples like the Hittites, the Hivites, the Moabites, and others. Such groups were characterized primarily by their distinctive languages, cultures, and lands, their presumed original family ties having long before become a matter of folk myth. Their life-styles centered about certain values which were reflected in saga, celebrated in rite, and expressed through their institutions.

Sociological reflection such as this helps us understand the extraordinary richness of Jewish life in our time. It comes from our having an ethnic heritage. Jewish life does not exhaust itself only in synagogue activities and home rituals but includes a complex fabric of style and attitude. This unverbalized ethos substantially shapes the individual Jew in terms of the historic experience and ideals of the Jewish folk. At its most basic social level it might merely be expressed as a concern for other Jews and their needs. It can become a passion for Jewish survival; at its height it involves dedicating the Jewish people and its activity to a universal, messianic ideal.

However, the Jews are not simply another ethnic group. Jewish ethnicity stands out in human history for its utter involvement with the one real God of the universe. Until Emancipation times, what moderns call nationalism and religion intermingled with little distinction in Jewish life. The classic folk language, Hebrew, was early called, "the holy tongue." The Torah describes the Land of Israel as God's gift to the Hebrews which they might occupy only as long as they observed God's laws. Despite recent decades of unbelief most of our people's distinctive activities take place in relation to religious rites. And we remain the only ethnic group one joins by religious conversion.

For me, then, the ideal Jew cannot be someone who believes

in God but has no concern for the Jewish people—as some spiritual but Unitarian types among us once contended—nor someone who loves Jews and Jewish culture but denies or ignores God—as did the Yiddishists and classic Zionists of yesteryear and the Israeli nationalists of today. Only in the relationship between God and the Jewish people, the Covenant, does authentic Judaism appear. My good Jew, then, believes in and lives in the Covenant.

These two beliefs carry with them a special attitude toward beings in general. Ancient Judaism declared that all people can know God and respond to what God demands of them: the mix of justice and mercy which creates a life of holiness. With all their creaturely limitations, people are free and thus have responsibility for their actions. Joining with one another, they comprise the groups which dominate and direct history, most often, unfortunately, by violent means to sinful ends. This creative iniquity sets the messianic problem: In the face of human defiance, how can God's rule become effective on earth? Judaism also proclaims that, despite peoples' failings, God has made them capable of starting afresh and doing the good. So to speak, God so "loves" the possibility of free human righteousness that, when people sincerely repent of their misdeeds, God grants them forgiveness. Judaism has as realistic and optimistic view of humankind as that. Hence working with all human beings to improve our world must be considered the necessary corollary of modern Judaism's doctrine of the Jewish people's own special service to God.

The Tradition We Have Created and the Duties It Teaches

Conscious of existing in Covenant, of being a people closely related to God, the Jews produced the teaching known as Torah. The Bible and the Talmud are its classic depositories; for the liberal Jew everything in Jewish life produced as a result of the Covenant relationship with God should be called Torah. The vast literature created by Jews over the centuries must therefore be supplemented with all the homey details of folklore and practice, all the ethnic attitudes and standards, all the non-verbal cues and signs one faithful Jewish generation has passed on to the next. Jews living under the Covenant today largely recapitulate and renew a heritage of three millennia and more, for the Covenant relationship did not begin with us. With so bookish a tradition, Jews consider study a Jewish religious duty, with enriched religious living its goal.

Liberal Jews consider Torah historical but not time bound. We associate it particularly with Mt. Sinai but we understand it also as a continuing creative stream of Jewish spiritual search and self-expression through the ages. We know it can find authentic forms in modern times as it did in yesteryear. Often the tales and practices which come from ancient times and distant places not only express our Covenant sentiments but instruct us in their proper depth. Sometimes continuity falls short of our needs or even impairs living out our faith. Then out of our immediate sense of Jewish duty we creatively add to the repertory of Jewish teaching and living.

As to beliefs, then, I see a good Jew having a living relationship with God as part of the people of Israel and therefore living a life of Torah. Three major areas of Jewish responsibility arise from this situation.

First, the Covenant obligates Jews to sanctify their lives and their relationships with others. Of all such duties, none has a higher place than that of being ethical. We may even say that this command rests more heavily upon Jews than upon all humankind, for the Jewish people claims to represent God in history. The primacy of ethics in Jewish duty flows naturally from the faith that all humanity has but one God and that God "cares" about nothing more than that people treat one another with righteousness.

Other duties flow from grounding one's life upon God's reality as a Jew: daily prayer, study, and religious observance. The week moves toward Sabbath observance, the year is punctuated with Jewish holy days; each life has its beginning, end, and other major moments marked by special rites. All these events have more than purely personal significance. They have a communal dimension, for life under the Covenant involves the Jewish people as well as God. The Jewish family provides the critical link between the individual and the folk at large, so Jewish duty largely centers on participating in a rich Jewish family life. A good Jew participates in the synagogue for there the community regularly renews the Covenant through liturgy, deepens it in study, and refreshes it by association. That institution, in turn, leads Jews on to serve the

Jewish community locally, nationally, and worldwide—and, through it, all humankind.

Ours being a time of special Jewish peril and attainment, the good Jew will be especially concerned about the survival of the Jewish people everywhere, most particularly in the State of Israel. The Holocaust mandates an overriding Jewish concern for other Jews. We cannot depend on others always to be of help to our tiny people. So wherever a Jew cries out for help—Argentina, Iraq, and, most dramatically recently, in the Soviet Union—other Jews need to be listening and active in their response. Or, more positively put, a good Jew ought to support every activity which upbuilds and enriches Jewish life anywhere.

Our Duties to the Israelis and All of Humanity

The State of Israel crowns our folk existence. Through it our people has given its response to the Holocaust and proclaimed to the world that Jews propose to live and not die. It sums up centuries of Jewish social aspiration and vision. In its humane response to the excruciating political and economic pressures it has faced, it proposes a Jewish model for humankind's collective behavior. A good Jew identifies with the State of Israel, attends to its needs, works for its betterment, learns from its culture, and contributes to its Jewish self-fulfillment.

The Covenant, being a collective endeavor, can best be lived as part of a self-governing Jewish community on the Land of Israel. A good Jew will seriously consider the possibility of *aliyah,* immigration. At the same time, the Jewish relationship with God can authentically be lived out elsewhere. Jews who choose to live outside the Land of Israel must necessarily adapt their community life to their specific situation while benefiting from a close relationship with the State of Israel. While Jewish life will differ in the Diaspora and the State of Israel, the same Jewish standard should rule all our communities: faithfulness to the people of Israel's continuing Covenant with God.

For all that, the good Jew's concern cannot, in my view, be confined, even largely so, to the Jewish people alone. As a matter of belief, we are part of humanity and its historic concerns are also our own. Pragmatically, too, Jews cannot escape what happens to our country and the world. At the very least, Jews should work at improving the world as a matter of self-interest; ideally, we ought to do so in order to realize something of our messianic vision. Some Jews argue that we do not have enough energy to also undertake such global responsibility. They see us so burdened as individuals and so periled as a people that they believe we cannot reasonably be expected to do more than be responsible for our own kind. Perhaps that may be necessary as a temporary survival strategy. I do not see that it can adequately fulfill what a generation of free Jews owes its society and dreams of in its messianic faith.

Finally, a good Jew will not despair. Realism about humanity's potential for evil has become so steady a message of our time that it leads many people to cynicism about human striving. That has not been the Jewish way despite what the nations have done to us. Our instinctive response to the Holocaust was to take life and renew it. Our experience in establishing and maintaining the State of Israel proves that the historically improbable can sometimes yield to stubborn idealism.

That, despite everything, the Jewish people lives proclaims a uniquely positive message about the continuing capabilities of people, the remaining possibilities of history, and the enduring reality of God. A good Jew hopes—and if the dreams of one day are shattered then an age-old, hard-won, Jewish aspiration asserts itself. A generation may be defeated, the Jewish people survives; our plans may fail, God's sovereignty endures and will not forever be denied. The messianic era will yet come and the universal well-being for which our people has waited and worked for centuries will one day arrive.

Who do I think is a good Jew? Someone who lives in Covenant, whose existence takes shape from a relation with God as part of the Jewish people; who lives by Torah, carrying out in traditional and modern ways ethical and other religious duties of a personal, familial, and communal sort; who is dedicated to the survival of the Jewish people and the enhancement of its way of life, particularly in the State of Israel; yet who is devoted to the betterment of humankind generally and determinedly hopeful that a messianic fulfillment awaits us.

That is my considered opinion. Would you say something much different?

PART
· II ·

THE GOD
WE AFFIRM

Part Two: The God We Affirm

·1·

HOW CAN WE TALK ABOUT GOD?

The problem of communication can hardly be avoided these days. In industry, workers and supervisors speak the same language but often have difficulty understanding one another. In education, teachers and students alike regularly complain that no one hears what they are saying. And family members so frequently antagonize their loved ones that we now have encounter weekends to teach spouses and children new habits of listening and speaking.

Much of our failure to communicate with one another arises from our inability to pick up the unspoken part of what is being said to us. The more significant the message, the greater the gap between what we truly mean and actually say. Often we count on the context to clarify the intent. "God bless you" may be an empty response to our sneeze; the same words from someone you've just helped through a family emergency will touch us deeply. Mostly we give cues so our hearer can appreciate the deeper message. For instance, a genuine smile signals that our impertinent remark is a teasing way of expressing affection, not a serious attack.

With many of our social problems stemming from failures in communication, a good deal of recent thought has focused on the many ways we communicate our meanings. In contemporary philosophy this approach is called linguistic analysis. It has forced thinkers to clarify just what they may mean by what they say or, alternatively, just what they are doing when they are speaking allusively or by implication.

Much of this book is a study of Jewish religious language, that

139

is, of the way Jewish thinkers talk about what they believe. In these chapters on God I shall be analyzing what liberal Jews believe they can properly say about so exalted and abstract a topic. The first step is to explain the contemporary understanding of symbols. To begin, let us put our religious concerns to one side and consider the role of symbols in ordinary communication.

Symbols Transcend Their Simple Content

As far back as we have documents, people have found it difficult to convey a rich and complex thought. To escape that predicament they have substituted something simple, concrete, and near-at-hand for the difficult message they wished to transmit. Thus, for thousands of years, people wishing to express how deeply (sic!) they cared about someone have said simply, "I love you with all my heart." They knew that a person is far more than a cardiac organ, yet, because they believed the heart was the seat of human feeling, they associated their richest emotions with it. Today, study has made plain that the heart is mostly muscle and hardly as involved in our feelings as is our brain or nervous system. No matter. The heart is the symbol we use to convey our love. Someone who insisted on declaring love in terms of the body's neurological network would be considered a pedant—or worse! Referring to the heart is our concise, understandable way of pointing to all the things we feel and want one another to know but cannot easily put into words.

There is something magical about symbols. By referring to commonplace objects we can communicate extraordinarily complex meanings. A flag is only pieces of colored cloth, stitched together in a certain pattern, but it stands for my country, so I will get quite upset when someone burns the cloth which is my flag. Leather sheets sewed together making a long roll on which someone has written seem an odd object to stir the emotions, but a Torah scroll represents our Jewish tradition as almost nothing else can. A bunch of flowers, a trophy, a diploma, all stand for something greater than themselves. They convey more than their physical essence and thus we call them symbols.

Words are an extraordinary class of symbols. If I say the sounds "heart" or, more ingeniously, if I write the letters h - e - a - r - t you, as someone who knows English, will understand that I am referring to our blood-pumping muscles. The sounds or letters are not the thing itself but a convenient representation of it.

Language, the system of word sounds-and-letters, is a wonder. It enables us to understand our world and to communicate about it with one another. In a few syllables I can describe a vast realm, e.g., the sun is ninety-three million miles away from the earth. Good symbols have a magical, creative quality. Scientists use them to describe atomic and galactic realities we cannot see. Poets and novelists use them to evoke sensibilities we largely ignore or to bring into being worlds that never existed. In our Bible, God creates simply by speaking. The phrase "And God said . . ." is the most frequent way the Bible authors symbolize their experience of God's commanding presence.

Symbols Are Mainly the Creation of Groups

There is a social and historical dimension to symbols. They will not work for you unless you are part of the group that shares them. Someone who only speaks French will not know what h - e - a - r - t means until it is translated into c - o - e - u - r. Confronted by a small *matsah,* most non-Jews will assume it is a cracker for cheese or jelly, not a flat bread which speaks of slavery and liberation, of family celebrations and Jewish hopes.

We begin to feel at home in a new culture not just when we can use its language but when we begin to respond emotionally to its symbol world. Its art and its celebrations, its special places and its favorite phrases gained their emotional power over a long period. They are the result of history and there is something about their age and their repetitive use which gives them special impact. Most of us today wouldn't think of going to school in a cap and gown, yet, because of the centuries of their use as the scholar's garb, it seems quite right to wear them when one receives a degree. Some symbols survive for long periods and seem to extend their usefulness. Justice as a blindfolded woman holding scales in her hand is what we call a "living" symbol. Others seem to die out for reasons which are not quite clear. Columbia, the female figure atop the United States Capitol, no longer seems to mean much to most citizens of the United States.

Many groups within a society—athletes, political parties, teenagers—create their own system of symbols. This identifies their group and expresses some of what they value. In a similar fashion religious groups conceived and perpetuated symbols.

The great religions have rich historical backgrounds. As they arose and spread from one culture to other cultures, their forms were elaborated in new terms. The same seated figure is common to all Buddhism but in the passage of that faith across Asia, from India to Japan, all sorts of subtle changes were introduced to it, often then to be picked up and carried on by new generations of Buddhists in other countries. The Jewish symbol system is unusually rich because of our people's many migrations. Our earliest sacred tales are reminiscent of ancient Near Eastern saga, the *seder* is like a Hellenistic festive meal, our greatest law books have a Babylonian style, much of our synagogue poetry is based on Moslem models. Jews in many cultures have adapted and created forms for their continuing faith.

God-Talk Is Necessarily Symbolic

Religions are concerned with symbols for more than cultural and historic reasons. They want to talk about God. But, if God is greater than the greatest thing any person knows or can imagine, how can one possibly use human language to talk about God adequately? God surely is beyond any words that we might create. This sense of God's grandeur and human limitations goes back quite far in the Jewish tradition. In the Talmud, Rabbi Jeremiah ben Eleazar interpreted Psalm 65, verse 2, to say, "For You, silence is [the proper] praise." (Er. 19a) At least in the stillness there is nothing to detract from God's greatness whereas, as Abraham Heschel put it, our most extravagant phrase for God would necessarily be an understatement.

I suppose that sentiment explains why most people consider the silent prayer the most meaningful part of Jewish worship. Then nothing, not even our words, gets between us and God. Yet, despite the evocative limitlessness of silence, people generally feel that what we care about most deeply needs to be put into words, even inadequate words.

Paradoxically, people often *talk about* the virtues of silence. We do so because using words is one of our greatest human talents. We utilize them to help us be truer to ourselves and what we esteem. Religions, most certainly Judaism, have often seen language as a link between God and people, another sign of our being created "in God's image." In this excerpt from *The Kingly Crown* note how Solomon ibn Gabirol (1021–1056 c.e.), the Spanish Hebrew poet, plays on what can and cannot be said about God:

> Who can understand the mystery of Your acts?
> For You have given our bodies the means to do Your work.
> You gave us eyes to see Your signs,
> Ears to hear Your wonders,
> A mind to comprehend some part of Your secrets,
> A mouth to speak Your praises,
> A tongue to tell everyone Your mighty acts,
> As, today, do I,
> Your servant, the son of Your handmaid,
> Who tells, according to the limit of my tongue,
> A bit of a part of Your greatness.

I will return later to the special virtues of poetry as religious language. First, let us see how the theory of symbols helps us resolve the paradox of talking about God: All words are inadequate yet we want to speak of what is most dear to us. We begin by acknowledging that our words about God are not meant to be taken literally, as if we were saying, "This is what God actually is." Our language about God is highly symbolic. That is, we take our words for everyday things and press them into service as symbols, using them to point beyond themselves to that ineffable reality, God.

The Apt Symbol Speaks of the Otherwise Unsayable

My favorite example of a Jewish symbol for God is "rock," as in the phrase, "God is a rock." Put so badly it is difficult to believe that any Jew ever said such a thing, much less believed it. Yet the term occurs again and again in the Bible. We know it best from the prayer book use of Psalm 19, verse 15, "May the words of my mouth and the meditations of my heart be acceptable to You, O Lord, my *rock* and my redeemer." Other psalms call on God "to be a rock" or praise God for being a rock. God is called "The rock of Israel" in 2 Samuel 23:3 and before that the question is asked "Who is a rock besides our God?" (2 Sam. 22:32) At the end of the Torah, the poem ascribed to Moses calls God simply, *Hatsur*, "The Rock." (Deut. 32:4) And, of course, at Chanukah our favorite song is *Rock of Ages*.

The difficulty as well as the genius of symbols is suddenly apparent. If you take a symbol literally, it is ridiculous, even blasphemous. Someone who does not know Judaism or its symbols (or a Jew who has forgotten about them) and hears us call God a "rock" will think our religion crude and primitive. This outsider would probably be quite astonished to discover that Judaism absolutely prohibits the worship of idols, that no object of any size, shape, or form can be allowed to serve as an image of God. It makes no sense that a religion that often calls God a "rock" adamantly refuses to use a stone object to stand for God. Of course, if our inquirer understands the theory of symbols, the difficulty could be resolved quite quickly. We only need explain that we use the term "rock" symbolically when we refer to God. Indeed, in Judaism, our words for describing God are always meant as "figures" of speech.

The trouble with symbols, then, is that someone may take them literally. Judaism like other religions assumes that risk because it wants words (and objects and acts) which will communicate some sense of the God who so greatly transcends us. Religion proliferates symbols in the effort to communicate a bit more of God's infinite nature. They represent efforts to share an intuition of ultimate reality. Through symbols such insights can be transmitted to many people and shared over long stretches of time, each generation adding its layer of understanding to old symbols or creating new ones.

Exposing a Symbol's Multiple Meanings

Let us analyze what the term "rock" might convey to Jews about God. We can get some idea of its significance to the Bible authors by noting the terms they associate with it. They coin phrases such as "a rock of strength and refuge," "an everlasting rock," "my rock and my fortress," and "the rock of my salvation." Living close to nature, these poets found their imaginations engaged by rocks, especially, I should imagine, the gigantic ones we see in the mountains of Judea or in the Negev. These impressions evoked something like their sense of God. Stone lasts a very long time. It is a dependable material, whether you build out of it or on it. You can hide behind rocks or, if they are huge and craggy, you might be able to hide in them. You can make yourself very secure by building a fort on top of them, like Masada. In some such fashion, talking about God as a rock, for all its incongruity, communicates much of what we feel about the ultimate, enduring power behind the universe. And all in one word.

These meanings and more are conveyed in so simple a way that one does not need to be a theologian or a philosopher to talk meaningfully about God. Everyone knows what a rock is and can easily learn how to apply that term to God. And different people, reflecting their individual personalities and experiences, will hear the word suggesting special meanings to them. The generations will then pile their associations on the old, living symbols until they seem to speak with inexhaustible meaning. Then we will say the symbol is "rich" in meaning. For religion that is particularly important for the God of which it wishes to speak is unutterably great.

To understand some of the content of a symbol one must move from the literal level of its meaning to that of its implications. Often our tradition helps us by teaching us what others have found in the term (or act or object). Mainly we need to allow our imagination to "play" with the symbol, seeing what it suggests and whether this or that sense of it seems true to our religious sensibility. We should not stop with one compelling interpretation, as if that were "the" meaning of the symbol. Good symbols say many things at once. We need to allow the many notions which come up from the various layers of our consciousness, or which history has loaded on the symbol, to suggest their validity to us now. On another occasion, this symbol may "speak" quite differently to us, symbols are that "alive."

Some Contours of Judaism's Symbol System for God

The Jewish tradition employs many symbolic terms for God. I would guess that our ancestors recognized that no matter how rich any one term might be it alone could never convey all our sense of God's greatness. Instead they employed diverse terms to speak of God, each with its own aura of meanings, hoping this would keep us open to God's infinity. Trying to bring these many

rich symbols together to create a coherent Jewish concept of God
is difficult indeed. But in our inability to smooth over all the
jagged intersections of our tradition's varied intuitions about
God we are forced to confront the gap between human imagination and God's greatness.

To gain some insight into what Judaism has taught about God
one needs to become acquainted with its main symbols for God
and their implications. To me, the familiar terms "king," or
"lord," or "master" speak of God's preeminent position and
incomparable power, a status that gives God the right to "set" the
rules for nature and humanity and to "demand" their observance.
Other words, like "father," "husband," "lover," or "friend" remind us that God is not only powerful and commanding but good
and caring, that God "loves" us.

In the last few pages I have utilized a common English gram-
matical device to signal you about a problem I was having. I used
quotation marks in two different ways. The first was for the ordinary case, when I wanted you to know that the words that followed were not my own. I also used them to call to your special
attention that the words "set" the rules, "demand" their observance, and "loves" us were being used *figuratively*. Ordinarily, one
counts on the reader to pick up a figurative usage: she's a brain
(rather than "brain"). The religious use of human activity to
describe God often disturbs moderns. They are troubled because
they are not certain how much of their childhood literal acceptance of these terms remains part of Jewish teaching. I therefore
signaled you that I was employing these personal terms symbolically. Usually, once the author communicates such a special sort
of usage, the reader will not object.

We could probably avoid the risk that people might take our
symbols for God literally if we always put quotation marks around
them: O "Lord," my "rock" and my "redeemer." However, that
pattern disrupts our reading too much. (Imagine what our prayer
book would look like: Our "father," our "king," "hear" our prayers.) As a result we limit its use to important cases. I have allowed
myself some liberties in this regard in this book. Should you feel
that I was overly generous, please keep in mind that I felt there
were many more times when I should have inserted them to make
certain you knew I was conscious of speaking symbolically.

Poetry, Our Most Explicit Form of High Symbolism

Another way we might signal that words are being used in a highly imaginative sense would be to print them in the form of poetry. Years ago we knew we were reading a poem because of its rhyme or regular rhythm. With poetry very much freer in style these days it is often difficult to know when we are being presented with a poem. Sometimes the layout on the page is the only indication.

Should you be sensitive enough to recognize that there is a poem before you, you will approach the words less for their prosaic meaning than as stimuli to your sensibilities. Because we know it is a poem, we are not dismayed when Shelley defies the evidence of our eyes and begins *To a Skylark* with, "Hail to thee, blithe spirit, bird thou never wert." As factual prose such a contradiction of reality would be abhorrent. As poetry we are delighted that Shelley has used a bird in flight to make us feel the joy that comes with being free.

Similarly, religious language uses the prosaic to transcend itself, to testify not about things but about God, their creator. Hence religious language often takes the form of poetry. I would contend that even when it is written in the form of prose it is so full of images and symbols that we should treat it as a special case of free-form poetry. I think we would all be far less likely to take our prayer book literally if all its pages were set as poems are.

Music, so closely associated with early poetry, is another device for signaling that we should reach for multiple, imaginative meanings. Note that until recent years, one never simply read a Jewish text, one chanted it. Intoning words indicates we are not to constrict our sense of what is being conveyed.

The Judaism I know speaks of a truth so rich that it finally eludes verbalization, though we have a number of helpful contemporary symbols for it. I shall try in these pages about God to be as clear and coherent as possible. Yet I know they must be read more in terms of what they evoke of your personal experience than for what they explicitly say.

What Shall We Do about God's "Body"?

No set of symbolic words has troubled people more than the anthropomorphisms, the ones which speak of God as if God had a human ("anthropo") form ("morph"). The Bible often refers to God's hand, arm, eyes, nose, mouth, and face, once even mentioning God's hair! The Bible also speaks of God having feelings ("pathos"), some common anthropopathisms being God's love, hate, anger, sadness, forgiveness, and rage. While we have no special term for it, God is also described as doing other human acts, listening, watching, talking, walking, sitting, and even laughing. Obviously, without continual quotation marks, people may take these terms literally and think of God as another human being, only a much greater and grander one.

The motivation to do so is very strong. Children, for example, think literally and, in that respect, some part of all of us never grows up. Freud clarified the psychological mechanism called projection. Children take the most powerful things they know, father-mother, and project them into the heaven as the God who controls the universe. Reading the frequent anthropomorphisms of the Bible and prayer book, adults often believe Judaism speaks of a God only a child or the child-in-us could accept.

Whatever the cause, taking the anthropomorphisms seriously has often undermined or shattered belief when one matured. The scientific view of the cosmos makes the notion of God as a gigantic human being absurd. Or discovering that much of what we feel about God stemmed from our unconscious, childhood fantasies about our parents, we give up God together with our infantile notions about God. The anthropomorphisms seem to prove that belief is incompatible with sophistication. Logically, this reasoning is as cogent as saying that since I cannot believe in the tooth fairy I also cannot believe in love.

The Jewish Tradition's Fight against Literalism

Our sages also were troubled by anthropomorphisms. The rabbis of the Talmud, though they regularly used them, created terms to indicate their figurative usage. Often they introduce them with the words "as if" or "so to speak." And many of their interpretations of biblical texts help us see what the personal language about God intends to symbolize.

In the Middle Ages, Maimonides led an unrelenting fight against giving naive credence to human descriptions of God. He won the intellectual battle and most thoughtful Jews in later generations realized that talking about God in bodily terms could be quite dangerous. Yet they went on using anthropomorphisms. Apparently people found them indispensable for communicating certain critical intuitions about God's relation to humanity, like God's goodness and concern.

In our time, Jews unaware of the history of this question think that Judaism takes its anthropomorphisms literally. They then point to these terms as proof that, instead of God creating us in God's image, we human beings have created God in our image. We liberals agree that people created the language in which God is described. But inventing words for something, even if the words differ from one culture to another or from one era to another, does not prove that the words point to nothing. Creating symbols for God is not the same as creating God. Being our creations, they are surely inadequate to God's fullness—but when they are living symbols, they have the power to point to the ultimate reality beyond us.

Our Contemporary Struggle with the Ancient Symbols

Some modern thinkers insist that our scientific world view makes it imperative for Judaism to dissociate itself radically from the traditional anthropomorphisms. Obviously, we cannot rid ourselves of them completely as long as we continue to use our traditional literature. Nonetheless, thinkers who advocate a rational view of God would like us to be quite explicit and indicate that we believe in an impersonal God. They urge us to symbolize God as a cosmic idea, process, or intelligence, or as the ground of all being.

Other thinkers believe that once we acknowledge the symbolic nature of religious language the anthropomorphisms might still be useful to us. They might enable us to discern those aspects of Divinity which come into clearest focus in human personality and action.

Both groups of thinkers agree that these humanized depictions of God yield their meanings in the same imaginative way that other symbols do. God's "hand" can imply the ultimate power which energizes and orders nature; God's "hearing" means at least God's connection with nature and perhaps God's responsive concern for humankind; God's "will" evokes our sense of the moral structure of creation and perhaps, too, its movement toward a time of perfect love and justice. If we can learn the process of "unpacking" our people's classic symbols for God, we can then share the wisdom generations of Jews have stored in them. We are then likely to find that much of what we modern Jews intuit about God is already expressed in Judaism's age-old religious symbols, including its anthropomorphisms.

I do not think that it is possible to continue to carry forward with full force every traditional Jewish symbol for God. With the democratization of our social order, words like "lord" and "master," which once referred to everyday relationships, have lost much of their symbolic power. Most of us do not know shepherds and we think of kings as anachronisms some countries have not yet outgrown. But few modern terms will give us the old symbolic effect. Certainly it will not do to try to say, "The Lord is my supermarket manager; I shall not want" or "Blessed are you, O Lord, president of the universe." Many of the old terms, for all their diminished vitality, are better than any modern words we have. We shall just have to wait and see which symbols will die out and which will retain or even gain in power. One of the great, imaginative religious tasks of our time is to create new, rich, living symbols for our God.

The Most Troublesome, the Most Moving Symbols for God

Certain old symbols for God are particularly disturbing to us, most notably today the ones that speak of God as masculine. They seem to say that being a man is somehow more perfect than being a woman. That contradicts liberal Judaism's fundamental ethical commitment to the equality of all human beings. Language or habits are sinful when they reinforce the old notion that women are less than men and should not receive equal human opportunity, respect, and responsibility. Having pioneered the equality of women in the synagogue, liberal Jews have a special responsibility to lead the search for new, more ethical, symbolic terms for God. Our preliminary efforts in this regard, despite some success, have indicated how nettlesome a problem we face. It is not clear how much Jewish history and the English language will allow us to formulate a religiously evocative, non-sexist language for God. Thus, it will not help us to change God the king to God the queen and the term dictator, for all its lack of gender, is morally repugnant to us. "Sovereign" serves us far better, yet it sounds antique to many ears. Obviously, if we can create a new-old language of Jewish prayer we shall have made another great contribution to Jewish religious life.

Some of our symbols for God will surely only deepen with the passage of time. For over two thousand years Jews have made it a special act of faith to declare that God is one. For us, too, the term "one," for all its simplicity, turns out to be unfathomably rich in meaning.

Let us try an easy experiment in symbol interpretation. Think of as many ways as you can in which we use the word "one" in our everyday lives—and then apply them to God.

By "one" we usually mean: not nothing but something; not a fraction but a whole; not partial but complete; not many but single; not split up but united; having an identity; being unique; the beginning of things; the chief of things; the number which goes into all other numbers but no number but itself goes into it.

When we say, "The Lord is One," all these meanings as well as our modern associations with unity may well up in our "hearts." And yet, paradoxical as it may sound, despite the richness of the many traditional and modern interpretations of the term, sensitive Jews know that much more remains to be expressed about God's unity. We know that we are not the first to utter this phrase. Thousands of years of Jewish experience and faith are concentrated in it. When we pronounce it, we speak for all the Jews of the past as for ourselves. And for the martyrs who died saying it.

And we are adding to its power. We now bring to it our enlarged sense of God as the unity pervading the galactic reaches and the relationship of subatomic particles. We also see God as that cosmic wholeness that draws us on to integrate our fragmented selves and that constitutes all the nations and races of this

·2·

HOW DO WE KNOW
GOD IS REAL?

Belief in God seems to be no problem to some people. They simply know God exists and nothing, not even tragedy, shakes their faith. Leo Baeck seemed to be such a person. Though this great Jewish thinker was in a concentration camp during the Holocaust, he came through the experience with his belief unchanged.

Most of us are not like that. We would like to believe in God and sometimes we think we do, only soon to find ourselves questioning what a few moments before seemed relatively certain. At such times particularly, we wish we had reasons we could point to for our belief. This experience seems to me to lie behind our yearning to "know" that God is real.

I cannot promise to satisfy that desire in this chapter (or elsewhere, for that matter). That is, I do not know any way today to convince you that God is real so that you will never again have any doubts about it. Our lives are too changeable and God is too complex for permanent answers. Modern Jewish thought can help us see that there are reasons for believing in God. It cannot guarantee that we will not have future questions about it.

One thing we can be sure of gaining by studying the Jewish teaching about God's existence is a sophisticated sense of what we mean by having faith. I find that many of the problems we have about religious belief come from our misconceptions of what faith in God means in Judaism. I hope, too, that as you read about our religious thought you will learn about yourself. You may

153

discover that one of our theologians has articulated your inner-most religious feelings. Or, in disagreeing with a given philosopher you may realize that you believe something rather different. Perhaps, by clarifying and expressing your own ideas about God, you will be able to help the rest of us gain a stronger sense of God's reality.

Doubt Is often a Part of Jewish Faith

To begin with, let's be clear that, for Judaism, belief in God has not usually meant complete and unwavering certainty. The authors of the Bible often had doubts about God. Surprisingly, their uncertainties and complaints are part of our Sacred Scriptures. The Book of Psalms, the most personal book of the Bible, is replete with the anxieties of believers.

> Pity me, O Lord, for I faint;
> Heal me, O Lord, for my bones melt and my spirit
>   dissolves in me.
> And You, O Lord,
> How long will You wait to help me? (6:2–3)

> Why do You stand far off, O Lord,
> And hide Yourself when we need You? (10:1)

> How long, O Lord, will you continue to forget about Me?
> How long will You continue to be absent when I need
>   You?" (13:1)

The Bible yields many more examples. Abraham and Job question God's justice and directly confront God about it. Jonah cannot understand why God is so forgiving. I often feel chagrin when I read such passages in Scriptures or later Jewish literature. What I thought was some secret difficulty of mine with God not only occurred to some Jews centuries ago but has long been an accepted part of Jewish religious life.

We modern Jews, living in a skeptical age, are likely to include a greater proportion of doubt in our faith than did Jews of earlier times. Many people feel their disbelief so keenly they cannot give much credence to their occasional sense that there is a God. No one has yet clarified just how many or how serious our questions must become for us to lose faith. I have known people whose trust in God was shattered by what seemed to me and to others only a trivial matter; at the same time, I have seen people tested far beyond what I think I could bear and yet they emerged from their trial more deeply believing people. In Judaism faith in God is that dynamic; it is not an all-or-nothing, static state of being.

Distinguishing Jewish and Christian Views

Judaism and Christianity have substantially divergent doctrines concerning gaining faith in God. For us, believing is less an event than a deep and quiet lifetime process. We are born Jews and by that fact begin our lives within our people's Covenant with God.* Technically, one is not born a Christian. One must become a Christian and does so by the act of baptism. The Roman Catholic and some Protestant churches will baptize infants, thus making them proper Christians. Many Protestant groups insist that one must responsibly accept the Christ before coming into the church. They only baptize adults and, knowing the terrible consequences of not finding salvation through the church, always seek to "bring people to Christ" (that is, God).

By contrast, people who are born Jews do not have to "get" something or undergo a special ceremony to enter their people's ancient relationship with God. True, we circumcise male infants —but not if a doctor rules that the operation would be dangerous for a particular child; such an uncircumcised baby is still fully a Jew. Bar and Bat Mitzvah and Confirmation ceremonies are a joyous welcome to Jewish responsibility but having missed out on such celebrations does not make one less a Jew. The Midrash says that when Moses spoke of making a Covenant between God and the Jews including "all those who are not present with us this day" (Deut. 29:14) he was referring to all the generations yet to be born into this people. (Exod. R. 28:6)

When Jews speak of finding faith, then, their reference is generally developmental. They are talking about gaining an adult sense of belief after education and experience have made their childish notions of God untenable. In presecular times, belief was so natural to most people that Jews strengthened their faith simply by studying and practicing the Torah. Modern Jews once thought

*For a discussion of the special nature of the Jews, see Part One, *The Jewish People*, chapter 1, "What Sort of Group Are the Jews?"

human reason was the only way to arrive at a mature faith in God. More recently, we have become open to the possibility of finding God through personal experience. Since this subjective approach to God is relatively unfamiliar to most Jews and is easily confused with certain contemporary cult notions, I want to make a few special comments about it.

Jewish Faith and the Revival Experience

Knowing God as a matter of personal experience has some respectable Jewish precedents. The Bible is full of poetic images testifying to its authors' powerful inner sense of God. There is also an old, rich tradition of Jews who had mystic experiences of God. This should not be confused with the evangelical Christian notion of being "born again." Protestants of this sort, so often seen on television, seek to repeat the extraordinary religious experience of Saul of Tarsus. While he was traveling to Damascus, the Christ appeared to him in a blinding light and with overwhelming gracious power. He had "seen the light" and was converted, taking the name Paul. For Protestants who believe God must seize people at their deepest level, coming to know God is a life-changing event. Theologically, the sinner is saved and freed to live righteously. Psychologically, someone who was miserable and self-destructive becomes courageous and strong.

Jewish teachers do not entirely disagree with this view of the effects of belief in God. Anyone who has a steadfast sense of God's nearness can face the joyous and bitter moments of life with special power. In Jewish experience, such people do not suddenly find all their previous problems solved. Faith often transforms us. It does not reverse history or change the social order. Problems like pollution, hunger, arms-control, and peace remain as intractable as they were before we had a strong sense of God's reality. Judaism does not suggest faith as "the answer" to all the problems of being human. As an activist religion it insists that belief in God will motivate us to struggle energetically for the right and carry on with undiminished determination despite the many defeats we are likely to endure.

A word also needs to be said about the cults which have carried the notion of personal experience to its extreme. They suggest that the reality of a person's belief is proved by the intensity of the emotion it arouses. They promise to provide the greatest "high" and thus the ultimate truth. Jewish teachers have rarely associated invigorated belief in God with an engulfing sensation of bliss or encompassing ecstacy. Modern Jews are skeptical of so emotional an approach to mature belief. Clever leaders can easily manipulate our feelings, and people might come to believe almost anything—even that they should commit mass suicide, as did the Jonestown community in Guyana. Religious experience may be the best way to a solid sense of God's reality. If so, most Jews will want to balance its subjectivity with a tough-minded intellectual analysis of the feelings being appealed to and the beliefs derived from them. Both the head and the heart have a role in attaining a profound Jewish faith in God.

Biblical Arguments for Belief in God

Let us make a brief survey of how our forebears talked about believing in God. The Bible's authors do not often speak directly of their reasons for believing in God. The prophets experienced God's revelation and the other writers had a tradition of God's giving the Torah. God's reality was self-evident to them even as most other people then accepted Divinity, though they expressed it in the form of idols.

When the Bible writers occasionally give reasons for their belief in God's reality, they refer to three themes. One is creation. They stand in awe at the grandeur of nature and amazed at its dynamism and orderliness. They know that God must have started it all and now keeps it operating properly. A second motif is a historical event, the Exodus from Egypt. Our people, enslaved by one of the mightiest empires of the time, left Egypt to become a free and independent nation on its own soil. The Jews could not imagine that they had produced so extraordinary an occurrence by their own power alone. They knew God had "taken" them out of Egypt. (Incidentally, the miracle of the splitting of the Sea of Reeds is the only miracle Jews of postbiblical times referred to in arguing for their belief in God. Predominantly, however, it is the Exodus as a whole, not specifically the miracle-at-the-sea, which Jewish writers cite. In general, then, we may say that Judaism's great teachers do not believe in God primarily because of miracles.) The third biblical theme associated with faith is the authors' experience of God's aid to them personally and to their people. As we have seen, they often did not receive God's help when they wanted it or in the form they sought. Nonetheless, they recognized God's presence in their lives and in the awe-inspiring survival of the Jewish people.

The Philosophical Reasoning of Medieval Jews

Ever since biblical times Jews have repeated some or all of these reasons for believing in God. A different dimension was introduced into Judaism when, about the ninth century, Jews were challenged by Moslem science and philosophy. This forced Jewish thinkers to develop for the first time highly technical, abstract, logical arguments for God's reality. The favorite early one was adapted from Aristotle's ideas about cause and effect. Nothing happens—an effect, like smoke rising—unless it has been caused, as fire creates smoke.

We can apply that rule to the cosmos. There could be no universe if something hadn't caused it to be. The philosophers called this the First Cause, the cause from which all the later effects followed. Moslem, Christian, and Jewish philosophers naturally identified the First Cause with God. Thus they had given a rational proof of God: the cosmos must have its ultimate cause, God, whom religion calls the Creator. (This argument gives an "answer" to the perennial question of adolescents, "Who created God?" One thinks back to the First Cause, by definition therefore the Uncaused Cause, and that alone is God.)

Later, when more of Aristotle's books were discovered, the philosophers were shocked to learn that he did not believe in a creation. Maimonides owes much of his greatness to accommodating Judaism to the new Aristotelian ideas. Instead of proving God via creation Maimonides gave new arguments for the existence of God. Later medieval thinkers, Thomas Aquinas among them, followed Maimonides in this regard.

I wish I could spend a few pages spinning out some of the intricate, elegant arguments for God's reality which medieval Jewish philosophers elaborated. They have an extraordinary range, from Yehudah Halevi's paradoxical use of philosophy to argue that only history and tradition are reliable, to Gersonides' heavy debt to medieval science, and on to Crescas's intellectual defense of love as the proper bond between us and God. Though that would give me much pleasure, I must confess that most of these medieval arguments are of no direct help to modern Jews. We are simply too skeptical to accept them; or, to put it another way, the premises of their thinking take very much more for granted than we can. We consider it a sign of sophisticated thinking to try to have as few assumptions as possible for our thought. René Descartes is generally credited with having started this modern pattern of philosophy. He brought the medieval style of thinking to an end when he declared that, as a matter of principle, a good thinker should doubt everything that could possibly be doubted. Descartes based his system only on what uncontrovertibly presented itself to him as clear and distinct, his famous, "I think, therefore I am." From his time on, methodical doubt became a central ingredient in modern philosophy.

How Can You Be Modern without Being Skeptical?

This radical questioning of our assumptions is basic to contemporary life and has given rise to our cultural heroes: the people who rejected an accepted premise and thereby created a fresh and productive way of looking at reality. Galileo challenged the old science; Darwin the understanding of how life developed; Marx our blindness to the relation between power and money; Freud our confidence that consciousness rules our minds; Einstein the notion that time and space are absolute; Cezanne and other Impressionists that art had to be representational; Schonberg and the Atonalists that music had to be written in a given key.

We moderns are as skilled at disbelief as the medievals were at believing. Even if we're not sure we mean it, we try to question everything. When that system works well, it gives us the evidence by which we can reach our own decisions rather than accept them because of tradition or because "everyone does." Rigorous unbelief also causes us great problems. Many people never get beyond questions to conclusions and one cannot live positively as an unrelenting skeptic. If one wants to act one cannot forever be asking questions.

Think of your feelings when a child persists in asking you "Why?" Finally you have to say, "That's just the way it is," or "Everybody agrees about that." One of our special difficulties today in talking about God—or anything else very deep and fundamental—is that it is no longer clear what it is that "everyone agrees about." The old answer to insatiable skepticism was an appeal to "common" sense—in Maimonides's time, a rough version of Aristotle. Today some people do not hesitate to challenge everything. In literature and art, in ethics and etiquette, our modern love of questioning has brought us to the point where it's difficult to know what, if anything, still remains certain to most people. With skepticism so much a part of our intellect, with so little certainty with which to begin, how can we hope to find a compelling and unchallengeable knowledge of God?

One valuable by-product of exploring modern Jewish reasons for believing in God is discovering what certainties you still have. Each approach to God is based on certain assumptions. If you share one particular Jewish philosophy, that indicates something about your view of reality. If you don't, that's almost certainly because you have different assumptions about the ultimate nature of things. Often what we can specifically believe about God has less to do with God than with what we assume people can properly *know* or *say* about God.

The Modern Rationalist Ways to God

We may usefully divide contemporary thinkers about God into two groups. One bases itself on the assumption that we should rely on human reason when thinking about God. Its members are called rationalists. The other group, the nonrationalists, begins' with the assumption that our grasp of religious truth stems from some broader sense of human experience than solely our ability to reason.

While many Jews have worked from the assumption that our minds are the best basis for thinking about God, almost none has relied on the so-called three classic proofs—the arguments from design, purpose, and the very definition of the term "God." In this respect Jewish thinkers have followed the general trend of modern philosophy of religion. I shall not explore these academic developments but will limit myself to what Jewish thinkers have been saying. With the exception of Alfred North Whitehead's metaphysics, all the recent general theological positions which could be adapted to Judaism have had major advocates in our community. I have limited my presentation to theoreticians whose distinctive approaches to knowing God have had a book-length exposition which has engendered some years of discussion. There is much else of interest going on but it cannot be considered here.

Jewish rationalists have commonly based their knowledge of God on science. At the root of all our scientific activity is a concept of the unity in nature. Although things appear to behave quite erratically, investigation shows that there are uniform patterns, "natural laws," governing them all. Thus, though no laboratory could demonstrate it, one might reasonably believe that there is one fundamental entity behind all the diverse processes we call nature, namely, God.

Something like that faith animated Einstein and it continues in those scientists who are determined to find a way to integrate what appear to be the four or five ultimate forces operating in the universe. Orderliness alone has not generally seemed to Jewish thinkers a sufficient basis for thinking about God, for the natural order, scientifically speaking, is morally neutral. Despite science's mechanistic view of things and the evils of history, almost all modern Jewish philosophers have argued that the universe is fundamentally ethical.

The First of the Five Major Modern Jewish Ways to God

A masterful demonstration of this scientific-ethical approach to God was given by Hermann Cohen (1842–1918), the greatest Jewish philosopher of this century. He worked out a tightly drawn argument that thinking people require a proper concept of God in order to have a fully coherent world view. This notion, that religion could be rational and that every fully rational person (in Cohen's sense) needed a God-idea, became the dominant idea of liberal Jews until recent years.

Cohen was not a rabbi though he had studied to become one. He taught philosophy at the University of Marburg and revived the ideas of Immanuel Kant with such cogency that his work received international academic attention. Cohen's neo-Kantian thinking was based on a premise: We cannot understand reality *as it is in itself* but only how our mind might best think about reality. A fully rational mind operates in three distinct realms:

science, ethics, and esthetics. (The poetic concerns, "the true, the good, and the beautiful," echo this division of labor in the mind.)

It will be simpler for us to deal with Cohen's argument if we limit ourselves to the relationship between science and ethics. We confront a major intellectual difficulty in trying to bring these disciplines together in a unified view of the world. They contradict each other. Scientific thinking assumes that nature is fully determined—sodium and chlorine can't choose to combine and form sugar rather than salt. Ethical situations are different. When we are tempted to commit adultery, we know we are commanded not to do so yet we remain free either to give in or to resist. There is moral law but it is not deterministic. We remain free—and it is precisely what we do with our freedom which is the crux of ethics.

But now we have a paradox. Ethical people act in a natural world. How can the freedom of ethical living be integrated into an un-free, scientific nature? Without determined law, we do not have science; without our freedom in the face of moral law, we do not have ethics. We must have both science and ethics in our lives if we are to be truly rational. To bring these two realms together into the harmonious world view that reason demands, we must introduce a new idea into the system. This idea must be more significant than either science or ethics. In this way it won't merge into the one realm or the other and thus destroy either the order of science or the freedom of ethics. This idea also needs to be more comprehensive than either science or ethics so it can bring them into the unified world view we seek. Thus, Cohen demonstrated that every rational person (in Cohen's sense), to make intellectual sense of the world, needs a transcendent, unifying idea, what religion has called God.

In one form or another, Cohen's rationalistic argument for God dominated Jewish religious thinking until recent decades. Not many people understood or utilized Cohen's technical, philosophic argument, but for years almost everyone who was not Orthodox called Judaism a rational religion. Instead of talking about God, they referred to Judaism's God-idea or God-concept. In other chapters of this work we shall see how this universal ethical approach to God shaped many of the virtues and problems of liberal Judaism.

A Second, Naturalist Approach to God

Cohen's rationalism was based on his certainty about the accuracy of the neo-Kantian description of the necessary way a mature mind operates. That premise was rejected by much of European philosophy after World War I. In the same period a new, American sense of how we ought to think came into prominence. Out of the thought of William James and John Dewey, an intellectual movement emerged which suggested that the scientific way of studying nature ought to be the model for philosophic thinking. Philosophers should consider ideas a way of exploring reality and test their validity by seeing how they worked out in experience. Truth would be found not by working out an airtight mental structure but by the continuing process of testing our ideas in life. The philosophers who adopted this point of view are called naturalists.

With science as their model, the naturalists denied the neo-Kantian notion that ethics carried the same rational authority as scientific thinking. The naturalists were not opposed to ethics but believed ethical ideas arose as a result of our human experiments in living, what we commonly call human growth. Obviously, this made their ethics flexible—with all the assets and liabilities associated with such a stance.

In the works of Mordecai Kaplan (1881–1983) naturalism received its fullest Jewish exposition and application. Kaplan contends that modernity and scientific thinking are indivisible. Only if there is a scientific basis to our understanding of Judaism will it have any chance of appealing to Jews in our time. Already in the 1920s he saw the newly emerging science of sociology as the best guide to understanding our people and our religion. (Other Jewish naturalists have argued for God from the sciences which deal with the formation of stars or the development of evolution or even from the assumptions in any scientific thinking.) Kaplan developed his thought around sociology because it focuses on the importance of human groups and thus would provide a modern theory of the Jewish people.

Traditional Judaism teaches that God brought the Jewish people into being. From the early sociologist, Emile Durkheim, Kaplan learned the idea that groups created religions. They did so quite naturally and without any heavenly revelation. Thus, in every society anthropologists studied they found a religion. Upon analysis it became clear that these religions served an important function in their social orders. By ritual and teaching they clarified the values the society cherished and put a sense of cosmic power behind its laws and institutions. Kaplan considered this a scientific law: every society must have a religion to give authority to its cultural practices. Our modern society also must have religion, one which harmonizes with our social ethos. For us, that means being in harmony with science, our major way of dealing with reality. For Kaplan, then, modern Judaism needs to be reconstructed so that it can function in our society. Religiously, it must now be built from a scientific understanding of human experience rather than from divine revelation.

Kaplan applies that general understanding to our search for God. We moderns understand human nature in a dynamic way, as involved in a continual effort for self-fulfillment. We do not hope to accomplish this in isolation but as part of our group and its culture. We rely on our group to help us in that quest and it, in turn, works best when it helps individuals find greater fulfillment.

All this human activity is based on an assumption that the universe permits, even encourages human growth. To be human, to plan and grow over the years, involves a fundamental trust that there are processes in nature which can help us develop our humanity to its highest level. We couldn't be true to our very selves as human beings if we did not have that faith. Once we have expressed it in this appropriately modern idiom, we have the kind of religion Jews need today. And as Jews in other cultures defined God in their terms, we have every right to say that by God we mean all those processes in nature which cooperate with personal fulfillment. Kaplan's point of view, elaborated in many writings over four decades, remained constant to this vision.

A Third View, Incorporating Our Religious Consciousness

Rationalism dominated Jewish thought for the first half of the twentieth century. It still has many adherents although, in my opinion, this is more cultural lag than continuing persuasiveness. The Jewish reaction against rationalism began in the 1920s in Germany. The wholesale slaughter of World War I seemed to refute the thesis that human beings are fundamentally rational creatures. That post-rational stance did not gain many adherents then in the United States; it did not become widespread here until the social disruptions and scandals of recent years. If anything, American Jews have held on to rationalism and naturalism far longer than has the academic philosophic community where its decline was already visible in the 1950s. We will approach the thought of the nonrationalists by first analyzing the system of Leo Baeck (1874–1965) who tried to bridge the gap between the two groups of thinkers.

In 1905, when Baeck published the first edition of his greatly admired book *The Essence of Judaism,* he seemed very much a disciple of Hermann Cohen. The 1923 edition, greatly expanded and revised, showed he had moved a considerable distance from the rationalistic views of the Marburg philosopher. Cohen's emphasis on God's unity and human ethics still dominates the book. With Cohen he continues to proclaim "ethical monotheism" as the essence of our faith. But Baeck no longer relies on arguments from human reason alone. He wants us to place as much reliance on our religious sensitivity as on our rational capacity. Baeck has left philosophy and the strictly cognitive reasoning of Cohen for what we today would call the realm of religious experience (which Baeck carefully differentiates from highly emotional or ecstatic states).

Baeck directed our thinking to what underlies our rational, ethical selves. He felt this opened us up to a subtle consciousness we have of being dependent on something in the universe far greater than ourselves. We are fleeting, yet reality endures. We are inconstant, yet the good is unchanging. We may fail, yet goodness will triumph. This sensitivity to what undergirds us in the universe cannot be rationally deduced. It stems rather from our precognitive consciousness of reality, our elemental feeling of what it is to be a person in the world.

Baeck is saying that when we move beyond reason we find ourselves surrounded by a sacred mystery. We cannot hope to comprehend the wonder of existence by the exercise of our minds. More important, we should not shield ourselves from the truth of this perception simply because we cannot turn it into a philosophical system. We need to give credence to this personal experience for it is the experience of the holy and the root of all religion. From our inner lives, Baeck says, we can know the reality our tradition called God.

Baeck realized that exclusive reliance on a prerational consciousness might open the way to bizarre beliefs and perverse acts. As a result, he insisted that religious consciousness always had to be guided by the standards of reason. The God known through the experience of the sacred was served primarily through ethical action. Ethics and monotheism, in turn, were rooted deeper than our cognitive processes for they arose from our consciousness of the mystery which surrounds us.

The Fourth View, Buber's Personalism

Baeck's compromise between rationalism and nonrationalism satisfied neither group of thinkers. The philosophers were distraught by his introduction of feeling into religious thought. One cannot respond intellectually to someone who says, "But that's how I feel about it." The nonrationalists were unhappy because Baeck's system gave reason such a tight hold on proper religion that it lost the fullness of our personal response to God. In their view Baeck should have gone beyond regarding a person as essentially composed of a strong mind accompanied by strong feelings. The nonrationalists wanted to move on to the idea of the whole person. They said that we are, at our best, integrated beings. We are most ourselves when we bring our thinking and feeling and everything else in us together in a wholeness which is more than any of its parts. That is indeed a new sort of philosophy, one variety of the modern movement called existentialism.

This viewpoint found classic expression in Martin Buber's little book *I and Thou* (published in 1923, the same year as Baeck's revised edition; Buber lived from 1878–1965). Buber's thought still sounds strange to many American ears, although it has become more accessible now that we are accustomed to hearing people say they wish to be treated "like a person, not like an object." We will understand him better if we momentarily put his ideas about God to one side and concentrate first on what he says about human relationships.

How do you get to know someone is a "real person"? Mostly we begin by getting acquainted with them, by noticing their face, their hair, their habits, and then by going on to get an impression of their qualities, their concerns, perhaps even their dreams. All that will tell us much about them, but merely accumulating data will not tell us who they "really" are. Consider the feeling you have when sitting with a doctor after an intense examination. By studying your case history and laboratory records, the doctor knows very much about you. Yet, depending on how the doctor talks to you, you may feel that the doctor doesn't know you at all. You may be conscious of wishing there were a more human relationship between you.

We make that kind of judgment about our relationships, Buber suggests, because we have often had the opposite experience. Someone who apparently knows little about us may actually understand us very deeply and vice versa. Have you not had this experience? You meet someone casually but the exchange between you is so friendly and direct that you leave thinking, "There's a *real* person." With friends and those we love, this experience happens more often, which is the basis of our special relationship with them.

Buber's point is that human beings have two, very different ways of knowing. The analytic-detached relationship gives us facts and patterns; the open-empathetic relationship enables us to get to know persons. The two knowing systems constantly alternate in our lives. Buber urges us not to substitute the one for the other. We are more comfortable with the first, the "I-it" relationship because it gives us such great power. Through scientific technology, the "I-it" mode of action *par excellence,* we put people on the moon and transplant kidneys. It gives us the hope that we may one day rule all of nature. But if we treat people merely as objects we deny their fundamental humanity. True, that may allow us to manipulate them for our purposes, or merely to keep our distance and not become involved with them. That is the beginning of our sin against one another. We ourselves do not wish to be treated impersonally, as objects, for we know how rewarding it is when others treat us like real persons. When they in all their fullness address us in our individuality, we have a sense of worth and quality no awards or compliments could engender. The tragedy of our times, says Buber, is that we have allowed the "I-it" relationship to usurp the legitimate place of the "I-thou" relationship.

What holds true of our knowing others also holds true of God,

Buber suggests. People prefer to treat God like a thing for then they will not have to get too involved with God. In another, cruder time people made God into an idol. Then when they did not like what God was doing they could change the idol they worshiped. Our more sophisticated way of keeping God a thing is to turn God into an idea. That is abstract not concrete, but it still allows us to relate to "God" in a detached and manipulative way. We adjust ideas of God to fit our system of thought. Should we deem it desirable, we can change intellectual systems. Buber insists that this "I-it" relation to God is utterly inappropriate. It says more about our need to be in control than it does about God's existence.

We know God is real, says Buber, the way we know persons are real. When one is "open," God may be "met" anywhere. There is nothing emotional, wild, or mystic about this anymore than there is in having an encounter with a friend that reaffirms your relationship. It can be casual and short-lived, as in the fleeting feeling we often have that things truly make sense; it can be as qualitatively significant as the recognition that, for a moment, we stood personally in the presence of ultimate reality. God is not always present to us, but, as with those we love, we know God remains real and our relationship firm.

Fifth, Focusing on God's Glory, Not on Our Experience

Abraham Heschel (1907–1972) found this nonrationalism too timid. He deprecated any view of religion which still makes human experience the basis for our knowing God. He considered Buber's thought another example of the humanistic self-reliance he considered the major failing of modern religion, regardless of its taking a rational or a nonrational form. He chided modern Jews for not being radical enough in their approach to reality.

Liberal Jews think that by asking tough-minded questions or by paying close attention to our experience we can find final truth. Heschel inquired as to why we take our thinking or feeling for granted. By what right do we make them the assumptions of our religious life? That we exist at all, that we are conscious of ourselves and our world, that we can inquire about or react to them should utterly amaze us. Before uttering a word or formulating an idea we should be awestruck, overwhelmed at the glory of being.

Modern culture has robbed us of our natural awe, our spontaneous sensitivity to the wonders about us. Sounds are reduced to vibrations, colors to wavelengths, persons to chemicals, and history to the clash of social forces. We are taught not to respond but to do research, not to be surprised but only to explain or investigate. This process of teaching us how to strip the world of its holy dimension is called secularization.

If we are to reverse the effects of secularization, Heschel declares, it will not do to take half-measures with human pride and self-assertion, making even our relation with God subject to our ideas and experiences. We need an amazement so radical, so primal that we will make the grandeur of what has been given us the basis of our very existence. Then we can stop talking about arguments or evidence for God's reality. Had God not given us the extraordinary capacities with which we challenge God's existence, we could not be so skeptical. For Heschel, God's overwhelming goodness to us is the only proper assumption for our understanding of Judaism.

Buber and Heschel have often been attacked by rationalists as being mystics and therefore unacceptable to the modern temper. Both thinkers do emphasize inner experience but neither shows the classical sign of mysticism, personal union with the Divine at the climax of the religious quest. I would argue that both retain too strong an emphasis on the worth of human individuality to be true mystics, though Heschel is less concerned with this than Buber.

The mystic way to God has not received much significant attention in modern Judaism—the Chasidim having refused to adapt to modernity. Until recently, the few traces of mysticism that could be found among us were associated with Orthodox Judaism. The inner experience which validated God simultaneously authorized a traditional view of God giving the Torah, the Oral as well as the Written Law.* Liberal Judaism, which legitimated our human changing of the law when the times demanded it, seemed permanently wedded to rationalism and the authority of the human mind. As our confidence in science and philosophy has waned in recent years, some efforts have been made to open up a mystic way to God which yet retains some liberal self-determination. The mystic option is now alive among liberal as among

*See Part three, *The Bible and Tradition,* for a discussion of the differing liberal and Orthodox views.

Orthodox Jews. But it is too early to say very much about how the inner path might bring us, despite our many questions, to know God's reality directly.

I think these represent the major possibilities now before the Jewish community with regard to believing in God. Let me emphasize that much more is going on in the magazines, conferences, and classrooms which serve as the laboratory of modern Jewish thought than I have been able to summarize here. However, I feel I cannot close this discussion without describing and analyzing the significant change in mood about God which I have observed come over the Jewish community in recent years.

The Growing Failure of the Old Agnosticism

I understate when I say that many liberal Jews have long privately thought of themselves as agnostics. Perhaps in the 1930s a significant number of Jews considered themselves atheists. Since the 1950s, I contend, neither Marx nor Freud, neither anthropology nor science seemed so certain that we could confidently assert we knew there was no God. We also could not easily say that there was good reason for believing in God.

More important, coming to a decision about God did not seem necessary for we had other means of knowing our responsibilities. Our ethics and politics were commanded by our faith in the goodness of human nature and the obvious necessity of liberal social attitudes. At the same time our Jewish duties seemed self-evident. Locally, our move to neighborhoods without Jewish institutions mandated our creating them. Internationally, the crushing events of our people's suffering made the need to respond self-evident. We could afford to be agnostics then for the general culture gave us our values and our people's needs mandated our Jewish responsibilities. Had someone come along with convincing evidence for God's reality, we said, we would be happy to accept it. In the meantime, we suspended decision and went on with our lives. Agnosticism was intellectually comfortable—for some it was positively moral. What could be better than to be an open-minded yet committed person?

Many American Jews still feel that way. In the face of their long-ingrained agnosticism, I do not know how much of what I have written will be persuasive. There is little these Jewish arguments for belief can say to someone who gives others the burden of proof while, in this area, insisting that there is no practical reason for coming to a decision in the face of scanty evidence.

A sizable number of liberal Jews is now easier to address. They have discovered that the assumption which grounded the old agnosticism no longer is valid. Our experience in the past decade has been revelatory—and utterly disillusioning. We cannot depend on the secular culture to inculcate the values we know to be basic to worthy human existence. We once took it for granted that every intelligent person would have a clear and compelling ethic. Today, the empty way people speak of mind or conscience or human nature has given them the empty sort of ethics we see about us. Once we thought that people did not need to believe anything special to be committed to a proper set of human values. Now we are confronted with people who, believing nothing, feel free to try anything.

The humanistic, secular faith of the past generation has failed the test of history. The pathetic spiritual state of our civilization is shown by our desperate search to salvage some sense of meaning for our lives. We try self-help books, new therapies, diets, exercises. More radically we seek out spiritual masters or join an esoteric cult. More practically we become quiet fatalists, placating ourselves with such self-indulgence as we can afford, seeking to fend off by our pleasures the despair which comes from having no firm values.

The God Who Stands behind Our Affirmation of Human Values

But some people, Christians as well as Jews, know they must take a stand against the filth and violence, the emptiness and despair of our times. No matter what the majority of people decide to do, those few know that they must devote themselves to increasing justice and love. Such a demanding commitment is no longer mandated by our culture or intellectuality. Neither science nor philosophy nor the spirit of our age demands that we give the long-range dedication required to combat the prodigious human and social forces which oppose radically humanizing our world. A thorough-going determination to do so makes sense, then, only as a matter of faith. That may most easily be seen in its negative manifestation. Our revulsion at the moral and spiritual failure of our civilization arises from an intuitive knowledge that life *ought to be better,* that we *must* give our lives to making it better. When we insist upon knowing why that motivation comes with such power, we recognize we are responding to an ultimate authority, that a reality in the universe which transcends us has laid this command upon us.

This stirring of the self to something beyond it may not sound very religious, that is, not until we acknowledge how infinitely distant it is from not believing anything. For we no longer live in a time when it makes no difference what you believe. The old social consensus about human decency keeps crumbling. With every day's news we meet those who calmly kill others or destroy themselves. We never expected having no belief might empower such negativity. Confronting it, many Jews now realize that we, in fact, are not as void of belief as we took ourselves to be—and, in the face of the reality about us, we need to explore and strengthen the intuition we have of what we continue to affirm.

The Jewish community has come a long way since the early 1970s. Then, we were excited about the possibility that God might be dead. By the early 1980s that no longer seemed a liberating or morally commendable doctrine. Instead, a minority of Jews was pioneering a new quest for Jewish spirituality. For in their passionate dedication to a high humane existence they had discovered themselves linked to what the Jewish tradition had, by many names over the years, called God.

For those who like me share that quest, let me not make too many claims. We do not know much about the God we dimly sense we affirm (and perhaps believed in all along). We do know that because our God is not neutral but holy how we live is of ultimate significance, no matter what the pagans around us say. For all our doubts and questions, for all our tolerance and openness, we know that not every form of human conduct is equally worthwhile. Should our civilization be entering a period of fall and decline, we know we must still live by ideal standards of conduct. For we now recognize that personal existence gains its worth and dignity from a relationship with the God who "calls" humankind to transform history.

I would not insist that this search for the ground of our values is the only or the best road for modern Jews to take to know God.

There are other ways I find a new sense of belief coming into our community. I only find this question of the ultimate basis of our commitments more significant to Jews who are spiritually on the move than, say, our increased esthetic sensitivity. What is important, I think, is for the majority of our people to inquire about its old, hidden Jewish satisfaction with its agnosticism. The pervasive disbelief of another, more settled age, I contend, is now badly out of date. I find many Jews I have talked to believing far more than they have been willing to admit to themselves. Retaining great faith in the value of life, they now often discover they have a personal reason for talking about God. Today, the two beliefs cannot easily be separated.

This little spark of faith has not illuminated all the dark corners of our lives or history. That we also remain skeptical is no surprise, for we remain moderns. What impresses me is that, though disbelief still gets the spotlight, it no longer dominates the Jewish community. There is a small band of believers in our midst these days, and one in search of God can find Jewish comrades for the way. And, as we move along it, we feel we are continuing in our own fashion the pilgrimage taken by all those Jews who through the centuries have affirmed that God is real.

·3·

WHAT IS GOD LIKE?

The history of religions discloses a persistent desire on the part of some believers to ferret out what God is truly like. The motives behind this interest quickly suggest themselves. If God is the most important thing in the universe nothing could be more worth knowing about. From that perspective, it seems wrong to be content with mere symbols. They only point us toward God but they do not disclose God's full reality to us. Moreover, we want to understand God intimately so as to have the best possible model for our lives and then, living properly, to receive God's benefits. Thus some intrepid religious spirits have always sought a way behind the customary religious terms and acts so that they might discover God's true nature.

Two special religious phenomena are worth mentioning in this regard though the borderline between them is not very clear. One is the religious impulse called gnosis, the other the better known experience called mysticism. Each yields direct access to God but in a somewhat different fashion. The Gnostic religions (various cults of the first centuries of the Common Era) promised to let their adherents know God as God truly is, not as God is commonly described in ordinary religion. (Note the root: gno=know.) One generally gained the basic knowledge through a ceremonial initiation into the cult and received more as one rose in its ranks.

The rabbis often attacked the Gnostic teachings, apparently because they found them appealing to Jews. Gnosticism seemed to explain why life was so difficult and history so chaotic. In opposition to the Bible, the Gnostics declared that there are really two Divine Powers. The "god" who created the universe is really the lesser deity, and in his incompetence he had rather botched the job of creation, leaving the world full of evil. The Gnostics then promised to introduce one to the true God, the God-above-"god," who was altogether beneficent and would accept us in a blissful life-after-death. To many people in the Roman Empire this was an appealing message of salvation. The rabbis opposed Gnostic ideas because they contradicted Judaism's central doctrine—the unity of God—and the basic attitudes toward existence which flowed from it—the goodness of life and the significance of history.

The urge to gnosis, a knowledge of what God is truly like, has reasserted itself in Western civilization in many centuries, particularly in troubled times. The mystical impulse has been somewhat more constant. People everywhere have claimed that through an inner experience they reached an intimate personal experience of God. I can suggest a rough rule for distinguishing between mysticism and gnosis. Gnosis tends to emphasize content, the dualism of good and evil one will come to know. Mysticism seems characterized by an exalted inner event which brings one into blissful communion with God. Both impulses teach doctrine as well as method but the balance seems somewhat different.

Who Can Claim to Know God's Nature Fully?

Were I now to propose explaining what God truly is, I would have to claim the esoteric sort of spiritual knowledge which comes from gnosis or mysticism. A generation ago, the notion that Judaism might conceivably be discussed in such a context would have seemed utterly outlandish. Modern Jews then were proud that Judaism was a rational religion. They gloried in using human reason to free our tradition from its medieval accretions of magic and superstition.

We live in another intellectual climate. Rationality no longer seems the exclusive measure of all truth and intellect no longer seems omnipotent. Many thoughtful people agree that we must use various levels of our consciousness if we are to plumb any richly significant human truth. Mysticism is no longer an outcast in the Jewish community and one can detect gnostic inclinations in a number of American writers, or in the bizarre satanic cults which occasionally surface. Personally, I find a nonrationalist approach to religion meaningful. That is, I believe that our cognitive capacity must be integrated into a more fully rounded-out personal approach to reality. Nonetheless, faced with the extraordinary claims some modern cults make about having ultimate truth, I react with typical modern skepticism. I do not see how they or anyone can know what they claim to know and know with certainty about God. I also remain doubtful of truths revealed by mysticism, for my more modest sort of experience of God leaves me with no arcane doctrine and a need for more answers almost as great as the certainty it gives me.

I suppose the issue here is just how much you believe any human being can know about God. When, as often happens these days, visionaries proclaim they have the final truth about God, they are making an astounding claim. If they suggest they have thought this out, then they are telling us that their minds are great enough to encompass all reality. If they claim to have had a vision or revelation, they are saying that their experience must be given priority over all other human claims to truth, including Jewish tradition with several thousand years of experience behind it.

For all our openness to new ideas, most moderns have been quite cynical about such prophets. Many of them turn out to be charlatans, taking advantage of people's desperate desire to be free of doubt and know the truth. Intellectually, their doctrines are unbelievable because they often contradict the rest of what we know and know most clearly. Besides, the claim to know God fully is a claim to final and unchanging truth. What we see in history is a series of ideas which come and go as they meet the intellectual demands of a given era. As we view the human situation, concepts must always grow and change if they are to stay alive. We cannot believe that any human being can give us ultimate truth now. The most we can hope for is a theory adequate to our present knowledge and experience. Equally disturbing, we often find the new forms of spiritual salvation radically turning us in on ourselves, thus deflecting us from the sort of social responsibility Judaism has taught us is critical to a worthy life.

Jewish Faith Does Not Claim to Know Everything

Once again I must assert the paradoxical thesis that a measure of skepticism is part of Jewish belief in God. Jews in Bible times knew that when seers or visionaries proposed to show you "God," that is, an idol, what they said was inherently unbelievable. When someone today proposes to teach you about the real God who is far different from the God of Judaism, such self-exaltation is literally incredible.

Should some modern prophets promise to disclose to you what God is truly like, do not believe them. If you have a Jewish sense of God you know they cannot do that. Our God is one, hence there is no one and no thing exactly "like" God and *vice versa.* That is so obvious to Jews that they have never bothered giving an answer to the biblical question, "Who is like You, O Lord, among the gods?" (Exod. 15:11) For all our arguments over other religious matters, we agree that human beings cannot know God's essence. Characteristically, our mystics, for all their many detailed teachings about God, acknowledged that, ultimately, God was *En Sof,* Without Limit, the One about whom we can say nothing substantive.

Judaism balances this relative silence about God's intimate nature by instructing us in elaborate detail about what God "wants" us to do. The proper Jewish balance in our relationship with God was epitomized by the chasidic master Abraham (he died in 1776). He was so accomplished a mystic that the Chasidim called him "The Angel." He once gave this interpretation to the phrase "Everyone tall shall bow before You": when a mystic climbs the heights of the spiritual life, becoming all a human being can be, he learns humility, that the most important thing one can do is simply serve God.

The Biblical Balance of Faith and Ignorance

The Bible reflects a similar sense of what we can and cannot know about God. In the main it tells us about people, how they lived, or how they should have lived. The biblical books are for the most part history, laws, prophecies, proverbs, poems, or stories. There is very little in them which is abstract and speculative, almost nothing like the Greek metaphysics or Indian philosophy of the same period. Our prophets are quite reticent when it comes to saying what God is truly like.

The nature of the Hebrew language seems itself to make such disclosures unlikely. Literary critics, such as Edmond Wilson, have commented that biblical Hebrew is oriented to action rather than to things or ideas. The language is built around verbs, and its nouns commonly derive from verb roots. Hebrew seems impoverished when it comes to abstract terms like "being" or "process" or "infinite,"—terms that we moderns like to use when trying to describe God.

In one, bewildering story, God is reported to give a self-description. Moses asks to see God's glory and is told he can only see God's back. (Exod. 33:18–23) When God goes by the cave in which Moses hides for this disclosure (Exod. 34:6–7), God proclaims: *"Adonai, Adonai,* God, merciful and gracious, long-suffering, abounding in goodness and truth, giving mercy to the thousandth generation of those loyal to God, forgiving all sin and iniquity, yet giving some punishment to the guilty and punishing sinful families to the third and fourth generation." Typically, God's great self-identification recounts only what God "does" not what God's nature is.

A widely accepted talmudic interpretation of these verses understands them to say as much about human duty as it does about God: as God is called merciful and gracious so people should be forgiving and generous. (Sifre Deut. 49) From God's "acts" they deduced some cardinal Jewish obligations, giving clothes to the naked and money to the poor, visiting the sick, burying the dead and comforting the mourner. For the rabbis, "knowing" God largely means knowing what we must do.

The Medieval Philosophers Knew How Little They Could Know

Some centuries later, when Jews learned of Greek philosophy (through Islam) and began to write philosophies of their own, they could not ignore this question of what we may say God truly is. As so often was the case, Maimonides thought this matter through in a way that had a lasting influence on later Jewish writers. Maimonides insisted we be strictly logical. To say God is one means that God is unique, that God is the only member of the class of things we may call "true gods." That means nothing else is God the way God is God. There is nothing then strictly parallel to God. Logically, God isn't "like" anything we know. What God truly is must always remain significantly beyond even the grandest or most abstract concept human beings could create.

Maimonides would seem to have created an unbridgeable gap between God and people. Fortunately he could overcome that difficulty by reminding his readers of the Torah which God had given the Jews. It is quite explicit about what God wants us to do. Righteous action, not speculation on God's essence, is basic to Jewish living. Though our reason can say nothing about God's ultimate nature, Maimonides pointed out that it can reflect on what God has done in nature and thus gives us a model for human responsibility.

We may sum up the classic Jewish attitude toward knowing God in a somewhat paradoxical way. Compared, say, to Christian theology's detailed analysis of God as substance or of the interrelationships of the persons of the trinity, Jewish belief is *relatively* unknowing, "agnostic." We do not assert that we know much about God's essence, surely not nearly anything like what we believe we understand about God's will for human action. The four parts of this work reflect that balance in Jewish faith. Two parts are devoted to Jewish duty and what it means to be a member of the Jewish people. One part deals with Torah; in effect, how we know what God wants of us. Only this one part discusses our teachings about God—and many of these chapters concentrate on how we should respond to God.

What Have Our Modern Rationalists Said God Is Like?

Having given this topic its proper Jewish limits, let me now review for you what the previously introduced modern Jewish thinkers have said about it. I feel free to do so because I have elaborately warned you what not to expect from them. I want to share with you what they believe can be said about God's nature because many inquiring Jews today are curious about it. Before they are ready to take their struggling faith in God very far, they would like to know what our thinkers are saying God might be like.

The four major theories I want to explain, as you might suspect, are those of Cohen, Kaplan, Buber, and Heschel. Baeck's thought, it turns out, is not of much help to us here for an interesting reason we will consider below.

Intellectually-inclined Jews have held that we should think of God as the most fundamental, integrating concept of all the ideas a mature mind needs to understand the universe. Hermann Cohen, the late nineteenth-century reviver of Kant's thinking, is the best exponent of this understanding of God among modern Jews.

Cohen, like other rationalists, argued that human beings are primarily distinguished from all other creatures by their ability to reason. Creating true ideas is an extraordinary accomplishment, for only through such general intellectual patterns can we get our notion of "the world." In Cohen's neo-Kantian way of looking at things, as we said, we can only be certain of how our mind works properly and not what reality-in-itself is like. Thus for Cohen a true idea about the world is as close as we can ever come to knowing what is real.

In the philosophy of Cohen and others, the notion of a "complete system" is critical. For them, by definition, rational activity requires that all our partial ideas be brought together in a harmonious whole. Logic rejects contradictions, so rationality drives toward a "complete system." Thinking people will therefore continually seek to integrate their thoughts in a comprehensive concept of reality. As we saw in the previous chapter, Cohen had demonstrated that in such a harmonious world view we would need one fundamental, unique premise from which all the other ideas would grow. Cohen identified this supreme idea with God. Cohen's God, then, is an idea, our most basic and significant true concept. For people who do not care deeply about intellect that seems to be a relatively unimportant thing. For Cohen and others like him, to say God is an idea is to ascribe to God the highest sort of reality of which human beings can rationally speak. It also gives God the greatest possible importance in our lives. Our God-idea is then the chief instrumentality through which we understand the world and find our place in it. This may be a radically different way of talking about God from the way of the Bible or Talmud. But Cohen felt that he had explained in the terms of contemporary rationality what the authors of the Bible and Talmud were seeking to describe in their more richly symbolic fashion.

Kaplan's Naturalistic View of God

A second rationalistic approach to what God is like begins from what we know about the way human beings live. Mordecai Kaplan turns our attention to what he believed science had demonstrated about our human drive to fulfill ourselves. To be human is to make plans and through them project ourselves into the future.

This ceaseless striving to grow and develop ourselves makes sense only in terms of a basic faith. That is, we base our lives on our trust that nature, in which we must work out our purposes, gives some support to our striving. Were the universe inimical to our plans, no rational person would seek to accomplish any long-range goal. Fortunately nature is not anti-human but contains many processes which aid and even prompt us to fulfill our humanity. God means to us all that in nature on which we rely for our development. For Kaplan, when we say "God" we refer to all the processes in nature which enhance human growth.

Kaplan's view sounds even more untraditional than did Cohen's. Kaplan acknowledges this but considers it a compliment. For his thought is based on the assumption that while we need religion we cannot accept religious ideas which go against the basic thrust of our culture. Modernity is science-oriented. We cannot be expected to believe in a God who is supernatural, say, in heaven. We need to find God in the only place where we moderns believe there is reality, in nature. Kaplan's theological creativity consists in showing us what it is in nature that we trust ultimately and therefore call God.

Cohen's and Kaplan's theories of God are called rationalistic because they believe that our Jewish understanding of God's nature must be intellectually understandable and persuasive. The strength of their position is that, in principle, there is no barrier to a rational person's comprehending what is meant by God. If you had a problem understanding Cohen's and Kaplan's philosophies, it suggests I simply haven't explained them well enough or that you may need to develop some new ideas to cope with them. They did not ask you to do anything "religious." They did not appeal to special emotional states or mystical insights. They only asked you to reason, which you do all the time; though generally not on so abstract a level. Any thinking person can therefore know what sort of God the rationalists have in mind and be able to make an intelligent decision about believing in such a God.

Why Is There a Conflict over the Place of Rationality in Religion?

Ironically, the power of rationalism is also the source of its weakness. Rationalistic thinkers deal only with what can be described by intellect and conveyed by unambiguous language. The nonrationalists deny that life is that simple and intelligible. They do not believe that the human mind, for all its power, has the capacity to comprehend and express the nature of ultimate reality. People are far more than intricate thinking machines. Even trying to understand ourselves requires us to move beyond pure reason to a more comprehensive if less precise way of knowing which, for the moment, we'll call intuition. Thinkers who work from this standpoint generally do not deny the virtues of reason when appropriately applied. They do not call on us to act out of passion or whim, for they know how quickly thoughtlessness leads us to destroy ourselves and others. Rather they want us to use our minds in terms of what it means to be a whole person and not as a substitute for it.

The nonrationalist position of thinkers, such as Martin Buber and Abraham Heschel, has become much more acceptable to Jews in recent years as part of our general cultural disaffection with human reason. This has not altered the commitment of Jewish rationalists to their own point of view. They criticize the nonrationalists because one can never quite know what they are referring to when they talk about our going beyond reason. When you can figure out what sort of experience they rely on, you may also discover that you haven't had it—as I said about myself concerning mysticism. Not sharing the nonrationalists' special sort of openness to reality forecloses any further discussion of their views. From a practical point of view too, when we see today the odd religious beliefs and peculiar standards of behavior of people who call on us to follow our feelings, we are led to recognize the virtues of rationalism.

The nonrationalists remain unpersuaded despite these criticisms of their position. To take the last matter first, they argue that many of the major evils of our time—the fouling of our environment, the exploitation of the powerless, the depersonalization of our lives—are not the result of following our intuition but of over-reliance on reason. The Holocaust itself was not a subjective passion but a coldly planned and managed operation. Our society doesn't need greater emphasis on technical analyses; rather it needs the restoration of sensitivity and personal openness to our relationships.

Surely when it comes to God, the most complex reality we could hope to try to understand, we must realize the limitations of our reason. Religions have never been philosophic societies, although they have had their thinkers. Students of philosophy, by contrast, even when they have ideas of God, have rarely been noted for their piety. What Judaism has had to say in relation to God usually took the form of story, poem, song, ritual, prayer, and even silence. There is a good historic warrant for modern Jews to seek God with more than their minds.

Our community has not resolved this debate about how best to try to understand what God is like. Both positions still attract firm adherents among us as they do in other religions. Some people seem naturally to emphasize the intellectual aspect of their lives, others respond to things in a more fully personal way. Neither the rationalist nor the nonrationalist approach may claim to be the only appropriate one for Jews to take, and we shall probably continue to receive new interpretations of belief in God from both of them.

Baeck's Effort to Find a Way between the Extremes

Leo Baeck tried to bridge the gap between the rationalist and nonrationalist ways of thinking about God. He accepted Cohen's conception of God as the grounding idea of our rational world view, but he felt that notion needed to be made more personal.

Baeck focused on the kind of questions which sensitive souls often ask but reason cannot answer: Why are people so fragile yet so significant? Where are our lives heading? What is the goal of human striving? And, most important of all, what is the source of ethical command and its unique power? Baeck agreed that reason explains much to us, but he insisted that our lives are more basically grounded in our sense of the mystery around us. True religion begins with this special consciousness.

Baeck saw an immediate advantage to bringing back an appreciation of mystery into Judaism. Against Cohen's rationalism, this new view mandated an intimate personal involvement in religious life. Baeck kept this new nonrational element from leading us into wild emotionalism by balancing it with a strong emphasis on the rational-ethical element in Judaism. For Baeck, then, God is what we sense standing behind the mystery which we are conscious of in our everyday life.

Baeck's approach has appealed to many liberal Jews. It seems to unite the best elements of rationalism and nonrationalism while removing the faults of each by that combination. Like most efforts at synthesis, it satisfies neither of the positions it seeks to transcend and supplant.

For our discussion the most immediate problem is that Baeck has not told us what God is like. All he has done is to pinpoint the human feelings which serve as the basis of our faith in God. Despite his desire to go beyond the rationalists, Baeck apparently accepts the central Kantian premise: We can have certainty only about how our mind works, not about reality itself.

Baeck's antagonists extend this criticism. The nonrationalists contend that we can find a way to go beyond describing our inner experience. Though they eschew mysticism and lay no claim to gnosis, they believe we can have a personal if limited knowledge of a God who is independent of us. The rationalists are even more disturbed by Baeck's procedure. By bringing religious consciousness into his system he has destroyed the power of logical argument. Once one values mystery, what may not be asserted?

The followers of Baeck respond that there is a limit to what can properly be said about God with certainty and we should openly acknowledge it. They are not perturbed that a balance of reason and consciousness may not be good philosophy. That was not Baeck's purpose in creating his system nor should it be our central concern. He wanted to give us profound insight into the central affirmations of classic Jewish belief, the essence of Judaism, and he did just that.

Martin Buber's Uniquely Personal Understanding of God

If Baeck may be said not to tell us what God is like, we may then call the teachings of Martin Buber and Abraham Heschel the third and fourth modern efforts to do so.

Buber's way of talking about God is radically different from that of Cohen and Kaplan. They do not hesitate to speak objectively about God. That is, they describe God's nature as careful observers, and thus in a rather detached and analytic way. Buber thinks taking such an attitude toward God is utterly inappropriate and he proposes to say what he can on this matter in a most unusual fashion. Since his suggestions are quite subtle let us proceed by way of an analogy. For the moment, let us set aside our religious questions and reflect on our experiences with someone we know as a real friend.

When people are very close to you it is difficult to explain to others what they are truly like. Whatever you say hardly conveys what you know them to be. If you talk about their hair, or eyes, or personality, or intelligence, that will not make clear what it is about them that makes them "them." When you are with them or think back to some special times you have had together, just who they are seems to be clear. They are also people on whom you feel you can specially depend. You expect them to know what you are going through, suffering or triumph—and that is true even if you haven't mentioned anything about it. You can say about such persons that you know them in a way that you know very few other people and you know they know you that way too. Such knowing is reciprocal.

Buber says that this experience with people is our best guide to what we may say about God. We know we would violate what is most precious to us in our friends if we tried to describe them in an objective, impersonal fashion. In the same way, speaking of God as if God were another thing that human beings could examine and depict is an error that verges on blasphemy. It is a verbal form of idolatry, the classic instance of treating as an object what should be addressed in a personal way.

Now we can see where it would be difficult for Buber to answer our question "What is God like?" That is an impersonal question. He thinks we can talk properly about God only in a personal fashion. If we insisted on an answer to our question we would have to say something like this: "God is the Universal Friend"—and, like our best friends, not an undemanding one. I would be more accurate, I believe, if I said: "Universal Lover"—but I am afraid that the contemporary erotic connotations of that term would trouble people. Buber is never that informal, but I will claim some Jewish warrant for employing this usage. The rabbis read The Song of Songs as a dialogue between God and the Jewish people. And the Yom Kippur poem, "We are Your people, You are our King," reaches a climax in the line, "We are Your friends, You are our Beloved."

Contrary to what death-of-God thinkers said a decade ago, many of us occasionally have the sense that God is with us. As with friends, this need not involve great emotional upheavals, just a sense of intimacy and nearness, of us to God and God to us. If that happens on a number of occasions we develop a "friendship" with God, that is, a relationship. For Buber what once was called "having faith" should be termed "having a relationship." One's friend does not always need to be present or sympathetic or even understandable to remain our friend. The relationship is greater than any moment's experience. So it is with God.

We can't say much *about* our Friend but we can say that God is greater and more important than anyone else we know. Unlike all other friends, God never becomes a mere object to us. God, when present, is always there as Friend. God is Always Friend—Buber's special contribution to the meaning of God's being one and unique.

This is quite different from the God-ideas of Cohen and Baeck. Buber says God is quite independent of us. God is other than us in the same way that our friends and loves are not merely our ideas or experience of them but independently real-in-themselves. And, against Kaplan, Buber asserts that God is not merely our reference word for diverse processes in nature. The One we come to know in relationship is at least as integrated and whole as we are, for that God is capable of relationships.

Heschel's Vision of God's Infinite Grandeur

Abraham Heschel believes that views such as Buber's still place too much reliance on the human element in understanding God. The besetting liberal sin is taking too much for granted. Heschel denies that we may simply make an assumption of our human capacity for religious experience or inquiry.

Heschel begins by attacking the liberals' basic premise. Why aren't we awestruck that we are creatures with the ability to have the ideas, or the consciousness, or the relationships out of which we then create our religion? Rather than start with human experience and see how that might lead us to God, we ought to be filled with wonder that we exist at all and are so nobly endowed. We are too self-centered, we moderns. We require the theological equivalent of shock therapy. Then we will understand that God is not the goal of our religious search but its most basic premise. Nothing comes before God. What could? God is the ground of all our experience, our ethics, our rationality, our growth, our relationships, even our very will to search for God!

When we gain this insight, God's greatness is almost overwhelming. Compared to God's proper glory, anything we might try to imagine God to be like is paltry, perhaps blasphemous. We should respond to the old biblical song, "Who is like You among the things people call 'God'?" with an awe-filled cry, "No one. No thing. You are one, *Adonai,* unique and unparalleled. We know You best when we worship You in humility and seek to do Your will in the world. You are truly the Holy One."

We may say, then, that for Heschel God is the Ineffable One.

I could easily expand this catalog of the ways Jewish thinkers describe what God is like. God being so great, there seems always to be room for fresh interpretations of God's nature. Some thinkers point to God as the intelligence which structures the universe, including its morality. Some identify God with the power which drives the evolutionary process through nature. Others speak of the ground of being whence all things emerged and to which they return. And, as various philosophies, social sciences, or cultural moods open up some new dimension of reality, our thinkers will utilize them to articulate more adequately what we know God to be like.

The God of the New Search for Jewish Spirituality

I want to conclude this chapter by saying a bit more about the new openness to belief in God which I have found in the Jewish community in recent years.

Its root is the loss of our old substitute-faith, that humanistic Western culture would mandate and foster the human values we cherish. We now find our civilization full of theoretical and practical nihilism, the rejection of any set of values as binding upon us. Freud and Marx, anthropology and history, the experience of modernization in all its diversity—all these awakened us from the absolutism of traditional religion and forced us to see how relative many of our standards were.

We could not remain orthodox in knowledge, life-style, or religion. We embraced diversity. We wanted to be open to many possibilities—but the nihilists are open to anything! We may reject dogmatism but we will not say there are no limits to what people should do. These days believing nothing is permission to try everything. We may not believe much, but we do not believe nothing. We insist there are things one cannot do and remain properly human. And we know, for all that we cannot easily specify them, that there are positive obligations one needs to undertake to fulfill one's humanity.

When, against much of the current temper, we lay such heavy demands on our lives, when we insist on obeying this intuition despite the institutions and interests which press their amorality upon us, we sense that we are responding to something other-than-ourselves. If this dedication were only a matter of childhood conditioning, of psychic introjection, of class interest, of cultural bias, of historical mood, it could not long command or empower us. Or, if our imperatives still pressed in on us, we would be wise to deprogram ourselves from what would then be quixotic dedication. Nothing in us or our culture can any longer demonstrate why we are right to feel spiritual disgust with the quality of life in our time and why we ought to dedicate our lives to changing it. But, if we recognize a transcendent claim to quality which emanates from the core of the universe, we and our culture stand under its judgment. And we then know that we and our society must be transformed.

This is not an academic issue. To do good or evil confronts us often in our daily decisions. To join or not join our culture's drift to paganism is the persistent temptation of our lives. With the social sources of our commitment to humane values collapsing, our persisting dedication to them must have a basis which is more than human. For all that we have closed ourselves off to such knowledge, we now dimly perceive that we are responding to something in the universe greater than us or our society.

I see no compelling reason not to call this cosmic, commanding otherness, God. For such as us, God is the Ground of Value. This God might also be Buber's Friend or Heschel's Ineffable One. I think that only a fully independent, existent Deity can make the ultimate claims upon our lives that we sense being made of us. For me that bars identifying God with Cohen's Idea or Kaplan's natural Power. Other thinkers, of course, see matters differently. On issues as abstruse as this, I view such theological pluralism most positively. The Jewish people as it faces history will measure the worth of these ideas against the realities of life and, in due course, will render judgment upon them, not the least by eventually creating better ideas than those we now possess.

·4·

WHY IS THERE EVIL?

Rabbi Yannai said, "We cannot explain why some evil-doers enjoy satisfying lives while some good people must endure severe suffering. (P. Av. 4:15) Though Rabbi Yannai lived about 1,700 years ago, Jewish teachers have still not found a satisfying answer to the problem of evil. They have given us some creative new ideas about God's justice and some helpful insights into understanding and living with suffering. But, if you want a theory which ends all our questions about why God permits anything other than goodness, then that is more than Judaism, traditional or modern, can supply.

Our perplexity arises from an intriguing mixture of logic and faith. The Bible teaches three ideas which traditional Judaism firmly asserted. First, the one God who rules the universe is good. That seems so obvious an idea we can easily overlook the distinctiveness of this Jewish teaching.

Consider the alternatives. God might be morally neutral. In that case God would not ultimately be involved with questions of good and evil in the world. Much of Asian religion teaches that at the highest spiritual level God is beyond all differences, including the distinction between good and evil. Or, surprising as it may seem, a religion might assert that "God" is evil. The Gnostic religions of Roman times contended that the creator "God" of the Bible was malevolent, not benign. (They then claimed that through their mysteries they would introduce you to the God-above-"god" and thus save you from evil.) In either case, with God neutral or evil, there could be no problem of evil. If the ultimate reality in the universe was not good, the created order

190

would reflect that and thus might be neutral or evil or even occasionally, accidentally, good. By contrast, if God is good, God's world should be good. Then the presence of any evil in God's world is a major religious problem. Because biblical Judaism was based on the premise of God's goodness, it had the problem of evil.

Second, the Bible teaches that, in principle, God has all power. Not all religions have agreed. In Zoroastrianism the God-of-good is opposed by the God-of-evil. These two gods constantly struggle, but neither is powerful enough to gain a permanent victory over the other. When the God-of-evil momentarily has the upper hand, evil rules in human affairs. The God of the Bible does not share divinity but is the one ruler of the universe. God can be described as "able to do all things." (Job 42:2) If God is powerful enough to prevent it, why does God permit evil in our world?

Third, the biblical authors do not doubt that the evil we see around us is real. Some faiths consider evil an illusion; it is only our mistaken way of looking at things. Christian Science teaches this even about illness. In many Hindu traditions the troubles of the world are unworthy of serious spiritual concern. They are merely *lila*, the play of the gods. They do not reflect the absolute One which is all that truly exists. Such views of evil's unreality would end our problem, for anything we could point to which contradicted God's goodness would simply not be real. The Bible takes evil seriously, which may account for its extreme sensitivity to suffering and injustice.

On these three matters our forebears had a forthright faith: God is good and God is powerful and evil is real. Separately these beliefs seem quite compelling; put them together and we find ourselves believing a contradiction. How can any thoughtful person affirm at the same time that God is good and powerful and that evil is real? That is the biblical tradition's classic problem of evil, what theologians call theodicy, justifying God. It has the form of a logical conundrum but it is not an academic issue. It crashes in on us when we or our loved ones have been badly hurt. Then we do not need intricate theological formulations to explain our doubts about God.

The Blunt Honesty of Biblical Religion

The most common human strategy in the face of an agonizing question is to evade it. The biblical authors and rabbis rejected that tactic. They admitted that their faith created problems for them. Many psalmists want to know why the good God does not help righteous people but allows evildoers to flourish. The prophet Jeremiah records his anguish that God, who cares so much for the people of Israel, is now determined to punish them. And, climactically, the Book of Job—a beautiful but very difficult series of lengthy poems—challenges the rest of the Bible's teaching that God rules the world in justice.

None of the authors of these works is an atheist. Had they not believed in God so devoutly they would not have been so troubled by evil. They share their turmoil with us openly and eloquently. They do not understand why God does not end the evil. They are troubled that God delays so long in aiding the good. They complain of their exhaustion waiting for God to act. They remind God of the Ruler's responsibilities and they threaten God that continued inaction will lead to a loss of God's reputation. That realism and candor are part of their religion—and ours. Jews do not consider it impious or heretical to be perplexed by the problem of evil. To the contrary, we call these troubled authors' words holy and enshrine them in our Sacred Scriptures.

Occasionally, a biblical author goes a daring step further and challenges God directly for not acting better. In one breathtaking story Abraham is depicted as reminding God of the meaning of justice. In respectful but strong language Abraham notes that it ill-behooves a good judge to destroy even a few good people while punishing the wicked ones in Sodom and Gomorrah. (Gen. 18:20–23) Many of Job's speeches are a direct demand to God to appear and explain the injustice in the world. Some talmudic rabbis were so upset by Job's *chutspah* that they called him a sinner who deserved his suffering. But the biblical account is unequivocal for God describes Job as "My servant . . . there is none like him in the earth, a whole-hearted and an upright man, who fears God and avoids sin." (Job 1:8)

God's goodness is so central a tenet of Judaism that when God does not seem to be doing good one may dispense with propriety and call God to account. Not many Jews in our history have had the courage—and the record of righteousness—to issue such a challenge, but Jewish tradition contains accounts of such figures. Levi Yitzhak, the chasidic *rebbe* of Berditchev, once even threatened to summon God before a Jewish court for not living up to God's promises to the Jewish people! I hear something of this in the Yiddish folk saying which is so modern a mixture of religious belief and exasperation: "If God lived in our shtetl, people would throw stones through His windows."

About What May We Properly Complain to God?

Most Jews have not felt that they had lived so uprightly that they could dare debate with God. Instead, they sought consolation in one or another of the several "answers" that Jewish teachers worked out. To simplify our consideration of them I have arranged them in something of a logical order. This reflects my judgment that they depend on one another and progressively explain aspects of evil the prior theories left untouched.

Let us begin our analysis by considering the old Jewish wisdom that people often get angry at God over matters that shouldn't be called evil at all. In our dark moods we can grow furious with God for making us frail rather than robust, or compulsive rather than easy going. Such traits, or others, may trouble us but they are not evil. Frail people and compulsive ones, like robust and easy-going types, can still be splendid human beings. To attack God's goodness or justice over a matter of temperament or individual difference testifies only to our false values.

That observation should be extended to other things people regularly and wrongly consider important, the chief of which is money. Judaism does not consider poverty a virtue; having little or moderate means is a difficulty, not an evil. If righteousness depended upon affluence most Jews throughout history would have been doomed to sin. For Americans, it seems an intolerable evil to lose one's money or undergo a major decline in one's living standards. The reactions to such economic setbacks range from shame to depression to suicide—as if giving up one's cars, jewelry, investments, or country club membership changed one's character. (Abject poverty can exemplify the true problem of evil but, for the moment, let us consider only its false forms.)

When we are confused about the goodness God exemplifies

and commands, we will see evil in countless places where it does not truly exist. Judaism proposes to teach us perspective. It sensitizes us to the difference between what is desirable and what is good, what is pleasant and what is worthy, what is nice and what is right. Looking at the world with wise Jewish eyes would save us from the unnecessary torments induced by human frailty and intensified by our acquisitive culture.

Often What We Call Evil Is Evil—the Holocaust

I consider the preceding analysis a good example of the way the Jewish heritage can help us with the problem of evil. This "answer," that we often have false standards, does teach us a valuable lesson. It resolves one part of what troubles us—but only one part. Many of the values we have are not false. We know them to be true because they are based on what we know of God. Life is such a value. Because God created human beings and let them uniquely share in God's creative power, Jews will do almost anything to preserve life. Therefore, when God "takes" life, especially from young people, we question God's goodness and ponder the problem of evil.

Surely one cannot give the answer that we have false standards when we ask why a good God "allowed" the Holocaust.

Perhaps you have wondered why I did not mention the Holocaust earlier. Some Jewish thinkers insist it ought to be the chief case considered in any discussion of evil. Elie Wiesel, Emil Fackenheim, Irving Greenberg, and Richard Rubenstein have gone so far as to assert that the Holocaust was qualitatively unique among the evils of human history. They argue that we cannot think about it as another, if quantitatively extreme, instance of evil, and thus apply classic Jewish wisdom to it. A horror without parallel, they contend, demands a response without precedent.

After many years of debate, most Jewish thinkers, I among them, have disagreed. The Holocaust, for all its unprecedented suffering, for all that it distended the proportions of the problem of evil, did not utterly transform it. By taking this stand we do not mean to diminish the tragedy of what happened but only to acknowledge how radically any serious evil disrupts faith. Every human tragedy poses an ultimate question to God. Our unutterable pain under the Nazis seems not to pose a radically new set of questions but rather to make the old ones press in upon us with infinite ferocity. For us the Holocaust agonizingly reawakens the old biblical cry, "Why do the righteous suffer?"

Perhaps the Evil Is Not Ultimately Real

Another Jewish answer, given by a few theoreticians, was the denial of evil's reality. I suppose they were so full of the love of God or so overwhelmed by God's grandeur that they could not give evil any genuine status in God's creation. Among philosophers Maimonides argued that evil should be understood as only the absence of good and nothing substantive in itself. We get shadows where the light does not enter but they have no substance of their own. A similar view has been common among Jewish mystics and is a part of much chasidic teaching today. Zusya of Hanipol is reported to have lived in utter misery most of his life. However, he was so full of the beneficent presence of God that when asked about evil he responded, "What, is there then evil in the world?"

Had most of us any temptation to deny the reality of evil, the Holocaust would make that unthinkable. It was not something we imagined; certainly it was not the mere absence of good. It was real as goodness is real. Precisely because of its powerful reality we have learned to take the problem of evil with new seriousness and to resist evil with new determination.

So much, then, for Jewish efforts to resolve the problem of theodicy by reinterpreting the Jewish premise concerning evil. Let us now see what we can learn from the various treatments of God's goodness.

The Problem of Evil as the Problem of God's Justice

The overwhelming response of Jewish teachers to the problem of evil has been that God is just. Most of the biblical authors insist that the evil that befalls us is the punishment we deserve for our sinful behavior. We cannot blame God for our suffering since we brought it upon ourselves. Instead, we should accept it in love, for justice is surely a part of God's goodness. We would properly despise an unjust God; we would be right to neglect a God who was utterly indifferent to our deeds. By contrast God's chastisement reveals God's nature. God punishes us for our benefit because by it God teaches us what is bad and encourages us to turn from it.

The prominence of God's justice in human affairs is a central theme of the Bible and the Talmud. Their statements about it are often put in a categorical fashion. The Book of Deuteronomy is noted for this tone. Observant Jews were reminded of God's justice daily as they recited the second paragraph which traditionally followed the *Shema.* It proclaims, in effect, if the Jews perform the commandments God will send rain, but if they don't God will bring a drought. (Deut. 11:13–17) Similarly the Book of Judges has a simple rule of history: When the Jews sin, God gives their neighbors power over them. (This causes the Jews to repent and God to send them a leader, a judge, who saves them, until the cycle starts over again.) In rabbinic times, we frequently hear the rule, "As people did, so was it done to them."

Occasionally the rabbis, who often use hyperbole to make their point, press the efficiency of God's justice to the furthest extreme. Thus, they can explain extraordinary natural phenomena as God's way of executing justice. The Babylonian master Samuel relates that he once saw a frog ferrying a scorpion across a river. This was no chance event. The scorpion was being taken to sting a man whose death had been decreed by the Heavenly Court. (Ned. 41b) In my judgment, most modern descriptions of our tradition have underestimated classic Judaism's pervasive commitment to the efficacy of God's justice.

God's Justice Is Not Pavlov's Conditioning

Having said that, I want immediately to avoid your misunderstanding that traditional doctrine. The authors of the Bible and the rabbis did not believe God's judgment was automatic, unvarying, and instantaneous. Such mechanical justice might be easy to understand but it would defeat God's greater purpose. This requires some special analysis.

Ezekiel gave God's goal concise formulation when he said, "Have I any pleasure at all in the death of wicked people, says *Adonai,* God, and not rather that they should change their ways and live?" (18:23) God's goal is not punishment. That would be, so to speak, too easy. God desires righteous living which means our freely choosing to do the good. An automatic justice would destroy our freedom. If we bit our tongue every time we forgot to say a blessing before eating and if we felt our muscles shape up every time we said a wake-up prayer, we'd soon do these things automatically. Only we wouldn't be doing them like human beings but like laboratory rats conditioned to avoid electric shocks and press a button for a bread pellet.

God created persons with the awesome power to choose between good and evil—that is a Jewish belief as old as the story of Adam and Eve in the Garden of Eden. If we are truly to be free God must give us some leeway in our decisions. Specifically, God must permit us to choose evil without immediately punishing us for it. Is that not true in a family? If children are ever to grow into mature adults they must learn to risk choosing for themselves. They cannot do that unless parents give them some freedom to make their own decisions and not instantly punish them for every mistake they make. A certain measure of forgiveness must be built into the relationship if the parents want their children to learn to use their freedom responsibly.

The Baal Shem Tov, the founder of Chasidism, compared God's situation to parents teaching their child to walk. You put out your hands to help the child but you must also take them away. If we are to walk, we must occasionally fall. God is like such parents. They seem to be doing evil allowing the baby to hurt itself enough to cry. But if the parents do not grant the possibility of a choice which may lead to suffering, the child will not walk— and, if that freedom is not progressively increased, the child will never grow up.

If We Choose to Do Evil, Is God to Blame?

Much of the real evil in the world is not God's fault but ours. We misuse our freedom, choosing foul ends, thus damaging ourselves and others. Shall we then protest that God has given us free will? Would a good God have denied us this capacity and made us, instead, like animals? Jewish thinkers have not thought so. They consider humankind's freedom a special sign of God's goodness to us. Indeed, there is something startling about this Jewish notion of God: it asserts that the all-capable Master of the universe restrains the use of the awesome divine power so that people might be free. (Thus, of course, gaining a partner who can join God in a covenant to complete the creation of the world.) This sense of God's apparent self-limitation so as to give human beings independent spiritual power is not a creation of the modern intellect. It is integral to the Hebrew Bible's earliest notions about God.

Then much evil is not God's fault but ours. The right to choose is a great good but we often use it to be creatively malicious. We drive too fast and maim careful drivers and innocent pedestrians. We destroy reputations, squander resources, abuse power, and make the world the worse for our freedom. Some people even choose to be Nazis and engender a Holocaust. They were not compelled by God to do so. They did it freely. They faced their moral responsibility and rejected it, abusing human freedom worse than anything else we know in human history.

Who Brought About the Holocaust?

A number of Jewish thinkers have therefore not seen the Holocaust as an indictment of God but of humankind. Leo Baeck, the only great modern Jewish thinker who was in a concentration camp during the Holocaust, found his faith confirmed in those terrible years. Decades earlier, in his major work, *The Essence of Judaism,* he had put forth this ethical thesis: Evil is essentially a challenge to humanity to learn to live morally. Nothing he experienced under the Nazis led him to shift the blame from people to God.

Abraham Heschel likewise ascribed the responsibility for the Holocaust directly to humanity. Early during World War II he wrote, "Where is God? Why didst Thou not halt the trains loaded with Jews being led to slaughter? It is so hard to rear a child, to nourish and to educate. Why doest Thou make it so easy to kill? Like Moses, we hide our face; for we are afraid to look upon *Elohim,* upon His power of judgment. Indeed, where were we when men learned to hate in the days of starvation? When raving madmen were sowing wrath in the hearts of the unemployed? Let modern dictatorship not serve as an alibi for our conscience. We have failed to fight *for* right, *for* justice, *for* goodness; as a result we must fight *against* wrong, *against* injustice, *against* evil. We have failed to offer sacrifices on the altar of peace; thus we offered sacrifices on the altar of war. . . . God will return to us when we shall be willing to let Him in—into our banks and factories, into our Congress and clubs, into our courts and investigating committees, into our homes and theaters. For God is everywhere or nowhere. . . ." (*Man's Quest for God,* pp. 147–151)

(Some people have wondered why Heschel, some of whose immediate family died in the Holocaust, wrote so little about it although he was continually in print until his death in 1972. I am convinced that having delineated sharply the human will to choose evil he felt little more needed to be said while much ethically had to be done.)

Does Our Responsibility for Evil Exonerate God?

I do not see how we can deny that a large proportion of the evil we complain about is our fault, not God's. I also believe that the suffering we bring on ourselves when we have behaved badly is often properly called God's judgment on us. If you overdrink, you will get sick; keep putting yourself first and you'll be unloved; stop growing and you will become a bore. Don't blame God; you're getting what you deserve—don't forget, by contrast, that all along God has been giving you strength, intelligence, sensitivity, life itself. No wonder we say God is good. Considering the treatment we deserve for our continual misdeeds, God punishes us very little. God is abundantly merciful and forgiving to most of us. When we can open ourselves to all that God does for us, even skeptical moderns can see that there is much justice and a lot of mercy in God's world.

Nonetheless, the problem of evil remains unresolved. A God who has all power should not create a world with only "much" or "partial" justice. Though we cherish freedom and spurn an automatic dispensation of rewards and punishments, what we see around us is very "rough justice" indeed. The charge against God is direct. Children, too young to be seriously guilty, are in torment. Thoroughly decent people die slowly and painfully. Sinners prosper and villains live out their years in comfort. Where then is God's justice?

And what of the Holocaust? The Lubavitcher Rebbe and Rav Yitzchok Hutner, among others, have reiterated the Book of Deuteronomy's teaching and said that the Holocaust was God's punishment of our people for their sins. Richard Rubenstein speaks for the overwhelming majority of Jews when he declares that such a faith is obscene and unbelievable. Most Jews cannot conceive that any sins committed by the past generation or two were horrible enough that it was just to permit the murder of 6,000,000 of us, 1,000,000 of them probably children. And that does not yet mention the slaughter of some 6 or 7 million non-Jews and the suffering then and now of all those who lived through the Nazi bestiality.

With Job we proclaim that sometimes there is no justice and no mercy. A good and powerful God should allow no exceptions whatsoever. Besides, though we may want freedom, must it be allowed to lead at times to such vile consequences? Why can't God find a way to set limits to how much damage we can do? Why can't evil quickly self-destruct? If God cannot in any way infringe on our freedom, no matter how great our depravity, then let God at least be personally present to comfort the victims of evildoers or be with us when we suffer. Alas, not the least of our pain then is that we feel God has deserted us.

The Instrumental Explanation of Evil

Jewish teachers have gone on to argue that much evil that cannot be explained as our just punishment can be understood as God's means of refining our character. Go back in memory to what you consider the most important lessons of your life. Are they generally associated with your triumphs or with your bitter disappointments? For most of us, suffering has been the greatest teacher—we grew as we overcame a difficult family situation, a troubled love, a business reversal, a physical ailment, a soul-searing insight into our deep-seated frailty. Through such suffering, people often develop what is richest in their humanity.

Evil may be said to have another good use. It sets off and distinguishes what is good. Sickness points up the glory of health. Death reminds us to appreciate life and therefore utilize our time for worthy ends.

That is a somewhat harsh doctrine, so many talmudic teachers noted that God sends the cures along with the diseases. The rabbis' favorite therapy was God's gift of the Torah. If we devoted ourselves to it, they argued, we could overcome our Evil

Urge.* As the Yiddish proverb puts it, God smites us with one hand but blesses us with the other. In this kind of explanation, though the evil remains, it is justified by the good it eventually creates.

Alas, not every evil has beneficial consequences. Have you not seen people broken by tragedy and those around them never recover from what took place? Death often takes a loved one with such a wrench that we cannot then help ourselves or anyone else. Suffering seems as likely to diminish as to enrich us. A powerful God could surely find less hurtful ways of instructing us. Certainly we cannot explain the Holocaust in this fashion. True, it taught us never again to underestimate the human capacity to do evil or to dream that democracy and culture could alone bring the Messiah. God surely could have taught us that at far less a price than the Holocaust.

Can Evil Be Properly Compensated for?

When the argument about the usefulness of evil leaves many cases unexplained some thinkers then argue that God makes up for the evil by later sending us some great good. Thus it has been argued that the Holocaust, not the many years of Zionist effort, made it possible to establish the State of Israel. The greatest suffering the Jewish people has ever endured was followed by the greatest accomplishment in 2,000 years.

This effort to justify the Holocaust has been indignantly rejected by thinkers such as Elie Wiesel and Emil Fackenheim. Could anything make up for what Hitler did to us? Had someone said, "You may have a Jewish state if you will sacrifice 6,000,000 of your people in foul butchery," we would have spurned so vile and debased an offer. To suggest that a God with all power would need a Holocaust to create a state for us seems ridiculous. The Bible says God has twice made possible a Jewish state without anything approaching such tragedy. The extraordinary accomplishments of the State of Israel and the greater glories we hope it will yet achieve cannot begin to wipe out the enormity of the Holocaust.

The traditional version of this compensation argument was

*On our proclivity to do evil, see Part Four, *Living as a Jew*, chapter 1, "The Human Will-to-Do-Evil."

that the sufferings of this world are made up to us after death in the rewards of the life of the world-to-come. Since I shall deal with life-after-death in detail in the next chapter, I will be brief here. If we firmly believed that God would reward us personally in our afterlife for the injustices of this world, I think that most of us would accept with little murmuring the troubles that confront us. That was the attitude of most Jews until relatively recent times. Evil disturbs us so greatly these days because most of us find it difficult, if not impossible, to believe in life-after-death. With no other existence to look forward to, suffering is a terrible experience in the only life we shall have. Could we overcome our disbelief, there are surely some cases, most notably the Holocaust, where the suffering was foul to the point of being irremediable. Even if we could accept the idea of this world as a vestibule to eternal, utter blissfulness, a God who is good should not create so evil a world as ours can be.

The Radical Modern Answer, a "Limited" God

Our consideration of God's goodness has given us no fully satisfying answer. That leaves only one further area in which to find a solution to our problem, the premise of God's complete power.

Some Jewish thinkers believe we must break with the Bible's faith in God in one respect. Their seemingly revolutionary proposal is that God is not omnipotent. Though God is good, there is real evil in the world because, for all the power God has, God is not strong enough to overcome it. God may be the greatest thing that is but even God is not perfect. God is limited in power.

Henry Slonimsky took a dynamic approach to God's finitude. He argued that we should think of God, like the best things we know, as growing. God will be "complete" and evil will disappear only in the Days of the Messiah. Then as Zechariah said, "The Lord shall be one and His name shall be one." (13:9) For Slonimsky, Mordecai Kaplan, and other thinkers who argue that God is limited (or finite), our responsibility for human destiny has now been greatly enhanced. Not God but humankind is the major agent that will bring the Messianic Age. Indeed our moral action becomes the means by which God achieves perfection, that is, victory in the world.

We can find hints of such a solution to the problem of evil in the classic Jewish sources. The Bible's strong appreciation of human freedom implies a limitation on God's omnipotence. The Talmud and Midrash often describe God as weeping over the destruction God brought on Israel, as if God did not have the power to do otherwise. One rabbi can picture God giving this self-description, "Woe to the king who in his youth succeeded but in his old age failed." (Lam. R., Intro. 24) Other rabbis suggest that human sin or virtue, as it were, detracts from or adds to the divine power.

The Jewish philosophers, from Saadya Gaon on (he wrote about 920 C.E.), also limited God by saying that God could not do the illogical. That has consequences for the problem of evil. Logically to have a world requires having matter. Things made of matter are necessarily perishable. God, despite having the power to do everything that logically can be done, could not create a world without decay and death. Thus, traditional thinkers acknowledge that there are limits even to what God can do. Today we should have even less timidity in fearing any diminution of the divine might for we know how much people can do to create the good. Affirming that God is good but acknowledging that God is not infinitely capable of effectuating goodness explains why there is real evil in the world.

If God's Power Is Limited, No Wonder There Are Nazis

I believe this theory is the only intellectually satisfying answer which has been given to the Holocaust. God "allowed" it because God didn't have the power to stop it. God was not strong enough yet to prevent this torment and we did not use our moral capacity to compensate for God's weakness.

The same may be said of other evils we face. God is doing all the good God now can do. We cannot blame our suffering on a God who, like ourselves, does not have all power. Psychologically we can easily understand that people in previous ages imputed to God the omnipotence they wished they had. This new theological position claims to be a more mature understanding of God. It calls us to give up our infantile fantasies of All-Powerfulness and replace these with the reality of human moral growth and cooperative effort.

Hans Jonas takes this approach when he describes God as the originating, ordering reality of our universe that now affects it only as an attracting moral goal. Harold Schulweis will make no claims about reality but suggests that we use the word God to describe what is most godly in human beings and thus is affirmed as worthy of our devotion. In these and other versions, most notably Harold Kushner's statement, many modern Jews have found the concept of a limited God deeply satisfying as they have faced life and history.

For all my appreciation of its intellectual sophistication and its Jewish roots, I do not finally find the doctrine of a limited God acceptable. I keep wondering who is in control of the evils over which God does not have power. I am so taken with the Jewish notion of the oneness of God that I do not see the universe as having more than one orderer—and that means I do not envision the awesome power of evil as excepted from the one cosmic order which God rules.

I also question whether a limited, so to speak, a weak God is worthy of worship and daily trust. Can such a God grow strong enough, as our tradition puts it, to bring the Days of the Messiah? After the Holocaust particularly, I find it difficult to trust human goodness sufficiently to say that we will supply what God lacks. A limited God plus fallible human beings hardly seem worthy of my deep-seated Jewish faith that goodness will triumph in history and God's Kingdom will one day be established upon earth.

There is, however, much in this new theory for Jews like me to admire. It does not evade the harsh reality of evil. It does not mitigate the goodness of God. And it calls upon us to utilize our moral powers to the fullest. I find this position far more realistic and admirable than sensational announcements that, after the Holocaust, Jews can no longer believe in God at all. But for all its attractiveness, I find this theory creates more religious problems than it solves.

The Surprising Death of the Old Agnosticism

Paradoxically enough, instead of driving us to atheism, the discussion of the Holocaust in the 1970s has prodded Jews to faith. Most Jews would have dispensed with God after the Holocaust if they thought such disbelief would leave their commitment to personal value and social quality undiminished. Until recently, we took it for granted that one need not believe in God to be dedicated to human betterment. One could count on people's innate goodness, particularly as channeled by modern education, popular culture, and a society concerned with human welfare, to produce high character. Most liberal Jews could afford to be agnostic because we were certain of the spiritual quality of Western civilization. We could welcome the death-of-God because we had a substitute source of value.

Gradually it has dawned on us that our old optimism about human nature and culture is no longer warranted. What has died for us is not the God of Jewish tradition. We hadn't believed in that God for some time. Rather we have lost our faith in our old real "God," humankind. The Holocaust and the subsequent social traumas we now associate with our disillusionment smashed our idol. Reason was applied to mass murder; esthetics lightened the off-duty hours of murder camp guards; European humanism could accommodate itself to nazism; and the best of the democrats knew what was happening and kept quiet. Since the mid-1960s we have increasingly lost our faith in the moral purity of America. No institution in our society, no branch of our government, no human relationship we trusted in has shown itself free of the possibility of corruption if it has not already demonstrated it. And we ourselves have turned out to be the biggest question mark of all. Is there anything left to be disillusioned about? Our world seems empty.

Then shall we say that the Holocaust merely reflects reality? That it demonstrates that there is no meaning to the universe? With no values inherent in it, naturally some people will arise from time to time to exemplify its ultimate nothingness.

Such theorizing "explains" the Holocaust but does so with a horrifying consequence. It says that it is quite natural to be a Nazi, that, in a neutral universe, one has as much right to be a Nazi as to be a Jew! That goes too far in disbelief for many of us. We may believe little, but we believe more than that the world is empty of values. The Holocaust has taught us we have at least this faith: we must never obliterate the utter qualitative distinction between the killers and the killed.

Denying the Void, Reaffirming the One

I am convinced that as some Jews gained this consciousness a new spiritual self-awareness arose in the Jewish soul. It is one thing to say that I believe nothing—but, of course, I take it for granted that all reasonable, sophisticated people can be counted on to be humane. It is quite another thing to run into people who, because they believe there are no ultimate standards of human decency, feel they may do as they please. Today no-faith quickly leads to no-limits. Compared to such a nihilistic stance our previous affirmation that we believed nothing was an exaggeration. We may not believe much but we do not, most of us, believe nothing. In affirming a cosmic standard of difference between Nazis and Jews—and the everyday commitment to righteousness which is its corollary—we respond to a reality that far transcends us or our culture, both of which it brings into judgment and calls to responsibility. On some such inner path as this, many in our time have found their way, tentatively but strongly, to what our ancestors called God. Ironically, the Holocaust, which led us to protest against God, has by its exemplification of absolute evil brought us back to a perception of the primacy of absolute good.

That leaves us in a most difficult situation, the familiar one of Jewish tradition. The evil is real and God is good. If there is ultimate unity in the universe then it must mean, somehow, that God is the embracing power of all that is, including the evil. "I form the light and create the darkness. I make peace and create evil. I am *Adonai* who does all these things." (Isaiah 45:7) We are back where we began, with three beliefs which separately seem compelling but which will not fit together logically.

What Holds a Paradoxical Faith Together?

Most Jews in the past have held that faith although it was not logical. Despite their pride in thinking for themselves and their high appreciation of intellect, they did so, I would guess, out of piety. They trusted God even though they did not understand God. Perhaps we may say that when life and logic pushed them to the limit they trusted their intuition of God more than they trusted their reasoning about God.

This piety was reflected in their way of life. The commandments encouraged them to be aware of what the good God was doing for them in everything that happened to them. Each portion of food, each unusual sight, each event, from seeing a king to excreting one's bodily wastes, was an occasion for blessing God. Jewish life overflowed with acknowledgments of God's beneficence.

When one lives with such a pervasive sense of God's gifts, the evils we endure generally appear few and small compared to all we have been given. To almost all of us, God has been overwhelmingly good and generous. Because of that perspective, most Jews have been able to say with the pious Job, "Shall we then take all the good God gives us and not accept some evil?" (2:10)

Even during the Holocaust, Eliezer Berkovits reminds us, the believers often retained their faith in God. The dramatic proclamations of God dying in the Holocaust were made mainly not by people who were in the death camps but, much later, by those who had been safe, miles away. We should not be surprised at such unbelief as occurred, Berkovits contends, for it is the common modern condition. What should evoke our religious admiration to the point of awe, he insists, is the faith that did not waver even in Auschwitz. In such lives the sacred manifested itself in hell. We owe these saints the benefit of such belief as we can muster. In faith, not in disbelief, we perpetuate their spirit.

Many modern Jews find they cannot easily respond to life in a spirit of awe and gratitude, particularly when they think of those whose lives are filled with unmerited suffering. Others recognize that God's goodness to us and our responding duty to do the good we can must ground everything else we know and do. Thus, like generations of Jews before them, they first affirm God's goodness and then try to overcome or accept evil.

How shall we conclude this chapter when we cannot end the discussion? I turn to a message which was found after the Holocaust on a cellar wall in Cologne: "I believe in the sun even when it is not shining. I believe in love even when I do not feel it. I believe in God even when He is silent."

·5·

IS THERE LIFE
AFTER DEATH ?

Many religious topics carry strong emotional overtones. Our feelings about Jews may be defensive or
aggressive as a result of growing up in a gentile world. Our
attitudes to sin can hardly be separated from our techniques for
handling our guilt-feelings. Psychoanalysis has indicated that
even our relationship with God is unconsciously influenced by
our deep-seated love-hate feelings for our parents. Rarely can we
talk deeply about our beliefs without doing some surface psychotherapy. That most emphatically holds true of discussions about
life-after-death. In my experience, no question concerning one's
personal faith evokes more troubling emotions. While my expertise and interests are intellectual, I want to begin this chapter with
a few words about our emotional difficulties with this topic. Perhaps some things I can say will encourage you to do some self-
exploration of your attitudes concerning death—and talk them
out with your rabbi and fellow-congregants.

Most of us have such strong feelings about dying that we cannot stand confronting them. I will not argue that everyone is like
that. Some people can accept the fact of death, theirs or others',
with equanimity. I do not find that to be true of most people. I
have a dear friend of broad-ranging intellect who finds it almost
impossible to visit the desperately ill or make a *shivah* visit (pay
a condolence call). I am certain you know people who, when the
conversation turns to death, become quite uncomfortable and
quickly steer the discussion to something else. Others appear to

208

be hiding something from themselves when they say with self-assurance that they have no particular feelings about death. I have spoken to too many people stricken far beyond their expectation long after a death to be impressed by such bravado.

The Challenge of Facing Our Strong Feelings

Perhaps there is something of these feelings in you, and reading this is more attention to death than you've ever permitted yourself away from a funeral. I understand such emotions. Death destroys what we know best and treasure most, life. Even young people shudder in the presence of death—but not for long. Their biological juices quickly propel them back into activity and they can rationalize that death is mainly for the old. With each added year, though, death becomes a personal threat. Our parents die, our friends and acquaintances begin to go, and our diminished vitality and new aches steadily signal our mortality. Facing death becomes more difficult to avoid.

Life itself can then become a problem, for death refuses to be abstract. It will happen to me. As the reality of my dying presses in on me, I might panic, at least for the moment. The major human strategy for dealing with inner terror is flight. We try to look young and stay busy. For many reasons, American culture encourages us in this denial, leaving us all the more unprepared for the death of those we love or for our own.

Much of what disturbs many of us is related to our early childhood fantasies about who might kill us or whom we might murder. The unconscious mind contains the oddest notions and ones that still have great influence upon us, which is why we ban them from our consciousness. If you have great difficulties talking about death, if the topic disturbs you greatly, you will benefit by getting some sympathetic help. Explore your feelings with your rabbi. Perhaps some sessions with a psychotherapist are in order to relieve you of some troublesome infantile imaginings which unconsciously still weigh heavily upon you. If you do not wish to do this for yourself, consider what a gift it would be to your family. Instead of transmitting your fright to another generation, you might help them face death's real anguish without a host of imaginary fears. When, together, we are able to talk about death, go to funerals, visit cemeteries, and accompany loved ones to the end of their lives, we make our love available when it is often deeply needed but not easily asked for. Ethically, too, we ought to cultivate sufficient maturity with regard to death to begin to reform our society's absurd attempt to shield us from the inevitable.

Death Sets a Limit to Our Religious Experience

One fear about death is so illogical that only a neurotic would pursue it. Don't try to use your imagination to conjure up images of what it is like to "be dead." You can't do it. All you'll come up with is some kind of nothingness, a void so opposite to life that it gives you the shivers. If you then imagine being in a coffin or buried in the ground, that adds suffocation fantasies to the horror. But you can't "be" dead. To be dead is not to "be" at all. Dead is, by definition, without feeling or consciousness or sensitivity. Dead really means dead, like a stone. If that's it, if death is the end, if there is no life-after-death, then you needn't worry about being uncomfortable. There won't be any "you" to have any idea of what is going on. The only way *you* can have any personal experience after death is if you have some form of afterlife, and that's not "being dead" but living in another way.

To speak of life-after-death creates a major intellectual difficulty for us. Almost all of modern religious thought is based on some aspect of human experience. When we spoke about God, for example, our thinkers taught us first to focus on something we commonly do. Thus, Hermann Cohen had us look at the operation of our minds; Mordecai Kaplan began with our will to live abundantly; and Martin Buber worked by analogy to our richest interpersonal relationships. We arrived at God from something we knew in our own lives.

We cannot follow that pattern if we wish to talk about life-after-death. We have no experience of "after-death." The conception of an afterlife thus becomes particularly troublesome for modern thinkers, for there is nothing in our lives analagous to it. As a result, we must be more open and tentative in our discussion of life-after-death than of any other theme we shall deal with. The technical term theological writers apply to a subject that stretches beyond our understanding is "mystery." Life-after-death remains one of the greatest religious mysteries, like the problem of evil. In both cases, Judaism has much useful to teach us.

Some years back, that would have concluded a liberal introduction to this theme. In recent years, science, which once made life-after-death seem incredible, has provided data which may give us some "experience" of our survival after death. I have many questions about this material, but I think it significant enough to merit some mention here.

Do We Now Have Experience of Life-After-Death?

On occasion, doctors now can revive someone who, technically speaking, died a little while before. Such cases are rare, but there are enough of them so that research has been done on the experience of surviving death. In one investigation of several hundred cases, many of the people involved reported rather similar happenings. They knew themselves to be out of their bodies and had some detailed idea of what happened to them. They had no sense of pain or confusion but, if anything, they "felt" rather peaceful and calm. They were met by friendly beings who summoned them to an area of great goodness and abundant light, but they then chose to return to life and subsequently were revived. Not all the subjects reported the same occurrences and some accounts were very much richer than others yet there was considerable consistency between the reports. Not surprisingly, since the publication of the data, many more people have come forward who report something similar having happened in their lives when they were on the brink of death or beyond it.

I do not wish to press this argument very hard. A major human mystery is not so easily resolved. Besides, I am highly skeptical of all such data. For some decades now people have been seeking scientific verification of life-after-death. Mostly this psychical research has taken the form of investigating messages which are alleged to have come from the next world. The mediums and spiritualists who have conveyed these communications have generally been fakes who preyed on the desires of people to know that their loved ones were still alive. Their occasional extraordinary performances which cannot be explained by known scientific processes seem better considered to be astonishing coincidences or problems for future research rather than proof that we live on after death.

Our new data seems to be of a different sort. What impresses me most is the contrast between what the trained medical observers and the revived persons say. The doctors and nurses report that their patient had died. That is, the person was utterly without consciousness in the period before the revival, sometimes for many minutes. Not infrequently, such patients who were later revived described in detail just what the medical staff had done and said in the time they had been "dead." The attending medical personnel have then corroborated the details.

I find that inexplicable and evocative but it does not prove to me that we have an afterlife. We have only a small number of such cases and few researchers have been involved in this field. It may be that we know less about the end of human consciousness than we thought we did. We need much more critical study in this area before we move beyond our common skepticism.

Yet the present investigations should at least make us ask how open-minded we are on this topic. I find many Jews quite dog-matic about the impossibility of life-after-death. Perhaps, in a time when it seemed certain that some laboratory would, sooner or later, discover everything important about life, a closed mind was warranted. Today, many people, I among them, believe that we exist on many levels simultaneously. If that is so, only a science that accepts more evidence than ours now does can adequately uncover the several dimensions of reality. We can at least say that our new data refutes the notion that a scientific attitude to life is utterly incompatible with life-after-death. The question is, at least, an open one.

The Bible's Changing Views of the Afterlife

Something of our modern tentativeness toward this belief may be seen in its slow and winding development in Judaism. The Bible says very little about life-after-death, concentrating almost exclusively on what God wants people to do while alive. That yielded the characteristic Jewish attitude: concentrate on this world. Had God thought it important for us to be concerned about the next world, God would have revealed some of its se-crets to us. Instead, God's Torah gives us extensive direction on how to live here and now; it promises but does not emphasize or describe afterlife.

Some observers find it strange that Judaism could center itself largely on ordinary human existence and hold only marginal regard for the next world. It does not seem that odd to Jews. The Baal Shem Tov, the founder of Chasidism, epitomized our Jewish sense of balance in this regard when he said, "If I can love God here and now, why do I need to worry about the life of the world-to-come?"

A few statements in the Bible seem to rule out life-after-death. Job, fortifying his arguments against God's justice, says, "As a cloud fades away and disappears, so a person goes down to the grave and doesn't come up from it." (7:9) Many other Bible authors do mention personal survival after death. They call it "going down to Sheol" but they never give us a clear description of Sheol or of life there. Their parenthetical statements about it hardly make it attractive. They refer to it as something like a great pit under the earth, a place of darkness and silence, one where there is no prayer or praise of God.

Surprisingly enough, we are once told of someone returning from Sheol. The witch of En Dor magically brings the prophet Samuel back to earth at King Saul's command. The account is as fascinating as it is unique to biblical literature. Astonishingly, Samuel then complains that he has been bothered by being raised up from "the pit." (1 Sam. 28:15)

Biblical Glimpses of a Positive Life-After-Death

Some few places in the Bible point to a more welcome sort of afterlife. In a highly visionary chapter of Isaiah we read, "And God will destroy the covering that is thrown over all peoples and the veil that is spread over nations. He will swallow up death forever. *Adonai,* God will wipe away tears from off all faces and the reproach of His people He will take away from all the earth. *Adonai* has said it." (25:7–8) That does not explicitly say that those who had died will now live, though the vision of a revival of the dead might easily be connected to it.

Another evocative passage occurs in the psalm ascribed to Hannah, the mother of Samuel. "The Lord kills and brings to life, brings down to the grave and brings up from it." (1 Sam. 2:6) That suggests that as God causes death so God gives life after death. Perhaps, though, the verse does not describe a literal sequence but is only an extravagant appreciation of God's power to heal the gravely ill.

The Book of Daniel puts all such ambiguity to an end. It notes that, in the end-time, "many of those who sleep in the dust of the earth shall awaken, some to everlasting life and some to everlasting reproach and rejection. Those who were wise will shine on, bright as the sky. Those who led others to righteousness will be like stars for ever and ever." (12:2–3) Much of the rabbis' later teaching seems stated in this passage: At a distant time and in an extraordinary way, corpses return to life, are judged for their previous acts, with everlasting glory for some and complete destruction for others.

Modern scholars generally agree that the Book of Daniel is one of the latest biblical books written. It was probably composed during the Hasmonean rebellion against the Syrians, about 170 B.C.E. By then, the concept of individual life-after-death in some positive form had become an explicit theme in Jewish teaching. Since we find the historical development of ideas valuable, it would be helpful if we could clarify the passage of Jewish belief from a dismal Sheol to a gleaming eternal life. Despite a number of ingenious scholarly theories about this evolution, we simply have too little data to do much more than speculate how that transformation occurred. Whether the latest stage was a borrowing from the Persians, an ideological device to strengthen the will of the Judean rebels against the Syrians, a response to individual fear of death, an outgrowth of the classic Jewish trust in God, the inspiration of a genius, or simply the revelation of God, we cannot be certain.

The Talmudic View of the Next Life

In the period after the destruction of the Temple, 70 C.E., the doctrine of afterlife was a major and characteristic part of the Pharisees' interpretation of Judaism. Josephus reports that their opponents, the Sadducees, rejected a belief in life-after-death. The Pharisaic teaching was quite specific. The Pharisees expected a resurrection of the dead in the Days of the Messiah.

Though rabbinic literature (which almost totally reflects the Pharisees' point of view) contains many views which differ on matters of detail, we can roughly draw a composite picture of what the rabbis believed happens to us after death. God takes our souls when we die, and they enter a period of purifying punishment. (In later lore, this lasts no more than twelve months; a mourner says the *Kaddish* prayer daily only during this period.) The term, *olam haba,* the world-to-come, is often applied to this status.

God then returns our souls to a heavenly "treasury" where they await the earthly coming of the Messiah.* Some time after that event, the graves are opened and the bodies, made perfect and pure, arise from them. Their souls are restored to them, completing the resurrection of the dead, *techiyat hametim.*

The revived person then comes before God for a final judgment. The righteous go straight into the life of the world-to-come, the other usage of *olam haba* (a state also referred to as *atid lavo,* the future-to-come). The wicked are punished until they are purified and permitted entry into the world-to-come or else are doomed to destruction and denied the bliss of eternal life.

The Mishnah declares (San. 10:1) that all Jews have a share in the life of the world-to-come. The rabbinic attitude to non-Jews is ambivalent. One source, much quoted in later times (Tos. San. 13:2), is positive toward individual Gentiles. It rules that "the righteous people of any nation have a share in the life of the world-to-come." The general rabbinic expectation concerning "the nations" (of Gentiles) is negative, consigning them to annihilation.

To this day traditional Judaism teaches this doctrine of the afterlife. Over the centuries fantasy and folklore have decorated it with many imaginative embellishments but have not changed its basic pattern.

Pharisaic Teaching and the Story of Jesus' Resurrection

The prominence of this teaching in first-century Judaism helps us to understand the teachings of the early Christians who were, of course, Jews. Because they believed Jesus had been resurrected they felt they had a new and unexpected proof that Jesus was the Messiah. To Christians the event was so unprecedented in history that, in due course, it suggested to them the idea that Jesus was no ordinary mortal. He was, as later Christian doctrine put it, God as well as man, the Son, who with the Father and the Spirit are

*For Judaism's teaching about the Messiah, see Part One, *The Jewish People,* chapter 4, "What Do We Expect in the Messianic Age?"

the Trinity which, in the central Christian mystery, is at the same time the one God. Easter, not Christmas, is therefore the major holiday of Christianity for on it the messianic promise suggested in Jesus' birth stories was fulfilled.

Jews can see that the story of Jesus' resurrection is told against the background of Pharisaic belief. Despite this our people has never had difficulty rejecting it. Our Bible is quite clear that the chief sign of the coming of the Messiah is a world of justice and peace. No prophet says the Messiah will die and then be resurrected as a sign to all humanity. Except for the small number of converts to Christianity, Jews in ancient times did not believe Jesus had actually been resurrected. Modern Jews, who believe in the immortality of the soul or in no afterlife at all, similarly reject the Christian claim.

Rabbinic Judaism contains an even greater variety of opinion on life-after-death than on most other Jewish beliefs. Rav (early third century C.E.), one of the founders of the Babylonian study style which resulted in the Talmud, taught: "The world-to-come is not like this-world-of-ours. In the world-to-come there is no eating or drinking, no procreation, no business, no envy, no hatred, and no competition. Rather, the righteous sit with crowns on their heads and bask in the splendor of God's presence." (Ber. 17a) About the same time, one of the great teachers in the Land of Israel, Rabbi Yohanan, said: "All that our prophets told us about the end-of-days concerned only the Days of the Messiah. What will happen when (after the resurrection and judgment) we go on to the world-to-come, we do not know. As Isaiah (64:3) said, 'No eye beside Yours has seen, O God, what you will do for the person who has hope in You'."

Two Marginal Conceptions of Life-After-Death

Two other ideas about afterlife appear at times in Jewish literature yet never were sufficiently accepted to set required Jewish practice. The older notion is the immortality of our soul, the other the reincarnation or the transmigration of souls.

All during the rabbinic period, substantial numbers of Jews lived in the various cities around the Mediterranean Sea. Despite Roman domination, Greek long remained the language of cultured people. Jews in this Diaspora (a Greek word for "dispersed") wrote in Greek and incorporated Hellenistic ideas in their thinking. The rabbis found many of these Greek writings religiously objectionable and excluded them from the authentic Torah-tradition.* We know about these books today from collections called the Apocrypha and Pseudepigrapha. They were preserved by Christians who found some of their own doctrines anticipated in them.

A number of these Hellenistic Jewish writings teach that our soul alone survives our death. As in much Greek thinking, the soul is immortal. Only our body can die for it is made of matter. Our soul is somehow made of a spiritual substance which is indestructible. Theologians use the word immortality to refer to our soul's surviving our body's death, as contrasted to resurrection in which body and soul are eventually reunited.

In the Wisdom of Solomon, the hope for immortality is expressed this way: "God created people to live forever and made them to be just as eternal as God is. . . . The souls of the righteous are cared for by God and no trouble shall come to them. Fools think people die and their passing from this life hurt them, that their dying brought them to ruin. But they are at peace. Though people think they've been punished by dying, they have every right to hope for life after death." (2:23, 3:1–4)

This closely follows much Greek thought with its sharp distinction between the soul and the body. This easily becomes dualism. The pure soul is unhappily confined to the impure, material body as its temporary dwelling place. Because the body has emotions as well as animal functions, we are unable to live in proper spirituality. When one begins with such an understanding (which we can trace back as far as Socrates, fifth century B.C.E.), bodily life can easily be disvalued, and death, which brings us to a proper spiritual existence, can seem a benefit.

A more popular idea grew up among the Jewish mystics. While our first traces of mystical Jewish traditions are found in early rabbinic literature, our evidence for their belief in reincarnation comes centuries later. Most mystic doctrine being secret, it is passed on only privately by a master to a responsible disciple. As a consequence, we have no knowledge what personal or religious experiences may have led to the adoption of this idea. Intellectu-

*On the issue of what constitutes the proper extension of the Written Torah, see Part Three, *The Bible and Tradition,* chapter 5, "How Has Change Come into Judaism?"

ally, its root seems to be the Talmud's notion that, for unspecified reasons, there are a finite number of souls in God's treasury. With so many people to live until the Messiah comes, God recycles these souls from body to body, reincarnating them in different generations. (This belief is also known as the transmigration of souls.)

Most traditional Jews have found reincarnation a questionable doctrine, not the least for the problems it seems to create for the resurrection and judgment day. Nonetheless the Chasidim still largely affirm the transmigration of souls.

How Modernity Changed Jewish Belief about Afterlife

When the Jews emerged from the ghetto, they found all these ideas increasingly challenged by modern science. Evolution closely connected human beings with other animals. Medicine showed our life was intimately linked to specific organs and structures. More recently, the unraveling of the chemistry of genetics has lent spectacular confirmation to the intuition of several generations of scientists that life is basically chemical. If our having life means that we are a mass of fabulously intricate interrelated molecules, then death is the decisive disruption of that interaction. And there is no "us" left to survive it. Our chemicals, in their separate and changing forms, will find their way into other parts of nature. Our genetic material is carried on by our offspring, if we have any. We, individually, having been a fantastically wondrous concatenation of chemicals, come to an end when our specific chemistry loses its integration. Moreover, science denies the existence of a soul, a spiritual substance which by medieval definition is so fine it cannot be detected in any laboratory. Since the chemical theory explains life quite satisfactorily, why add unnecessary unobservable entities like the soul?

Some liberal religious thinkers have forthrightly accepted this scientific view. They have compared belief in an afterlife to other mythical matters in traditional religion, like the earth being the center of the universe. Psychology helps us understand how previous generations came to such an idea. They wished it were true, and out of their pain and anxiety they made it true. We have rejected other traditional Jewish beliefs which reflected an earlier world view. We should now also acknowledge that a mature view of reality requires us to give up the belief in personal survival after death.

Fortunately, the Jewish tradition has not emphasized life-after-death; there seem strong currents in our tradition that have largely done without it. Modern Jews, then, feel they have good Jewish warrant for denying the classic views of the afterlife. Having done so, we can emphasize the good that people need to do while they are alive and can thus intensify our sense of human responsibility. We can find long-range satisfaction in the good we have done that will survive our death and in the knowledge that the Jewish people will carry on our ideals long after we are gone.

How an Old Belief Died Out

On no other topic, I would guess, has naturalism, thinking about religion in terms of science, enjoyed a greater success. For some time now most Jews seem to me to have effectively given up belief in life-after-death. At the least, they have been more determinedly skeptical on this belief than any other.

Something of modern science's veto power in this connection may be seen in Reform Judaism's struggle to reinterpret afterlife in a modern fashion. The early nineteenth-century Reform prayer books in Europe already omitted references to the resurrection of the dead. Modern Jews could not be asked to believe that God would one day restore bodies which had disintegrated in the earth. Reincarnation, too, was utterly incompatible with their rationalism but they found the notion of the immortality of the soul congenial.

By soul, the early Reform Jews did not mean the medieval sort of inner substance which modern science had discredited. Instead they had recourse to nineteenth-century philosophy's emphasis on the human "spirit." Unlike other animals, human beings can think, propose, choose, and create, all in full self-consciousness. In these powers the Reform teachers saw the unique functioning of the human spirit. They pointed to it as our likeness to God and suggested, in a poetic rather than descriptive fashion, that this spirit in us survived the death and dissolution of our body. To the best of my knowledge, no modern thinker ever described what such immortality might be like. It was generally spoken of as "returning to" or "being with" God and rarely carried connotations of judgment or punishment.

Belief in such immortality of the soul faded in the mid-twentieth century. Science seemed well on its way to explaining all of life, and naturalism displaced the philosophies which proclaimed the uniqueness of the human spirit. An old Jewish belief seemed to be nearing its end.

In recent years something has changed. A different mood has been moving through much of Western culture. Science is no longer a god whose truth we blindly accept. Its benefits have serious limits, including the new problems it always seems to create for us. It knows much about facts but little about purposes or values. Science may be indispensible to our understanding of the universe, but insofar as it is unconcerned with what is good or just or loving it cannot fully describe human existence. The richness of the day-to-day reality we know ourselves to be confirms that a person is far more than laboratory measurements can show. Naturalism is no longer the obvious, undisputed way of talking about life—and of what succeeds it.

The New Openness to Personal Survival after Death

The center of much thinking today is our appreciation of what it is to be a genuine human being. "Real persons" do not always automatically try to do what social convention dictates or what is fashionable. While being concerned for others and society as a whole they manage to remain true to themselves. They are genuine individuals though they richly partake of relationships of trust and love. Such people have integrity and in their presence we can sense that their personal depth is unfathomable. When we are with them, we know we are in contact with what is most "real" about being human.

Any effort to explain such personhood exclusively in chemical terms seems self-contradictory. Molecules move without choice, in set ways, with no consciousness or conscience, no sense of beauty, and no ability to love. The great chemical conglomerates, the proteins, do show unexpected powers. Life emerges from the apparently lifeless, the adaptation to nature becomes extraordinarily complex. Still nothing we know about the development from chemicals to plants to animals prepares us for human beings. A qualitative gap remains between the most intricately organized molecular processes and living as an authentic human being.

For all that I am intricately related to my body, I know myself to be a person and not merely a chemical structure. I do not say I have a "soul" for in today's culture I would not know how to substantiate the existence of such an entity. Still, there is something about me that enables me to share in God's reality. I know a bit about God. At my best, I consciously serve God and my acts help complete God's work of creation. I occasionally have a glimpse of what God wants of me and all humanity. Sometimes I am capable of rising above the frailties within and social ugliness without to dedicate my life to a purpose far transcending my small existence. This exalted human capacity deserves as much attention as does the chemistry of our life stuff—or more, for it is what makes us characteristically human. And it is the experiential base of our sense that we are like God and thus may be privileged to share in God's eternal life.

Naturalism hoped to find what is truly real by reducing everything to its smallest physical constituent. The other view, mine, and I think that of Jewish tradition, sees reality most clearly in the most complex thing we know, a person. The one perspective breaks everything down to impersonal energy. The other says we see ultimate reality more clearly as we build upward from human nature to that which transcends and fulfills it. If God is the most real "thing" in the universe, then we may hope that, as we make our lives ever more closely correspond to it, we may personally share God's eternity despite our death. And knowing ourselves to be most fully human through our individuality, we trust that the God who is one will preserve our oneness and grant us personal survival after death.

Life-After-Death, a Personal Statement

That belief cannot be ruled out by saying, "You believe in life-after-death because you want that to be true. You turn your wish into an assertion of fact." Not every wish is unrelated to reality. Some motivate us to reach for what can await us. I yearn for redemptive love and social justice. My wanting them to be real does not make them false hopes even as hoping alone does not bring them into being.

Despite Marx, my desire for life after death will not desensitize me to social evil but actually will intensify my struggles in this world. Being a liberal I am dedicated to humankind's significant role in achieving God's purposes. With that sense of faith, I am unlikely to give up my activism and patiently wait for the life of the world-to-come. True, because I do not consider people the only agents of fundamental change, I will not bring a messianic enthusiasm to every immediate social struggle. But should my projects fail I will not be as dispirited as many one-time liberals have now become. Believing there is only one life, they have grown discouraged, even bitter because they were not able to bring the Messianic Age in their time. Often they now despair of human progress altogether. Why should they spend their only existence suffering continual defeats, why sacrifice their precious few years to the painful task of resisting evil?

Believers who do not expect vindication in this life alone are saved from the spiritual rot that easily sets in when humanity proves obdurate to change or malevolent in interest. They trust God to reward them in another existence for what they have suffered for God's sake in this one. They may even be strong enough to see their defeats on God's behalf as joining them to God's reality. Their lives will be fulfilled no matter what happens in this world for they have a life with God yet to come. And, trusting God, they know history will one day be redeemed by the One who will not ultimately be defeated.

I do not know much more than that, how I shall survive, what sort of judgment awaits me, or what I shall do in eternity. I am, however, inclined to think that my hope is better spoken of as resurrection rather than immortality for I do not know my self as a soul without a body but only as a psychosomatic self. Perhaps even that is more than I can honestly say, though in the use of this term I may lean upon Jewish tradition with which I share so much else. Ultimately, I trust in what I have experienced of God's generosity, so surprising and overwhelming so often in my life. In such moments I sing whole-heartedly the last stanza of the hymn, *Adon Olam,* "In God's hand I place my soul both when I sleep and when I wake, and with my soul, my body. God is with me. I shall not fear."

·6·

WHY DO RELIGIONS DIFFER?

In Judaism some theological questions can be answered directly. Is there a God? Yes. Is God plural? No. But some other theological questions have no answers in our religion. What was God doing before creating the world? What will we know about God when we attain the "knowledge of *Adonai*" promised us in the life of the world-to-come? Our teachers do not know the answers to these questions. They would say such matters are not worth worrying about when one considers what we do know and ought to be doing.

Some religious questions, such as "Shouldn't we all really have one religion?" receive what theologians call a dialectical answer, "Yes . . . but. . . ." Dialectical because two voices sound in this response, one speaking positively, the other, negatively. Neither alone gives the proper answer. Only in the *dialogue* of the two is the full truth heard.

Judaism takes a dialectical approach to the desirability of one religion. Its required daily prayers conclude with a fervent plea for the advent of a common faith. But it also asserts that such unity of belief and practice is possible only after "the coming of the Messiah."

Such dialectical thinking troubles many people, particularly those who want a clear-cut authorization to pursue either a universal or a particular religious life. "If Judaism favors one religion, then why not create it right now by giving up what separates us from others?" Conversely, "If Judaism maintains that we cannot have one religion until the Messiah comes why don't we stop diverting our efforts to non-Jewish and interfaith causes?" To

223

partisans of the theological left and right, I respond dialectically, *"Yes* you are right in part *but* you fail to see the whole truth." Traditional Judaism is universal *and* particular; liberal Judaism, in response to democracy, has added to Jewish universalism while trying to maintain a balancing particularism.

The Power of Dialectical Belief

I propose, shortly, to argue for both sides of that Jewish dialectic. Before I do so, I wish to dispel the fear that to hold a belief in so balanced a fashion will give us a lukewarm and inconsequential faith.

I agree that unqualified belief can powerfully summon our energies for life and, if need be, for death. It can also lead to zealotry and fanaticism. Liberals consider it a sign of maturity to recognize that there are few matters today worthy of unqualified devotion. Our resultant doubt and hesitations do make life, with its multitude of decisions, troublesome. Trying to be true to the varied values we affirm may fill us with conflict. It also makes us more responsible. Working at our self-fulfillment while being faithful to those we love, bettering the lot of humanity while furthering the interest of our ethnic group may tear us apart at times. Yet living in a world where such a dialectic of duty exists is the sign of our wisdom.

This pattern also applies to our hope for one religion. History has taught Jews that "the Messiah may tarry," but the best of our people, despite their secularization, remain deeply devoted to perfecting the world and steadfast in their refusal to concede victory to the amorality around us. Nature seems indifferent to our aspirations and history often looks like random activity, yet Judaism teaches that goodness is inherent in creation and powerful in human affairs. Despite centuries of persecution, and now astonishingly, after the Holocaust, we dare to affirm a messianic dream. Our idealism transcends our realism. To belittle our hope for one religion as "only an ideal" misunderstands the commanding power of Jewish hope.

The Two Reasons for an Ultimate Single Faith

Jews recognize two compelling arguments for the coming of one religion. We have hinted at the theological one above: with only one God in the universe, there should ideally be only one religion. The logical consequence of monotheism is that day "when the earth shall be full of the knowledge of *Adonai* as the waters fill the sea." (Isaiah 11:9)

The other argument stems from our bitter experience with religious difference. Ever since the seventeenth-century Enlightenment, religion has been chastised by its secular critics as doing more harm than good. In God's name wars were fought and believers were urged to treat infidels heinously. Despite our contemporary climate of disbelief, this ugly underside to religion still makes itself evident in Ireland, India, and the Middle East. And there are few American cities where interreligious tension need not be taken into account in social planning and perhaps in one's personal relationships.

Jews have a special sensitivity in this regard. Many passages in the Christian Scriptures show animus against the Jews, inducing or validating later Christian hate of Jewish neighbors. The Koran contains passages similarly derogatory of Jews, leading the followers of Islam to expect Jews to live among them on an inferior level. These teachings remain the background of the anti-semitism which suffuses the societies shaped by Christianity and Islam.

On the whole, people hate one another for many more urgent reasons than religious difference. The social sciences have shown how religion is brought into social disputes largely as a matter of "scapegoating." When we feel economically exploited, socially degraded, ethnically oppressed, humanly deprived, morally hounded, or otherwise disturbed, we seek an outlet for our aggression. We can't strike out at the nearest target for we have been taught to respect other people. Religion can resolve our tension by authorizing us to hate the unbeliever or heretic. Even when we no longer seriously believe in a religion we are happy to utilize its cover to hate and hurt others. Hitler could not have succeeded in his political exploitation of anti-semitism had religion in a prior time not authorized despising Jews.

One Religion Would Mean the End of Religious Hatred

To end this practice, people suggest we merge our separate religions. Were there only a teaching of human solidarity, scapegoating would lose its greatest validation and stand condemned as a sin. Compared to such gains, our comfort in maintaining our particular ways of serving God hardly seems significant. Thus, some Jews see ending religious difference as an immediate way of wiping out anti-semitism. They cannot understand why other Jews are not as enthusiastic as they are about our giving up all signs of Jewish distinctiveness so as to achieve this great goal.

Every time I confront religious chauvinism, in Jews or other groups, these arguments spring powerfully to mind. Unfortunately, that happens rather often these days. We Americans once carefully hid our prejudices since they were considered undemocratic. Today, with the glorification of ethnic self-interest, the racist slurs that once might have occasionally slipped out are rather easily spoken and perhaps put into print. The Jewish community, despite its self-image as immaculately tolerant, is no exception to this practice. Many an issue of *The Jewish Press* of Brooklyn, perhaps the Diaspora's largest selling English Jewish newspaper, has seemed to me to carry derogatory ethnic innuendoes. In this and other such phenomena, religion, the source of our belief in one humankind, is used to foster contempt of others. Religion can so easily be co-opted by what is worst in human beings, that liberals insist their faith manifest an active universalism.

The first half of our dialectical attitude to one religion, therefore, has a solid theological and historical underpinning.

We Cannot Avoid the Issue of Practicality

There are five arguments against trying to realize the universal ideal in the here and now of history.

The first contention is that it cannot be done. We find it difficult to get the members of a neighborhood association or a congregation to agree on anything of significance. We often cannot establish a common way of life even in our families, where love rules. Human difference is not easily overcome. It shows its resistive quality as soon as we begin to think of uniting specific individuals in any important enterprise. In temperament, sensitivity, insight, and intuition, people are simply too varied to follow one religious way.

The historical record is clear. Every effort to create a universal religion has turned out merely to have begun another "church." If it survives some generations, later observers see how obviously it reflects the particular time and place of its origins. The universal of one century appears quite particular to another. We human beings have no way of vaulting out of the concreteness and specificity of history into the universal love and openness of the Messianic Age.

Moreover, it is folly to hope that giving up our separate religions will substantially wipe out human hatred. The roots of human viciousness go too deep into our personal dynamics and our social concerns for such quick therapy. To end the pretext of hatred will not affect the repressed hostility behind it; the rage will find another way to make itself felt. It seems far more sensible to place our major energies behind an attack on the personal and social breeding grounds of prejudice. Then perhaps we can successfully utilize religious power to teach that prejudice against others is a sin against God.

One Religion Means No Serious Disagreement

The next two reasons against trying to institute universal religion stem from its negative consequences.

The first of these binds liberal Jews with all who are fearful of the effects of allowing only one religion to be right. In that situation everyone believing something else is in serious error. That can lead to the classic formulation "error has no rights," and then whatever is done to bring the unbelievers to the one truth is justified for it is for their own best good.

The examples of the tyranny that results from having the only correct understanding of religion are numerous. The men of the First Crusade were not following sophisticated church teaching when they massacred Franco-German Jewry. They merely did not see why they should wait to fight God's enemies in a distant land when heretics were living nearby. In Florence, Savonarola terrorized his fellow Catholics, insisting that they do what he knew God demanded of them. They finally rebelled and overthrew him. The similarly repressive rule of Calvin in Geneva remains a major blemish on the record of that Protestant reformer.

In our time effective orthodoxy is more commonly political than religious; its characteristic form is totalitarianism. Most notably in communism, where the secular transformation of the messianic hope is readily apparent, the doctrine of one truth has led to the ruthless suppression of difference and dissent.

Liberalism in religion arose mainly as a protest against institutions which insisted they had the one truth all people ought to follow. By contrast, liberals value pluralism in religious ideas and practices because they look to individual conscience as the sole arbiter of spiritual reality. They remain convinced of the limits of all human thought, so they passionately espouse each individual's right to religious freedom, and hence to religious difference.

The Terrible Toll of a False Messianism

Jewish experience also knows the high spiritual cost of premature messianism. Ever since the savage repression which followed Bar Kochba's messianic rebellion against Rome in 133 c.e., our teachers have condemned "forcing the End." When the exalted hope of a messianic movement collapses, despair sets in and the adherents often cannot resume their proper social responsibilities.

Consider the case of Shabbetai Zevi. Until the Holocaust, no internal event so debilitated the Jewish people as did his career. In 1654 he announced that he was the Messiah and would shortly introduce the historic changes which Jews traditionally awaited. He aroused such excitement in Jewish communities across the world that historians still struggle to explain its roots. Astute entrepeneurs liquidated their businesses and sold their homes in preparation for being taken to the Land of Israel to live in the reestablished Davidic kingdom.

The sultan of Turkey, not interested in sharing his rule, jailed Shabbetai Zevi in 1666 and eventually gave him a choice between conversion to Islam or death. Shabbetai Zevi then became a Moslem. Jews everywhere were stunned. Some were so desperate to preserve their faith in the new Messiah that they followed Shabbetai Zevi into Islam. They hoped that this great sin would precipitate his messianic return. Most Jews suffered a serious loss of faith, even despairing that God would ever save them. Contemporary writers spoke of living in a time of "black despair" and it was as an antidote to this mood that the chasidic movement arose.

A failed utopia engenders such disappointments that we cannot even utilize such power as we ourselves have to make things better. The hope of instituting one religion is very likely to create more harm than good.

Does Not Difference Enrich Existence?

There are two positive reasons for maintaining separate religions until the Messiah comes. One is practical, that such variety is a natural, valuable aspect of human existence. The other is theoretical, that there are major disagreements between religions about the nature of reality and human responsibility.

The practical argument extends the commonplace observation that people seek diversity. I shall never forget the experience I had years back walking through the extensive collection of pottery from the biblical period in the Rockefeller Museum in East Jerusalem. For centuries people made their pots from the same material in about the same way. Quite instinctively they kept altering them. They made them fat then skinny, with handles then without, with decorations then without, colored and not, fluted and plain, incised or bulbous, and on with more variations than I can describe. And these were not art pieces made by ceramists for collectors but pots for everyday use. All this individuality was being made manifest long before self-expression had become a major value.

Religious difference reflects this human proclivity. Most people get special satisfaction from doing things the way they have been done in the community in which they grew up. Sociologists contend that such attachment to community style is demonstrably more persistent than the beliefs which engender it (though the two cannot altogether be sundered, in my opinion).

The contemporary American celebration of Easter is a good example. Many people who are skeptical of the resurrection of Jesus still enjoy maintaining the folkways of the holiday. They want to wear their new spring clothes, have a special dinner, and get together with their family. To give up Easter might make them more like the non-Christians who are the majority of humankind but they know their lives would be the poorer for it.

Most people enjoy their group's special style, its singing, feasting, parading, studying, joking, gossiping, mourning, celebrating, eating, drinking, fasting, and all the other social practices that make it their group. Our ethnicity imparts a special flavor to our otherwise ordinary lives. Americans find such group activities so attractive that they often seek to participate in them. Surely American culture would be less exciting if there were no separate groups among us to charm us with their different foods, festivals, and celebrations. At the same time the power of belonging may be felt in the difference between celebrating St. Patrick's day as an Irishman and as an outsider who joins in the wearing of the green.

Christmas Means Exclusion to Some Jews

An analysis of the Jewish celebration of Christmas is unavoidable in this connection. Nothing so symbolizes the Jewish desire for religions not to separate people as the effort by some Jews to find a way to observe Christmas. They do not believe that the day marks the birth of the Messiah, indeed of humankind's Lord and Savior. Proud Jews though they may claim to be, they still want to have a tree, exchange presents, and celebrate joyously. After all, they argue, is not the message of goodwill universally ethical?

For all its surface plausibility, this stand has little to commend it. Secularizing Christmas is an offense against the Christian faith. A large number of Christians properly resent having a major holiday of their religion subverted by commerce and sentimentality, and, not infrequently, by our contemporary paganism.

Jews who participate in Christmas observances also demonstrate a lack of Jewish self-respect. Any day devoted to the supposed birth of the Messiah necessarily separates Christians from Jews. Not to acknowledge that is to deny our people's faith and history.

That many Jews nonetheless are avid to be part of Christmas testifies to some deep need within them. They are not responding to the intrinsic beauty of the carols or trees, both of which they can easily do without in all months but December. And they do not need Christmas to remind them of the worthwhileness of peace on earth. What they long for is an end to being different. They are tired of being outsiders. They want to be included, even if the expressions of goodwill are superficial and trite. For Jews in a democracy, what our tradition called "the pain of the Exile" takes this form.

Do We still Need to Be Jews?

That is also the hidden agenda behind the idealistic yearning of many Jews for one religion. They want an end of the burdens separateness imposes. If there were only one religion, Jews would no longer be different but would be just like everyone else. In fact, this is a morally acceptable way people can use to call for an end to the Jewish people.

The assimilatory intent buried in this proposal emerges from the plan suggested for its implementation. This almost always assumes that the Jews will give up their practices for those of other groups. Oddly enough we take it for granted that distinctive Jewish observances are unworthy of adoption by the rest of humanity, e.g., a universal Yom Kippur day. An equality that demands sacrifice of your individuality is only subservience. One would think self-esteem meant acknowledging that being a Jew is not the same as being a Christian, a Moslem, or a vaguely undifferentiated American—and then reaching out to one's neighbor in rich human openness. Midnight mass cannot be the same experience for Jews as for believing Christians. Likewise, a moral chasm separates Jews who attend that service as appreciative outsiders from those hoping momentarily to lose the pain of Jewish distinctiveness.

I often get the impression that such self-sacrificing universalists have little experience of Judaism's enriching power. Let me take a difficult example. We lament our lavish Bar/Bat Mitzvahs and weddings, but those who have celebrated them in a Jewish spirit know that they have been touched on many levels. We may eat and drink and dance too much, we may get bored catching up with distant relatives and annoyed by getting involved in old family squabbles and personal rivalries. We may also exercise our traditional Jewish right to complain that the service was too long, the sermon boring, and the rabbi pretentious. We will rate the decor, the dress, and how people look. We may get a little senti-mental about our parents and grandparents, the quick growth of our children, the passing of the years. We may be touched that another generation now does what other Jewish generations did. At some moment or another the whole thing—and our lives—may make sense. All these impressions, positive and negative, say something real of what it is to be a Jew. One who has not felt their impact simply does not know Judaism.

I am not suggesting that only Jews do these things or that we do them utterly differently than anyone else. Being human, we engage in the same sort of social activities all ethnic groups do. We then transform them in terms of our special history—dis-crimination and exclusion, immigration and social climb, Holo-caust, Zionism, and survival worries—and our folk tradition with its affirmation of God and humanity, of individuality and family, of moral courage, personal accomplishment, and undying hope. For all that the resulting American Jewish style cannot be defined or pinpointed; most Jews find it uniquely rich and appealing. It adds so much to our existence—or could, if we would actively participate in it—that it seems particularly insensitive to suggest we would be more fully human by giving it up. Separateness may have its pains but they cannot be adequately evaluated until one has tasted the compensating joys and values unique to the Jewish community.

The Most Evocative Religious Language Is Particular

The theory of symbols is also relevant here. Symbols are not universal. The cross, the crescent, the Torah are the products of groups. To those to whom they are "alive," they say far more than can ever be expressed objectively and they have added to their power by encapsulating centuries of experience. As a result, they are highly resistant to change. Despite all our modern expertise in communication, we have rarely gone beyond projecting an image to creating a deep and lasting symbol.

Religions continue to be separate because people do not want to give up their symbols. They do not believe that someone else's symbol will grant them the insight disclosed by their own. That is not simply a matter of childhood conditioning, of being accus-tomed to a cross, say, rather than a crescent. Symbols carry a considerable substantive as well as intuitive content. In a synagogue, the tablets of the Ten Commandments direct the worshiper to a commanding God who brought a special people out of Egypt, a God who is more concerned with their acts as a whole than with their worship. Perhaps a crucifix incorporates these truths, but the image of Christ dying on the cross immediately suggests devotion as self-sacrifice. A statue of the Buddha, the empty niche in a mosque, the lingam and yoni of Siva and Shakti worship in Hinduism direct the believer to the central truths of their faiths. To surrender them would mean sacrificing the unique vision of the transcendent which they mediate. But that brings me beyond the practical argument to the theological one: the great religions have radically different intuitions of ultimate reality.

Is My One God Your One God?

Liberalism, having taught us humility about our religious wisdom, has made us open to the spiritual truths in faiths other than our own. Often we can find significant guidance in them. With all that, the similarities between religions have often been overstated. It simply is not true that all religions believe in one God. For instance, Theravada Buddhism involves no god at all. Religions which say God is one can mean by that anything from the Trinity of Christianity to the absolute monism of Vedanta Hinduism. We use the same number to describe God but we differ significantly in the substance of what we believe.

A similar diversity is found in the parallel ethical injunctions of the faiths. Put into religious context, the golden rule, for example, helps create a different quality of life for Buddhists than for Christians or Jews. The basic detachment of Buddhists produces a different quality of compassion than that created by the involvement of Judaism and Christianity. The interreligious situation is best described dialectically. The worldwide faiths share many beliefs and are likely to move closer together as our world contracts. But there are limits to their accommodation for they also radically disagree.

At this point, protagonists of Judaism usually demonstrate where it differs from other religions and show why Judaism has the most adequate perspective on reality. I shall not attempt that although I consider such comparative work a useful if challenging task. I do not see that any such argument of mine can be convincing. In a few pages, it cannot be done seriously. More important, it is instantly countered by the skeptical retort, "What else do you expect from a rabbi?" I am, of course, not a disinterested party in such a discussion and therefore subject to the charge that I have manipulated the data so as to make Judaism appear more distinctive and attractive than it is. Most Jewish accounts of other religions unconsciously compare the best in Judaism to the worst in the religion under study, probably in compensation for Christian treatments of Judaism in like fashion. To avoid any such difficulty, I shall analyze the theological differences between several non-Jewish religions.

There Are Incompatible Views of Ultimate Reality

Religions remain separate because they envision the transcendent in fundamentally different ways. Islam teaches that the Almighty created the world and controls it. Its adherents take the world, individual life and human history, quite seriously for it is the arena in which God's purposes are being worked out. Most Moslems have been so respectful of God's sovereignty that they see God's will in everything that happens. Since Allah has so ordained it, they accept whatever occurs as best for them and for humankind. To outsiders, this humble acceptance of the reality and wisdom of the Almighty's rule seems to border on fatalism. To the follower of Mohammed's teaching, it is so fundamental they call their faith Islam, the "reverent acceptance of" or "submission to" God's sovereignty.

Most of the faiths we roughly group together under the title Hinduism hold the opposite to be true. The world and history are not real. How could they be? Everything we see around us is changing. It soon passes away. Some things last a long time, some a very long time indeed, but no thing is permanent. They cannot then be ultimately real. So, too, our individual lives, to which we attach such importance, are ephemeral and cannot have true existence. They are only one phase in a series of migrations to which the soul is committed until it attains salvation from the ceaseless cycle of life. If we could gain true spiritual insight, we could release ourselves from the relentlessly revolving wheel called history and unite ourselves permanently with the Absolute. It is the only reality, beyond all change, all distinctions, all limitation. Beyond space and time and self is the One, Absolute and Infinite, the self-contained Reality-Itself. Nature, life, and history are only an illusion, what some Hindu mythology has called *lila*, "the play of the gods." The first step in spiritual enlightenment is to distance ourselves from ordinary affairs and concentrate on the inner growth which alone might enable us to transcend falsehood. For there is in us a spiritual reality which links us to the Absolute and, if we can give ourselves wholly to it, we may become one with the only One.

If my sense of Hinduism and Islam is reasonably accurate then their world views seem substantially contradictory. None of our usual strategies can reconcile the difference between them. They don't "really" mean the same thing; they can't satisfactorily meet half way between their diverse positions; and adherents of each would deny that the other system contains their teaching. They are divergent intuitions of the nature of reality and the meaning of life. Islam and Hinduism remain separate religions because they teach distinctively different doctrines. All the similarities we can find between Moslem and Hindu ethics and their vision of the oneness of ultimate reality cannot compensate for this fundamental division in their teaching.

There Are Incompatible Views of How to Live

Religions also radically disagree about the essential attitude we ought to manifest in our lives. For Christianity, Jesus' crucifixion sets the ideal of human existence. In the traditional interpretation, Jesus, being God as well as human, could have claimed all earthly glory. Instead, he took our burden of guilt before God on himself, giving himself up to suffering and death to make atonement for us. For Christians, therefore, our suffering should be seen as an exceptional opportunity to serve God. Christ-like, we should accept our personal crucifixions as our special way of dedicating our lives to God. This is particularly true when we sacrifice our happiness or even give our lives for others as Jesus did.

Buddhism has a diametrically opposite view of human suffering. The Buddha considered it the major problem of human existence and his enlightenment came when, after many fruitless efforts, he discovered how to gain release from it. The source of all human grief, he realized, was desire. We yearn for many things: wealth, fame, love, immortality. Other teachers said our unhappiness arises from desiring the wrong things or from having unworthy priorities. The Buddha says our anguish stems from desiring anything at all. The antidote to suffering, then, is detachment from all yearning. Ending desire we overcome disappointment and despair. Should we be able to complete the full spiritual journey charted by the Buddha and his followers, we would reach Nirvana, the ineffable realm in which one is blissfully beyond all reaching and getting, all plans and all goals. Its symbol is the Buddha-statue, with the master seated in a calm, contented manner, radiating serenity.

In Christianity, the greatest man who ever lived found suffering his chief means of serving God and freely underwent extreme pain, humiliation, and death to fulfill his life's mission. Buddhism centers around a man who found suffering the most significant problem of existence and discovered the spiritual truth by which humanity might escape it. These two approaches to life and duty differ radically. I do not see how one can make them both the basis of one's existence. Either one accepts suffering as a fulfillment of one's love of God, or one devotes oneself to gaining a philosophy of life which will enable one never to suffer. On this matter, one must choose between Christianity and Buddhism. They continue to be separate religions because there are such basic doctrinal differences between faiths.

Some Intimations of Judaism's Special Character

Perhaps now I may be permitted a few words about Judaism's unique way of understanding and relating to ultimate reality. Unlike the Asian faiths, Jewish belief is centered on a God who is concerned about people and their everyday conduct. Its daughter faiths, Christianity and Islam, share this distinctive ethical monotheism. Yet Judaism is more monotheistic than Christianity and more activist than either of its offspring, since it emphasizes serving God through many specific acts.

That is about as much as can usefully be said here. Beyond that come a host of academic problems concerning method, content, and adequately qualified statement. Because of these, there is a serious disagreement among Jewish thinkers as to how this work of comparison may best be done. This has given us a number of views of what constitutes the uniqueness of our religion. Let us glance quickly at the opinions of the philosophers we have met frequently before.

Hermann Cohen said Judaism was the first religion to intuit a rational God-idea and to make it the continuing basis of a people's life and history. Leo Baeck agreed, adding that this was a self-conscious matter which no other ethnic group felt nearly so keenly, thus making us a "chosen" people. Mordecai Kaplan dissented sharply from these views. He argued that true ideas are necessarily universal and not the special possession of any single group. Rather, he insisted, the Jews are different in the same natural social fashion that all ethnic groups are, by having their own distinctive culture, through which they express their universal beliefs. Martin Buber argued that the Jewish people's relationship with God is unique in the history of human religion. No other ethnic group transformed its entire folk existence in terms of a direct and non-mediated involvement with God as did the people of Israel in its experience of the Covenant. Abraham Heschel contended, rather traditionally, that God gave the full Torah, the Oral as well as the Written Law, to the Jews alone, thus setting us apart from all other nations and faiths. The philosophies of Judaism developing today will each produce its own answer to this question of Jewish distinctiveness.

Must We Get This Deeply Involved?

At this point in the discussion, a cry sometimes goes up. "Do we need to take religion this seriously? If we could only get down to the basics, one God and ethics, we could retain what everyone believes and do away with the religious divisions which spawn such hatred." I understand the anguish behind this statement and agree with its goals but not its view of religion. A faith which does not engage us in our uttermost depth is unworthy of us. Triumph and tragedy, goodness and guilt, hope and despair, that is, life, should not be met with superficial wisdom. To make the least common denominator of universal belief the standard of our existence is to take our lives too lightly. To refuse to specify what we mean by God or ethics for fear of arousing controversy buys us a dubious peace at the price of denying our minds and our special spiritual vision. Many Jews who say, "One religion for all humanity," effectively mean "little or no religion for anybody." Under the guise of a noble universalism, secularization, self-hate, or a passion to outwit anti-semitism often manifests itself.

Believing Jews want human community without the sacrifice of group identity. We reach out to all people of goodwill to demonstrate the oneness of humankind despite the diversity of temperament and culture we naturally manifest. If we are not for ourselves or if we are only for ourselves, we are nothing. Being true to ourselves and open to others is not always easy but it reflects the dialectical relationship between the particular and the universal which is at the heart of Jewish belief.

PART
·III·

THE BIBLE
AND TRADITION

Part Three: The Bible and Tradition

·1·

DID GOD GIVE THE BIBLE?

A different understanding of Torah, rather than of God or the people of Israel, critically divides liberal from traditional Jews. The authors of the Bible—and those of the prayer book echoing them—say God gave the Torah to the Jews; liberal Jews take such statements symbolically. The issue goes beyond the first five books of the Bible, the Torah proper, though that alone would be no small matter. Traditional Judaism claimed God's authority stood behind the words of all the rest of the Bible and of the Oral Torah, the rabbinic law, which was presumably also revealed to Moses on Mt. Sinai.

Jewish liberalism is characterized by a radical break with a doctrine that had been the foundation of Judaism for about two thousand years. Jewish Orthodoxy, that is, the formal statement of a position of correct Jewish belief, arose in the nineteenth century in response to this revolutionary liberal position.

To appreciate why liberal Jews took so daring a stand, let us first seek to understand the traditional view of Torah.

God's Book in God's Own Words

The Torah text says repeatedly that it is God's words which God "personally" gave Moses to transmit to the children of Israel. "When God had finished speaking with Moses on Mt. Sinai, God gave Moses the two tablets of the testimony, tablets of stone, written with the finger of God." (Exod. 31:18) Later, it adds, "The tablets were the work of God and the writing was the writing of God, engraved on the tablets." (Exod. 32:16)

241

As important as these ten laws are, they are but a tiny part of all that God revealed to Moses at Sinai or during the forty subsequent years of wilderness wandering. Moses received laws and guidance for the wilderness trek, others that applied after they entered the Land, and a correct account of history from creation until Moses' death. Moses wrote all this down under God's guidance. "When Moses completely finished writing the words of this Torah in a book," he told the Levites to put it into the Ark of the Covenant. (Deut. 31:24–26) Rabbi J. David Bleich, a contemporary Orthodox authority, has said, "The text of the Bible as we have it today—that of the Torah Scroll which is read in the synagogue—is identical in every significant detail with the original Scroll of the Torah written by Moses in the wilderness." Thus today, after the scroll is read, the open book is held up before the congregation which chants, "This is the Torah which Moses set before the children of Israel, [written] at God's dictation by the hand of Moses."

The accuracy of the Torah text is of special concern to Jewish tradition because the Torah specifies the fundamental laws of Judaism. A slightly lesser aura of sacred authority surrounds the rest of the books of the Bible. David, Amos, Nehemiah, and other authors do not claim as intimate a relationship with God as Moses had. "Never again did there arise in Israel a prophet like Moses whom *Adonai* knew face to face. . . ." (Deut. 34:10) Nonetheless, every sentence in the Bible comes with God's own authority behind it.

Though the Torah does not say so, the earliest rabbinic traditions assume that, in addition to the Written Torah, the *Torah Shebichetav,* God gave Moses an Oral Torah, the *Torah Shebeal Peh.* They are fully complementary, the one as text, the other as its interpretation and supplement. The Oral Torah not only has an independent content, e.g., that Jews should kindle lights and make *kiddush* as *Shabbat* arrives, it imparts a method for amplifying Torah law and extending it to new situations. Thus all the laws requiring Jews to separate meat and dairy foods derived from the injunction not to boil a baby goat in its mother's milk. (It is given in three places: Exod. 23:19; 34:26; and Deut. 14:21.) Thus, too, in most recent times, the ordinance forbidding throwing an electric switch on *Shabbat* is an extension of one of the thirty-nine categories of work the rabbis specified are not permitted then.

All through Jewish history, when an acknowledged authority renders a formal Jewish legal decision, his ruling is, so to speak, the latest development of the dynamic Torah God revealed at Sinai. Over the ages, Jews stubbornly resisted "the ways of the nations" and refused to yield to their persecutors because of this faith: God had mandated every detail of Jewish observance. Believing Orthodox Jews today continue this ancient Jewish trust. Some extend it even further. Rabbi Moshe Feinstein, chairman of the Council of Torah Sages of Agudath Israel and a leading halachic authority for Ashkenazic Jewry, has asserted: "The Torah leadership of every generation, then, always possesses the ability to perceive the needs of the time and to initiate individual acts or even sweeping ordinances to meet these needs. And these ordinances bear the full weight of an actual *halachah*. . . . One might well say that ignoring the advice of a *talmid chacham* [sage] is far worse than transgressing a *lav* [a negative commandment] clearly expressed in the Torah. . . . When one does not heed the advice of a *talmid chacham,* he denies the superior wisdom of the Torah personality."

Are There Not Reasons for the Commandments?

With God as the giver of its law, Judaism had little need of reasons as to why Jews should follow it. Long before the Emancipation, some Jews did ask why they were required to obey laws whose provisions seemed arbitrary, *chukkim,* as rabbinic literature terms them. "There are laws which the Evil Urge and the idolatrous nations complain about, to wit, not eating pigs, not wearing garments of mixed fibers, the release of the childless brother's wife, the purification of lepers, and the scapegoat ritual. Therefore the Torah says here (Lev. 18:4), 'I am *Adonai,*' [teaching] 'I have made these ordinances [*chakakti,* literally, issued *chukkim*] and you are not allowed to complain about them'." (Sifra 86a) Though neither the Bible nor the rabbis rigorously refuse to give reasons for following a law, they generally do not do so. On the whole, the rabbis discourage our inquiring why we are asked to do just this or that. (Pes. 118b) It is enough to know God has commanded us to do so.

The medieval Jewish philosophers, because of their high concern for rationality, did seek to give reasons for various laws. Maimonides, the most determined of the Jewish rationalists, argues that there is always a logical explanation though we may not be wise enough to discern it. Yet even he, in his great legal code, placed the ultimate emphasis upon obedience. "It is right that a man study the laws of the holy Torah and seek to understand their full meaning to the extent that he is able. Nevertheless, a law for which he finds no reason or sees no cause should not be trivial in his eyes. Let him not 'break out, rebelling against *Adonai,* lest *Adonai* break out upon him.' [Paraphrasing Exod. 19:21–22] Let him also not think about the Torah as he would think about secular and everyday matters. . . . [If the sin of expropriating even trivial things designated for Temple use is heinous] how much more should a man be on guard not to rebel against a command decreed for us by the Almighty, only because he does not understand the reason. He should also not ascribe incorrect things to God or regard the commandments as ordinary matters." (Mishneh Torah, Hil. Meilah 8:8)

This view has been repeated in modern times. Rabbi Samson Raphael Hirsch (1808–1888) was the first great German language proponent of Jewish Orthodoxy. In his commentary to Psalm 119, Hirsch utilizes verse 66 to argue that only one who accepts the authority of the commandments may validly inquire as to their reasons. The usual procedure, he contends, proceeds in the opposite direction and creates a false impression. After one has, in fact, rejected the law's commanding quality one claims that because there is no rational reason for Jewish practice one has become nonobservant. Hirsch approves of only one motive for asking for a rationale for the laws: to understand God's will better.

The Need for Change and Rise of Liberalism

In Hirsch's case for the Torah's authority we can already see the special problem raised by the Emancipation. If God gave the Torah then the rabbis could rule against adaption to the new freedom with God's own authority. But the liberals insisted change was necessary for Jewish survival. This was one of the two major lines of reasoning which combined to convince most Jews to deny their inherited doctrine of Torah. They had a deep intuition, first, that innovations prohibited by their rabbis were necessary for Judaism to remain meaningful. And they found, second, what seemed to them a better way of thinking about the Bible than that of the Jewish tradition. Let us consider each of these developments in some detail.

Whether traditional Judaism was inherently incapable of as radical a self-transformation as the Emancipation required or whether the early nineteenth-century rabbinate lacked vision is a moot question. In America we are accustomed to a large Orthodoxy which accepts the onetime liberal "heresy" that Judaism can accommodate to modernity, in dress, language, education, and style, as long as it remains faithful to the law. But a smaller group of Orthodox Jews retain the old hostility to liberal accommodationism and are profoundly suspicious of modernization. In various degrees, they reject not only the university and careerism but the demeanor, bearing, and tone associated with modernity. They identify Judaism with one or another of its self-isolated European patterns which they seek to re–create here. For them, modernization necessarily leads to assimilation, so they fight it.

This anxiety as to the fate of Judaism, should change be allowed, dominated the consciousness of the early nineteenth-century European rabbis, accustomed as they were to Jewish separatism. The modernizers heard them saying that Jews would now have to choose between the old, proven Judaism and the opportunities of the threatening if beckoning world. The "logic" of this choice, which led to the rise of liberal Judaism, may become clearer when we consider what happened to an early effort at Jewish modernization.

During the years 1780–83, Moses Mendelssohn and some associates published a translation of the Torah into cultured German. Two purposes animated this endeavor. First, Mendelssohn sought to provide young Jews who no longer knew Hebrew well with a responsible Jewish translation of their basic book. Second, Mendelssohn wanted to acquaint them with the enlightened level of language becoming standard around them. An unexpected aspect of the publication provides further insight into the isolation of the community: the German translation, printed alongside the Hebrew text, was in Hebrew characters.

The Mendelssohn translation was repeatedly attacked by leading rabbinic figures, notably Ezekiel Landau of Prague and Phinehas Horowitz of Frankfort. Bans were pronounced on all who utilized the translation. The attacks would probably have been

worse had Mendelssohn not arranged to have various rulers sub-
scribe to the book.

No attack was made on Mendelssohn personally. He was not
only fully observant but was widely recognized in the Jewish
community as an authoritative interpreter of Judaism. Moreover,
no Jewish law prohibits translating the Torah. Most of its opponents objected to the translation because it taught Jews proper
German and thereby facilitated their entry into general culture.

From this and similar examples, it becomes clear that to many
Jews of the first half of the nineteenth century it was unthinkable
that one could be fully modern and traditionally Jewish. As a
consequence many emancipated Jews converted to Christianity.
Heinrich Heine's case is typical. He admitted that he did not
believe in Christianity but without joining the church he did not
see how he could participate fully in the benefits of Western
society.

The Intuition of Development in Search of a Theory

The liberal approach to Judaism was born out of an instinctive
rejection of both horns of this tragic dilemma. Daringly, some
Jews insisted that Judaism did not have to remain premodern and
that Christianity was not the only way of entering the social future. They proclaimed it possible to be Jewish and modern—
though how this would work in practice they could learn only by
experiment. On a theoretical level, Moses Mendelssohn once
again pioneered their path, in this instance by a significant failure.

Appreciating Mendelssohn's immense cultural achievement is
difficult today. We take Jewish social expertise for granted and are
surprised should any incident break the acceptance to which we
are accustomed. Though Moses Mendelssohn became one of the
most famous figures in European intellectual life, he, like all Jews,
had to apply to the police annually for a renewal of his permit to
reside in Berlin. This went on for nearly two decades before the
king of Prussia granted him residence rights. So, too, despite his
winning first prize in a philosophical competition of the Prussian
Royal Academy of Sciences—Immanuel Kant was runner-up—
and later being elected a member of that body, the king refused
to ratify his appointment. Most people had never imagined Jews
were capable of such feats of intellect. This short, ungainly genius

proved them wrong and by his accomplishments made a powerful case for the emancipation of his people.

Mendelssohn became recognized as one of the great philosophical minds of the late eighteenth century. His book on the immortality of the soul, *Phaedon,* caused such excitement that it was translated into all the major European languages. Even more remarkable for a self-taught business man brought up in the segregated Jewish community of Dessau, he became a recognized authority on German language and literature, and thus a major arbiter of what was culturally acceptable.

Mendelssohn's Philosophy of a Modern Judaism

Mendelssohn was clearly a modern man years before emancipation began to affect large numbers of Jews. Unlike those few others of his people who had made their way into general society, he remained a devoted Jew. Though he eschewed religious polemics, a Christian challenge forced him to explain publicly how someone as enlightened as he was could still remain a pious Jew.

Mendelssohn based his theory of the compatibility of Judaism and modernity on the fundamental distinction he contends Judaism makes between intellectual truths and religious duties. With an unstated polemical thrust at Christianity, he points out that Judaism has no dogmas, that is, no formally required beliefs. Rather, he declares, Jews are free to reach whatever religious truth their minds and consciences commend to them. He could say this with considerable confidence for in the culture of the Enlightenment mature rationality led to the conviction that there is one God, freedom of the will, commanding ethics, and immortality of the soul. Judaism, Mendelssohn argued, had always encouraged an impartial search for the truth. Modernity could enter Judaism through its openness to ideas—which for Mendelssohn necessarily included a corollary hospitality to contemporary esthetic expression.

Though ideas and cultural forms might change in Judaism, he opined, its laws could not, except as they themselves provided. Its intellectual life was determined by the free human spirit seeking truth. Its practices were ordinances of God imposed upon the Jews by God's unprecedented revelation at Sinai. One remained

Jewish by virtue of observing this eternal law as continually reinterpreted by the legal masters of every generation. In our terminology, Mendelssohn was liberal in his philosophy except for his theory of revelation; yet he was Orthodox in practice.

The Unhappy Consequences of Mendelssohn's Ideas

Mendelssohn's merger of modernity and Judaism came with a heavy price. So to speak, his theory split the Jewish mind into two utterly separate areas. On one side of the wall, the Jew was free to learn from science, culture, and metaphysics. Of course, any rational person could do this, for it concerned the realm of universal truth. On the other side of the wall, the specifically Jewish one, everything centered about God's unique act, the giving of the Torah. What distinguished Judaism from universal human activity was law, and Judaism was a religion of law-followers.

In later years, this theory of Mendelssohn was used against Judaism by Christians arguing for the supremacy of their faith. For us a more important issue is the failure of Mendelssohn's theory to find many adherents among Jews who were modernizing. Simply put, they rejected the notion that they should live by two standards, one valid for all humankind, the other true only in the case of Judaism. They were not leaving the ghetto to take up a schizoid existence. They balked too at the odd barrier Mendelssohn put into the inquiring mind. The truths of reason applied to all humankind, except for the revelation at Mt. Sinai. If the modern intellect could satisfactorily deal with all other questions, why could it not also help us understand the central claim of Judaism?

This rejection of Mendelssohn's ideas helped the liberals unconsciously set a goal for their philosophy. They were seeking an *integrated* view of their humanity and their Jewishness. What applied to the one must apply to the other, at least in a general way.

The first phase in the development of their new theory of Judaism was a negative one. They abandoned the literalistic notion of God giving the Torah and stressed instead the human role in its creation. (In the next chapter we shall consider the second stage, the liberals' positive theories of phrases like God "giving" the Torah or "speaking" to people.)

The Bible as a Human Document

The early Jewish liberals did not begin by proclaiming a new theory of authority. They were interested in action and carried on experiments in Jewish modernity. Politically, we may say, they democratized Jewish power by letting anyone try things. Theologically, they were asserting that God "spoke" to Jews in every age. Practically, their activism reflected the explosive growth in human self-confidence that occurred in the nineteenth century. Slowly, at first, but then with little hesitation, instead of speaking about what God "gave," they referred to what people discovered.

Nothing justified their new way of looking at Judaism so well as the success of their humanism in resolving their problems with the Bible.

Already in the seventeenth and eighteenth centuries, the rise of rationalism had engendered a critical approach to the Bible. Scholars began studying it not in terms of its own claims of God's authorship but as if it were another human document. Spinoza, one of the earliest modernizing Jews, wrote in 1670 that he sought to read the Scriptures "in a spirit of entire freedom and without prejudice." The early Bible critics did not deny God's authorship but they pointed out and sought to explain a number of peculiar characteristics of the Torah narratives.

One of the most puzzling of these was why God should want to relate stories twice or in two closely related forms. The creation is described as a sequence of grand daily events in Genesis 1:1–2:4. It is then described again, this time in rather more earthy fashion. The story of Abraham telling the king of Gerar that Sarah was his sister (Gen. 20:1–18) is told more concisely about Isaac and his wife Rebekah (Gen. 26:1–11). In the account of the flood, Noah is called upon in Genesis 7:1–5 to bring into the ark seven pairs of ritually clean animals and one pair of unclean animals. In Genesis 7:6–9, he apparently only had to bring in one pair of animals, clean or unclean, and this seems part of another history of the flood.

A closely related issue is the occurrence of contradictions in the texts. The wives of Esau are not the same in name and lineage in Genesis 26:34, 28:9, and 36:2–3. According to Numbers 18:18 first-born cattle belong to the priests but Deuteronomy 15:20 says all Israelites may eat them in the place *Adonai* will choose.

Deuteronomy 24:16 forbids fathers or children being executed for the other's crimes but Exodus 34:7 presupposes that vicarious punishment is just. Most astonishingly, though they are each supposed to be the exact words God "personally" spoke to all the people at Sinai, the fourth, fifth, and tenth commandments of the Decalogue vary from Exodus 20:9–12 to Deuteronomy 5:12–16.

Duplications seem strange in a book written by God. The rabbis had not overlooked these problems and the others that we shall raise. But accepting in advance that it was God's writing, they drew a logical conclusion: God must want to teach us something special by this seemingly unnecessary material. And they then used their spiritual ingenuity to draw lessons from these texts.

The Deeper Challenges of Content and Context

More troubling to the moderns, as they began to doubt God's "personal" responsibility for the Bible, were some of its descriptions of God. It is unethical of God to harden pharaoh's heart, and its stated purpose, that God might gain greater glory, is utterly unworthy of "The Holy One of Israel." (Exod. 7:1–5 and elsewhere) In the self-reference made in the Ten Commandments God uses the term *"El Kana."* The second word, the modifier, normally means "jealous." The elaboration here that God will punish the second, third, and fourth generations of those people who reject God bears this notion out. (Exod. 20:5) This note of vindictiveness is manifest in another account of God's self-disclosure when God "passes by" Moses proclaiming the divine names. (Exod. 34:7) A somewhat similar mood is repeatedly mentioned when the people of Israel sins. Then God is depicted as having a blazing anger, one which can barely be restrained by Moses' intense pleas and which, should it burst forth, will be destructive without measure. (Exod. 32:9–14 and elsewhere) These notions would be immoral in a human being, perhaps merely a sign of utter immaturity. They seriously compromise God's right to be worshiped and contradict all the rest the Bible writers teach us about their unique God.

The matter is further exacerbated by commands which seem contrary to what God otherwise demands we value. The classic personal example is the demand to Abraham to sacrifice his son

Isaac. (Gen. 22:2) If, as modern apologists say, the purpose of the story is moral, to abolish child sacrifice in Judaism, a good God should not use such an immoral means to that end. Similarly, if as the text indicates, this is a test of Abraham's faith, it is a profoundly revolting one.

The outstanding example of a corporate command which seems inconsistent with what else we are told about God is the one directed at the seven Canaanite nations. The invading Israelites are told to exterminate them without pity. (Deut. 7:1–2) Even though their idolatry poses a fundamental threat to the Jews' Covenant with God, the command to "show them no mercy" converts prudence to ruthlessness and thus demeans God.

An external challenge to the divine revelation of the Bible came from archeology. All through the nineteenth century archeologists uncovered Near Eastern documents and artifacts bearing on the Bible. Believers were astounded that some of the writings closely paralleled the biblical texts. Were that not troubling enough, these semitic materials predated the Bible and hence seemed closer to their even prior common source. The much-vaunted uniqueness of the Bible seemed unsustainable after learning, for example, that our Noah story was but one version, though an uncommonly moral one, of a whole family of Near Eastern flood narratives. Even though much of the archeological evidence has confirmed the accuracy of the Bible, this has not refuted the liberal rejection of the traditional doctrine of its origin. It only confirmed the virtue of locating the biblical writings within their social milieu. (We shall shortly take up the conflicts of the Bible with archeological finds in chapter 3. We shall also consider the issue of miracles there. Both matters also made God's personal authorship of the Bible untenable to the liberals.)

Explaining the Anomalies in the Text Proper

Once the critical method began to take hold the textual peculiarities of the Torah manuscripts provided additional reason for thinking the Bible was written by people. Thus before and after Numbers 10:35–36 we always find the letter *nun* written upside down. Seven further examples of the inverted *nun* are to be found in Psalm 107 but nowhere else. At the very least, these inexplicable signs appear odd in God's own sacred texts. Something of the same feeling strikes one who discovers that the *nun* in Menasheh of Judges 18:30 is always suspended over the letters. One might critically explain this as an editorial insertion to protect the good name of Moses *(Mosheh)*. It would suggest that the man leading Danite idol worship was not Moses' grandson. That will not explain the suspension of the letter *ayin* in Psalm 80:14 and Job 38:13 and 15. To this list of oddities in the text we may add the many letters which must be written in a somewhat contorted way or those which have a series of dots over them.

A more esoteric arrangement is the tradition of writing the text one way but always reading it differently. In some instances this is simply scribal shorthand, as when the last syllable of Jerusalem is not fully written out though always properly pronounced. The most famous case, the name of God, is a matter of piety. But there are a number of places, e.g., Ruth 3:5 and 17, where the arrangement makes up for what in another document we would call a faulty text. These scribal matters are called "lower criticism" whereas the question of the human sources of the various books is called "higher criticism." Both sorts of study, I am arguing, contributed to the revolutionary idea that the Bible is as much, if not more, a human document as it is one of God's revelation.

An Alternative Explanation of the Torah's Source

The humanistic view seemed incontrovertible when late in the nineteenth century scholars reached a consensus as to the probable origins of the Torah books. Adapted from Julius Wellhausen's formulation, the Documentary Hypothesis recognized four basic layers to the Torah. The earliest, called J after its use of the tetragrammaton for God, was set down in the tenth-ninth century B.C.E. An E document, eighth-seventh century B.C.E., so termed because of its preference for the word *Elohim* for God, appeared one hundred years later. By mid-seventh century B.C.E. these had been edited into a single document. This was supplemented late in the seventh century B.C.E. with the D strand, substantially the Book of Deuteronomy, but not limited to it. A priestly set of traditions, P, was set down in the sixth-fifth century B.C.E. Finally about the year 400 B.C.E., the Torah as we know it was complete.

The Documentary Hypothesis seemed irresistible. It clarified why we might have two versions of a given story or conflicting commands. It made it seem perfectly natural that there were vocabulary preferences in certain narratives and that various texts would have a somewhat different religious point of view. And in a stroke it explained the textual anomalies as human error, accident, or innovation. To think of the Torah text developing over centuries seemed far more simple than the rabbinic reasons why God had revealed the ultimate truth of the universe with so many surprising peculiarities. Moreover, the Documentary Hypothesis explained the Torah in the same way moderns dealt with all other texts. It fit in with all the rest of the expanding knowledge emancipated Jews were acquiring and so made their religion true in the sense all other things were true.

For most of the twentieth century, the academic acceptance of the Documentary Hypothesis seemed to prove the necessity of a liberal interpretation of Judaism. Time has eroded much of its certainty. Today scholarly critics point to its internal inconsistencies, its erroneous historical assumptions, and the archeological data which upsets some of its older conclusions. Yet contemporary Bible students have found no theory which better integrates all the data; they still rely upon it but with considerable caution.

This change of scholarly tone has not decreased the liberals' commitment to the human origins of the Bible. Although a specific theory is no longer certain, the approach which undergirded it remains very much the same. Thus, Form Criticism looks at the Bible in terms of the literary patterns common to the ancient Near East: treaties, unqualified and qualified laws, proverbs, ritual formulae, songs, and the like. All assume that we shall understand the Hebrew Bible better if we see its basic units in terms of their life-setting, perhaps by analogy to other Semitic cultures.

Restating the Fundamental Issue

In sum, liberals argue for their humanistic, developmental concept of the Bible because of its simplicity and integrity. It clarifies all the problems in a way that seems natural and that is no different from our way of understanding other things. When God is asserted to be the author of the Bible, its anomalies are disturbing. The pious reader therefore requires explanations to make them say something other than what they appear to say. This has elicited a great deal of ingenious interpretation over the centuries, but the very elaborateness of the defense proves to liberals how faulty the premise of God's authorship is. By contrast, if people are primarily responsible for our texts, most of the previous problems no longer trouble us. We would expect as much of books created by authors over a one-thousand-year period and transmitted for years orally before being committed to writing.

Equally important, Jews could now describe their religious history in much the same terms one would use to describe any other human history. Unlike Mendelssohn's theory of modern Judaism, no dogmatic claim now needs to be made for the uniqueness of Jewish experience. It reflects only the individuality common to any people in history. The same knowledge of human psychology, of social development, of the interplay of economic, political, and other historic forces which we apply to other peoples and religions we equally apply to ourselves. So, too, whatever we learn about humankind may help us better understand ourselves as Jews. By accepting the concept of the human authorship of the Bible, liberal Jews had integrated their religion into their new intellectual world view.

The practical point of this theoretical discussion must not be forgotten. If the basic documents of the Jewish faith are essentially human, then so is the authority behind Jewish law. Now God cannot be claimed as the final arbiter of what must remain fixed in Jewish observance and what can be altered. In the new view that becomes a matter of our human decision today, in response to God, to be sure, but one in which our minds and hearts will have priority over ancient precedents. When the early liberals intuitively rebelled against the traditionalists' rejection of modernity, they were simply reasserting the age-old Jewish religious quest. They were seeking to serve God as Jews under the conditions of emancipation, even as previous generations had done so in the Land of Israel or in the ghetto. The Jews of those times had adapted their religious insights to their social situation. Modern Jews were merely doing the same. In asserting the humanity of the Bible, they were also putting forth a claim for the Jewish authenticity of their own modernization of Judaism.

With all these extraordinary gains, the liberals incurred one great loss. They could no longer say God wanted Jews to follow Jewish law in all its details. If the sacred texts were always human, a distance had opened up between God and any specific verbal formulation of God's will. Its virtue was that it allowed for human creativity in the face of changing circumstances. But it also raised the issue of the lasting significance and authority of the Bible in liberal Judaism—and, of course, the practices derived from it. To see how liberal Jews responded to this challenge we must now probe deeper. We must analyze the second of their arguments for their right to introduce change in Judaism, their theories of how God still played a central role in their faith. For the liberals also had to explain what it meant to them when they read each week in the Torah the critical words, "And *Adonai* spoke to Moses saying. . . ."

·2·

HOW DOES GOD
SPEAK TO PEOPLE ?

W hen the Torah scroll is read in the synagogue,
again and again we hear, "And *Adonai* spoke to
Moses, saying. . . ." In many places in the Bible God appears and
talks to people; the prophets specifically credit their speeches to
God.

The claim that God communicates this directly with people is
most uncommon in the great world faiths. In much of Hinduism
and Buddhism, the Ultimate is not conceived in terms which
would allow for what theologians term "revelation." So, too, the
Chinese traditions of Confucius and Lao-tse are too humanistic
for such a notion. Even Christianity, which relies on Hebrew
Scriptures for much of its self-understanding, makes no claim in
the Gospels or Epistles that God revealed them. Only Islam proclaims itself to be founded on God's verbal revelation, in its case,
to Mohammed, "the last of the prophets." Our question, then, of
what we might mean by asserting God once spoke or still speaks
to people, touches on a distinctive characteristic of Judaism.

When our religion must fit in with all else we know, we are
nonplussed by the notion of revelation. Nothing of that sort has
ever happened to us or any responsible individual we know. The
people who have declared God spoke to them have had a message
so self-serving, bizarre, or inane that it was self-discrediting.
Many, we must judge, have been emotionally deluded.

How can one make sense out of God speaking? The language
implies that God has a vocal apparatus with which to generate
sounds. Such gross anthropomorphism is doubly offensive for its

256

sexist overtones, God's voice is "naturally" a rich baritone—a soprano is unthinkable! And there are people who imagine that God only communicates in Hebrew.

To refute this skepticism by pointing out that we are not prophets violates our liberal commitment to one standard of truth and a common human experience in history. To claim that one person, or group, has been granted privileged access to God takes us into the realm of dogma where submission is the most appropriate attitude.

The critical issue, of course, is not anthropomorphic usage but religious authority. With "God spoke" as its central premise, Orthodoxy can claim God's own power for its dicta. The rigorous humanistic position argues that all religious commands and teachings were the creations of people. They therefore confront us with nothing more than the genius or fallibility of their human author. Since some people have exceptional spiritual capacity, their teachings can be our best religious guide. For much of the past century and a half, many moderns lived by some such faith.

Most liberal Jews find themselves midway between Orthodoxy and humanism. They do not believe God gave people verbal instructions as the Orthodox do, but they are also not as skeptically unknowing as the humanists. For them, the words, "God said," do reveal more about human religious perception than about God's utterances. But these human texts are also responses to the Sacred Other, in whatever modern sense we understand God. Some liberals interpret revelation almost exclusively in terms of human religious intuition; they feel on sure ground only when speaking of themselves and their own kind. Others prefer to emphasize God's role, for all the difficulties involved in discussing it. They believe religion's distinctive value lies in helping us transcend our humanity but by helping us make contact with the Sacred.

I intend to introduce you to five different contemporary Jewish interpretations of revelation. We will, I think, appreciate the liberal thinkers' accomplishments more deeply if we understand the traditional doctrine they inherited.

In the Bible, God Speaks in Many Ways

Scholars estimate that the various books of the Bible were written in a process that went on for over a thousand years. In all that lengthy record of Jewish faith and anguish we do not find one explicit inquiry about *how* God spoke to people. To the ancient Hebrews revelation may have been special but it was not unnatural, for religion was an organic part of life and God seemed close. We do not then find in the Bible any significant discussion of the process by which God communicates.

Scripture does mention many ways in which *Adonai* makes contact with people. The most astonishing of these is God's "personal" speaking of Ten Utterances to the people of Israel encamped at the foot of Mt. Sinai. The setting was awesome, "Mt. Sinai was all in smoke for *Adonai* had come down upon it in fire. Smoke rose like the smoke of a kiln and the whole mountain trembled violently. The blare of the horn grew louder and louder. As Moses spoke, God answered him in thunder." (Exod. 19:18–19)

Psalm 29 likewise describes the greatness of God's voice. "The voice of *Adonai* shatters cedars. . . . It makes Mt. Lebanon skip like a calf. . . . The voice of *Adonai* kindles flames of fires. The voice of *Adonai* convulses the wilderness." (Ps. 29:5–8) Moderns read these texts, so to speak, in reverse. That is to say, people, feeling the power of natural phenomena, get a hint of God's overwhelming might and, thus, of what it would be like for God to speak. But for the most part, the Bible authors write of God speaking to individuals in apparently more modulated fashion.

The most common direct case of God's revelation is the communication of a message to a prophet. The prophet's role is aptly described in this passage about Moses and Aaron: "You [Moses] shall speak to him and put the words in his mouth . . . and he shall speak for you to the people. Thus he will serve you as a mouth and you will serve him, as it were, as a god." (Exod. 4:15–16) A true prophet does not originate his message in any way. He only transmits what God has told him.

Varieties of Indirect Communication

Sometime the disclosure by God comes by way of a vision. Jeremiah sees a boiling pot and "the word of *Adonai*" comes to him with a message of judgment for the people. Occasionally, God shows the prophet something, as when Amos is variously confronted with locusts, a plumbline, and a basket of summer fruit, leading to a message from God. (7:1–7; 8:1) The gentile prophet Balaam describes his experience this way:

> The word of Balaam son of Beor,
> the word of a man whose eye is opened.
> The word of him who hears God's speech.
> who sees visions from the Almighty,
> prostrate, but with eyes unveiled. (Num. 24:3–4)

In Zechariah the visions are more dreamlike, with flying scrolls or chariots with red horses. (5:1; 6:2) The most extraordinary visions come to Daniel who sees bizarre beasts and dreamlike events. (7:1–28)

The Torah proclaims Moses the greatest of all the prophets, explaining that his contact with God was uniquely direct and unmediated. "If there be a prophet among you, I, *Adonai,* make myself known to him in a vision or speak with him in a dream. Not so with Moses, My servant. He is trusted throughout My household. With him I speak mouth to mouth, plainly and not in riddles. He beholds *Adonai*'s likeness." (Num. 12:6–8)

Sometimes God speaks through what appear to be ordinary people, as was the case with Abraham's three visitors. (Gen. 18:2 and following) Samson's mother calls her visitor a "man of God" who looked like "an awesome angel of God." (Judg. 13:6) But we are not quite certain how to translate the last term, for the word rendered "angel" is the ordinary Hebrew term for a messenger. So to speak, God can also communicate by messenger.

One last reference to God's speaking cannot be omitted, it is so evocative though cryptic. Elijah challenged the prophets of Baal to a public contest of religious truth and proved them false. Threatened with death if Queen Jezebel's agents can find him, he flees to the Judean wilderness and asks God to take his life. After a miraculous meal, he goes forty days and nights to a cave at "the mountain of God at Horeb" where he spends the night. The next day God asks why he has come and Elijah pours out a bitter complaint. He alone is left of all God's prophets and now they seek his life. " 'Come out,' God called, 'and stand on the mountain before *Adonai.*' And lo, *Adonai* passed by. There was a great and mighty wind, splitting mountains and shattering rocks by *Adonai*'s power. But *Adonai* was not in the wind. After the wind, an earthquake. But *Adonai* was not in the earthquake. After the earthquake, fire. But *Adonai* was not in the fire. And after the fire, *kol demamah dakah.*" The old Jewish translation rendered it as "a still small voice." The new version is "a soft murmuring sound." I prefer Martin Buber's more literal reading, "the voice of a fine silence." (1 Kings 19:1 and following) And that is all the response Elijah gets, except for a command to go back and proceed with God's work. Despite Psalm 29, God also speaks with *kol demamah dakah.*

The Concept of Seizure by God's Spirit

The authors of some biblical books, like King David, to whom many psalms are ascribed, and King Solomon, the author of the Song of Songs, do not say their books were composed because God spoke to them. Yet obviously they are part of *Kitvei Kodesh*, Sacred Scriptures, because they were, in some sense, revealed by God.

The rabbis, who made the decision as to which books were to be included in the third section of the Bible, the Writings, had a simple standard for their decision. Was the book written by the *ruach hakodesh*, the holy spirit, or not? Unfortunately they do not explain in any detail what they meant by this or how they applied it. (They accepted the Song of Songs and Ecclesiastes, about which questions had been raised, but they excluded the book of Ben Sirach.) We can get some idea of what they meant from the biblical notion on which they based themselves.

A number of the prophets use the expression "the spirit of *Adonai*" to denote the source of their message. Micah says it has given him strength, judgment, and courage "to declare to Jacob his transgression and to Israel his sin." (3:8) Isaiah hopes that it will fill the ideal king so that he may rule with true discernment. (11:2) Ezekiel uses the term "a spirit" as he does "the hand of *Adonai*" to explain the source of his prophecy. (1:2; 2:2)

The term "the spirit of God" can also refer to what we would call ecstatic possession, as in the striking tale about Saul. Leaving the seer Samuel, after being told that he was to be the first king of the Hebrews, Saul saw a band of prophets coming towards him. "Whereupon the spirit of God seized him and he prophesied among them." (1 Sam. 10:10) In a number of other biblical accounts, the "spirit of God" refers to a sudden seizure which brings one transcendent understanding or personal power. By the time of the rabbis, the term had become "the holy spirit" and no longer designated an unusual psychological state. It now certified that a given message was revealed by God. To this day, our notions of "in-spiration" derive from this biblical motif.

The rabbis thought that "the holy spirit" had functioned only in a limited historical period. "Our masters taught that, after the later prophets Haggai, Zechariah, and Malachi died, the *ruach hakodesh* [in the sense of God's revelation] departed from Israel —but they still availed themselves of the *bat kol.*" (Sot. 48b) *Bat kol* literally means, "daughter of a voice," and it refers to an audible communication from Heaven or God. It was often heard proclaiming the reward of martyrs like R. Hanina ben Teradion and R. Akiba. (A. Z. 18a; Ber. 61b) On occasion a *bat kol*'s decision was accepted in a legal dispute among the rabbis (Er. 13b) and, on occasion, it was not (B. M. 59b). In any case, though the rabbis occasionally make comments about revelation, they do not tell us very much about their understanding of it.

Medieval Beginnings to a Modern Problem

About a thousand years ago, Jews came into close contact with Moslem philosophy and science. Recognizing the great power of human reason, they began to formulate abstract questions about religion and philosophical responses to them. Special difficulties arose because their "science" used rigorous cause-and-effect reasoning to explain natural phenomena. Specifically, they conceived of the cosmos as a series of utterly transparent crystal spheres, one nesting inside the other. The various stars and planets were suspended in one or another of the spheres, and their odd motions, as observed from earth, were explained by the special motion of their sphere. Everything which happened in the sphere below the moon (and thus on earth) operated in terms of natural cause and effect. God, so to speak, had to operate the universe from outside the total system of spheres. How then could people on earth receive divine communications?

Maimonides responded by taking a current philosophic idea and reformulating it to make it more effective. God, he contended, ordered the world by intellect—which explains why human reason can comprehend nature's laws. When one applies one's mind to the philosophy of religion, metaphysics, one can develop one's reason so that it is open to and activated by God's effecting intellect. Most people do not have the intellectual ability and devotion to rise to this level. Maimonides also believed that everyone could be taught the rudiments of metaphysics, thus insuring them of a lasting link with God. The thoughtful few, by rigorous study and thinking, could become channels for the intellect with which God suffused the universe. The utterly exceptional, in whom mentality was accompanied by morality and complete inner dedication to God, were candidates for the highest religious intimacy, prophecy.

At this point the great rationalist surprises us. He insists that human efforts alone do not produce prophecy. God must grant that culmination; one is a true prophet, Maimonides says, by the grace of God.

Though he did not give a rational explanation for everything, Maimonides made revelation plausible for his generation's questioners. "God speaks" now meant to them a human mind which had reached the stage of being fully influenced by God's activating intellect.

For the rest of this chapter, I shall be arguing that liberal Jewish thinkers have roughly followed Maimonides's strategy. They have converted "God speaks" into a version of "people understand." I think our challenge is more difficult than Maimonides's. Our scientific world view is much more impenetrable, and a pervasive secularity makes any talk of revelation seem irrational. Yet present-day science also supplies us with metaphors to explain our sense of revelation. God "speaks" like an FM radio transmitter—but most people listen to the world via AM. Religion seeks to change our sensitivity so we can get something of the message which surrounds us. And some few religious geniuses are uniquely well tuned-in to it.

Contemporary Jewish philosophers go beyond the creation of new metaphors and attempt to explain in detail what they mean by revelation.

Abraham J. Heschel's Theory: Modern but Not Liberal

Though it was created after the other four theories we shall consider, analyzing Abraham J. Heschel's ideas first will usefully set the bounds of our interest.

Heschel's theory is typically modern in seeking to explain God's revelation in terms of personal experience. For Heschel, modern science has robbed us of our instinctive surprise at the wonder that we or anything exists. If we can shed our secular programing, all of us can have a direct, personal appreciation of the incomparable grandeur of the God who created and sustains all being.

The prophets differed from us only in the unusually profound way they had this experience. They had the gift of what Heschel calls "sym-pathy." I have introduced the hyphen to distinguish Heschel's meaning from sympathy as the common sentiment of feeling the distress of a sufferer. Heschel wants us to take the term literally, sym = with, pathos = feeling; the prophet's sym-pathos enables him to feel along with God. He is totally identified with the divine purposes and that is the source of his message and authority.

Heschel's prophet does not literally hear words addressed to him. He does not have to. He is so intimate with God's "desires" that he can accurately verbalize them. He does this in terms of his personality and situation for he has not surrendered his individuality in this experience.

However, Heschel emphasizes that prophets do not invent or create anything they say. Heschel's notion of prophetic "sym-pathy" does not include imaginative reconstruction or literary embroidery. The prophets' involvement with God was too intimate for that and the greatness of God precluded their daring to intrude their own meanings upon God's. Rather their words accurately represent what they felt God undergoing.

Our God Is Not Indifferent to Our Deeds

Heschel does not flinch from the implications of this theory (whose essential Orthodoxy should now be apparent). The prophets continually speak of God in highly emotional terms. We should learn from this, says Heschel, that the God of Israel is a God of pathos, that is, of feeling. And he mounts an intense polemic against the notion that God would be more God-like if God felt nothing at all. That, Heschel tellingly points out, is a Stoic, not a Jewish notion. Instead of apologizing for the prophets by calling their highly-charged language poetic or exaggerated, we should recognize they are reliably transmitting God's response to our sinfulness and obduracy.

If its literalness were not enough to deter most liberals from

Heschel's theory of revelation, he further gives them pause by seeking to validate the depiction of God's anger. He argues that God's wrath is always controlled by God's moral purposes.

Most liberal thinkers do not see that in the texts. To the contrary, the prophets utilize the notion of God's anger to indicate that Israel's sinfulness will generate more punishment than justice warrants. In human beings, anger denotes an emotional state in which we throw off our usual restraints. The prophets are threatening their sinful people with that sort of "breaking forth" in God. To liberals, this understanding of God projects the prophets' distress better than God's reality. In this instance, Heschel's claims for revelation as "sym-pathos" demand too much deference to the text—and thus the whole case for the verbal reliability of the prophets fails.

In Heschel's defense we must note that he sought to limit somewhat the authority of the revealed texts. He pointed out that Judaism had comparatively little revelation and considerable interpretation, implying thereby that some needs of modernity could be met through the interpretive process. He also made a strong case for ethics as the central theme of prophetic revelation. I suggest that spending his first six years in the United States at the Hebrew Union College influenced him in this regard. But he never made clear how he would resolve a direct clash between a prophetic revelation (most particularly, those of Moses) and an ethical imperative. This matter has always been critical to the liberals. Equally troubling, he unqualifiedly cloaked the rabbinic tradition with the authority of prophetic revelation: "The prophet's inspirations and the sages' interpretations are equally important." In the face of such traditionalist consequences, liberals have generally not looked to Heschel for a modern understanding of revelation.

1. Revelation as the Ethics Reason Discloses

In the last part of the nineteenth century Hermann Cohen elaborated the first great modern theory of revelation. It was an integral element of his neo-Kantian ideas about God.*

For Cohen, using reason is humanity's greatest talent; using it properly enables us to gain an integrated concept of the three

*See Part Two, *The God We Affirm,* chapters 2 and 3.

distinct realms which comprise mature rationality—science, ethics, and esthetics. The basis of such a world view is the integrating idea which people traditionally called God. Thus, for Cohen, true rational philosophy is the same as true religion, a unity he called religion of reason.

Obviously, a God who is understood as an idea, cannot "speak." For Cohen, revelation is a term describing the human mind functioning at its best. Cohen attached the highest importance to the creative powers of reason, of the mysterious way a mind originates a new idea, particularly one which extends our unified understanding of the world. To get a fresh comprehensive concept was, in effect, to gain greater knowledge of God, the unique, integrating premise. Equally, to discover the way in which the God-idea rationally requires certain consequences in thought or action may also be termed, for Cohen, a "revelation." All such insight is a perfectly rational and, therefore, natural process.

Cohen becomes quite passionate about the connection between God and ethics. The rational person, he asserted, experienced the commanding power of the ethical as a "categorical imperative," to use Kant's famous term. Like all the highest products of the mind, it had the form of law, in this case of moral law. Therefore, a critical sign of one's rationality was one's responsiveness to ethical duty. This is so ordinary a human experience that it seems an exaggeration to call the demands of conscience "revelation." Yet, insofar as they directly instruct us of what the God-concept requires of us, they are everyone's ongoing "revelations."

As liberals popularly came to understand Cohen's theory, "God reveals" means "our conscience requires." Cohen judged Judaism to be the great historical exemplar of religion of reason. He therefore considered its ethics to be its lasting, commanding element. He called for unequivocal abrogation of any Jewish law which conflicted with them, as for example the prohibition against transgressing the Sabbath to save a gentile life as against a Jewish life. Where laws were not directly ethical but conduced to ethical behavior, like prayer, he considered them valuable. Where they had no direct or instrumental relation to ethics, one might feel free to keep or discard them as one wished.

As long as liberal Jews had great confidence in the power of human rationality, Cohen's theory of revelation was highly influential. Residually, ethics as essence remains the basic belief of most American Jews. But other rationalistic thinkers soon saw the need to modify Cohen's view in two directions. Leo Baeck sought to give it greater appreciation of religious feelings, and later Mordecai Kaplan presented an American form of rationalism which put authority entirely into the hands of the Jewish people itself.

2. Leo Baeck: Revelation and the Religious Sense of Mystery

While Cohen begins with philosophic ideas and then applies them to Judaism, Leo Baeck does the opposite. Baeck, who was a young rabbi in Cohen's later years, starts with the lived experience of Judaism and only afterward looks for concepts to explain its unique genius. Baeck agreed that Cohen had exposed much of Judaism's central truth, but his preoccupation with the intellect prevented his doing justice to its piety. Judaism clearly encompassed more than doctrine and ethics. It taught trust and confidence, dependency and aspiration, resignation yet joyous optimism. These emotions and more suffused the life of believing Jews as much as did the concept of ethical monotheism.

To bring feelings back into Judaism, Baeck joined the notion of religious consciousness to Cohen's theory of rational religion. Baeck believed faith began with our sense of mystery about human origins and destiny. Paradoxically, our lives, which seem so temporary, also appear to have lasting significance. Though we know we were created by a power far greater than ourselves, yet we share its extraordinary capacity to create, particularly in doing an ethical deed.

For Baeck, revelation derives from our awe at being alive and empowered, as well as from our reason. Sensitivity and not merely conscience instructs us. Baeck's liberal Jew must respond to God in more than intellectual and ethical ways. Prayer and ritual mean much in Baeck's Judaism, for they are our appropriate response to the mystery which surrounds us.

Should intuition and rationality conflict, Baeck insists that ethical judgment be sovereign. Allowing our religious consciousness to be paramount might easily lead us to romantic emotionalism and self-indulgence. That having been said, Baeck quickly reasserts the passional side of the dialectic. In Judaism the subjective aspect of faith must be a full partner to ethical rationality, lest we create a sterile, moralistic sort of religion.

Baeck's stature as a thinker has been enhanced in recent decades as cultural developments have shown his fears of emotionalism and secularism to be well grounded. We have seen how relying largely on one's feelings can itself dehumanize people, and how conscience without a religious foundation has itself gradually lost our confidence.

3. Kaplan's Reworking of Vox Populi, Vox Dei

Both Cohen and Baeck base their thought on the individual. As a result, neither could assign the Jewish people a central place in his thought. Mordecai Kaplan, speaking out of the American immigrant experience, agreed with Cohen's and Baeck's rationalism but rejected its focus. For him, the folk would have to receive greater priority than the individual mind or religious consciousness.

Kaplan's thought derives from American naturalism which seeks to understand people in terms of their interaction with the world. For Kaplan this meant the way in which culture shaped human individuality. Individual self-fulfillment inevitably involves one's folk, for it gives one one's very language and horizon of achievement.

All cultures known to us have a religion. It functions to promote the society's chief values and to help individuals rise to the highest level of development. Thus, the individual, as well as the folk, needs religion to provide a sense that the personal values they cherish are worthy of their trust. Should one lose faith in one's goals, one's humanity begins to die. Healthy people therefore manifest an intuitive trust that the best in them is sustained and furthered by many natural processes. Modern Jews should use the word "God" to refer to this unity of the inner and outer thrusts toward human betterment.

Only slowly did higher religious intuitions develop and become part of people's lives. In many places they are barely recognized even now. Religion like all the other aspects of human life must be considered a process of growth and discovery. For us moderns religion must be rational. We will believe only what we can under-stand.

For Kaplan, then, revelation is the process by which people discover the highest truth about themselves and their world, a largely but not entirely rational matter. Since almost all of us receive our stock of ideas—even our rebellious ones!—from our society, one's people, rather than one's self, is revelation's most reliable source and repository. Consequently when our people honors its individual members by making decisions democrati-cally, we ought to do what it says. This makes Kaplan a liberal Jew, for as the Jewish collectivity changes its mind, so ought modern Jewish law.

4. Martin Buber: Revelation as Relationship

The three preceding liberal theories center on the human role in religion. God has so little independent function in them, we might do well to consider these theories a humanistic overcom-pensation for an Orthodoxy dominated by God. At an opposite extreme, we can understand Heschel's deprecation of the human role in revelation as his effort to correct the liberals' excessive humanism. Martin Buber stands somewhere between Heschel and the liberals. He is more humanistic than Heschel, more God-oriented than the rationalists.

For Buber, as we have previously noted,* God is a reality not ourselves. We can come to know this God, Buber teaches, only if we desist from treating God like an object to be analyzed and learn to relate to God as we do to another subject.

To understand what revelation might mean to us today, Buber utilizes the experience of friendship or love. (Franz Rosenzweig also used the love-metaphor, but Buber's thought is more acces-sible so we will speak only of it.) When you are very close to someone, that person has a powerful effect on your life. You care what they think, want to do what they desire, are fearful of their judgment, and concerned to make amends for whatever you have done that offends them. Perhaps they specifically spoke to you about these matters, but they need not have. Merely by your intimacy you and they will have a mutual sense of command and

*See Part Two, *The God We Affirm*, chapters 2 and 3.

responsibility. Indeed, it often happens that they will feel their relationship with you damaged if they must say what deeply concerns them. If you truly cared, you should have known. Even without words, love communicates and demands responsive understanding.

The basic Jewish commandment is not to love our minds, our consciousness, or our highest self, but God. Not everyone is capable of a great passion for God, but all of us can grow into friendly intimacy. Our moments of closeness with God are the basis of our religious life. Whether ours is a great or only an ordinary love, its effect will be the same. Our closeness will increase our understanding and our responsibility. God does not speak words to us, but knowing that God is present with us engenders our knowledge of what we must do to stay close to God.

Heschel obviously learned a good deal from Buber, with whom he worked in Germany, but he disagreed with him on one vital matter. Heschel insisted that the prophet's self was radically subordinated to God's greatness and thus his message was not creative. Buber had taught that in a true relationship one partner does not sacrifice self to the other. Both partners remain independent selves though most intricately linked. That individuality can be most fully realized in the most involving relationship is the mystery of mature love.

Buber also believed that nations, like individuals, confronted God in their history. Such experiences formed the ultimate basis of their "nationality" and their culture. For the people of Israel, that had happened at Mt. Sinai and again and again, thanks to the prophets, during the course of biblical history. More important, the Jewish people as a whole came to accept the traditions of these "revelations" as the basis of their folk existence. But against Mordecai Kaplan's later theory, Buber always insisted that individual Jews must give priority to their personal relationship with God, not to what their people says it ought to be.

How then Might Liberal Jews Read the Bible?

These four liberal thinkers deny that God communicates words. They agree that the statements attributed to God are human creations, arising out of human religious experience as they variously explain it. For liberals, revelation is a human response to God's reality. And it continues today as it did in the past.

How then will you find the lasting religious truth of the Bible?

If you agree with Hermann Cohen, you will read the Bible with a strong appreciation of its incomparable early understanding of ethical monotheism.

If you follow Leo Baeck, you will also resonate to the sense of personal mystery and exaltation which our ancient forebears felt in relation to God.

If Mordecai Kaplan's rationalism explains things best for you, the Bible will become an incomparable source of your people's decisive early intuitions of nature's support for humankind's proper self-development.

If you share Martin Buber's experience of the power of relationship, you will read the Bible with the same sort of openness you bring to a trusted friend or love, knowing that from its words you may relieve now the experience which lies behind the words before you.

If Abraham Heschel has convinced you that in the face of God's greatness we are best off accepting what the prophets have told us, as interpreted by our sages, you will study the texts in an accepting, grateful way.

What you believe about God and humankind and the people of Israel will effect what you believe revelation can mean today. And from that definition will stem your understanding of what constitutes proper authority in contemporary Judaism.

·3·

HOW TRUE IS THE BIBLE?

A curious controversy has recently divided Protestant fundamentalists in the United States. While all fundamentalists agree that the Bible is the word of God and, as such, altogether true, they cannot agree on just how inerrant that makes it. None of them suggests that the Bible is only symbolically true. But, once one says it is literally true, problems arise.

Let us take an apparently trivial matter: Where can we find the correct meaning of the Christian Scriptures? Surely not in one of the English versions for they are translations from the Greek. If we agree we are interested in the Greek text's message, we quickly discover it can be read in different ways, some of which have credal implications. Thus, the very virtue of fundamentalism, that we possess God's specific guidance, is shaken by the ambiguities of an ancient tongue. But which Greek version is the right one? There are many small discrepancies between one manuscript and the next, and even more between one family of manuscripts, as they are called, and another. The truth is that we do not have "the" or even an "original" manuscript of the Christian Scriptures. Our earliest documents appear at a very much later date than the time of their composition.

And, if I may be indulged for a bit of pedantry, some scholars argue that the Gospels were originally written in Aramaic. If so, all we have are Greek translations! We cannot presently recover the earliest authentic accounts of Jesus' life!

Clarifying Our Concern about the Truth of Our Bible

I hasten to add that all these problems hold true of Hebrew Scriptures. Jews have studied the Bible from what they termed the Masoretic text (from the word *"masorah"*), that is, the "received" or traditional text. Considering the intricate procedures the sages had worked out to safeguard the Bible, one might think the Masoretic text had been transmitted perfectly over the ages. Once again, the scrutiny of biblical manuscripts proves this is not so. The texts vary and the earliest ones show a certain fluidity in their readings. Our oldest complete manuscript is about a thousand years old—but that places its text about a thousand years after we believe the last biblical book was written. The various partial older manuscripts we have, including the Dead Sea Scrolls and fragments, show considerable variance from our "official" Bible text. It may be a small point but we cannot be absolutely certain which set of words it is whose truth we are inquiring about.

I do not mean to suggest that Orthodox Judaism's belief in verbal revelation closely parallels that of Protestant fundamentalism. Both do believe the Bible gives God's explicit guidance. Both would question any religious position which substantially departed from it. But traditional Judaism reads the Bible with the guidance of the rabbis. It is thus not limited to Scriptures' exact words and is not "fundamentalist" in a Protestant sense. Moreover, the doctrine of the Oral Torah presumes that God's revelation is many layered. The rabbis read the Bible "midrashicly" and glory in revealing another of the Torah's "faces." While traditional Protestantism displays something of this respect for the richness of biblical language, the difference between these two orthodoxies is quickly apparent.

The problems that trouble liberals about the Bible arise in another area. Chiefly we want to know what to make of the troublesome instances where the Bible contradicts what we otherwise know to be facts or well-established scientific theories. If we resolve that issue by asserting the Bible's essentially human authorship, we beget a corollary question: In what sense do we say these old Semitic documents are uniquely valuable? That is, does a human Bible retain a unique place in our religious lives, one unmatched by other great human classics?

Let us begin our investigation by first reviewing the factual question. Then, having further understood the liberals' case for the humanity of Scriptures, we can take up the issue of the Bible's enduring religious worth.

The Major Clash: With Modern Science

For much of the past two centuries the discoveries of science have proved "revelatory." The new medical knowledge saved lives, the new understanding of energy radically improved them. On every frontier, understanding became more detailed as well as more comprehensive. The fundamental descriptions of nature became ever more simple and, hence, more satisfying. One could not be modern without adopting a scientific view of the universe. As a consequence, the project of integrating Judaism and modernity faced a special obstacle, the scientific untenability of the Bible.

The conflict should not be overstated. Whole books of the Bible, like the Psalms or Proverbs, do not contain any major contradictions of science. Even in the Torah, aside from an occasional miracle, the difficulties arise primarily with the first few chapters of Genesis, the account of creation and early human history. Overwhelmingly, the Bible does not conflict with science —but, if God is its author, none of it should.

One set of problems arises from the claim that God created the universe. As various modern cosmologies have held sway, the very notion of God's creation appeared unscientific. Today, with scientists less dogmatic, the so-called "big-bang" theory of the universe's origin has made the notion of creation less objectionable. Theoreticians can speculate with some degree of accuracy as to what happened once the energy ball exploded. Where the energy that acted this way came from and why it followed certain mathematically describable patterns is necessarily a mystery to them. In a somewhat surprising turn of events, considering the struggle between modern science and religion, some scientists allow their faith to fill that gap of explanation with a religious notion of creation.

None of this congenial speculation resolves the contradiction between the scientific view of the age of the universe and that given by the Bible. The range of scientific estimates for the time of the primal explosion is from about four to two billion years ago. There is no unconvoluted way of squaring these numbers with the figure of five thousand, seven hundred plus years which traditional Judaism, based on the Bible's dates, reckons to be the age of "heaven and earth."

The more famous conflict between science and the creation stories has been over the appearance of humankind. The second chapter of Genesis tells how God fashioned a man out of dust and a woman from his rib. The first chapter, though it has a sequence for the emergence of the creatures, says that God "personally" created man and woman on the sixth day of creation. The Darwinian theory of the evolution of humankind, regardless of its revisions and modifications, directly discredits both accounts. All the natural species we know, including humans, emerged from one another or certain common ancestors. They did this in response to environmental circumstances over a long, if not geological, time span. *Homo sapiens* almost certainly came into being not from one pair of progenitors but from the evolution of our mammalian ancestors in several parts of the globe.

While many early liberal Jews initially found these scientific views too upsetting to accept without a struggle, their fundamental commitment to modernity eventually overcame their discomfort. The Bible's faulty science then became a major support for their view that the Bible transmits the words of people, not of God. Of the ancient Hebrews, we might reasonably only expect ancient science and that is what the Bible gives us. That, of course, as we shall see, says nothing about its religious insight.

The Contradictions with Facts Known to Be True

Strictly speaking, creation and evolution are not matters of proven fact but only highly respected scientific theory. The Bible's conflict with reasonably well established data has also been a challenge to its truthfulness.

The chief example from the field of archeology may well be the problems concerning the conquest of Jericho. They begin with the complexities of trying to determine a rough date for the Exodus. In 1 Kings 6:1, we read that there were 480 years from the Exodus to the construction of the Temple by Solomon. That accords well with Jephthah's comment in Judges 11:26 about the length of time since the entry of the Hebrews into Canaan. These references yield a date of about 1450 B.C.E. But the archeology of ancient Jericho shows no major destruction then, though there were ravages a century earlier and a century later.

This early date for the Exodus also is at loggerheads with the report that the enslaved Hebrews built the cities of Pithom and Raamses. (Exod. 1:11) If the latter may be identified with a similarly named city erected by the Pharaoh Raamses and the Exodus took place in his time or that of his son, it must be placed in the thirteenth century. While there is good evidence for the destruction of many Canaanite cities in the thirteenth century, there is not for Jericho. If anything, the city seems not to have been inhabited in this period (which is also true of the city Ai, whose conquest is described in Joshua 7–8). If that were not trouble enough for reconciling the account in Joshua 2 and 6 with the archeological data, when the city was standing the remains indicate it was unwalled! Some scholars suggest that it had a wall made of mud bricks and these offered little defense against Joshua.

Two literary cases are also pertinent. We can date the Assyrian kings quite accurately. King Sennacherib's attack on the Kingdom of Judah, which Isaiah describes in chapters 36 and 37, took place in the year 701 B.C.E. The prophet was then an adult. Later in the Book of Isaiah, there are two references to Cyrus, king of Persia. (Isaiah 44:28 and 45:1) He came to power in 559 B.C.E. and ruled for thirty years. If the prophet is contemporary with Cyrus, as the text seems to indicate, Isaiah was then well over 140 years old. Most modern scholars resolve this difficulty by attributing Isaiah, from chapter 40 on, to a later prophet (or two), referred to as the Second (or Deutero) Isaiah.

An even more puzzling set of conundrums confronts us in the Book of Esther. There is no king Ahashuerus in our detailed lists of the Persian kings. The closest parallels to his empire are those of Artaxerxes, who died in 425 B.C.E. or Artaxerxes II, who died in 328 B.C.E. But the Book of Esther says that Mordecai came to Babylon with the exiles in 597 B.C.E. (2:6) At the least, he was over 170 years old. More surprisingly, the beautiful Esther is described as his cousin. (2:7) If we can ignore the chronology, we face the challenge of our records of the Persian royal court. These indicate its meticulousness in matters of lineage. The Persian king could not marry an alien woman. He could not appoint as his prime minister an Agagite, like Haman, or a Jew, like Mordecai. The historical facts therefore suggest that the book is fiction. Accepting that conclusion speedily exposes the difference between accuracy in data and true spiritual worth. For what this unhistorical tale says about Jewish vulnerability and survival remains true today as in centuries past.

And What Shall We Make of the Miracles?

For many people, the most unacceptable part of the biblical record has been its miracles. The number of dramatic "signs" or "wonders," as the Bible authors refer to them, is not very great. Most of the Bible histories recount events in much the same fashion a religious person might do today. The only Bible miracle that is mentioned in later Jewish practice is the splitting of the Sea of Reeds. Traditional Christian faith depends far more heavily on God's one-time acts. The virgin birth, the incarnation, and the resurrection are central to classic Christianity. No biblical miracle has anywhere near similar status in Judaism.

Probably the single largest collection of miracle tales is connected with the Exodus. The plagues come and go at Moses' command, not by natural onset and departure. (Exod. 7:1–12:36) The climax of this unparalleled display of God's power comes at the Sea of Reeds where wonder follows upon wonder. Moses stretches out his hand and the sea parts. The Israelites walk through on dry not wet ground. The waters stand as walls on either side of them. When the Egyptians pursue the Israelites, their chariot wheels lock. Then the waters come back and drown them. Not one of them survives. The Egyptian corpses are then thrown up on the shore so that they are visible to the Hebrews on the far shore. (Exod. 14:21–30) The result of this is that "Israel saw the wondrous power *Adonai* had wielded against the Egyptians. Then the people feared *Adonai,* and they believed in *Adonai* and His servant Moses." (Exod. 14:31) In one place, the text says God utilized a strong east wind, but this one naturalistic aside only emphasizes how unnatural and providential the rest of these acts were.

A far more dramatic display of God's care for the Hebrews occurs during Joshua's attack on the Amorites. Needing more time to complete his victory, Joshua prays to God to extend the daylight. God complies and "the sun stayed in the midst of the heaven and did not move to descend for about a whole day. There was no day like that before it or afterward. . . ." (10:13–14)

For reasons which are not clear, very many miracles are associated with the prophets Elijah and Elisha. (Something like their special powers is ascribed to various other prophets in these historical books.) Thus, to cite a few instances, Elijah calls down fire on unfriendly messengers (2 Kings 1:9–12), gets God's fire to consume wet sacrifices (1 Kings 18:38), goes forty days and nights on one meal (1 Kings 19:8), divides the Jordan with his mantle (2 Kings 2:8), and ascends alive to heaven in a fiery chariot (2 Kings 2:11). Similarly, Elisha divides the Jordan, purifies water with salt, draws the water out of the land of Moab, fills from one cruse of oil every empty vessel a widow has, purifies a deadly stew, and makes iron float (all in 2 Kings 2:14, 2:22, 3:20, 4:1–7, 4:41, 6:4–7).

Orderly Science and the Religion of Singularities

These miracle stories demonstrate God's greatness because God alters nature's normal way of operating. Nothing could more directly oppose the cumulative wisdom of science. Experiment and generalization demonstrated that nature operated by unvarying patterns, "laws" as the nineteenth-century scientists called them. These laws do not change, a fact attested by research over some centuries and therefore assumed to be true for all time and space. We therefore confidently extrapolate from the patterns we presently observe to determine what happened, for example, when the "big bang" occurred, or what now transpires in the far reaches of space.

The Bible authors also had a sense of nature's regularity. The miracle stories make their point because God momentously interrupts it. The break in the order demonstrates God's sovereignty. In direct opposition to this, modern science rigorously insists upon the orderliness of the universe. It cannot admit occasional lapses in the structure lest its entire system of explanation break down; one could always then claim that certain phenomena are exceptions to nature's "lawfulness." Odd phenomena may require further research, a revision of an old theory, or the statement of a new "law" to include them—but they cannot be arbitrary events. Miracles proudly make the violation of nature's order the sign of God's greatness. But, as science progressed, religion's grandest proof became its chief liability. It seemed far easier to understand the miracle tales as human overstatement rather than as historical fact and religious evidence.

I must add that the scientific stand against miracles is less hostile these days than it once was. Much of the philosophy of science now talks in terms of probability rather than of natural law. The highly improbable is most unlikely to occur—but that does not mean it is impossible. Eccentric events might have occurred. But liberals feel it would strain our limited modern capacity for faith to assert that miracles had occurred and are integral to our Judaism. Rather they have preferred to see God's power manifest in the extraordinary orderliness of nature.

Setting the Miracles in Human Context

Students of the history of religion have noted that all cultures have wonder tales. On the simplest level they reflect the human proclivity to play and be imaginative. Add a certain element of wishfulness and the tall-tale soon makes an appearance. Recounting such narratives over generations—recording them is always a late stage—conduces to elaboration. And as every storyteller knows, a little exaggeration makes for greater excitement. Centuries later we have a legend, a story embroidering the historical kernel at its core.

All that holds true of folk heroes and national epics. We can discern an additional layer of meaning to religious stories. People in every environment have utilized tales to answer some universal human questions: How did the world begin, why must people suffer, what happens when we die? Naturally, each culture's tales will reflect what it values most and express its concerns in terms of its environment.

By labeling these religious narratives "tales" or "stories," we indicate that we take them to be fiction. As history or science they are likely to be false. They generally speak out of a mentality which sees structure in the universe far differently from the way modern science does. But if the stories mainly address perennial concerns of the human soul, and not issues of fact, we must reopen the question of their truth.

We must not be put off by matters of form. People everywhere have utilized their imaginations to answer their most profound questions. They did not respond to them with abstract, intellectual analyses. Most people do not think that way today, and an even smaller proportion of the population did so in ancient times. It takes considerable sophistication to think philosophically. It is far simpler to tell a story. Everyone not only likes a good story but they can also benefit from it in their own individual ways.

The story-form has another advantage. It speaks on many levels at one time and conveys rich meaning in a simple way. (So do many of the other literary forms religions often use, like poetry and adage.) A good narrative can fascinate critics for a long time, with new commentators coming along to discover fresh layers of meaning hidden in it. Religious truth is almost always characterized by its complexity and limitless significance. Some contemporary theologians doubt that any abstract philosophy could ever adequately articulate it. Hence they urge that we go back to the Bible authors' way of conveying their meaning and retell their stories when we wish to speak of our faith.

In contemporary discussions of religion the technical term for an imaginative tale which seeks to convey spiritual meaning is "myth." On the mundane level, the word implies something known to be untrue, as when we say, "That's only a myth." But if we can be subtle enough to separate the story's religious purposes from its premodern view of the natural order, we may find its spiritual meanings as deep as any truth we know.

Let me present an example from the creation "myths" we previously discussed. Scientifically, we would not say that all human beings are descended from one couple. Therefore, the Genesis accounts are false. But what religious concerns motivate the Adam and Eve stories? One is that all human beings are members of one family. By projecting that metaphor, a powerful ethical perception was made basic to Hebrew religion. I would not deny that the modern love of democracy may prompt my interpretation, but two thousand years ago the rabbis read Genesis very much the same way and made their interpretation basic to Jewish law. History aside, the stories of Adam and Eve are, in this respect, true. Indeed, they are importantly true, particularly in our time of hatred and violence. And I have educed only one truth from the multiplicity of valid spiritual insights contained in these historically false tales.

A Liberal Attitude toward the Sacredness of Scriptures

A special task now develops upon liberal Jews who study Scriptures for their continuing religious meaning. They cannot assume, as traditionalists do, that every verse conveys God's own truth. Because the text was written by humans it may not only be factually in error but convey a faulty or immature Jewish view of God and our obligations to God. Seeking the Bible's lasting spiritual content now becomes an intensely dynamic process. When the answer is not self-evident, readers must repeatedly ask, "What religious meanings might this text point to?" And they can learn to find answers to that question by keeping in mind their sense of the relationship between God and the Jewish people. Assuming that it was essentially the same 2,500 years ago or so, they look for it in the words before them and read the text in that spirit. I shall shortly be more specific about this.

The Bible does not contain many full-blown "myths." The creation stories and the miracle tales are the most obvious ones. Some accounts of Hebrew history which show a heavy religious interpretation may be said to have a mythic component. But very much of the Bible is not patently imaginative. Nonetheless, the same religiously activist reading must be brought to laws and poems and prophecies and histories as to the explicit myths. Knowing that humans stand behind them all, we must deal with them as we would with any other great human literature. But seeking religious guidance from them we need to ask more than technical or literary questions of our texts. We need to be open to the spiritual messages they still communicate regardless of the form in which they are expressed.

Two related general principles should help us in this contemporary religious quest. Neither asserts a claim for Jews that could not be argued by other people about themselves or their scripture alone. Both come from our common cultural understanding of human beings, though Jews may apply them in ways that other peoples do not. First, we believe the Bible is a work of incomparable religious genius. Second, we value it as the founding religio-ethnic saga of our people. On both counts, Jews will have a lasting intimate involvement with Hebrew Scriptures.

The notion of genius seeks to explain a curious but well known human phenomenon. In almost every endeavor, certain people seem able to accomplish extraordinarily much more than even their great colleagues. Newton, Mozart, Rembrandt, Freud— such people are qualitatively unique. They create works which later generations keep returning to for they find them brimming over with meaning. What made them capable of such supreme statement or why others of their family, station, time, or opportunity, did not do as well or better is inexplicable. They were as human as anyone else and yet soared far beyond the usual limits of accomplishment.

Liberal Judaism makes a similar claim for the authors of the Bible. They were geniuses in the field of religion. Though they lived thousands of years ago and spoke in the language and culture of their time, their words are classic. For millennia people have turned to them and found them incomparably instructive and exalting. Through Christianity, their influence has gone far beyond the Jewish people and affected people in the most varied circumstances. That this old Judean work still "speaks" to people in jungles and in wintry climes, in technologically advanced and in relatively primitive states, in freedom and under oppression, is an abiding wonder. Abraham Heschel said that the greatest miracle of the Bible is its universal influence. No religious or humanistic works of modern times, for all their greatness and value, are likely to show such continuing worldwide relevance.

This claim for the Bible's lasting quality does not contradict what was previously said about having to grapple with its words to elicit and evaluate their meaning. Even geniuses can falter. But when we know we are dealing with the products of uncommon ability, we learn to make proper demands of ourselves so as to appreciate what the authors of the Bible are communicating. And, as we come to know and trust their capacity to guide us, we can develop a certain patience with our frustration when we find we cannot understand them.

The first declaration concerning the substantive distinctiveness of the Bible is abetted by one less likely to arouse debate: The Bible is the Jewish book *par excellence.* From it we learn the origins and early history of our people. It has given our folk its distinctive character and shaped our unique way of life. It has been the basis of the nations' appreciation of us and is the foundation of our special status in countries that honor Hebrew Scriptures. One cannot live a rich Jewish life without knowing and cherishing the

Bible. Therefore, for folk reasons if for no others, Jews should give the Bible a unique place in their lives.

Liberal Jewish Ways of Reading the Bible

We do not need to leave our claim for the Bible on this general level. We have already studied four contemporary liberal theories of revelation. We can now apply them to inquire how each of them would guide us to find religious meaning in the Bible. Each sensitizes us to a way the sacred texts reflect the human interaction with God. Each gives us empathy with the religious experience of the people who brought these texts into being and enables us to share their religious insights in full personal depth.

For Hermann Cohen, religion results from the enlightened human mind and conscience responding to the oneness it finds in the universe, particularly in the ethical imperatives identified with it. Readers with this rationalistic view will rejoice in the utterly atypical monotheism of the prophets and their devotion to the religious primacy of ethics. These readers will be sensitive to the ethical dimensions of texts that readers without their focus might well miss. The commandment to observe the Sabbath, for example, includes one's servants as well as one's family. For the ethically minded, this teaches that morality transcends all class and economic lines. It also instructs us to apply our ethics to those over whom we hold power.

Leo Baeck adds to this concern for ethical monotheism an appreciation of the awe and mystery one properly has at being part of this vast cosmos. For Baeck, the religious consciousness reaches out to God not only through its rationality but beyond it to the beneficent Unknown which surrounds us. Baeck can therefore resonate with deep religious appreciation when he reads of the otherwise mythic "glory of God" appearing to the people of Israel. And his expanded sense of religious experience enables him to comprehend how someone like Job, who has been given an intimation of God's transcendence, can accept in humility and faith the ultimately Unknowable.

Mordecai Kaplan's rationalism also goes beyond ethical monotheism to attune us to the manner in which the Hebrew folk continually seeks to redefine itself in terms of its intuition of God. It could not, therefore, be content to be like other Semitic nations, though its natural inclination was to sink to their level of idolatry and licentiousness. In an extraordinary process of self-transcendence, the prophets of Israel reprove its leaders and masses for impeding the full human and social development of their nation. Their vision of a proper human existence is not confined to a private life embellished by a few rites or priestly services. It embraces the whole human being within his folk and through it as part of all humankind. Our ideals must therefore be robustly social, encompassing economics and culture, human relations and law, ecology and world government. And our people's ancient saga, when we read it in such social appreciation, can continue to inspire us to work for these goals.

Martin Buber would have us be far more personal and less mental as we read the Bible. He asks us to approach its words with something like the open mood we bring to old love letters or our collection of souvenirs. Of course, we must have intellectual respect for the words before us; we do not abandon knowledge and rationality in seeking to be the fullest possible person. Only we must not come to the texts as detached analysts if we hope to know something of the experience of those who wrote them. We need to open ourselves up to them. If we have learned how to reach out to other people and to God, we can read the Bible as an effort at recapitulating now something of the intimacy its authors had with God. The content of such encounters will vary with each of us but such variegation of religious experience has been part of the classic worth of Scriptures. Sharing these insights with fellow Jews has enriched our existence as a folk and our understanding of our Covenant with God.

Whatever means we utilize in perceiving the Bible's truth for us and our people, one conclusion strongly impresses itself on liberal Jews. If these are "only" the words of people, how astonishing it is that they so often radically transcend their time and place! What a depth of sensitivity and a breadth of compassion again and again infuses these ancient Hebrews! Reading their writings thousands of years later in a thoroughly transformed world, we, the best educated generation the world has ever known, are instructed and exalted by them. Would that our sense of truth and virtue were as reliable and lasting as the Bible authors' has proven to be.

·4·

WHY ARE THE PROPHETS
ESPECIALLY IMPORTANT
IN LIBERAL JUDAISM?

In the synagogue on *Shabbat* we follow some instructive customs with regard to Scripture. A portion of the Torah, the *sidrah,* is read. In the course of a year, the *sidrot* will have taken us through every word in the first five books of the Bible. The reading from the Torah Scroll is followed by a shorter reading, called the *haftarah,* from the prophetic books. Despite the similarity in sound, the word has nothing to do with the Torah. It derives from a verb whose basic meaning is "to set free," "to open." In its liturgical usage it has the sense of "a selection" or "portion." The term *"haftarah"* indicates that after one year's readings we shall not cover all or even one of the prophetic books of the Bible; we read but a fragment of a much greater literature. Incidentally, in Jewish usage, "the prophetic books" refers to the entire second division of Hebrew Scriptures—Joshua, Judges, Samuel, and Kings as well as the three extensive ("major") prophets, Isaiah, Jeremiah, and Ezekiel and the twelve briefer ("minor") ones.

The Jewish dedication to the words of the Torah extends much beyond reading them annually. Traditionally, during the reading a prompter stands beside the one who is chanting the unpointed text—that is, one without vowel, punctuation, or musical notations. The prompter follows the reading in a modern printing containing every help. Should the reader mispronounce even a vowel, the prompter immediately corrects the reader who then repeats the phrase correctly. Should the prompter hesitate in spotting a mistake, people in the pews, also following the *sidrah* in printed texts, will call out the correct pronunciation. But there is neither an official prompter nor a community effort to correct slips in the chanting of the *haftarah*.

These usages indicate the exalted place of the Torah in Jewish piety. The prophetic books are indeed holy, as the blessings recited before and after chanting the *haftarah* indicate. But, as the synagogue practices show, they are clearly of subordinate importance. All the Torah was God's dictation to Moses, the greatest of the prophets. The prophetic books contain speeches giving God's words, but much else besides.

I do not think I am exaggerating the gap between the two sections of the Bible. Before the Emancipation, the Prophets had no special relevance to the situation of the average Jew. Only after Jews entered general society did the prophetic literature, with its emphasis on social responsibility, become the most immediately relevant part of the Bible. I shall be explaining this with some enthusiasm in the following pages but I do not wish to create misunderstanding. Though they liked to call their belief Prophetic Judaism, liberal Jews did not replace the Torah with the prophetic books. In their synagogues, the Torah Scroll, not the prophetic literature, reposed in the ark. It remained the fundament of their Judaism.

Emphasizing the Interpersonal Rather than Worship

Let us now explore, somewhat impressionistically, five motifs which prompted this liberal devotion. Where they perceived the Torah to center about worship, institutions, the sacred community, structures, and the eternal present, they judged the prophetic books to focus on ethics, society, individuals, change, and ultimate goals. Searching for the Jewish religious component of their modernity, they made the Prophets their primary teachers.

We need not delve deeply to understand the first of the contrasts they found between the Torah and the Prophets. Once the people of Israel has been accounted for, that is, after the Exodus stories, the Torah texts overwhelmingly concern themselves with laws and records. In wearisome detail, the last part of the Book of Exodus recounts the erection of the wilderness tabernacle, and the Book of Leviticus dissects every aspect of the sacrificial service there (and thus, by implication, later in the Temple). The Book of Numbers is packed with lists and legal detail, while Deuteronomy, as the name indicates, reviews much of the previous legislation, adding distinctive themes of its own, like the indispensability of a central sanctuary.

Many of these commandments can no longer be observed today. Once the Temple in Jerusalem was destroyed, the tabernacle/Temple/holiness commandments could no longer be directly observed, for the only place where sacrifices might properly be offered was not available. Instead, studying the regulations for the cultic service kept it alive in our community, at least in memory and aspiration.

To Jews beginning to modernize, most of Judaism already seemed so outmoded they saw no virtue in memorializing an obsolete set of rites. Moreover, the sacrificial system was abhorrent to them. To kill animals, catching their blood in basins so that it could be poured out at the altar, to skin and eviscerate them so that the fat of the entrails or even the whole animal could be burned to make a "savor pleasing to *Adonai*" seemed primitive and its long disuse progress.

The Ethical Thrust in the Prophets

Being concerned with the wide world which had opened to them, they responded enthusiastically to the prophets' call to give ethics religious preeminence.

> Woe to them that devise iniquity,
> who design evil on their beds.
> When morning dawns, they execute it,
> because they have the power.
> They covet fields and seize them
> houses, and take them away.
> They defraud men of their homes
> and people of their land. (Micah 2:1–2)

> Hear *Adonai*'s word, O people of Israel,
> for *Adonai* has a controversy with the people of this land
> because there is no truth or mercy

or knowledge of God in the land.
Swearing and lying and murder
and theft and adultery abound.
They break all limits
and blood touches blood. (Hosea 4:1–2)

Isaiah, after a touching parable about a farmer who plants a selected grapevine but only gets wild grapes, articulates God's complaint against the people God tenderly brought up from Egypt and planted in this land.

He looked for justice,
but behold, violence!
For equity
but behold, iniquity!
Woe to those who join house to house
and add field to field
till there is no room
and you must live alone in the midst of the land!
. . . Woe to those who rise early in the morning
that they may chase liquor,
that stay up late at night
until wine inflames them!
Who have lyre and lute, timbrel and flute
and wine at their feasts
but pay no attention to God's work
and have no interest in God's doings!
. . . Woe to those who call evil "good" and good "evil,"
who call what is dark "light" and what is light "dark,"
who call what is bitter "sweet" and what is sweet they call
    "bitter."
Woe to those who are wise in their own eyes
who are, by their own opinion, so clever.
Woe to those who are heroes at wine bibbing
and champions of mixing drinks.
Who, for a consideration, vindicate the wicked
and wrest the right of the righteous from him. (5:7–8, 11–12,
    20–23)

Such passages gave ancient Judaism immediacy in the modern world. What had once been said for the Jewish community applied universally, to humankind as a whole. Living by such behests, one would not only be a good Jew but the sort of citizen everyone would respect.

How Great a Gap Separates the Torah and the Prophets?

Before considering the four remaining themes, I should like to point out how this first contrast, like the others we shall consider, overstates the case.

To begin with, the Torah clearly demands and frequently prescribes high standards of human morality. From the story of Cain and Abel to the last passages in Deuteronomy denouncing Jewish sinfulness, the Torah knows the human condition well and shapes it to God's exalted criteria of human goodness. Indeed, we might argue that the Torah teaches righteousness far more effectively than the Prophets, for it turns values into law. The Torah not merely commends but commands not stealing, or cheating, or lying, or swearing falsely, or withholding a day-laborer's wages, or cursing the deaf, or tripping the blind, or taking vengeance, or bearing a grudge, but loving our neighbors as ourselves. (Lev. 19:11–18) Exhortation may rouse us to action and break through our defenses against greater responsibility. Good habits are more desirable and the Torah seeks to inculcate them.

For their part, the prophetic books demonstrate a serious devotion to worship. The postexilic prophets call for the restoration of sacrifices. The last eight chapters of the Book of Ezekiel detail the prophet's vision of the rebuilt Temple and its community. Some decades later, Haggai and Zechariah led the effort to rebuild the Temple. Malachi even denounces the people for bringing blemished offerings to the new Temple.

> A son honors his father
> and a servant his master.
> If I am a father,
> where is My honor?
> If I am a master,
> where is My respect?
> [This is what] *Adonai* of Hosts says
> to you, O priests who scorn My name.
> You ask, "How have we scorned Your name?"
> You offer up polluted food on My altar.

You ask, "How have we polluted You?"
By saying, *"Adonai*'s table is contemptible."
When you offer the blind for a sacrifice, [you say] "It is not
    evil"
and when you offer the lame and the sick, [you say] "It is not
    evil."
Present them now to your governor.
Will he be pleased with you?
or show you favor?
says *Adonai* of Hosts. (1:6–10)

And, in many places, those who prophesied before the destruction of the Temple show their high esteem for worship.

The contrasts I am drawing attention to are at best emphases, not absolute differences. To the generations in exodus from a segregated existence into general society, these distinctions were of immense importance. They validated the liberal Jewish boast that Judaism could adapt to modernity and still remain true to itself.

In What Sense Did the Prophets Teach Ethics?

One further comment about the prophets' "ethics" must be made. The liberals read the prophets as making ethics the essence of Judaism—and the Jewish followers of Kant widely popularized this interpretation of their heritage. As we shall see, some grounds for such a judgment exist, but people so easily distort the concept of prophetic ethics that some specific clarification is in order.

By ethics people usually mean a natural human capacity for discerning good from evil. We can then think of prophetic ethics as based on a purely human sense of moral right and wrong.

Such an interpretation of prophetic ethics utterly contradicts the prophets' views. They know of no independent realm called "ethics" and the word, as such, never occurs in the Bible. It couldn't, for it is a coinage of the Greek philosophic tradition. The "ethics" of the prophets derive from God. They result from applying God's criteria to human conduct. One should always bear in mind that the interpersonal judgments of the prophets, so important to us, take second place in the prophetic books to the denunciations of idol-worship. They unequivocally consider idolatry the root sin. All iniquity derives from it for, once one has thrown over God's rule, God's commands no longer obligate, including "ethics." The behavior of the nearby nations proved this to them, which explains why the prophets incessantly excoriate them. Insofar as the prophets have an "ethics" it is thoroughgoingly religious. It has no relation to the modern notion that ethics and belief are two distinct realms.

A Social Rather than an Institutional Focus

Very much of the Torah centers about the Temple and its cult or the organization of the Hebrews in the wilderness. The prophets, while referring to the Jewish community in which they lived, can be read as having a more encompassing social vision.

Very many prophecies indict the ruling classes. Consider the sweep of Micah, chapter 3. In verses 1–3, his list of charges begins:

> I said, "Listen, you rulers of Jacob,
> you chiefs of the House of Israel,
> you, who ought to know what is just,
> who hate the good and love evil,
> who tear the skin off [the people],
> and the flesh from their bones,
> who eat the flesh of My people,
> and flay the skin off them
> and break their bones. . . .

He then moves on in verse 5:

> Thus said *Adonai* to the prophets
> who lead My people astray,
> who cry "Peace"
> when they have something to eat
> but launch a war against one
> who fails to fill their mouths.

In verse 7 he includes seers and diviners in his condemnation. The chapter concludes with these charges (verses 9–12):

> Listen to this, you rulers of the House of Jacob,
> you chiefs of the House of Israel,
> who abhor justice

and pervert all equity,
who build Zion with blood
and Jerusalem with iniquity,
your rulers give verdicts for payment,
your priests make rulings for a fee,
your prophets foretell for money.
Yet they rely on *Adonai,* saying,
"Adonai is in our midst,
No evil can come upon us."
Assuredly, because of you
Zion shall be plowed as a field
and Jerusalem become ruins
and the Temple Mount
like a shrine in a forest.

Jews attaining citizenship in the nineteenth and twentieth centuries found such attacks particularly pertinent to leaders who condoned evil or promoted it. Jews had long suffered from unjust treatment and still had a long agenda of oppressions to overcome. With other disadvantaged groups in their fledgling democracies, they carried on a struggle for greater equality. With the words of the prophets ringing in their ears, they could feel they were helping their countries live up to their highest ideals while they were following the most valuable part of their religion. It was an ideal fusion of modernity and Judaism.

The Prophets as Moral Heroes

The stories of the prophets reinforced the new Jewish duty of challenging governmental injustice. Nathan, one of the earliest of the prophets, nobly defies his all-powerful king and patron David. He charged David with arranging the death of Uriah the Hittite after having seduced Bathsheba, Uriah's wife. He ostensibly submits for David's judgment the case of a rich man who seizes a poor man's only she-lamb to prepare a feast for a guest. When David, enraged, said, "That man deserves to die," Nathan replied, "You are that man!" (2 Sam. 12:1–7)

When Queen Jezebel, by perjured testimony, had Naboth killed so that King Ahab could seize Naboth's vineyard, which Ahab coveted, Elijah confronted the king. *Adonai*'s word had come to him with this message, " 'Will you murder and then take possession?' Thus said *Adonai* [about you], 'In the place where the dogs lapped up Naboth's blood, the dogs will also lap up your blood!' " (1 Kings 21:19) Unlike our modern experience of "stonewalling," both kings acknowledged their guilt and repented for it, surely one reason the stories are part of Sacred Scriptures.

Amos's case does not involve the king but, so to speak, a spiritual colleague, Amaziah, the chief priest of the royal sanctuary at Bethel. Amos had gone there to declaim his dire prophecies about the punishment *Adonai* would bring upon the sinful Kingdom of Israel. Amaziah first reported this "treason" to King Jeroboam and then confronted Amos, insultingly suggesting that he go earn his prophet's fees in the Kingdom of Judah. Amos replied, "I am not a professional prophet or a member of a prophetic guild. I am a cattle breeder and a tender of sycamore figs. But *Adonai* took me from following the flock and *Adonai* said to me, 'Go, prophesy to My people Israel'." (7:10–15) The same sense of divine compulsion is heard in chapter 3, verses 3–4, 8:

> Will two walk together
> without having made a date?
> Does a lion roar in the forest
> when he has no prey?
> . . . A lion has roared,
> who can but fear?
> *Adonai,* my God, has spoken,
> who can but prophesy?

Of all these moral heroes, I find Jeremiah the one who best reflects the situation of the modern social dissident. Perhaps I am impressed by the relatively more extensive records of his personal life or his continual involvement in issues of war and peace. We certainly can identify with the range of threats and punishments to which he was subjected. He once went to the Temple and prophesied that, because of the society's iniquity, God would destroy it as God had already done to the Temple at Shiloh (in the Northern Kingdom). When they heard this, the priests, prophets, and ordinary folk there threatened to lynch him. (26:4 and following) When King Jehoiakim had a scroll of Jeremiah's prophecies read to him, he found the message so distressing that he personally cut off and burned every few columns of it. He then sought to arrest Jeremiah but the prophet was in hiding. (36:21–26) More than once we read of Jeremiah being seized, beaten, and thrown into jail (37:15), or lowered into a pit to die (38:6). And his crimes? He attacked the people's self-righteous notion that the Temple would excuse their sinfulness (chapter 7), he accused the nobility of immorality (e.g., in 22:13–17, the speech to Shallum, also known as King Jehoahaz), and he called for peace, if necessary by surrender, in a time when everyone favored war.

These lonely fighters for justice who suffered greatly for their moral courage served as models for many modern Jewish idealists. Their contemporary social devotion might appear purely political, but they could identify it with an old and honored tradition of their people.

Some liberal Jews took this prophetic stance as a challenge to the people of Israel as a whole. They proclaimed that the Jews had a "prophetic" mission to teach the world an ethical vision of society and bring it into being. Not unexpectedly, the nations not only refused to accept this high ethical purpose but persecuted the Jews for bringing it. Jewish suffering results from being God's messenger.

Appealing to the New Individualism

We have already broached the next theme, the prophets' individuality, which made them newly appealing. The Jews received their rights in secular society as single selves, not as in the medieval system where groups or communities were enfranchised.* Individual political entitlement now powerfully inflated self-concern where earlier Judaism had stressed the Jewish people as a corporate entity.

The perennial appeal of the Book of Genesis largely derives from its focus on individuals. The rest of the Torah, though concerned with Moses as a person, focuses largely on the wilderness community and its program for living on the Land of Israel. The prophets are far more individualistically oriented. They not only concentrate on interpersonal relationships but tell us about their personal situations.

A number of the prophets are intriguing human beings. Where

*See Part One, *The Jewish People,* chapter 1, "What Sort of Group Are the Jews?"

Isaiah seems almost suave and worldly, he is so at ease with kings, Elijah is addressed by King Ahab as "you troubler of Israel." (2 Kings 18:17) Jeremiah was obviously a well known social nuisance, and Ezekiel behaves so bizarrely and makes such ordinarily inappropriate references in his prophecies that we might judge him deranged.

I usually find Jonah humorous in the touching, pathetic way he relates to God. When told by God to go to Nineveh and prophesy against it, he promptly books passage on a boat to Tarshish, the opposite direction. (1:3) Moses, Isaiah, and Jeremiah, among others, were also reluctant to be prophets, but Jonah is the only one of God's messengers who imagines he could flee from God. When he finally does prophesy the doom of Nineveh, he is furious at the result. The Ninevites, those hated enemies of the Jews, listen to him! They sincerely repent—note, please, that their sins involve ethical issues—and God forgives them, canceling their punishment. (3:8–10) Jonah now peevishly claims that this was why he hadn't wanted to go to Nineveh in the first place. When he stays to see what God will do to the city, God causes the *kikayon* plant to give him shade and then die, exposing Jonah to the hot sun. Now Jonah is doubly exasperated and again asks God to let him die—leading to God's compassionate message that even Ninevites are infinitely precious. (4:1–11) Jonah's petulance makes me laugh at myself for all those times I am concerned with self-justification rather than God's purposes. And I should like to think that something like this, rather than "the great fish," has made him precious to other liberal Jews as well.

The most touching if mysterious personal story of the prophets is that of Hosea. *Adonai* commands him to "take a whoring wife and children of whoredom, for the Land goes whoring, away from *Adonai.*" (1:2) The prophets often use the metaphor of marriage to describe the relationship between God and the Jews. And adultery or whoring is their biting image of Israel's sinfulness. Hosea had three children with Gomer, his wife, and they bear symbolic names of the judgment to come upon the Jews. We cannot tell from the following chapters what happened to their relationship. But the speeches are distinguished by moving insight into love and forgiveness. No other biblical book explores the tension between love and judgment as tenderly as does Hosea's writing. Much of our contemporary anguish in facing up to the demands of faithfulness in relationships appears in these chapters.

The Dynamic Implications of Prophetic Judgment

A difference of tone also distinguishes the Prophets from the Torah. So much of the Five Books of Moses lists details of law and structure that their Judaism seems timeless and unvarying. The prophetic books expose us to religion as a dynamic force.

In large part, the prophets' commitment to change manifests itself in their preoccupation with the punishment God threatens to bring down upon the unrepentant people. Habakkuk suffers because God delays in executing it.

> How long, *Adonai,* shall I cry out
> and You not listen?
> Shall I shout to You, "Violence,"
> and You not save?
> Why do You show me iniquity
> and make me look at unrighteousness?
> Spoiling and violence are before me,
> strife continues and contention goes on.
> Therefore the law does not function
> and justice never emerges;
> For the wicked outmaneuver the righteous
> and justice emerges deformed. (1:2–4.)

From the very first of the writing prophets, Amos, we hear of the judgment God will exact on *Adonai*'s Day. Society simply cannot be allowed to remain in its present, sinful state. Zephaniah continues the tradition, saying it must be transformed, beginning with an awesome punishment.

> Be silent before *Adonai,* my God,
> for *Adonai*'s Day is approaching
> . . . "I will punish the officials and the king's sons
> and all who clothe themselves in alien garments.
> I will also punish on that Day
> everyone who trespasses a threshold,
> who fill their master's house with violence and fraud.
> In that Day there shall be,"

declares *Adonai*,
"a loud cry from the Fish Gate
and howling from the Mishneh
and a sound of great anguish from the hills. . . .
At that time
I will search Jerusalem with lamps
and I will punish those who rest easy on their lees
Who say to themselves,
'*Adonai* will not do good, neither will He do evil.'
Their wealth shall be plundered
and their homes become desolate.
They shall build houses but not live in them,
they shall plant vineyards and not drink their wine." (1:7–13)

These teachers rejected the notion that things could never change. Rather they knew that because God ruled our social practices could not be allowed to remain as they had been.

Changing the Hierarchy of Jewish Values

Of all the lessons the liberals derived from the prophets, none affected them more profoundly than the principle that ethics are more important than worship in Judaism.

Above, I mentioned Jeremiah's attack on the notion that, as long as the Temple functioned, no harm could come to the people despite their unrighteousness. Here is some of what he said in the course of his speech: "Do not trust lying words, saying, '*Adonai*'s Temple, *Adonai*'s Temple, *Adonai*'s Temple are these [buildings].' No, but if you thoroughly mend your ways and your actions; if you thoroughly execute justice between one man and another; if you do not oppress the stranger, the orphan, and the widow; if you do not shed the blood of the innocent in this place; if you do not follow other gods, to your own hurt; then I will cause you to dwell in this place. . . . Will you steal, murder, commit adultery, swear falsely, sacrifice to Baal, follow other strange gods, and then come and stand before Me in this House which bears My name and say, 'We are safe!' " (7:4–10)

The Isaiah of the Exile had a similar message.

[You ask] "Why, when we fasted, did You not see?
Why when we afflicted our bodies, did You pay no heed?"

Behold, on your fast day you pursue your business and op-
    press your workers!
Because you fast in strife and contention
and you smite with a fist of wickedness!
You do not fast this day
so as to make your voice heard on high.
Is this the fast I desire,
a day for men to afflict their bodies?
Is it to bow one's head like a bulrush
and to lie in sackcloth and ashes?
Will you call that sort of fast
a day acceptable to *Adonai?*
No, this is the fast I desire:
To loose the fetters of wickedness,
to undo the bands of the yoke,
to let the oppressed go free,
to break off every yoke.
It is to share your bread with the hungry,
and to bring the wretched poor into your home;
When you see the naked, to clothe him
and not to hide from your own kin. (58:3–7)

Perhaps the favorite of all these prophetic passages demanding
human concern more than ritual performance is from Micah,
chapter 6, verses 6–8. When *Adonai* complains about the faithlessness of the people of Israel, the prophet has them respond:

"Wherewith shall I present myself to *Adonai?*
And do homage to God on high?
Shall I present myself with burnt offerings,
with calves a year old?
Will *Adonai* be appeased with thousands of rams,
with ten thousands of rivers of oil?
Shall I sacrifice my firstborn for my transgression,
the fruit of my body for the sin of my soul?"
He has told you, O man, what is good
and what *Adonai* requires of you:
Only to do justice
and to love mercy
and to walk humbly before your God.

Whatever authorization modern Jews needed to pay greater attention to their ethical rather than to their ritual behavior, they found in passages such as these. By mandating this newly congenial ranking of their religion's values, the prophets also validated the liberals' determination to revise the Jewish practice they had inherited.

Changing the Jewish Spiritual Horizon

One final theme cannot be omitted from our discussion, the sense of religious vision the liberals derived from the prophets. The Torah texts seemed to them almost provincial in their concentration on the present and on the Jewish people. By contrast, the ultimate goals of human history, and thus the destiny of all humankind, constitute a major motif in prophetic literature. For those no longer restricted to the affairs of their own folk, these were liberating ideals.

Contemporary scholars remain deeply divided as to whether the prophetic texts which allegedly point to the coming of the Messiah are merely a limited kind of political hope or a truly eschatological ideal. The liberals who, as we have seen*, gave up the idea of a Messiah in favor of the coming of a Messianic Age were not troubled by such niceties. The "Messianic" texts of the Bible spoke to them of a world they would like to live in. And now that they were free of the ghetto, they envisioned it as a world that they could create together with their fellow-citizens.

At the very least, it would be a world in which people could dwell in security. Ezekiel speaks of David being their shepherd and God then truly becoming their God. "I will grant them a covenant of peace and banish evil beasts from their land. They shall live safely in the wilderness and sleep in the forests. . . . I will send the rain in its season, rains that bring blessing. The trees of the field shall yield their fruit and the land shall yield its produce. [My people] shall be safe in their land. They shall know that I am indeed *Adonai* when I break the bars of their yoke and have delivered them from the power of those who enslaved them. They shall no longer be a spoil for the nations and the beasts of the earth shall not devour them. They shall dwell secure and untroubled. . . . They shall no longer be carried off by famine and they

*See Part One, *The Jewish People,* chapter 4, "What Do We Expect in the Messianic Age?"

shall not again bear the taunts of the nations. They shall know that I, *Adonai,* their God, am with them and they, the House of Israel, are My people. So declares *Adonai,* God." (34:23–30)

The ideal ruler is described by Isaiah in chapter 11, verses 2–9:

> The spirit of *Adonai* will rest on him,
> A spirit of wisdom and understanding,
> A spirit of counsel and valor,
> A spirit of devotion and reverence for *Adonai.*
> By that reverence will his intuition function.
> He shall not judge merely by what his eyes see,
> Nor decide merely by what his ears hear.
> Thus he will judge the poor with equity
> And decide justly for the lowly in the land.
> With the rod of his mouth he will smite the land,
> With the breath of his lips he will slay the wicked.
> Justice will be the girdle about his loins,
> And faithfulness the girdle about his waist.
> The wolf will dwell with the lamb,
> The leopard lie down with the kid.
> The calf, the young lion, and the fatling [will flock] together,
> With a little boy to herd them.
> The cow and the bear will graze,
> Their young will lie down together,
> While the lion, like the ox, will eat straw.
> A suckling child will play over the hole of a viper
> And an infant pass his hand over an adder's den.
> In all of My Holy Mountain
> Nothing evil or vile will be done,
> For the earth will be filled with devotion to *Adonai*
> As waters cover the sea.

This sort of vision inevitably reached out to embrace the nations of the world as well as the people of Israel. The great messianic passage found in both Isaiah 2 and Micah 4 dreams of all nations living in harmony. Something of the same universal horizon is found in various prophetic asides. Isaiah can look forward to a day when "there will be a highway from Egypt to Assyria. The Assyrians shall join with the Egyptians and Egyptians with the Assyrians . . . and together serve [*Adonai*]. In that day, Israel shall be a third partner with Egypt and Assyria as a blessing on earth, for *Adonai* of Hosts will bless them, saying 'Blessed be My people Egypt, My handiwork Assyria, and Israel My inheritance'." (19:23–25) Zephaniah sees as the climax of God's punishment of the nations that "then I will make the peoples pure of speech, / So that they shall invoke *Adonai* by name / And serve Him with one accord." (3:9) And Malachi, chiding the people of Israel for their contaminated religious service, reminds them in God's name: "From where the sun rises to where it sets, My name is honored among the nations and incense and pure oblations are offered to My name everywhere. For My name is honored among the nations. . . ." (1:11)

If these hopes were not sufficient to arouse the passions of Jews for the first time becoming citizens of the world, there was some prophetic hint of an even greater human culmination.

> *Adonai* of Hosts will make in this land
> For all nations
> A feast of rich foods,
> A feast of choice wines,
> Rich foods seasoned with marrow,
> Choice wines fully clarified.
> And in this land He will destroy the shroud
> That covers the faces of all peoples,
> The covering that is spread over all nations.
> He will destroy death forever.
> *Adonai,* my God, will wipe the tears away from all faces
> And will put an end to the reproach of people over all the
>   earth.
> For *Adonai* has spoken. (Isaiah 25:6–8)

·5·

HOW HAS CHANGE
COME INTO JUDAISM?

I have devoted the previous four chapters to liberal Judaism's teaching about the Bible, for all religious authority
in our religion stems from it. Now we must face a critical fact:
Judaism is not primarily a religion of the Bible. Many of our
practices and some of our beliefs cannot be directly derived from
it. Christians, particularly fundamentalists, are often shocked to
discover that we no longer have a sacrificial worship or the Aaro-
nide priesthood. Not knowing about Judaism's vigorous postbiblical growth, they have no idea that the rabbis created the Jewish
religion in the form it has today.

One of the first great modern Christian scholars of Judaism,
George Foot Moore of Harvard, wrote a path-breaking three-
volume work on the beliefs of the rabbis in the period from 70
to about 200 c. e. In his opening sentence he explained the
purpose for his choice of these years—to study Judaism in the era
"in which it assumed definitive form as it presents itself in the
tradition which it has always regarded as authentic."

A half century later scholars argue just how "definitive" a
"form" Judaism attained in those decades preceding the Mishnah. The many heterodox writings of that era, the Apocrypha, the
Pseudepigrapha, and the Dead Sea sect documents, testify to the
competition for adherents rabbinic Judaism faced. It was no orthodoxy but had a slow and uneven acceptance as the Talmud
indicates. Yet I consider Moore's judgment basically correct. The
rabbis, not the Bible or the sectarians, fixed the fundamental

301

beliefs and practices of Judaism and, equally important, the system for adapting them to changed historical circumstances.

How Did We Get from Prophets to Rabbis?

I will add one qualification to the previous generalization. The rabbis did not invent everything they mandated that is not in the Bible. Many of their discussions analyze long-practiced traditions that they apparently inherited. But we possess little reliable information about the evolution of Judaism in the centuries immediately prior to 70 c.e.

Our last hard historical data from the Bible comes from about 450 b.c.e., the time when Ezra and Nehemiah rebuilt Jerusalem and reshaped Jewish religious life in Judea. Retrospectively, Ezra seems a proto-rabbinic figure. The texts identify him as "the priest, the scribe, a scribe of *Adonai*'s commandments and of His statutes to Israel." (Ezra 7:11) His work is neither priestly nor prophetic. Rather, the people asked "Ezra the scribe to bring [out] the scroll of the Torah of Moses, which *Adonai* had commanded to Israel. Ezra the priest brought the Torah before the congregation, men and women and all who could listen with understanding. He read from it from early morning until midday . . . [and various officials] explained the Torah to the people. . . . They read from the scroll of God's Torah, translating it and giving the sense, so that they understood the reading." (Neh. 8:3–8)

After this tantalizing glimpse of an innovative practice that sounds like the later rabbinic Scripture reading, classic Jewish sources provide no reliable historical data until the earliest rabbinic texts, the first century c.e. The books of the Maccabees (in the Apocrypha) written about the second century b.c.e. do provide us with some information. Mostly we must rely on Josephus, who, some time after 70 c.e., recounts to a Hellenistic-Roman readership what he has learned of the previous few centuries of Jewish history. From these records plus some scraps of inference from late biblical texts, we can speculate intelligently about what happened in the growing Judean community. All that still leaves us largely unprepared for the doctrine of the Oral Torah and its study process, which is utterly without precedent in the Bible.

We have no difficulty understanding why a system such as that of the rabbis came into being. A written law can never be fully adequate to life. One simply cannot put everything into words, even in a relatively restricted area; interpretation is always required. When the law must guide a society over time, it also requires a way of adapting to new circumstances. We may well presume, then, that the origins of the Oral Torah stretch far back into Jewish history. Its institutionalization began in the dark period between Ezra and the Maccabees. When, in the first century c. e., the concept and practice of the Oral Torah become clearly visible, they are quite mature.

The Greatest Subsequent Challenge to Rabbinic Judaism

Until modern times, only one substantial threat arose to the authority of the rabbis. The Karaite movement that began in ninth-century c. e. Babylonia-Persia constituted for several centuries a major alternative to rabbinic Judaism. The Karaites rejected the doctrine of the Oral Torah and accepted none of its rulings as binding. Instead, they based themselves upon the Bible and a certain measure of community consensus.

Modern Jews often suppose the Karaites sought to liberate themselves from the heavy burden of rabbinic law. This interpretation discloses more about their image of traditional Judaism than about Karaism. In fact, the Karaites by relying rigorously on the biblical text created a more severe kind of Jewish practice. Thus, Anan ben David, the founder of the sect, added fast days to the Jewish calendar, interpreted the rules prohibiting *Shabbat* work stringently, and erected new barriers between Karaites and their non-Jewish neighbors.

The case of the Karaites can help us comprehend the distinctive character of the liberal Jews' clash with rabbinic Judaism. Liberal Judaism does not break with the rabbis and substitute a biblical for a talmudic structure for our religion. Rather it arises from the judgment that the traditional Jewish system for change, or its leadership, has failed to adapt Judaism to the conditions of emancipation.

As we shall see in the succeeding chapters, some liberals believe the resources of traditional Jewish law are adequate to our changed social situation. They only need to be utilized courageously, though responsibly. More individualistically oriented liberals believe that, in this era of self-development, rabbinic law can only serve as a guide to contemporary Jewish duty. It can no longer expect the dissenting conscience to conform to its mandates. Whatever their degree of reverence for Jewish law, conserving and reforming Jews consciously base themselves on rabbinic Judaism, though they wish to continue its evolution.

Esteeming the Sages without Idolizing Them

Clearly, liberal Jews continue the rabbinic tradition because it makes such good Jewish sense. Contemporary Jews learn this most readily from the ceremonies which surround *Shabbat,* the festivals, and weddings—and, in their own way, those of funerals and mourning. In these moments of joy and sorrow, the rites prescribed by the rabbis express wonderfully well our ongoing sense of our people's Covenant with God. We can also identify with the rabbis as we see how they enabled Judaism to mature spiritually. This matter deserves some special elaboration. Because I shall return to the complaint that rabbinic Judaism failed to meet the challenge of the Emancipation, I want to make certain first that the resources of the *halachah* for change are properly appreciated.

Let me begin by presenting a positive example of the rabbis' creative legislation in an area where today they regularly seem insensitive: women's rights. They created the *ketubah,* broadly the Jewish marriage contract, but, more specifically, the legal instrument by which the husband promises to transfer a substantial amount of capital to his bride.

The Bible does not mention marriage contracts, though it assumes the groom will pay a price for the bride to her father. (Exod. 22:15) Legal documents for Jewish marriage long precede the contracts of which the Talmud speaks in elaborate detail. Papyri from the Jewish military community of Elephantine, Egypt, dating back to the fifth century B.C.E., make stipulations different from the later rabbinic *ketubah.* In the time of the rabbis, the husband must make a significant monetary pledge, not to his father-in-law, but to his bride. Rava said that this provision was instituted so that husbands would not lightly divorce their wives, which the law otherwise made possible. (Ket. 11a) The *ketubah* of the rabbis protects the wife, for, should her husband divorce her, he must pay this debt. It also grants her further security. In the event of his death, she has first claim on the assets of his estate for this amount. Otherwise, rabbinic law gave her no rights to her husband's estate.

Moderns perceive in this innovation of rabbinic law the rectification of a previous inequity. As the Jewish conscience matured, the legal disabilities of Jewish wives seemed inconsistent with other Jewish values such as the dignity of all human beings and the importance of family harmony. The Oral Torah made it possible for Judaism to grow beyond what it once had been. Many other instances could be given as even our brief mention of Karaite rigor should have indicated. For nearly two millennia, rabbinic Judaism used its resources to keep Judaism alive as it faced challenges from within and from without. Its methods for accomplishing this were quite ingenious.

Surviving the Loss of a Central Authority

Before the destruction of the Temple, the decisions of the Sanhedrin determined Jewish law. This body of seventy one scholars had a combination of judicial and legislative powers. It also had the sanction of the government behind its decisions and could compel obedience to them.

When Jerusalem was conquered in 70 c.e., the official Sanhedrin ceased to exist. The rabbis, first under Yohanan ben Zakkai at Yavneh, and then, from time to time, in various other places, convoked successor councils which ruled on troublesome issues. These bodies had no governmental status; their authority derived from the stature of those who participated in them and from the loyalty of those Jews who followed the rabbis' interpretation of Judaism. Though such assemblies were held until the fifth century c.e., they gradually became less significant, largely due to the decline of the Jewish community in the Land of Israel.

The Jewish people's survival of the first Exile and their continued existence after the loss of the Second Temple have often been termed small miracles. To me, the maintenance of Jewish unity over the fifteen hundred years or more, when no central Jewish religious authority existed, constitutes an equal wonder. Bear in mind that Jews had become widely dispersed in this period, lived in the diverse cultures found from England to Persia, and large numbers of them were forced every few centuries to migrate. Their achievement of recognizable continuity despite the need to adapt to ever new circumstances excites the religious imagination.

Three facets of the rabbinic doctrine of the Oral Torah made possible innovation with integrity and we shall give them the bulk of our attention. First, the rabbis created a method of studying and amplifying their traditions which continues down to the present day. Second, a body of literature came into being which, without formal promulgation, became classic for all Jews. Third, a system of individual authority became accepted, which, though informal, effectively guided Jewish life.

The Rabbinic Study Method, Transmission with Creativity

Prophets have revelation firsthand; they repeat, they say, what God told them. The rabbis have revelation only secondhand; they have the words of those who had the direct communication from God. Some of what has been transmitted to them is Written Torah and some Oral Torah. The former they can get from texts. The latter they must gain from a Master, a *rav,* through a system of arduous discipleship. (A "rabbi" is one who is "my Master," in Jewish law.) The Masters communicate what they got from their Masters, and so on back to Moses listening to God on Mt. Sinai.

The Oral Torah is both a content and a method. The content is cumulative, for many generations have added to the Oral Torah. In time a given term or phrase or statement may no longer be clear or its application may be ambiguous. A method is needed for determining the meaning of the law. The disciples, by studying famous problems of the past, by learning how their Masters reason, and by analyzing ever more complex issues of their own time, finally become competent scholars. Now they can find or be brought new problems and they can give old or new answers as the occasion warrants. If they are worthy, their words, too, may become part of the Oral Torah.

This system treats the past with great reverence. Precedent and received traditions have compelling power. In one sense, the greatest Masters remain disciples all their lives. R. Eliezer b. Hyrcanus is the most extreme case of the pure transmitter. He once said to a group of Galilean Jews pressing him for instruction, "You wish to force me to say something I have not heard from my teachers. All my life, no man came to the academy before me. I never slept or dozed there. I never left someone there when I departed. I never indulged in secular talk. And I have never in my life said a thing which I did not hear from my teachers." (Suk. 28a) This conserving tendency in rabbinic study gave great stability to Jewish life.

The greatest of the early rabbinic dialecticians was probably R. Meir. R. Aha b. Hanina said, "It is perfectly clear to God that in the generation of R. Meir there was none equal to him. You may well ask, then, why was the *halachah* not fixed according to his views? Because his colleagues could not fathom the depths of his mind. Thus, he would declare the ritually unclean to be clean and supply plausible proof. He would also declare the ritually clean to be unclean and also supply plausible proof." (Er. 13b) In a system founded on the premise that the Torah had infinite depths of meaning and minds could be trained to uncover them, a Master could meet new situations with creative intelligence.

A further opening for innovation comes from the practice of encouraging and remembering differing opinions. The early controversies between the Schools of Shammai and Hillel are among the most famous divergent interpretations of Judaism, but the method of clarifying by dialectical argument continues down to the present day. Moreover, preserving the minority position made it available to a later generation should it seem needed to meet new circumstances.

By these procedures some teachers clearly changed the law from the obvious intent of the Torah. Where it demands capital punishment for certain offenses, the laws of the Mishnah breathe a different spirit. In Mak. 1:10 we read, "A Sanhedrin that puts one man to death in seven years is called 'destructive.' R. Elazar b. Azariah says, 'Or one in even seventy years.' R. Tarfon and R. Akiba say, 'Had we been in the Sanhedrin none would ever have been put to death.' Rabban Simeon b. Gamaliel says, 'They would have multiplied murderers in Israel!' "

The Oral Torah Itself Became a Written Tradition

The second aspect of the *Torah Shebeal Peh,* which kept the Jews united despite dispersion, migration, and change, was its distillation into written form. How this happened continues to divide scholars. Perhaps as its contents grew, documentary help became indispensable. Perhaps the declining circumstances of Jewish life in the Land of Israel and the continued vitality of Diaspora Jewries made easily carried packets of authentic traditions necessary. Whatever the reason, about 200 C.E. Judah Hanasi, the Prince or Ruler, recognized by both Romans and Jews as head of the Jewish community, issued the Mishnah. In six major orders, containing sixty-three tractates, this prestigious teacher put into written form the major opinions of his predecessors. Another, less concise collection, which overlaps the Mishnah considerably, is called the Tosefta. But it did not take long for Judah Hanasi's Mishnah to become the basis of all future study of the Oral Torah.

As we have seen in the capital punishment citation, the Mishnah provides previous opinions of sages and such decisions as the study process engendered. By fixing them in written form, the Mishnah, like all law books, specifies the official legal tradition. Yet it also preserves the records of differing opinions and innovations. It therefore provides weighty precedent for refusing to be satisfied with the accepted rule when it clashes with pressing Jewish needs.

If anything, the subsequent emergence of the Talmud favored the analytic, individual aspect of rabbinic Judaism. In the Land of Israel, the records of its sages' Mishnah study received fixed form about 400 C.E. Its Talmud is popularly called the *Yerushalmi,* that of Jerusalem. The Babylonian Talmud, the *Bavli,* was compiled about 500 C.E. It became the more authoritative of the two, perhaps because it is more extensive, or because its community had greater influence over Diaspora Jewish life in succeeding centuries.

Where the Mishnah transmits relatively compressed statements, with a preference for conclusions, the Talmud, literally "the study" (of the Mishnah), primarily presents reasoning. The authorities presented in the Gemara, the rabbis' discussion of the Mishnah, constantly inquire about the basis of a given position, its sources, its further application, or its adequacy in the face of contrary evidence. It practically luxuriates in divergent opinion and its text wanders freely from a given topic to whatever tangent seems momentarily of interest. It touches far more matters than does the Mishnah. One may well say that nothing human is alien to it.

In the second half of the first millennium c.e., the Talmud gradually became the authoritative guide to continuity and change in Jewish life. What the talmudic sages had done to make the Mishnah relevant to their time, later teachers could now do to its texts in their unanticipated circumstances.

The Medieval Evolution of the Oral Torah

The study of the Talmud took a quantum leap forward with the completion of a commentary to it by Rashi, the eleventh-century French savant. In brief and relatively simple fashion, he set down the accepted interpretation of the often cryptic Talmud text.

Students with the Rashi commentary before them now had a Master in written form; there was no reason they could not now understand the whole Talmud as the great teachers did. In Rashi's own Franco-German Jewish community, his work quickly had an unexpected intellectual effect. Studious Jews, now comprehending the Talmud texts with relative ease, began comparing statements from one part of the Talmud with those in another. This enabled them to raise new questions as to what the law ought to be, whether in theory or actuality. When the Talmud was printed in the fifteenth century, the Rashi commentary was set on one side of the Gemara and the Tosafot, as the comparativists came to be known, were on the other side—and subsequent printings have followed this practice. The study of the Oral Torah had now reached a new level of competence.

A final layer of definitive literature eventually arose, the codes. In the centuries after the completion of the Talmud, the accumulation of opinion on given topics became so great that rabbis would write monographs on them to clarify the law. This sporadic process came to a climax in Maimonides. About 1180 c.e., he authored an incredible distillation of all the major decisions in Jewish law to his time! These he arranged, without precedent, in a logically ordered structure. The *Mishneh Torah,* literally, the "Second Torah," now set a new horizon for the reach of Jewish legal competency. It did not remain unchallenged, for Maimonides had not provided the classic sources on which his judgments were based. Critical commentaries to the *Mishneh Torah* (now regularly printed with it) were succeeded by new codes. The most authoritative of these are the *Arbaah Turim,* the "Four Columns," of Jacob ben Asher of fourteenth-century Spain and the climactic code, the *Shulchan Aruch,* the "Set Table," of Joseph Karo of sixteenth-century Safed.

Despite the variety of opinion in the several codes and the ideal that a sage would reason from the talmudic data, not the codes, it is difficult not to see codification rigidifying Jewish law. And the printing of texts furthered the thrust to standardization. Variety and innovation did not cease, but from the sixteenth century on, the internal processes of the Oral Law functioned more strongly for preservation than for change.

The Individual Power of the Master

A third formal aspect of Oral Torah deserves particular attention for it is the direct instrument through which continuity or change still comes into Jewish life. Having been deemed worthy to bear the title Master, rabbis have broad personal authority over the community that elected them. As authorized expositors of the Oral Torah, they speak, as it were, with the power of Sinaitic revelation. In a social emergency, they may contravene what was previously the law. Thus, despite the strong, explicit prohibition of writing the Oral Torah, the need not to forget any part of it brought the rabbis to set it down (in the name of a higher legal principle, preserving Torah). (Tem. 14b)

Perhaps the most dramatic case of individual rabbinic creativity is Hillel's *prosbul.* "This is one of the things that Hillel the Elder ordained. When he saw that people refrained from extending loans to one another (as the sabbatical year approached), . . . Hillel ordained the *prosbul.*" (Shev. 10:3; cp. Git. 36a ff.) By a judicial formula and confirmation, he made it possible for a private debt to become an instrument of the Jewish court and thus not subject to the sabbatical year remission of private debts. So, too, the official ban on polygamy in Ashkenazic Jewry is ascribed to an edict by Gershom ben Judah of Mayence about the year 1000.

Though this power still inheres in the individual rabbi, the great sages of modern times have rarely invoked it on a major communal issue. They have rather made their influence felt by the more common device of the responsum, the formal answer to a question put to an authority. This pattern goes back to the days when Jewish communities around the world sent inquiries to the Babylonian academies about the Talmud. Later, as rabbis became known for their erudition and piety, individuals as well as communities would turn to them with their questions. We know Maimonides as the great legal mind of Spanish Jewry and his responsa, *teshuvot,* were extensive. A more widely sought after Spanish *posek,* decisor, was the later sage, Solomon ben Abraham Adret (c. 1235-c.1310). He wrote over 1,000 *teshuvot* to questioners from all over the Jewish world. They still constitute a major source for determining Jewish law.

Being individualistic, responsa often reflect a *posek*'s local circumstances and personal predilections. Despite codes and precedents, he may see fit, in responding to a question, to modify in small or great part the usual previous interpretation of the law. A good example is provided by an aside by the highly regarded Rabbi Jacob Emden (1697–1776) on the issue of abortion. While dealing with a pregnancy resulting from adultery, he says, "With legitimate offspring too, there is room to permit abortion should there be [a legally determined] 'great need,' as long as the birth process has not yet begun. The reason need not be to save her life but only to save her from the excessive pain it causes her. But the matter requires further deliberation." (Sheelat Yaavetz, 43) Other more modern respondents have made reference to serious mental-health risks as being possible reasons for an abortion. Such statements may be utilized by later decisors to justify permissive rulings. But these positions stand at the margins of the great stream of responsa on abortion which are highly restrictive.

Utter democracy and informality characterize the realm of responsa. No communal body elects or appoints the authoritative leaders of the generation, the *gedole hador.* They become *gedolim* because other rabbis defer to their decisions or turn to them for opinions on difficult questions. They may be few or relatively many in a given country or era and no institution has the power to adjudicate between the ruling of one sage and that of another. Such openness in an orthodoxy is utterly uncommon yet it has been fundamental to the Jewish heritage for much of the lengthy history of rabbinic Judaism.

Because of the welter of questions raised for Jewish practice by technology and other new conditions of Jewish life, the *teshuvah* system continues to function with great vigor. The former Ashkenazic chief rabbi of the State of Israel, Shelomoh Goven, despite his governmental status, was not widely considered a leading *posek* for world Orthodoxy. By contrast, the responsa of the head of a comparatively small, lower Manhattan *yeshivah*, Tifereth Jerusalem, Rabbi Moshe Feinstein, receive respectful Jewish attention in observant Jewish communities everywhere. Most of his *teshuvot* apply Jewish law to modern questions with considerable stringency but he occasionally lends his authority to what liberal Jews would see as more lenient rulings. Thus, he rejects the prohibition by some *poskim* of a doctor's role in the artificial insemination of a woman with her husband's semen because of the laws of adultery. And he agrees that mental derangement is considered the equivalent of a physical danger to life, thus allowing for abortion in some special cases.

The Role of the Community in the Development of the Law

All this attention to the institutionalized patterns by which the law developed should not blind us to their necessary corollary: a community must follow the law. Even briefly, let us consider the informal ways in which the will of the Jews living under the law has also shaped it.

In every community tension arises between the populace and the law. While people follow most of its provisions, keeping the system alive, some statutes produce considerable resistance, generally because the laws were consciously made to interdict acts people wish to do. If the proportion of transgressors becomes high, the law becomes unenforceable. We may then repeal it, as happened to Prohibition in the United States.

Occasionally, the Jewish community has exercised such a veto on the continuation of a Jewish law. Thus, we read in the Mishnah, "When murders multiplied, the rite of breaking the heifer's neck ceased. . . . When adulterers multiplied, the rite of the bitter waters ceased. R. Yohanan b. Zakkai brought it to an end in accord with Hosea 4:14." (Sot. 9:9) Note the role of the sage in determining when to follow the lead of the people and when to resist it. Jewish law is not democratically determined. God formulated it and put its continuity into the hands of trained personnel. They must determine in any given instance whether to fight the people's sinfulness, momentarily overlook it, or authorize some change in Jewish practice.

In religion, particularly, the people often also create forms of such wide appeal that a significant addition is made to the inherited practice. The festival of Simchat Torah, as we now observe it, testifies to the creative power of the folk in Judaism. It did not exist in talmudic times but came into existence when the one-year cycle for reading the Torah became widely accepted. The reading of Joshua 1 as the festival *haftarah* may be dated to the ninth century; following the conclusion of Deuteronomy by the immediate reading of Genesis 1 began in the fourteenth century; about the same time we begin to hear of all the Torahs being taken out of the Ark; and a century later dancing with them in the synagogue receives formal authorization.

Nothing today better illustrates the power of custom than the emotion surrounding the practice of praying with covered heads. We have good evidence that as late as the thirteenth century some Jews prayed bareheaded. But covering the head for prayer became so common among Jews and so important for distinguishing them from Gentiles that it took on the force of law. The German Reform Jews, but not those in the Liberal movement, broke with the rest of the community and adopted the Western custom of showing respect by removing one's hat. (Paradoxically, women were expected to wear hats at services.) American Reform Jewry continued this experimental practice while the rest of modern Jewry rejected it. What was once only a custom had become so significant a part of Jewish practice that the bulk of the community considers it a valued sign of Jewish distinctiveness.

Most folk customs never rise to the level of law but they may become so dear to some Jews that they become as punctilious about them as about the requirements of law—and not infrequently confuse the two. A quick survey of contemporary Orthodox Jews indicates a clear division between two groups. One consists of those whose clothes, demeanor, and grooming proclaim that they believe European fashions to be integral to Judaism. The same signs in the other group indicate their belief that one can adopt American styles and remain fully faithful to Judaism. Even among liberal Jews folk custom has a powerful legislative effect. A family religious celebration at which no food was served would affront those attending, though no commandment requires us to make feeding family and friends a part of our observance. So, too, the accustomed emotional tone of the local synagogue service, so precious to those who are used to it, can be oppressive to visitors unfamiliar with it or to people who come to pray with other emotional needs.

Defending the Torah against the Community

This system of Oral Torah, which had worked so well to keep Judaism alive for eighteen centuries, lost the allegiance of most Jews after the Emancipation. Perhaps their flight into the modern world was so headlong that nothing the traditional leaders could have done would have redirected their ways. Perhaps the rabbinate was still so badly shaken by the worldwide Jewish experience with the false messiah Sabbetai Zevi (1626–1676) that it could tolerate no new proposals to change Jewish law. Sabbetai Zevi had given evidence of his exalted status by publicly altering certain Jewish practices. This led extremists influenced by him to call for greater sin as a path to higher holiness, and change was then doubly damned by the false messiah's eventual conversion to Islam. Surely, too, the depth of economic misery and population loss from which the Jewish community was just emerging by the beginning of the nineteenth century had depleted Jewish religious energy and initiative. And I suggest that the grant of freedom, for all its qualifications, so radically reversed fifteen centuries of segregation that the cultural discontinuity was more than the system or its leaders could cope with.

For all these reasons, the Orthodox sages now began to defend the law against a nonobservant community and confined their leadership to the minority who remained faithful to the Oral and Written Torah. Thus, these rabbis could have ruled, in full accordance with the law, that the use of the vernacular was permitted in services, as were sermons; and they could have eliminated those additions to the service which were not required and had little relevance to contemporary worshipers. Instead they strongly objected to these and other changes for they might encourage those who wished to introduce more radical changes or to abandon Judaism altogether.

The battle over the functioning of the old system of adaptation broke out most poignantly over the emancipated Jew's desire for a modern education. Today, modern Orthodoxy (but little of right wing Orthodoxy) coexists peacefully with higher Western education. A few generations back a student, found reading about world history or mathematics in a modern Hebrew popularization, would immediately be dismissed from his *yeshivah.* The rejection of modernity went that far.

But What if There Were No Genuine Notion of Change?

In all this discussion, I have suppressed one critical concept. Rabbinic Judaism, for all its knowledge of the various matters I have mentioned previously, denies that there is ever true innovation in Judaism. Against the central perception of the modern consciousness, it thinks of religious truth as permanent and unchanging. This sense of reality operates with such strength that the rabbis can hardly imagine that there was ever a time when Jews did not live according to the prescriptions of rabbinic Judaism.

The general principle is summed up in a statement of the *Yerushalmi,* the Jerusalem Talmud. "Even that which a conscientious disciple later teaches in the presence of his Master was already said to Moses on Sinai." (Y., Pe. 17a) Though no one has heard it before, this makes it the recapitulation of an ancient, perennially valid truth. Were it truly a creative statement of a later consciousness appealing to us on that basis alone, the rabbis would reject it out of hand. Change could come into rabbinic Judaism only if it appeared to be continuity with the past.

This notion, often so difficult for moderns to grasp, finds full exposition in the rabbinic treatment of the great biblical figures who lived before the giving of the Torah at Sinai. It cannot be imagined that a Jew as notable as Abraham, for example, did not live according to rabbinic law. In the course of a discussion in which the sages debate the legitimacy of deriving the law from the presumed practice of Abraham, the following exchange occurs. "Rav said, 'Our Patriarch, Abraham, kept the whole Torah, as it is said, "Because Abraham hearkened to My voice and kept My charge, My commandments, My statutes, and My laws." ' [Gen. 26:5] R. Shimi b. Hiyya said to Rav, 'Should you not rather say that he kept the seven commandments [given to the Children of Noah]? And, of course, that of circumcision.' [Rav responded] 'That cannot be the meaning of "My commandments and My laws." ' " To this is appended the statement, "Rava or R. Ashi said, 'Abraham, the Patriarch, kept even the [rabbinic laws] concerning the *"eruv* of dishes" [ordained by the rabbis to extend the Sabbath boundaries]. Note the exact wording. ["My laws" literally says] "My *Torot.*" He kept not only what was in the Written Torah but in the Oral Torah as well'. " (Yoma 28b)

In the Midrash, with its delight in the imagination, we hear of this sort of reasoning applied even to Adam, whom the rabbis agreed was not a Jew. The verse describing God's purposes in putting Adam in the Garden of Eden indicates that Adam was supposed "to till it and tend it." (Gen. 2:15) These verbs remind the "midrashist" of commands given to the people of Israel. He therefore triumphantly concludes that Adam was supposed to offer sacrifices and observe the Sabbath. (Gen. R. 16:5)

This devotion to permanence entails indifference to precise chronology or the sort of developmental history that moderns consider central to understanding phenomena. The great Babylonian teacher Rav was once quoted by a disciple as saying, "The Torah does not present things with a strict distinction between what came earlier and what came later." (Pes. 6b) Something of this attitude lies behind the rather surprising fact that, though much of the Bible consists of books of history, the rabbis seem to have little interest in it. Though they recognize some events as having historical significance and record some accounts of them, none of their books follows the model of Samuel or Kings.

When the Emancipation challenged the long-accepted patterns of Jewish life, this devotion to the perennial character of the Torah asserted itself as opposition to all change. A struggle between two forms of consciousness broke out. In the older one, change had obviously occurred but could, as it were, be subsumed under the general notion of the Torah's essential continuity. Moderns would say that it had been so organic a part of the community's way of life that it was unconscious of the continual innovations it had made.

Modernity came with a suddenness and ruthlessness that would not allow the old mind-set to function. The social transformation was so severe, the intellectual shift from the static to the dynamic was so contrary, that the consciousness of change could no longer be reinterpreted as "already said to Moses on Sinai." Rather adaptation became a value in itself, and creativity, not continuity, became the hallmark of worth. Liberal Judaism has wholeheartedly adopted the modern notion that things are always changing. It views truth, including religious truth, more as a process than a given, more an activity than a once-and-for-all-time event.

Could There Have Been Compromise Rather than Revolution?

Had the early liberals been less radical, had they made their changes more slowly, justifying them by talmudic rationale, and carefully seeing how much of past tradition they could conserve, would that have appeased the traditionalists? More importantly, would it have convinced those many Jews stampeding into the general society that they could truly be Jewish and modern? I sometimes wonder about such things. Mostly I do not see how we, who do not know the highly charged atmosphere they faced but extrapolate from our security in an established modern Judaism, can say with assurance how they should have acted.

We shall see in the following chapters how liberal Jews divide over the issue of the desirability of revitalizing the adaptive procedures of the Oral Torah. For the moment let us conclude this part of our investigation by reminding ourselves of what the liberals introduced into Judaism. They asserted a greater role for the people in determining proper Jewish observance than the traditional Judaism had previously known. They insisted on trusting the deepest religious intuitions of the Jews facing their new situation as much if not more than the Oral Torah's heavy weight of precedent. They had the courage to acknowledge and meet the radical historical transmutation which had befallen their people and to reform Jewish practice so that one could live fully as a modern person and a faithful Jew. And they had the daring to undertake the experiments which sought to give this revolutionary new conception of Judaism proper content. Let us then add one more hypothetical question to the many we have asked, "Where would Judaism be today without them?"

·6·

MUST WE OBSERVE
ALL THE COMMANDMENTS
AND TRADITIONS?

I begin with two assumptions. First, that the question about how much we must do as Jews does not come from people who have only a casual interest in Judaism. One need not be a trained anthropologist to perceive that the Jews who fill the pews of Orthodox, Reform, Conservative, or Reconstructionist synagogues have a polite indifference to what is demanded of them. Realistically, they will do what they please, and generally that isn't much.

Tepid Jews have only one interest in asking about the extent of Jewish duty: getting permission to continue doing very little. I doubt that anyone with such a mind-set would be interested in reading this book. But should some aspect of this widespread Jewish cynicism slither up from your unconscious, please understand that I cannot be of much help with it. When you love Judaism, you are not inclined to help people ignore it.

I also assume that we share a common ethical principle, namely, that people ought not be hypocrites but should live with integrity, acting on what they say they believe. In what follows, then, what you "must do" means, at least, that you ought to act in accord with your deepest commitments.

Linking belief and practice teaches us a good deal about the hidden agenda of many Jews. What explains the negative emotions Jews regularly bring to discussions of faith in God? Not, I

318

am now convinced, issues of intellect or ethics but, unconsciously, the conviction that to accept God would mean, for a person of integrity, restoring the yoke of the commandments, all of them. And we may fantasize that this includes East European immigrant styles and lower class manners. God, as it were, stands for the ghetto life we do not want to lead. Agnosticism liberates us from "all that" and preserves our life-style. No wonder Jews hold on to it with such intensity.

I shall indeed be arguing that our belief in God and the Covenant ought to have power over our lives. That is why I devoted the first two-thirds of this book to various modern interpretations of our faith. And, I hope, I have made perfectly clear our liberal Jewish principle that you, personally, ought to make your own decisions concerning them. Perhaps one of the best ways of judging what you should believe is to determine what you know you must and must not do. At the same time you will not grow as a person unless your faith and values lead you to try things you have not done before.

Traditional Belief and Traditional Duty

Let us begin with our heritage. Suppose tomorrow that God came to you and, to your own surprise, you knew it truly was God. Suppose further that God said that you deserved better guidance for living your life. As a result, God left a handbook for living at your front door. And, when you got there, you found it just as God had promised. Would you not then do your best to live by its prescriptions as carefully as you could? The logic is irresistible. If we unquestionably knew something to be God's command, we would devote our whole being to it.

All religious orthodoxies begin with such reasoning. Traditional Judaism, deriving as it does from the giving of the Torah on Mt. Sinai, may even be the prototype of this form of religion. As we noted previously, classic Judaism proclaims that God revealed an Oral as well as a Written Torah. A *believing* Orthodox Jew must then try to fulfill all those obligations which have been specified by the unbroken chain of sages down to our day. But that puts it badly. If, indeed, we possess God's instructions, they are not a burden but an exquisite privilege. Ordinary people doing simple things have by these acts become partners of the

Most High. No eminence granted by human beings could ever match such prestige.

This certainty of the possession of God's word powers all orthodoxies. Every religious deed can elicit a maximum effort. One's motivation is never sullied with ambiguity about why one must do it or do it in just this way. The pious also have great personal security. They are not only linked with God but with a community that serves God even though most other people ignore God. No ethnic "roots" could run so deep.

Much of the recent resurgence of orthodoxies has come from the willingness of disappointed liberals to accept their yoke and be rid of the responsibility for making all one's own critical decisions. Not infrequently, the old liberal agnosticism ironically reasserts itself here. Wanting above all the psychic serenity that comes from knowing what to do, people again sunder belief from action and glory in the security which comes from living as one of the chosen.

Commandments the Orthodox Do Not Observe

Let us, however, understand the limits of traditional Jewish obligation. Statutes exist which all authorities agree continue to make a claim upon us but which no one observes. The most obvious of these are the many ordinances concerning the Temple service. They cannot be carried out under present circumstances, namely, the absence of a Temple in Jerusalem. There is also considerable opinion to the effect that, even if the Moslems were willing to return the Temple Mount to Jewish hands, the central shrine can now only properly be rebuilt by the Messiah.

In general, the Torah recognizes that special circumstances may alter the way in which we carry out its prescriptions. In the absence of a *minyan,* we pray as individuals; since there is no water in the desert, there we may ritually "wash" our hands with sand.

Another large category of circumstantially unperformed commandments consists of those which apply only when one resides in the Land of Israel. Nowhere else do Jewish farmers have the opportunity of properly fulfilling the laws of the sabbatical year, as observant Israeli Jews do. Orthodox Jews comprise so high a proportion of Americans migrating to the State of Israel because it provides them with the maximum opportunity for fulfilling God's behests.

We may say of a few laws that they are no longer in practice because we are not certain how exactly to carry them out. Numbers 15:38 specifies that in the fringes attached to the four corners of a Jew's garment one thread was to be blue, specifically, *techelet.* This color was obtained by utilizing a dye from the *chilazon,* a snail found near Haifa and Tyre. When finding and processing these snails became difficult and counterfeit dyes made proper identification of the *techelet* onerous if not impractical, the rabbis ruled that a fringe of all white threads would be acceptable. (Men. 4:1)

A somewhat related case, and a charming one, is the Cup of Elijah at the Passover *seder.* Tradition requires four cups of wine to be drunk at the celebration; the community must help even the poorest Jew fulfill this obligation. (Pes. 10:1) A midrash relates this rule to the four terms for redemption in Exodus 6:6–7, "I will take you out . . . deliver you . . . redeem you . . . and choose you as My people." Later some rabbis pointed out that the phrase "I shall bring you . . ." is also used in reference to the Exodus. Hence a fifth cup should be drunk. The argument was not strong enough to persuade but was too cogent to brush aside. A compromise was reached. The rabbis had taught that, when Elijah the prophet returns to announce the coming of the Messiah, he will answer all our unresolved religious questions. (Mal. 3:23–24) Hence we put a cup of wine on our *seder* table in the hope that he will come and indicate whether we do or do not have the obligation to drink it.

In some highly specific situations, competent authorities disagree. Some permit and some prohibit. Both are fully traditional but two patterns of practice result. Such disagreements on the specific content of the Torah create the differences in observance between the "modern" and the "right wing" Orthodox. Thus, by the limited size of their families, the "modern" Orthodox have apparently accepted the Jewish legitimacy of contraception, once they have satisfied the basic law requiring a child of each sex. Those of the "right wing," however, continue to follow the older interpretation of the law, banning contraception except in special instances.

The Unusual Status of Custom among Jews

The list of "all" the practices that Jews should traditionally perform has another limitation, the ambiguous status of "custom." An act that has "halachicly" been identified as a *minhag,* usually translated as "custom," *must* be done, as is the case with wearing a *kipah* at services. But the word "custom" has such weak connotations in English—custom does not usually obligate—that we face semantic difficulties in this discussion. Perhaps the phrase "customary usage" will, for the moment, allow us to focus on acts traditional Jews regularly do and expect of other Jews, but which are not mandated.

Food immediately comes to mind, for it plays so great a part in our Jewish memories. The customary East European *Shabbos* dinner regularly included gefilte fish, chicken soup with noodles, and boiled or roasted chicken. When fruit compote came in as a desert remains a matter of debate, but tea and honey cake have an old claim on *Shabbos* gustatory affection.

This menu is not a matter of law, as witness its local variations in Europe. Its transmutations in the United States are startling. Who ever heard of a *Shabbos* salad?—with dressing yet! The common substitution of *matsah* balls for noodles has been denounced by palate purists as Jewish culinary heresy!

Any abrupt shift from fish-soup-chicken can cause family tensions, for many customary usages have an inner power of their own. But, if *Shabbat* should be the most honored day of the week, the meal which inaugurates it ought to be the most delectable of the week. With the extraordinary range of foods and spices available to us, why must we continue to eat a meal which East European poverty made seem like a celebration?

The Openness of a Tradition Based on Law

The *kiddush* wine cuts across the lines of law, *minhag,* and custom. Because of a practice that became codified, traditional Jews use only red wine for *kiddush.* For unknown reasons, Jewish ritual wine has for some time been sweetened with sugar. No law requires this and it has not acquired the status of an official, binding *minhag.* As affluence and experience have changed the taste of American Jews, they have sought out the *kosher* dry wines of

France, Italy, and the State of Israel. For the *seder,* at least, a shift is under way from serving only sweetened wine to providing dry wine for those who prefer it—and the white dry *kosher* wines are also reported to be selling well.

Not so long ago all traditional Jews could be identified by their lengthy jackets, *kapotes,* or the way they wore their beards. Today, the short jacket and the groomed beard have become acceptable even in right wing Orthodox communities. But many issues remain between them and the modern Orthodox. Can the Talmud properly be studied with English rather than with Yiddish? Can the Sephardic pronunciation of Hebrew be accepted among Ashkenazim? How much general education is not *bittul Torah,* neglect of the obligation to study Torah? Can a devoted Jew be satisfied with a small, knit *kipah* for his head-covering or must one wear a nice black hat, preferably covering a sizable black *yarmulke?* In many questions such as these the living quality of Orthodox Judaism's adaptation to modern fashion is being worked out.

One final word about the range of Orthodox Jewish obligation: The Torah does not tell us everything we need to do. It leaves a great deal up to us. How much time one will give one's children or how to treat one's help humanly, what one will do with one's leisure or how one will handle one's depressions, are all left up to us. Jewish literature may give us copious suggestions as to how we ought to live and we can gain much from our community and rabbi. Yet, in the last analysis, the quality of our life is ours to determine. As the Spanish sage Nachmanides once put it, one can be "a fool under the Torah," observing the law but being an ugly human being. Orthodox Judaism, like all religions, leaves much room within the law for temperament, situation, and personal choice. Individual Jews, not the law, must ultimately shape the texture of their existence.

I hope these various discussions have clarified that for traditional Jews, who have the privilege to be obligated to perform "all the commandments and traditions," there are internal limits as well as options as to what must be done.

When Religious Authority Derives from Humankind

Liberal Jews believe that human beings are responsible for both the Written and the Oral Torah. Our sacred texts and contemporary sages may have much to teach us but they do not legislate for us. Liberals insist on the freedom to determine for themselves which aspects of their inherited faith they will continue to observe and what in their belief now requires the creation of new forms.

To me, the history of the liberal Jewish use of this freedom falls into two overlapping periods. The one begins with its origins and extends into the present with declining influence. I would term this the period of *negative* freedom. In it, liberal Jews gloried in their right *not to do* what prior Jews had considered mandatory. The second period, whose first formal stirrings can be traced back to the late 1920s, and whose impact has been increasingly visible since the late 1960s, may be termed one of *positive* freedom. Now, the liberals utilized religious self-determination *to add to* their religious observance. They adopted previously neglected traditions and created new ones to express their growing Jewish religious sensibilities.

Most Jews popularly associate liberal Judaism with negative freedom. Modernizing Jews now felt they had the Jewish right to set aside long honored, central provisions of Jewish law. Traditionally observant Jews may not use electricity on *Shabbat* if a switch will be thrown in the process. Though the Talmud knew nothing directly about electricity, later rabbinic law bars utilizing a switch on *Shabbat* as a spark may well result (even if a minuscule one). This would violate, by extension, the prohibition of making a fire on *Shabbat*. Liberal Jews rejected the continuing validity of that ruling just as they did the prohibition of using an automobile on *Shabbat* for a purpose as worthy as getting to the synagogue.

Freedom to Do as Well as to Desist

Not every use of personal autonomy by liberal Jews was as defensible. Humankind being beset by what the rabbis called the Evil Urge, the freedom to choose became for many license to do as little as possible. Personal convenience or whim now often substituted for Jewish commitment or responsibility. But I have already stipulated that we will not talk about the superficial Judaism of the bulk of our community.

Negative freedom retains an important place in modern Judaism when it expresses a rich Jewish religious commitment. Some commandments and traditions may have met a previous era's spiritual needs. They need to be rejected when, as best we can determine it, they no longer convey any religious significance— like *chalitsah,* the ceremony of release necessitated by the refusal to marry one's childless brother's wife. Any generation seeking to avoid hypocrisy must insist upon the right not to be bound by the past merely because it is the past.

I hasten to add that the Jewish legitimacy of one's rejections is more fully established when it is complemented by the vigorous employment of the freedom to do more. Devoted Jews will manifest their caring by the acts with which they fill their lives. And considering how spiritually empty the experience of most American Jews has been, greater Jewish concern should mean much more Jewish doing.

The evidences of the positive use of liberal Jewish freedom abound from the Reform embrace of Zionism to its hebraization of the average synagogue service and the various rituals liberal Jews have brought into their homes. Many of these changes have, with some grumbling, been widely accepted. Some still bother liberals who cringe when they see some people now gladly performing rites they once were happy to be rid of. Reform Jews can still become highly emotional over the issue of wearing a *kipah.* To the objectors, this violates a simple rule: Reform Jews don't pray with covered heads. Many such people insist on identifying Reform Judaism with its negative use, to discard an old practice. Those who now choose to wear *kipot* have employed their liberal freedom positively in reclaiming this practice. Some do so for reasons no more substantial than nostalgia or a desire to change. Others believe Reform Jews should not isolate themselves from the rest of the Jewish world by following Western rather than Jewish custom in this regard.

The Earliest Efforts to Institutionalize Change

If irresponsibility constitutes the great risk of liberal Judaism, personal commitment to practice is its great opportunity. How might we best encourage the latter while containing the former? Specifically, where shall liberal Jewish religious authority—of a suasive sort, to be sure—be vested? I shall devote the rest of this chapter to the Reform Jewish experience. The approaches of

Conservative and Reconstructionist Judaism will be considered in the next chapter.

Since the early days of the movement, the leaders of liberal Judaism have puzzled over how to channel but not destroy freedom. A number of social realities helped limit their problem somewhat. In Europe, Jews tended to live in close communities where pressure from other Jews might still exert some influence upon them. The threat of anti-semitism also made some Jews less daring, though it encouraged others to advocate thoroughgoing assimilation into their host nation. The bourgeois ideal of most modernizing Jews likewise limited what they would themselves do or tolerate in others. Bad manners resulted in ostracism. These social checks on personal freedom probably seem more important to us, looking back from our permissive vantage, than they did to those Jews who were still excited by the daring of this or that *avant-garde*. Compared to the meager options available to their parents, their new freedom appeared radical.

The German liberal rabbis hoped that by organizing themselves into a deliberative body they might control the move to modernize Judaism. They held three conferences, at Brunswick in 1844, at Frankfurt in 1845, and at Breslau in 1846. The theoretical discussions about the need and possibilities for change at Frankfurt were rebutted by a statement of 116 Orthodox rabbis that no one was authorized to abrogate even the least of the Torah's laws.

The side effects of the practical decisions made at Frankfurt and Breslau show how difficult gaining consensus on change can be. When the 1845 session voted for the use of the vernacular in worship, with Hebrew retained for certain prayers, Zecharias Frankel withdrew from the meeting. (American Conservative Judaism has seen its European roots in Frankel's stand.) The meeting also approved of the abolition of the repetition of prayers in the service, favored the use of the organ, called for the delegation of references to Jewish Exile, and replaced petitions for the coming of a personal Messiah with hopes for a Messianic Age.

At Breslau in 1846, when the radicals proposed that the Sabbath be celebrated on Sunday, the body rejected it. However, the conference went on to accept riding to the synagogue on the Sabbath and even working then if one was dependent on it for one's livelihood. They also voted to abolish the second day of all holidays except Rosh Hashanah, to have a three-day rather than a seven-day mourning period, and omit many of the traditional signs of mourning. A strong report calling for the equality of women in religious matters was received but not acted upon because of lack of time. Despite all these changes, the radicals felt the rabbis had been too timid. They called for lay participation in future discussions, feeling certain that this would tilt the balance toward more forthright integration into the culture.

No succeeding meetings were held due to the troubled times which led to the German revolution of 1848. When conditions again became more settled, the opportunity for guiding the emerging movement had passed. The later occasional efforts to provide institutionalized guidance for German liberalism never got very far.

American Efforts at Institutionalizing Change

Isaac Mayer Wise clearly hoped to channel the development of all of American Judaism by establishing strong central institutions. He began by creating what he hoped would be a Union of (all) American Hebrew Congregations. His several efforts to found an American rabbinical school culminated in the opening of the Hebrew Union* College in 1875. He proposed to graduate models of indigenous Jewish religious leadership whose communal presence would set the stamp on acceptable Jewish modernity. Once he had a considerable number of alumni, he called for the establishment of a Central* Conference of American Rabbis. As the preamble to its constitution says, this body acknowledged that the previous European conferences, "by their deliberations and resolutions, have established certain norms, guiding principles, and precedents which have become recognized as an authoritative expression of the best intelligence and purpose of their respective times; therefore do we, . . . in obedience to the same natural prompting and urged by the same need and longings, organize ourselves for like purposes. . . ."

Isaac Mayer Wise expressed his goals for the Conference, of which he was president from 1889 until his death in 1900, in his first presidential address. "The united rabbis of America have undoubtedly the right . . . to declare and decide . . . which of our

*"Union" and "Central" meant inclusive of *all* Jewish groups.

religious forms, institutions, observance, usages, customs, ordinances, and prescriptions are still living factors in our religious, ethical, and intellectual life and which are so no longer and ought to be replaced by more adequate means to give expression to the spirit of Judaism and to reveal its character of universal religion. All reforms ought to go into practice on the authority of the Conference, not only to protect the individual [rabbi], but to protect Israel against presumptuous innovations and the precipitations of rash and inconsiderate men. The Conference is the lawful authority on all matters of form."

He was even stronger about the legislative purpose of the Conference in his second address. "We are the American *Bet Din,* with all the duties, rights, and privileges which the ancient expounders of the Law secured to the *Bet Din.*" And he reiterated the theme in his yearly messages thereafter.

The early *Yearbooks* of the Conference hum with the excitement of committees meeting to create services for each holiday and for the great events in the life of every Jew. Questions of rabbinical practice with regard to proselytes, confirmation, and the status of women are studied and debated. Within ten years most of these were satisfactorily answered and the Conference was ready to move on to more personal and detailed matters.

The turning point was reached with the Sabbath Observance Commission report of 1904. The commission had been formed to provide guidance to individuals in their observance of the Sabbath. But it never got to this matter. Instead, it lost all purpose in being when the Conference split evenly between those who wished to retain and strengthen the observance of the seventh day and those who wanted to try to turn Sunday into *Shabbat.* To have proceeded in either direction would have destroyed the Conference. Instead, it abandoned the subject and, at the same time, gave up its leadership in matters of religious practice.

Asserting the Right of Individual Self-Determination

Since those early days the occasional efforts to have the Reform rabbis' group act as a guide to Reform Jewish practice have had a limited effect. The Conference has had the greatest influence on Reform liturgy because it issues the official Reform prayer books. But no congregation is required to use them; they contain a variety of services; and individuals use the books as they see fit. On the rare occasions when an issue of practice comes before the Conference for a vote, as in the case of performing intermarriages, a sizable number of rabbis will vote against the proposal, regardless of the substance. They do not want the Conference to specify its members' religious duties in any way at all. By the time Isaac Mayer Wise died, a sizable number of his graduates and liberal colleagues had rejected his image of the Conference as "the American *Bet Din.*"

It is an exaggeration to say that the radical Reformers now took over the reins of leadership, though there is some evidence for this judgment. By 1900, one could hardly fail to recognize that Wise's "Unions" represented only Reform Judaism, which had evolved into a distinct party in American Jewry. It contained the Jews moving out most directly into the general society and it pioneered the American Jewish effort to continue as Jews in a society which granted the maximum freedom known. Perhaps to fulfill this function, Reform Jews began to think of their Judaism in highly individualistic terms. From now on, each rabbi would speak for himself—and, by extension, individual congregants would make their own decisions as to what they would do as Jews.

The new mood was spearheaded by the Conference. In its *Yearbook* for 1903 a heading appears for the first time on each page of its major papers: "The writer alone is responsible for views expressed in this article." The new individualism was emphasized, too, in the odd status assigned to the Conference's Responsa Committee. The answers it gives to questions addressed to it are officially not responses by the Conference but of the individuals who wrote them. Should they be read at the annual meeting, they may not be debated. These provisions apply to no other Conference committee.

In quite recent years, as Reform Jews have taken greater interest in having ritual guidance, the Conference—not without considerable qualms—has created a number of books to meet their need. These books treat of *Shabbat* observance, life-cycle events, and the like. They have been acceptable to the broad membership of the Conference because no one disputes their lack of authority. For all that they may speak of their contents as *mitsvah,* commandment, or be called by their enthusiastic proponents Reform *hala-chah*, they bind no one. They are resources for rabbis and lay people to utilize in full personal freedom.

What Is the Individual Reform Jew Expected to Do?

If, then, caring Reform Jews inquire about their religious responsibilities or, in the language of this chapter, if they ask whether "they must do all the commandments and traditions," the answer is simple but indirect. As honest people, they "must do" whatever follows from their Jewish religious beliefs. Thus, their obligations in matter of prayer and ritual will directly flow from whatever modern understanding of God they accept. As Jews, they do not serve that God in lonely solitude but as a member of the Jewish people. Now their belief in the people of Israel's relation to God comes into play. What mix of ethnicity and religion do they think best expresses its character? What, if any, uniqueness do they ascribe to its ancient alliance with God? And to all such questions must be added their view of Torah, in the broad sense. Does God "speak" to us as God did to the prophets or did they or do we have qualitatively superior levels of insight? And what weight do we assign to Jewish tradition in our religious life—almost compelling, highly instructive, significant, or merely advisory?

These theoretical questions probe too deeply for most of us. When we seek to determine what to do in a particular matter we rarely wish to investigate our theology. Now the advantage of belonging to a good congregation and having a rabbi in whom one has confidence becomes apparent. We are not the only modern Jews facing life from a Jewish perspective and our question has probably been asked before and resulted in experience we can now share. If one can find the caring minority with whom one feels comfortable, one will very likely find that what they have been doing often fulfills one's private religious striving. And, as mentioned, there are now books which can give us guidance by exhibiting the appeal of various Jewish practices.

In its 1976 statement, "Reform Judaism, a Centenary Perspective," the Central Conference of American Rabbis provided a formal answer to the question concerning a Reform Jew's religious obligations. It began by indicating that the Reform move-

ment, like the rest of Judaism, is a religion of "duty and obligation." It then delineated the areas in which Jewish responsibility
ought to manifest itself: "The past century has taught us that the
claims made upon us may begin with our ethical obligations but
they extend to many other aspects of Jewish living, including:
creating a Jewish home centered on family devotion; lifelong
study; private prayer and public worship; daily religious observance; keeping the Sabbath and the holy days; celebrating the
major events of life; involvement with the synagogue and community; and other activities which promote the survival of the Jewish
people and enhance its existence."

I wonder if there is anything in this list which your belief in
God, the people of Israel, and Torah would not mandate? Could
you be true to your Jewish religious affirmations, as best you
comprehend them, and not express them in each of these ways?

The rabbis went further. They suggested how you might determine in any specific case what you should do. "Within each area
of Jewish observance Reform Jews are called upon to confront the
claims of Jewish tradition, however differently perceived, and to
exercise their individual autonomy, choosing and creating on the
basis of commitment and knowledge."

Of course you should live as a self-determining person. Your
freedom to choose what you will do is the precious premise of
your humanhood, and your modernity consists mainly in acknowledging and acting upon it. As moderns who are Jews, we are
called upon to use our freedom in terms of "the claims of Jewish
tradition" upon us, for we are part of our people's millennial
relationship with God. I have begun each chapter of this book
with a survey of our Jewish heritage in joyous fulfillment of this
Reform Jewish obligation. Not everyone will read the Jewish tradition the same way and thus "hear" the same call being made
to them. We are too individualistic for that and it is too complex
for such uniformity. We should then approach it and decide out
of the depth of "knowledge" which befits a significant decision.
We should also do so in terms of our deepest "commitment" for,
when we ask about religious duties, we are speaking of the service
of God. Then whatever we choose from the past or create for the
present should rest upon us with the full force of commandment.
For only by being false to ourselves and to what we believe will
we be able to ignore or transgress it.

·7·

WHY ARE THERE THREE BRANCHES OF JUDAISM?

The accepted division of American Judaism into three major wings has its uses, particularly when we think in national terms. Roughly speaking, about a million Jews each affiliate with Reform, Conservative, and Orthodox congregations. There are also important social and intellectual divisions between these three interpretations of Judaism. Yet this gross labeling hides from our view the many divergent small groups which give color and vitality to American Judaism. If only in apology for not paying more attention to them, we ought to begin this study of the three great branches of our religion by taking some notice of the various smaller groups in our community.

Liberal Jews often do not perceive the considerable diversity found in contemporary American Orthodoxy, perhaps because it surfaces only in our largest metropolitan centers. Chasidic Jews stand out most readily because of their distinctive dress. Since Chasidim organize around individual *rebbes,* each projecting an individual teaching and practice, the lush variegation of American Chasidism defies easy categorization. The most outer directed are the Lubavitcher Chasidim who actively engage other Jews in an effort to bring them to greater observance. Most Chasidim are inner directed, having as little contact with nonobservant Jews or Gentiles as possible. Perhaps the most notorious isolationists are the Satamarer Chasidim, who fanatically oppose the State of Israel and thus hold themselves aloof from most other Jews. None of the chasidic *rebbes* will join with Conservative and

Reform rabbis for common action. With some exceptions, they have similar disdain for their modern Orthodox colleagues.

Another part of the Orthodox right wing has been called the *"yeshivah* world." It centers about the venerable leaders of certain esteemed *yeshivot.* By contrast to chasidic mysticism, this Orthodoxy considers talmudic erudition the highest Jewish virtue. Its followers devote themselves to ever greater expertise in the *halachah;* those who cannot fully devote themselves to study identify with and support those who do. These Jews also segregate themselves from the surrounding culture, not now to facilitate the development of mystical piety, but to enable them to observe Judaism without distraction. At the extreme, they seek to recapitulate European patterns of Jewish existence. Others accept a small measure of acculturation as compatible with proper piety. Attitudes toward the State of Israel vary from anti-Zionism to support, with substantial numbers non-Zionist in theory but pragmatic in practice. These groups have made common cause with certain Chasidim but have tense relations with modern Orthodoxy. They fear its Americanization has led to a damaging diminution of Jewish distinctiveness and even to breaches of the Law. They boycott joint activities with Conservative and Reform rabbis and denounce modern Orthodox colleagues who participate in them.

Modern Orthodoxy itself ranges over a considerable spectrum of observance and style. Particularly in the midwest and south, many of its congregations are indistinguishable from some in the Conservative movement. Its rabbis insist that their interpretation of Judaism faithfully reflects the demands of traditional Jewish law and carefully adheres to its canons of change. They regularly join with Conservative and Reform rabbis in communal projects but almost always deny their competence in matters of Jewish law.

What I shall be saying about Orthodoxy in the rest of this chapter mainly applies to the modern Orthodox, though it may characterize the position of some of the Orthodox right as well.

The Divisions in Conservative Judaism

The topography of the other branches of American Judaism may be far more easily mapped. Two wings have long been identified in the Conservative movement. They differ over the extent to which they believe Jewish law can allow for change in our demanding times. Their division appeared most noticeably in the debate over ordaining women as Conservative rabbis. The "right" wing argued that, at the least, so great a departure from previous practice deserved the most searching scholarly examination of the halachic issues involved. They insisted nothing should be done until the legal experts had completed their work, and no women should be ordained until they ruled it was halachicly acceptable. Other rightists insisted, on the basis of their investigations, that women could not legally be ordained and that, for pragmatic reasons as well, they should not be. The Conservative "left" responded that there were no direct, compelling legal reasons to prevent the ordination of women and such objections as were raised could be met by utilizing various halachic precedents. Besides, they contended, historical change and our ethics mandated an end to the previous denial of ordination to women.

In the 1960s, long before the ordination issue arose, the reluctance of the Conservative leadership to satisfy the demands of their far left followers led to the institutionalization of the Reconstructionist movement. Reconstructionism had previously been a school of thought founded by Mordecai Kaplan in the mid 1930s. Its adherents were also found in Reform Judaism though the far greater number were Conservative. Kaplan hoped that his ideas would move Conservatism, with which he was affiliated, to be more progressive and would make Reform more traditional. When it became apparent that the Conservative leadership increasingly considered his philosophy tangential to their movement, Kaplan and his followers founded a fellowship of congregations, and, later, their own rabbinical school.

I shall say more later about Kaplan's ideas about proper change in Jewish practice. Here I should like to point out that the Reconstructionist movement has grown to where it numbers several dozen congregations, mostly of modest size, but its number of affiliates continues to expand. Reconstructionist services are somewhat more traditional than those of Reform congregations and less so than those of most Conservative synagogues. As the immediate disciples of Mordecai Kaplan are succeeded by a new generation of leaders, Reconstructionism faces a time of new opportunities and risks.

The Variety of Jewish Experience on the Left

Reform Judaism, too, has been characterized as having a more traditional, "right" wing and a more radical, "left" wing, with most of its members congregating between the two. In the rabbinate, these divisions became manifest in a tense struggle of the early 1970s. Some of its members sought to have the Central Conference of American Rabbis revise its negative stand toward intermarriage. Those on the "right" wanted a strong reaffirmation of the Conference's position that rabbis should not conduct such ceremonies. The "leftists" wanted the synagogue to reach out to the many people who intermarry despite the Conference's disapproval. A not insubstantial number of rabbis in the middle didn't want the Conference usurping the individual rabbi's right of self-determination in decisions concerning religious practice.

The several years of deliberation on this topic particularly disturbed those rabbis who felt that Reform Judaism had moved too speedily toward greater traditionalism. They believed this shift to the right threatened the personal freedom that had long been Reform Judaism's pride. For a few years, they organized themselves into a caucus to further the cause of openness in the movement. It did not last long as it soon found itself without new threats to combat and no positive program of its own to suggest.

Some Reform Jews on the left remain disturbed that their movement is becoming "Orthodox." In my opinion, they err in identifying Reform freedom only with the right not to do—negative freedom, as I termed it in the previous chapter. They cannot accept the possibility that Jews as free as they are might equally choose to adopt traditional practices. But no Reform body sought to enforce greater traditionalism on any Reform Jew. To the contrary, the Reform rabbinate could accept the Conference's several books making detailed suggestions for Reform Jewish practice because everyone understood them to be resources not "laws." They did not presume to tell Reform Jews what they *must* do.

Several small groups hover at the extreme left of the Reform movement, finding one or another aspect of its general religious position unacceptable. The affiliates of Humanistic Judaism object to its affirmation of God. Those identified with Polydoxy as Jews exercise their freedom in complete autonomy without accepting the legitimacy of any claim upon them, including belief in God, the people of Israel, or Torah. Not part of Reform or any religious Jewry are those secularists who seek to maintain a strong Jewish ethnic identity. The dwindling native Yiddishists do so by means of language; the self-consciously Jewish Communists, Trotskyites, and other Marxists do so by their sectarian blends of the universal proletarian struggle and Jewish nationalism.

Greater detail I must leave to the sociologists and historians of American Jewry. With regret that I cannot present a more finely nuanced picture, I now turn to what divides the three great streams of American Jewish religious life.

Focusing on Social Not Theological Reality

For most human beings, social factors shape their lives far more effectively than do religious beliefs. That rule holds particularly true in periods of rapid transition—and Jews are no exception to either of these observations. If we are to understand what has predominantly motivated the differences between Orthodox, Conservative, and Reform Jews, we must focus on the time and pace of their acculturation to America.

The bulk of American Jewry derives from families that have been on this continent less than a century. For much of that time their primary goal has been to effectuate a speedy transition from immigrant alienhood to American belonging. In most cases their religion had to find a place in their lives subsidiary to their more urgent social agenda. Once we explicate their history and sociology we can fill in the ideology.

American Jewry has the unusual distinction of being the first community where liberal Jews established the major institutional forms. Though the congregations of the Colonial and post-Revolutionary periods in the United States were traditional, they had no strong rabbinic leadership well into the nineteenth century. When German Jews began immigrating here by the thousands after 1840 and found a society uncommonly open to them, they moved into it with special enthusiasm. Their rapid integration was accompanied by the burgeoning of an American Reform movement. By the start of the twentieth century, it had a well established national organization of congregations, a rabbinical school annually ordaining rabbis, a conference of rabbis meeting each year, and had worked out a way of being a liberal Jew in

America that set the basis for the later adaptations of other Jewish groups.

The diligence and creativity of the German immigrants enabled many of them to become unusually successful. A great social distance, therefore, separated them from those Jews who had not acculturated so rapidly or so well. An even greater gap set them apart from the next great wave of immigrants who came to the United States.

The Rise of an East European Liberal Judaism

In the early 1880s, East European Jews began reaching these shores at the unprecedented rate of 100,000 or more a year. Demographically, they overwhelmed the German-led American Jewish community. For social and economic reasons, they tended to settle in the great metropolitan areas of the eastern seaboard, with Chicago the one great middle western magnet. Because of their masses, they moved into the American culture at a relatively slow rate. Many preferred to acculturate cautiously because they had not been emancipated in Europe. For some decades they remained far more ethnically oriented and xenophobic than the descendants of the German immigrants.

The two groups clashed badly. There had been much antipathy between them in Europe—the German Jews considering the East Europeans uncouth, and the latter considering the *"Yahudim"* snobbish assimilationists. For many years marriages between prominent families of the two communities were unthinkable, constituting a sort of "intermarriage." In those circumstances, Reform Judaism was anathema to East European Jews.

The Conservative movement resulted from this communal clash. It can trace its roots to those Europeans who, like Zacharias Frankel, deemed the liberals to be modernizing too rapidly. During the rise of Reform, in the United States, a similar mood surfaced. The effective development of Conservatism here dates from the reorganization of the Jewish Theological Seminary under Solomon Schechter in 1902. The initiative to bring this prominent European scholar to the United States came from wealthy "German" Jews in the Reform movement. They wanted to provide East European Jews with a religious movement which would enable them to Americanize.

Many of the great strengths of Conservative Judaism arose

from the positive Jewish character of the community which embraced it. Jewish ethnicity, as manifest in devotion to Jewish languages, Zionism, and custom, provided a strong communal base, while the fabled East European devotion to Jewish learning set high intellectual ideals before the community. Above all, the movement could claim a unique social stance for itself among American Jews: less assimilated and "more Jewish" than Reform, more adaptive and modern than Orthodoxy.

Finally, the Nucleus Becomes Visible

The unexpectedly late development of Orthodox Jewish institutions in the United States followed logically from the defensive state of Orthodoxy in most of the modern period. Modernization appeared to constitute a mortal threat to authentic Jewish continuity. If that was true in Europe with its old, established institutions and communities, how much the more so was it to be feared in the "godless" United States. The leading East European rabbis, who guided what was the heartland of world Jewry until the Holocaust, decried emigration. America was an "impure" land, and a move there was as good as a decision to abandon the commandments. Most immigrants undoubtedly fulfilled this dire prophecy. The comparative few who remained fully observant became a minority among Jews and could not easily find a way to accommodate to the American way.

The situation of American Orthodoxy began to change with the increasing economic pressure on Jews in Eastern Europe, the growth of sizable Jewish communities in the United States, and the gradual development of American Orthodox institutions. By the second half of the twentieth century an accommodation had been worked out between Orthodox Jewish observance and American style; a decade after World War II, "modern Orthodoxy" began to flourish. Behind this efflorescence lay a social transition. Orthodox Jews—or, more accurately, Jews affiliated with Orthodox synagogues—had moved into the main stream of American economic and political life. American social perceptions facilitated the appeal of Orthodoxy to Jews. A broad ranging resistance to aspects of American culture became common among Americans. Ethnicity became fashionable; liberalism now found itself outmoded as orthodoxies came into favor. In the

Jewish community, the virtues of Orthodoxy became freshly apparent. And the educated graduates of the day school movement, pioneered by the Orthodox, gave substance to the new growth of Orthodoxy. The immigration of Orthodox survivors following World War II also played an important role in this development. Though they have most dramatically been identified with the Orthodox right, their intransigence has stiffened the resolve of modern Orthodoxy, to which other survivors have been attracted.

I hope that this sprint through American Jewish social history will explain the great inner contradiction of its religious life. We have three, energetic, useful religious movements which can easily be distinguished from each other ideologically. Their partisans are sufficiently devoted to them that the groups are most likely to continue for the foreseeable future. Yet the bulk of American Jews live with but minor ritual differences from one another. Most of them choose a synagogue less because of its theory of Judaism than for the social compatibility they feel with its congregants. Now that most of the community has completed its acculturation, it tends to live in pretty much the same way. And this absence of serious denominationalism and fanaticism reflects the fundamental American commitment to pluralism and suspicion of absolutism.

Intellectually as well, one discovers considerable overlap in the adjacent wings of the three movements. Orthodox modernists and law-minded Conservatives speak in similar accents. The Conservative left, the Reform right, and much of Reconstructionism may use different buzz words but they reach similar results. In sum, marriage between two average American Jewish families belonging to different religious groups is more likely to run into difficulties about class differences rather than about clashing interpretations of Jewish law.

Confronting Issues of Principle

This lengthy sociological overview should not be misconstrued. I think ideas play a significant role in separating the major branches of American Judaism and I now propose to discuss them. However, I have found over the years that advocates of a particular Jewish ideology speak less out of intellectual conviction than in defense of a social style they enjoy. As Marx said, their "philosophy" is an ideology, that is, an intellectual rationalization for their social status. In Judaism, the faith of a people, belief, and social situation cannot easily be separated. But I hope in what follows you will be sensitive to the potential distinction between what you truly believe and what you affirm because it is socially useful to you.

A major difference in attitude toward acculturation separates Orthodoxy and liberalism in all their divisions. Orthodox leaders remain highly skeptical of the Jewish utility of further integration into the general culture. God has revealed God's own law to us. No one should lightly alter it. Even its sanctioned methods of change should not be employed without the deepest sense of awe before God's judgment and the general consensus of the great masters of our time.

Moreover, they believe that the results of the accommodations made since the Emancipation have contradicted the high hopes held out for them. No Jewry in recent centuries has been as Jewishly illiterate, as unobservant, and as unbelieving as is our liberated community. The worst sin of our age has been its penchant for intermarriage, an act which threatens Jewish continuity even more directly than nonobservance. Our community has so little Jewish devotion, it accepts this life threat as our new normality. Is more evidence required to refute the call for more change? Should we not, instead, engage in a profound act of *teshuvah* and repentantly return to rigorous Jewish observance?

This grudging attitude toward further modernization may be epitomized in the old rabbinic notion of "a fence around the law." On occasion, the sages instituted regulations more stringent than actually required. This made certain that the basic law would not easily be transgressed. (For example, the Torah stipulates one may not eat the Passover sacrifice after dawn but the rabbis prohibit eating it after midnight.) We may say, then, that most Orthodox leadership today believes Jews need to build "a fence around the law" to protect themselves securely from the constant American pressure to contravene it. Only when we have irretrievably rooted ourselves in Jewish faith and observance will it be time to discuss some further limited borrowing from American culture.

The Liberal Rejection of the Orthodox Remedy

Reform, Reconstructionist, and Conservative Jews agree that modern Judaism has serious problems but deny that Orthodox stability will resolve them. Obviously, not every gentile fad should become part of Jewish practice but there is much that we can learn from our society to enhance our Judaism. We ought to acknowledge this forthrightly and without hesitation. Indeed the changes in Orthodoxy itself over the past century are clear proof of the validity of the unequivocal liberal Jewish involvement with the society.

Let us consider, for a moment, the most visible single practice which distinguishes liberal from Orthodox Jews, mixed seating at services. Liberal Jews clearly learned this from gentile practice. Should we now go back to the traditional segregation of sexes at services? The legal grounds for a women's section are most flimsy, stemming from a report of "levity" during a special Sukot celebration in the Temple. (Suk. 51b) To the modern Jewish conscience, awakened by the Emancipation, the practice says more about ancient Near Eastern sexism than about God's will. To seat women separately from men, preferably with a curtain between them, so that they will not sexually distract the men who alone are commanded to pray, is demeaning. To seat families together at worship enhances the experience of prayer and may then set a standard for the relationship outside the synagogue. Liberals broke with Jewish tradition in this instance to create a practice which would keep Judaism more vital than it could be merely by following precedent. To liberals the challenge of modernity will best be met not by changing as grudgingly as possible but by responsibly determining which innovations might improve Jewish life today.

At this juncture, the argument between the groups focuses on the proper methods for introducing and controlling change. At their most fearful the Orthodox agonize that once radical departures are allowed there will be no way of stopping them until all of Judaism has been sacrificed—and they then point to the evidence of gross assimilation in the liberal Jewish community. In that spirit, only the most minimal deviation from inherited practice would be allowed, and some Orthodox groups live by this strategy. Most Jews, including most American Orthodox Jews, refuse to be frightened into flexibility. Thus the debate now centers less on the desirability than on the method of innovation. On this matter, the liberals not only differ from the Orthodox but from one another, thus exposing their specific institutional postures.

The Conservative Jewish Esteem of Halachah

Orthodoxy maintains, as we have noted, that change may take place only as the Oral Torah permits and as the recognized sages of our time deem proper.

Conservative Judaism agrees with Orthodoxy that developments in Jewish practice ought to take place through the instrumentalities of Jewish law. Historically, the Jewish tradition grew in just this way. No contemporary Judaism can consider itself authentic if it does not remain faithful to this central institution of Jewish life. Were Orthodox decisors willing to interpret the law today in terms of the flexibility allowed them, there might be no need for Conservative Judaism. But an unfortunate rigidity has crept into the way they now read and apply the *halachah*. Specifically, scholarship clearly demonstrates that the great teachers of other eras met social discontinuity by significantly altering Jewish practice. Responsible Jews will do so today to meet the special threats of modernity to Judaism.

To protect against ill-considered and irresponsible shifts in Jewish observance, the Conservative rabbinate created a body to give guidance on issues of *halachah*. Its Commission on Law and Standards is composed of scholars who represent various points of view in the movement. Should they reach a unanimous decision on a matter, it is binding on all Conservative rabbis. Should there be a division of opinion, as often happens, the individual congregational rabbi is deemed the authoritative interpreter of the Conservative position on this law to his congregation.

The Reconstructionist movement stems from Mordecai Kaplan's rejection of the Conservative Jewish decision to have a scholarly elite make decisions for the community. Kaplan argued that law can function properly today only when the people actively participate in its reinterpretation and creation. Living in a democracy, as we do, the active involvement of those who will be called upon to follow the law must be primary to our social organization. Hence, Kaplan called for the community as a whole, through a democratically elected assembly, to legislate for American Jewry.

Kaplan enunciated his theory of a self-legislating community decades before his followers recognized that there was no chance of the Conservative movement accepting even a timid version of it. This led them to organize the Reconstructionist congregational group and rabbinical school. The movement has a democratic decision-making process, as Kaplan hoped, but it embraces only Reconstructionist congregations, not the whole community. In practice, most of the significant questions of observance have been the province of the Reconstructionist rabbinical group. Thus far, their decisions differ little from that of most Reform rabbis.

Testing the Theories: The Ordination of Women

I think we can best grasp what divides Reform Judaism from Conservatism by looking at a concrete issue, the ordination of women. As a matter of conscience, Reform Jews have long been committed to the equality of women in Jewish religious life. They early found the courage to express this in their synagogue seating, music, and education. Only at a much later period did women become synagogue trustees and presidents. Finally, in 1967, with feminist agitation high, a woman candidate for the rabbinate was admitted to the Hebrew Union College. When she completed the course of study in 1972, Reform Judaism gave American Jewry its first woman rabbi, Sally Priesand. Since then the College has graduated substantial numbers of women rabbis and cantors and they have been widely accepted in Reform congregations and on college campuses.

The Orthodox rabbinate remains steadfastly opposed to this practice. It considers it forbidden under the *halachah* though few explicit legal texts can be cited to substantiate this position. We may presume that traditional Jewish legists did not bother to proscribe a contingency they could not imagine. From various legal analogies, Orthodox scholars have argued that the *halachah* cannot countenance women as rabbis. Their unequivocal negativity created a dilemma for the Conservative right.

Much of the Conservative movement, rabbis and laity alike,

having seen the great benefits of educating its girls equally with its boys, was long ready for women rabbis. But Conservative ideology requires change through the instruments of Jewish law. It therefore needed the approval of its legal leaders for this step —only the Commission on Law and Standards had no authority over this matter. Ordination being a function of the Jewish Theological Seminary's faculty, its professors had to approve of the admission of women candidates for the rabbinate.

Two questions then arose. First, who may authoritatively decide this matter? Should opinions on Jewish law offered by professors of Bible and ethics, say, have equivalent weight with those of experts in Talmud and Codes? That issue had important practical overtones. Legal scholars tend to be largely uncongenial to the introduction of new practices because they are highly concerned about the juridic unassailability of whatever they do. The other question was also procedural. At what point would there have been adequate academic study of the halachic status of women in general and the issue of their ordination in particular to allow so weighty a decision to be made? These issues deeply divided the Seminary faculty.

To my eyes, it seems clear that the fundamental problem of Conservative ideology had here surfaced: Does *halachah* truly govern or only guide? Having said for years that the *halachah* can change to meet the needs of the times, the demand to ordain women confronted the authorities with the need to validate what some of them perceived to be a radical break with Jewish legal tradition. For all its willingness to modernize where it can, the Conservative right knew that if it agreed to this change it will have lost whatever halachic authenticity it has had with modern Orthodoxy. The Conservative left, however, viewed this as a classic instance where historic evolution and ethical development required halachic creativity. Responsible Jewish leadership necessitated a bold move into the future, by halachic means, to be sure, though the Orthodox would deny this particular step could be taken. Finally, the pressure exerted by historic change and ethical development could no longer be denied. In 1983 the faculty of the Jewish Theological Seminary voted to admit women as candidates for ordination as rabbis.

The Reform Commitment to Individual Conscience

Issues such as the ones we have covered in this chapter make plain to Reform Jews why they cannot be content with institution-alizing the need to change Judaism. In the case of women rabbis the ethical question could hardly have been plainer: Are women not to have equal religious rights with men? If Jewish law has not seen women as fully enfranchised Jews, that must be considered more an indictment of the law than a good reason for barring them from the rabbinate. After years of debate and experience, it seems utterly unconscionable to call for extensive further study or to demand we wait until a halachic argument has made systemi-cally plausible what is humanly self-evident. Some Jews consider the preservation of the methods of Jewish law so important for Jewish continuity they willingly abide by even its archaic and discriminatory provisions. The Reform movement exists because other Jews insist that moral imperatives must take precedence over outmoded institutional forms. Their determination to re-spond to the immediate spiritual needs of contemporary Jewry makes them willing to take great Jewish risks, by traditional stan-dards. They then pioneer the ethical and esthetic forms which the rest of the community may sense it needs but cannot bring itself to act upon.

In a sense the Reform movement stakes the Jewish future on the will, intelligence, and devotion of the Jewish people itself. That is, it denies that any authority ought to be empowered to tell individual Jews what they must do as Jews today. Rabbis should teach, persuade, exemplify, prod, exhort, and encourage Jews to know more, care more, and therefore do more. Congregations should provide settings in which personal varieties of Jewish doing may be enlarged and enriched, as well as find communal expression. The great national institutions should guide in-dividuals and congregations to transcend their local vision and join in the national and international tasks of our people. One can hardly set a limit to what can and ought to be done to help individual Jews be ever better Jews. A messianically-oriented reli-gion should not have a lesser goal. But, having had the benefit of the wisest, most learned, and most sensitive instruction, indi-vidual Jews, utilizing their minds and hearts and consciences, should decide for themselves what Jewish duties devolve upon them.

Facing the Criticism of Reform Judaism

The Orthodox and many Conservative Jews have not been persuaded by this Reform position. It has often been debased by Jews who have used it as an excuse to do whatever they felt like doing; calling Jewish minimalism creativity cannot mask its superficiality. Even at its best, when knowledgeable Jews seek to be faithful to God as part of the people of Israel's historic tradition, their individualism creates grave problems for the Jewish community. Specifically, by virtue of its conversions, intermarriages, and marriages of people without halachic divorces, Reform creates "Jews" whom tradition cannot accept as Jews, particularly for purposes of marriage. The Reform movement, it has been charged, is by these radical breaks with Jewish law bringing about a serious split in the Jewish community between those Jews with whom one can and these with whom one cannot marry.

I do not see how any Jew who cares deeply about the Jewish people and its central concerns can be unmoved by this grave problem. We face so many external difficulties that to add to our troubles from within the community is agonizing. There has been considerable soul-searching among Reform Jewish leaders to find some accommodation with the Orthodox rabbinate to avoid this problem. In some individual communities, where long experience with intergroup Jewish cooperation has bred mutual trust, local arrangements have been worked out allowing all the groups, with some bending, to follow one mutually acceptable practice.

I should like to think that, with great good will, some such universally acceptable practices might yet be worked out. But, for the immediate future, I do not see that this will prove practical. Not the least reason being the intractability of the Orthodox right and the Israeli religious leadership in particular. Believing themselves to be in full possession of God's law, they consequently see all Jewish efforts to break with it as the most reprehensible sort of heresy. They adamantly enforce their point of view in religious matters in the State of Israel. I do not see them soon becoming more flexible. Any significant compromise of their position would mean having to share some of their power with others, an eventuality no establishment cherishes.

Acknowledging the Limits of Liberal Accommodation

This religio-legal absolutism of Orthodoxy draws forth the liberals' equivalent ethical certainty. Consider the charge leveled against us. When a Jewess remarries without having received a Jewish divorce from her former husband, any child she conceives by her second husband results from what the *halachah* must consider an adulterous relationship. The offspring is therefore a *mamzer*. No Jew may marry a *mamzer* except another *mamzer*. There is no way to wipe out the stain of *mamzerut* and it continues in that person's lineage until the Messiah comes. Reform Jews, so we are told, are responsible for the Jewish horror of multiplying *mamzerim* among the Jewish people. To avoid creating *mamzerim*, Reform Jews should abide by traditional Jewish law.

Such reasoning explains why the Reform movement was called into being and must continue to exist. The laws of *mamzerut* are viciously immoral. They punish a spiritual crime with a biological taint. They provide a punishment that cannot be mitigated. They do not allow for repentance. They degrade an infant—just in the process of being conceived—for the "sin" of its mother. They perpetuate the racist notion that some people, simply by their lineage, are inferior.

Judaism should no longer have such laws—but contemporary Orthodoxy not only does, it enforces them when it finds the facts meet the stipulations. And these laws are a critical part of the Jewish marriage and divorce statutes. Set aside for a moment all the problems a person of conscience should have over participating in a system which grossly discriminates against women. Shall modern Jews, for the sake of unified Jewish legal procedures in matters of personal status, accept the continuation of the laws of *mamzerut*? Should they not rather protest against a system that cannot find a way to do with these unconscionable laws what it did with an eye for an eye or the Sanhedrin's right to impose capital punishment, that is, make them effectively inoperable for all future time? Bertha Pappenheim, leader of the German Jewish feminist movement early in this century, put the matter bluntly. Any leaders who can find a way to permit the equivalent of the forbidden practice of taking interest from another Jew, but who cannot manage a way around *mamzerut*, must be seen with suspicion by any Jew of conscience.

But I am becoming polemical, a stance I think Jews in this post-Holocaust era ought to shun. I only wish to indicate that liberal Judaism, for all its lack of dogma, has its own fundamental commitments and it cannot be asked to deny them by those who see only their own sense of certainty at stake.

The Liberal Dedication to Democracy

One further matter radically divides liberal Judaism from Orthodoxy, its thoroughgoing devotion to the practice of democracy. Throughout its history Judaism has had some rudimentary forms of popular participation in decision-making and a long record of sectarian division. Those practices did not involve the citizens' control of their government or the virtue of living harmoniously with people from whom one differed religiously, racially, politically, and otherwise. Jews learned about pluralism and democracy through their emancipation. Liberal Jews, having seen its benefits in the humane tone of American civil life and American Jewish community affairs, have enthusiastically insisted it must be a cornerstone of modern Judaism.

The relationship of Orthodoxy to democracy remains problematic. If God gives the law, no majority vote of the people can change it. If God's Oral Law decrees that the majority vote of the rabbis is God's law, then that much democracy prevails—but it has no effect on determining the gender of rabbis or what sort of ordination qualifies one to rule on the *halachah.* Jews who violate the provisions of the Torah are not mere social deviants; they are defying God. One should not lightly tolerate their sinfulness and one certainly cannot allow rival theories of Judaism to be expounded. There is only one true Judaism, though it has its own, internal plurality of interpretation. Orthodoxy ought not, as a matter of principle, authorize democracy of the sort we see around us.

Modern American Orthodoxy exhibits great appreciation of the virtues of democracy and the value of working as equals with people of divergent opinions. But it does not presently have the power to do much else, except withdraw from community affairs, as the Orthodox right wing tends to do. As yet, no Orthodox Jewish thinker has set forward a widely accepted reconciliation of Orthodox revelation and the practice of Jewish democracy. In the

State of Israel, where Orthodoxy has some areas of power, it has often demonstrated that its understanding of religion rejects the notion of Jewish religious pluralism. It not only denies other Jewish religious interpretations various rights but it employs co-ercion when it can to have its version of Jewish practice followed by everyone.

Liberal Judaism—Reform, Conservative, and Reconstruction-ist alike—has a positive, unequivocal commitment to democracy. It knows none of us possesses God's truth so fully that we have the right to force our version of it on others. It has such great faith in the individual mind and conscience that, in religious matters, it considers persuasion the only proper basis for religious deci-sion. It has learned so much from other people in the general society, and it has found its individual forms of Judaism so en-riched by sharing with Jews of other points of view, that it sees pluralism as a positive value to modern Judaism.

The divisions between Orthodoxy and liberal Judaism can run very deep—but that is not to gainsay the far deeper truth, that they share very much more in common. They stand in the same Covenant-relationship with God as part of the same people of Israel though they hear its imperatives differently. And as Or-thodoxy modernizes and liberal Jews become more traditional in their practice, the bonds between them can grow evermore strong.

The ideological arguments between Reform and Conservative Jews can easily move them to opposite ends of the liberal spec-trum. That should not blind them to their great sociological similarity. And, in their attitudes to God, the people of Israel, and the need for flexibility in Torah, they share the same range of faith. They are very much more alike than different from one another.

Perhaps, in time, we shall have only Orthodox and liberal Jews in America. Surely Jews ought to aspire to the Messianic Day when the entire Jewish people is united in spirit. But for the moment we American Jews are, at least, three great religious movements, a matter which should cause us some regret but one, too, which, if properly understood, may enrich and enlighten our community.

PART
·IV·

LIVING
AS A JEW

Part Four: Living as a Jew

·1·

THE HUMAN WILL-TO-DO-EVIL

Why do people behave badly? You may find that a rather negative question to begin a discussion of Jewish duty. So much of our teaching stresses the commandments of Judaism that I thought we should look into its converse: Judaism's theory of why good people do evil acts.

The topic has always intrigued Jewish thinkers but it strikes us with exceptional force. We are the most educated generation of human beings who ever lived and in many cases the best fed, housed, clothed, entertained, and usefully involved. Yet we seem to have created new forms of tyranny, exploitation, and self-destruction—and we live with the threat of nuclear holocaust. Individually and socially, depression and despair accompany our comforts and attainments. Our strange mix of moods will paralyze us less if we look at our situation in the context of Judaism's centuries-old wisdom.

In our heritage the problem of sin begins almost simultaneously with the creation of people. Living paradisiacally, with but few commandments to observe, Adam and Eve transgress. They eat the fruit of the forbidden tree of knowledge, good and evil. The story proceeds in such a way that we cannot evade the seriousness of their deed. We hear that they feel guilty, seek to hide, and, after a punishment more lenient than expected, are driven from the Garden of Eden forever. (Gen. 3) While the Bible authors do not often refer to this event, it clearly provides their model of our human condition. People, commanded by God to live in decency, turn violent and corrupt; the Hebrews, too, brought by God into a special Covenant, first worship a golden

353

calf and then generation after generation find other ways of defying God and God's law. Almost every prophetic biblical book centers on the Jews' sinfulness and God's anticipated response to it.

Sin looms so large in the biblical authors' perspective because it runs contrary to the unique Jewish religious experience: that the one Sovereign of the universe had made plain—indeed, put into words—how people are to live. Hence, they could not help being troubled by the human proclivity to sin. We shall not understand Judaism in all its robustness if we limit our study to its delineation of duty. We must also explore its unique attitude toward human rebelliousness. Four affirmations about humankind and one concerning God will provide the insight we seek.

1. Distinguishing Evil Feelings from Evil Deeds

For us rather than for historical accuracy, we should first note the old Jewish distinction between judging our feelings and judging our deeds. The Bible and Talmud contain few statutes about our emotions, the major exception being that we must not envy. It stood out so from the Torah's concentration on action that the rabbis generally limited it to passions which would actually cause one to sin. An early commentary says that merely putting one's desire into words does not yet transgress this commandment. Citing a parallel text (Deut. 7:25), an anonymous teacher rules, "Just as there only the carrying out of one's desire is forbidden, so here all that has been proscribed is carrying out one's desire in action." (Mech. Bah. 8) The rabbis—and apparently the biblical authors before them—knew human beings well enough not to summon us to discipline our feelings rigidly. They realized that one may experience conflicting emotions and yet do deeds which sanctify our lives and our society. This primary, enduring attitude forms the background of the modern Jewish affinity for psychoanalysis which we shall touch on fleetingly at the end of this chapter.

2. Carrying Forward the Bible's Insistence upon Human Freedom

We must give much closer scrutiny to the second affirmation, that human beings are reasonably free to choose what they will do. Consider the closing words of what is said to be Moses' last speech: "I call heaven and earth to witness against you this day that I have set before you life and death, blessing and curse. Choose life, if you and your offspring would live!" (Deut. 30:19) No doubt is raised here or elsewhere in the Bible that people can do what God has asked of them if only they choose to. Obviously, many motives may deflect our good intention. Again and again, the Bible authors describe people as prone to seek power, pleasure, goods, and ease rather than righteousness. The heroes of their stories are buffeted by hardship and misled by folly. None is relieved of personal responsibility for behaving badly. For the Bible holds us accountable for what we do, whatever our situation. The good we bring into being therefore testifies loudly to our God-like creativity—and we acquire true merit. By the same standard our transgressions lead to our condemnation. We might have done good, not evil. Hence, we must bear the guilt for what, in fact, we did.

Perhaps the puzzling appearance of the serpent in the Garden of Eden story mitigates this teaching. The authors seem to imply that we cannot understand the origins of evil solely from within the human psyche. Something external to us often lures us into evil action. But note that the serpent is not a demon or a malicious demi-god, only another of God's creatures, though apparently the shrewdest one. And temptation remains so serious because we do not have to give in to it but we often do.

Hardly any genre of postbiblical Jewish literature fails to emphasize human freedom. The Book of Ben Sirach (third century B.C.E.), which we find in the Apocrypha, describes it this way:

> Do not say, "God made me sin,"
> for God does not make that which He hates,
> and do not say, "God made me stumble,"
> for God has no need of evil men.
> Rather, the Lord hates evil and abomination
> and keeps them far from the pious.
> From the very beginning when God created man,
> He gave him power over his will.
> If you desire, you can keep the commandment
> and it is wise to do what God desires.
> Fire and water are poured out before you.
> Stretch out your hand to the one you desire.

Life and death are before man.
What he wants, that will be given him. (15:11–17)

The medieval Jewish philosophers provide impressive evidence of the Jewish commitment to human freedom. They acknowledged that significant aspects of our behavior derive from the vegetable and animal inheritance we bear. Nonetheless, our freedom distinguishes us from all other created things. Saadya Gaon (early tenth century) expresses the common philosophic view when he says, ". . . Our belief in man's superiority is not mere delusion, nor the result of our inclination to judge in favor of man . . . but it is something demonstrably true and perfect. The reason why God in His wisdom endowed man with this excellence can only be to make him the recipient of commandments and prohibitions." (Emunot ve Deot 4:1)

Maimonides similarly defends our freedom of choice and derides the notion that our character or deeds are predestined. "Give no credence to the idea expressed by foolish heathens and thoughtless Jews that when a person is born God decrees whether he is to be just or wicked. Not so. Every human being may become righteous like Moses our teacher or wicked like King Jeroboam; wise or foolish, merciful or cruel, niggardly or generous, and so with all other qualities. No one coerces him or decrees what he must do or draws him to either of the two ways. Every person turns to the way he desires. . . ." (Mishneh Torah, Hil. Tesh. 5)

Only rarely do we find sages who delimit or deny ultimate human freedom. Among philosophers, Chasdai Crescas (thirteenth century) may so be listed. Among mystics, some thinkers, particularly among the Chasidim, affirm that the human spirit contains evil within it, going so far as to preach predestination. Such views collide headlong with the bulk of Jewish teaching, causing a heavy fallout of criticism by Jews of many diverse perspectives.

3. The Talmudic Doctrine of the Two Urges

Over the centuries Jews avoided extreme views because they found the rabbinic understanding of human sinfulness quite persuasive. Where the Bible authors do not analyze human nature to explain the origins of our evildoing, the rabbis of the Talmud seem remarkably agreed on what we may call their "psychology." Knowing their own conflicts and candidly observing others, they described people as constantly buffeted by two urges, the urge-to-evil *(yetser hara)* and the urge-to-good *(yĕtser hatov)*. Sin abounds, they insisted, because the urge-to-evil is generally more powerful than the urge-to-good. Psalm 35:10 speaks of God delivering the poor from someone stronger, eliciting the rabbinic comment, "That is Israel and its spoiler is the urge-to-evil. How greatly does the urge-to-good move us to do the right but then the urge-to-evil comes and steals what would have been our gain. No thief is stronger than the urge-to-evil—but God delivers Israel from the urge-to-evil's power." (Pes. R. 32b) Another rabbinic dictum derives the superior strength of the urge-to-evil from its being born with us while the urge-to-good arises only when we reach the age of thirteen. (Eccles. R. 4:13)

The rabbis seem unable to say enough about the strength of the drive to do evil. They often cite the verse in Ecclesiastes, "No man on earth is so righteous that he always does good and never sins." (7:20) Rabbi Simeon b. Levi's hyperbole is typical: "The urge-to-evil waxes strong against a person day-by-day and seeks to kill him. If God did not help him, a man could not prevail against it." (Kid. 30b) They appreciate how slyly it can overcome us. "One trick of the urge-to-evil is to say today, 'Do this small thing,' and tomorrow, 'Do that small thing,' until at last it says, 'Worship an idol,' and we go and do that." (Shab. 105b) Neither virtue nor learning nor age makes us proof against its guiles. "The rabbis taught that we should not set an opportunity for sin before an honest man much less before a crook; it is like putting fire next to straw." (Tan. Buber, Metz. 26b) Of both R. Akiba and R. Meir we hear that they used to mock at the weakness of sinners. On separate occasions, the urge-to-evil presented itself to them as a gorgeous woman in an inaccessible spot. Both immediately made foolhardy efforts to get to her. When they were halfway the urge-to-evil called out, "If God had not just proclaimed, 'Respect the rabbi and his learning,' I wouldn't have given two cents for your life." (Kid. 81a) Abbaye once was embarrassed after he had been unnecessarily suspicious of a certain couple, knowing what he might have done in like circumstances. An "old man" then consoled him: "The greater the man, the greater the urge-to-evil." (Suk. 52a) The rabbinic attitude to human nature may be summed up in the common rule: When a rabbinic text mentions only an unspecified urge, the urge-to-evil is almost certainly meant.

4. For All Its Strength, Evil May Be Overcome

Reading the many talmudic citations on the insatiability of the urge-to-evil one might conclude that the rabbis had a pessimistic view of human nature. That judgment would be quite inaccurate. The rabbis were tough-minded. Had they not been, Judaism would not have long survived in human history. Rather, though utter realists, they remained idealists. Neither view of humankind by itself expressed their faith. Each, balanced by the other, gave a true view of humankind. All their lives people must engage in a fearsome struggle with themselves, one in which, however, they have the capacity momentarily to prevail.

The Torah enunciates this curious sort of optimism in God's speech to Cain before the murder of Abel. Cain was disturbed because God had not been impressed by his offering of produce. God then is reported to say to him, "Why are you distressed and why is your face fallen? Surely, if you do the good, it will be recognized. But if you do not do the good . . . [out of fear of their magical effects, one does not actually verbalize one's threats]. Sin is like a wild beast. It crouches at your door waiting to get you. But you can master it." (Gen. 4:6–7)

We shall better comprehend the rabbis' positive assessment of human nature if we keep in mind the context in which the urge-to-evil operates. People are made in the image of God; they cannot therefore be fundamentally evil. They stand in a covenant relationship with God; they therefore have inalienable dignity and may expect God's help in their lives. As the chasidic *rebbe* Shelomo of Karlin taught: "What is the worst thing the urge-to-evil can achieve? To make a man forget that he is the son of a King!"

With astonishingly modern insight, the rabbis even asserted that if God created the urge-to-evil it cannot be altogether evil. It too might occasionally be a means of leading us to do good. Nahman b. Samuel interpreted Genesis 1:31, "It was very good," as applying to the urge-to-evil. "How can that be?" he rhetorically asked. "Simple," he replied. "Were it not for the urge-to-evil a man would not build a house, take a wife, beget a child, or engage in business, as it is written [in Eccles. 4:4], 'All effort and excelling in work comes only of a man's rivalry with his neighbor'." (Gen. R. 9:7)

The rabbis could be positive about the human situation because they believed God had provided us with effective antidotes to the urge-to-evil's attacks. Chief of these was the Torah which they compared to a life-giving medicine. " 'As long as you occupy yourselves with the Torah,' says God, 'the urge-to-evil will not rule over you. But if you neglect it, then you will be delivered over into the power of urge-to-evil'." (Kid. 30b) Specifically, the rabbis meant that study of any aspect of Torah and attending the House of Study where scholars gathered would save one from sin. Obviously, too, observing the commandments, making them habitual, and associating with good people, all helped strengthen one in the unending struggle called life.

The Talmudic Doctrine of "The Turning"

With all the help people can get in staving off the urge-to-evil, the rabbis knew it would often overpower us. That does not end our relationship with God or our responsibilities as part of it. Based on biblical ideas, the rabbis taught we should then perform *teshuvah,* a notion so extraordinary it has no precise English equivalent. Usually, we render *teshuvah* as repentance, and it surely means that—except that the connotations of repentance are largely emotional. It means feeling sorry for having acted badly or being troubled by one's conscience for an evil act. If we do not go beyond this subjective mood to action, we shall not do *teshuvah.* Literally, that term comes from the Hebrew root meaning to turn back or to return. (The Hebrew noun *teshuvah* means an answer, that which you give back when someone asks something of you.) Thus *teshuvah* denotes action more than feeling. It points to the need to change one's direction (from a false to a true way). Many writers prefer to speak of *teshuvah* as turning rather than repentance though the usage is a bit odd in ordinary English.

However we translate the term, the rabbis taught that there are four steps involved in the process of *teshuvah.* First, we ought to feel proper remorse for what we did. The rabbis do not consider a bad act a triviality. We have abused our greatest talent, hurt others, added to humanity's woes, and affronted God. If we do not feel pangs of guilt we apparently do not recognize what we have done. Remorse may keep us from committing similar acts or letting this one become a habit. It ought to motivate us to try to repair the damage we did.

Second, we must now do what we can to remedy the effects of our wrongdoing. Ideally, we must sincerely ask the pardon of those whom we have offended (and, by Jewish law, they must grant it to us), make good their loss, and give up our sinful gains. When we cannot do that, we must still, to the extent we can, restore the order we violated. Only after we have exhausted our own power, may we reasonably seek help from others.

Third, we should confess our guilt to God. Doing evil estranges us from God even as violating an understanding with a friend changes our relationship. We need to say we're sorry if we are to "return" to the intimacy we once enjoyed. Putting our remorse into words—even in our hearts—and directing it to the One we have offended concretizes the acknowledgement of our guilt and redirects us to the standard of right we should follow.

Fourth, facing God, we need to resolve, as genuinely as we can, not to repeat this evil. This shift of concern from the past to the future seems to me characteristically Jewish. We cannot undo past history—but the time in front of us lies empty, awaiting our creative, transforming will. Jews believe we will redeem the past most fully by living the future well; it is a small messianic contribution each of us can make.

The Covenant in Action: When We Repent, God Forgives

The rabbis enthusiastically proclaimed that human *teshuvah* is met by God's loving acceptance. Sin is heinous but if we are willing to do *teshuvah* our covenant with God survives our evildoing.

The regular practice of *teshuvah* became as integral to Jewish living as doing good deeds. Rabbinic literature abounds in exhortations to Jews to do *teshuvah*. Thus, R. Samuel b. Nahman said, "The gates of prayer are sometimes open and sometimes closed —but the gates of repentance are always open." (Deut. R. 2:12) R. Eliezer b. Hyrcanus made it even more graphic. He instructed his disciples, "Turn to God one day before your death." They objected, "But does anyone know on which day he will die?" "Good," he responded, "then turn to God every day lest you die tomorrow. Thus all your days will be days of *teshuvah.*" (P. Av. 2:10)

The chasidic masters added an important theme to this teaching. They recognized that we can become so full of regret we cannot move on to the other steps of *teshuvah.* A motivating remorse has now been replaced by a paralyzing morbidity. Rabbi Bunam warned against this, "Dejection is not good and not pleasing to God. A broken heart prepares man for the service of God, but brooding corrodes one's service. We must distinguish carefully between the two." The ethical will ascribed to the Baal Shem Tov, the founder of Chasidism, cautions us against being too gloomy. "Do not increase detailed observance in any matter for the urge-to-evil wants a man to fear that he has not been observant and thus grow sad, for sadness severely hinders one from serving God properly. Even if one stumbles into sin, one should not be overly sad. . . . One should only be regretful and turn and rejoice in one's Creator . . . and consider that God inquires into one's intentions and knows that one wants to do one's duty but simply cannot."

The Differing Views of God and Humankind in Judaism and Christianity

The doctrine of *teshuvah* radically divides Judaism and Christianity. Consider the sort of God implied in the Jewish concept of *teshuvah.* God rules, commands, and judges—in the various traditional or modern ways these actions are understood—but this same God continually gives people another chance so as never to foreclose the opportunity for them to become righteous. And, since it is free human righteousness that God seeks, the sovereign God freely forgives.

Ezekiel gave this Jewish teaching classic form in chapter 18. He denounces the false doctrine that God punishes subsequent generations for the sins of their forebears. (That is, the Jews living after the destruction of Jerusalem by Nebuchadnezzar feared they would still have to suffer for the evils of a previous generation.) Ezekiel, with a clarity rarely found in his prophecies, proclaims that God judges individuals solely on their own merit. More important, says Ezekiel, God doesn't "want" to punish people for their sins. What God wants of them is good deeds. If God were concerned mainly with exacting punishment the world could not continue, people being such confirmed transgressors. But goodness, not mechanical justice, is God's goal. Ezekiel ringingly concludes his oration in God's name, "Cast away all your sins with which you have sinned and get yourself a new heart and a new spirit that you may not die, O House of Israel. For I do not want anyone to die, declares *Adonai,* God. Turn you, therefore, and live." (18: 31–32)

For the past two thousand years and more, Jewish practice has been shaped by this experience of the immediate accessibility of God. The second of the petitions in the daily service appeals for God's help in our doing *teshuvah.* Our community asks God's forgiveness on Yom Kippur. We personally approach God each day asking for God's compassion. Every Jew should do so, and to perform *teshuvah* we need no rabbi, no rite, no synagogue, not even a *minyan,* though they all are desirable. We only need to turn to God sincerely for we know that God so loves us that we will be forgiven.

> He has not dealt with us after our sins
> > punished us according to our iniquities.
> For as the heaven is high above the earth,
> > so great is His mercy to those that fear Him.
> As far as the east is from the west,
> > so far has He removed our transgressions from us.
> As a father pities his children
> > so *Adonai* has pity on His children.
> For He knows our urges [*yitsrenu*],
> > He remembers that we are dust. (Ps. 103:10–14)

Christianity reinterpreted these old Jewish ideas in such a way as to create a fundamentally different religion. Christian theology transforms the notion of a powerful but momentarily conquerable urge-to-evil into a flawed human nature. In its various permutations, the doctrine of original sin asserts that human beings, in their very essence, are tainted by sinfulness. No matter what you might do, you cannot overcome the iniquity which estranges you from God. Christian thinkers envision God as so holy and pure that the sinful human being cannot stand in intimate relationship with the Divine. Only an extraordinary act of forgiving love by God can bridge the terrifying gap between humanity and God. In the classic version, God, as one of three persons of the Trinity, enters history in the God-man person of Jesus of Nazareth. Because Jesus as God need not suffer and die, his willingly doing so makes restitution for humankind's primal iniquity. He thus saves people from God's judgment and restores them to God's favor. Those who believe in him join in the New Covenant, gain the strength to live in greater righteousness now, and are promised a later life in God's own Kingdom.

In Protestant Christianity, restoring one's basic intimacy with God depends solely on having proper faith. One signals this by the inner act of acknowledging Jesus as the Christ and thus joining the church. In Catholicism, one also lives out one's faith through the life of sacraments administered by the priests of God's true church. Though all Christians use the term repentance, they give it a radically different meaning from the Jewish one. Repentance has value in Christianity but it cannot by itself effectuate that supreme forgiveness which is available only through the Christ and his church. Judaism teaches that God is so loving and close that God immediately responds to anyone who performs genuine *teshuvah.* For Christians, God so loves people that, though they have utterly distanced themselves from the Divine through their sinfulness, God miraculously enters history, takes their sins as God's own, suffers and dies for them, and now grants them forgiveness and a new mode of existence. Throughout the centuries, despite the hardships they endured as a consequence, almost all Jews have rejected the Christian claim to improve on Israel's Covenant. Theologically, they found its views of human sinfulness, and of God's distance and love, unacceptable.

Modern Approaches to Human Nature

The past century has revolutionized our perception of individuals and society. Our new insights into human behavior have sharpened our understanding and improved our therapies so that we cannot employ the old rabbinic psychology unaltered.

Modernity has been most impressive in teaching us how many factors determine human behavior. All of us are very much the

creations of our nation, class, neighborhood, family, society, nu-
trition, environment, education, media, experience, and the like.
Our genetic makeup, animal inheritance, organic adequacy,
homeostatic dynamisms, neurological structuring, learning capacities, conditioned behaviors, and emotional balance, conscious and unconscious, substantially shape what we do. Serious
pressures from any of these elements will skew or alter our behavior. Now when we see or hear of aberrant acts, we do not immediately respond with a moral condemnation, as previous generations did. We are likely instead to inquire what force drove the
person to such a course of action. Some hard-line objective scientists, B. F. Skinner being the most notable, deny entirely that
freedom or dignity remain valuable terms to apply to human
behavior.

Liberal Jewish teachers believe this new view of humankind has
taught us two great virtues—though each led on to a new problem. The first is increased compassion. We become less cruel to
others when we perceive their troublesome acts as largely a destructive unwilled reaction to various impersonal factors. Frac-
tious school children may be hyperactive, or learning disabled, or
gifted, or emotionally disturbed, or badly taught, or any one of
a number of things rather than simply bad and in need of punishment. Applied to one's own family, friends, neighbors, community and country, in fact, to humankind, we learn to appreciate
human difference.

Even tolerance can go too far, as difficult as that is for a Jew to
say. One becomes so understanding one no longer holds people
responsible for what they have done. If nothing else shook our
determination not to be judgmental, the Nazis did. Of course
many forces from without and within impelled ordinary Germans
to carry out the Holocaust. Does that mean, then, that they bear
no guilt for what they did? Are there no standards which people,
despite intense pressure, should not transgress? Or should, at
least, make a supreme effort not to transgress? Jews, like many
other people, have come to recognize that the greatest dehumani-
zation occurs when we excuse people from moral responsibility.
We may not be as free as earlier generations believed but neither
are mature persons utterly un-self-determining.

This radically altered perspective also gave us new power to
help people. If nutritional deficiences or sensory deprivation or

emotional lack in the early months of life could permanently retard a child's growth, we might prevent such damage. Instead of relying on shame or pain or the threat of them to keep social incompetents in line, we could provide the therapies and conducive situations which turned previously intractable situations into healthy ones. With every revelatory insight our optimism grew at what science might empower us to do for humanity. We dared hope that, by therapeutically redesigning our bodies or ourselves or our social order, we might messianically transform human existence.

Many people accepted the secular promise of salvation with all the fervor they had formerly reserved for religion. Jews have been spectacularly overrepresented in the ranks of those seeking to create the ideal society through some new humanistic program. I see in this widely remarked upon phenomenon a subtle transformation of old Jewish beliefs. Where the rabbis thought study and commandments would make us fully free, the Jewish Marxists and psychologists, to mention only two obvious cases, proposed revolution or treatment to redeem us from our outer or inner slavery. To crusading liberals traditional Judaism often seemed utterly ineffectual. So they cast off a heritage they judged discredited by modern science and technique. In hindsight, we can say that they merely created a highly specialized urban, secularized, activist version of it.

The New Realism and the Old Struggle

The experience of the past several decades has discredited unbridled confidence in human competence. Science today is more divided in theory and less certain in application than we ever anticipated. Our triumphant therapies of another generation, social and individual, have all disclosed serious limits—and not infrequently created problems nearly as severe as those they solved. With all our insight into the human evils that can lead to nazism, the best and brightest among us—to borrow the title of a book on the Kennedy era—regularly behave foully.

Those Jews who can now bear to face the loss of their old liberal optimism have found a new appreciation of the rabbis' realism-with-idealism. A deep-seated urge-to-evil powers individuals far more than Marx ever dreamed, though Freud's late dark writings seem almost a reappropriation of the rabbis' bleak view of human perversity. The tide has turned so fully that we wonder how people without many illusions can have any great hope at all.

The rabbis believed people might rule over their capacity for evil but not because they esteemed human self-control. They knew us well enough not to trust in humankind alone. Despite our inertia, stupidity, malice, and aggressiveness they knew we remained God's covenant partners. They trusted God to help us even as we sought to do God's work. The rise of a new spirituality among liberal Jews, I am convinced, stems largely from our recognition that we share the rabbis' faith that trust in people cannot ultimately be dissociated from trust in God.

We also know much more about the effective motives for human behavior than they did. The rabbis believed that intellect, discipline, and will, reinforced by belief, rite, and community, would largely subdue our urge-to-evil. The high sanctity of many Jewish lives and of many Jewish communities over the centuries attests to the truth in their vision. But the way of rule and repression exacts a heavy toll. We modern Jews must take a somewhat different way. We propose to integrate our bodies and our emotions into our lives in ways the rabbis would have judged unthinkable. We need to alter our social relationships, particularly those which have been strongly hierarchical, to allow for greater self-expression.

We are creating a new, postmodern Jewish view of human nature and of the varied means of coping with our urge-to-evil. Our tradition teaches us realism about human nature and conditions us day-by-day in what we too must now see as the lifelong struggle with our darker side. Modernity equips us with a deep understanding of our urge-to-evil and with powerful techniques for reorienting and perhaps harnessing it. When we have integrated them, we will have freedom with direction, few illusions yet much hope, a view of life as an unending spiritual struggle balanced by the Jewish optimism that, with God's help, we can succeed in it.

·2·

DEALING WITH TEMPTATION:
MONEY, SEX, DRINKING

An anonymous American epigram proclaims that everything delectable is either illegal, immoral, or fattening.
Whoever put that oft-felt impression into words hinted at a great
moral truth: evil does not appear to us flashing warning lights of
pain or bitterness. Temptation works upon us because it presents
a desirable option. In this respect, nothing much has changed
over the several thousand years of Jewish experience. Take
money, for example. Its appeal has always been high. The Book
of Proverbs declares, "A poor man is hated even by his neighbor;
but a rich man has many friends." (14:20) In talmudic times,
R. Judah b. Shalom noted, "No one pays much attention when a
poor man comes to plead his cause but a rich man gets priority
as well as attention." (Exod. R. 21:4) And, nearer our own time
in the impoverished shtetl, the Yiddish proverb opines that "with
money in your pocket you are not only wise and handsome but
you sing well too."

Two social changes persuade me that the power of temptation
may be greater for our generation. First, our society tolerates,
perhaps even encourages, a wide range of behavior that people
once avoided for fear of community censure. In the sexual realm,
another era's deviance is now healthy experimentation, playful-
ness, or alternative style. What once only the adventurous tried
is today's common knowledge and perhaps commercial enterprise. Besides, we are richer than any previous Jewish community.
We can indulge our fantasies in ways that Jews, severely con-

367

strained by immediate survival needs, could not. As Moshe Leib, the *rebbe* of Sasov already understood: "How easy it is for a poor man to depend on God. After all, he has nothing else. And how difficult it is for a rich man to do so. All his possessions call out to him, 'Depend on us!' " The combination of amplified freedom and increased means has clearly intensified the old problem of temptation.

The Danger of Underestimating Temptation

One might think temptation had less appeal these days because we rightly fear addiction. We know that what may begin as desirable or even worthwhile can easily become a life-absorbing necessity. Hard drugs receive the greatest publicity. Jews, like other people, are more involved in the sedate self-destructions, like tranquilizer dependency or life as workaholics. And the older, widespread American addiction, alcoholism, now makes itself felt in unprecedented numbers among us.

Not all temptation leads to habit formation and character deformation. Most lapses, thank God, are temporary. That very fact leads the urge-to-evil to get us started on a slippery slope by saying, "Try it once," and then, "We all need to give in to ourselves once in a while." As R. Assi said, "The urge-to-evil begins as a spider's web but ends up as strong as cart ropes." R. Akiba said, "A ship's hawser." (Suk. 52a; Gen. R. 22:6) The pleasures of indulgence being great, we begin to live for goods, power, or pleasure. For their sake we may come to sacrifice family, friends, and responsibility. Even the modest addictions we see among our immediate acquaintances testify to the destructiveness which ensue from treating temptation lightly.

One age-old stratagem of the urge-to-evil is to persuade us that we can control our lust. Other people do not know when to stop but we, because of our education, shrewdness, experience, attainments, or such, are different. We shall merely warm ourselves at the fire but not get burnt. Or, we may take the route of self-pity. After all, others are having such a better life than we are, surely some slight indiscretion is only just compensation. "Besides," we intone, "we're only human."

The process of self-damage seems not to have changed much over the years, though the urge-to-evil now often validates permissiveness with seductive evidence from science or psychotherapy. The downward route remains what it was. This is how one midrash fancifully describes the origins of wine: When Noah planted the first vineyard (Gen. 9:20), Satan [God's accusing angel] appeared to him, offered to be his partner, and, to seal their bargain, sacrificed a lamb, a lion, a pig, and a monkey, whose blood then drenched the vineyard soil. Since then, before one drinks, one is docile like a sheep, not even complaining before one's shearers. When one drinks in moderation, one becomes like a lion, whom nothing in the world can withstand. But, when one drinks more than enough, one becomes like a pig, wallowing in filth; and, when drunk, one staggers around like an ape, uttering obscenities, oblivious of what one does. (Tan. Noach 13)

People sometimes argue that the time has come to reorder our old Jewish values. Previous generations deprecated wealth, sex, alcohol, and drugs because they were obsessed with God and Torah. They had comparatively little regard for bodily pleasures. When people's energies had to be directed to providing subsistence, religion performed the useful role of repressing people's natural desires. Our economy allows us to live in a less stringently constrained fashion. Our tradition may have been too restrictive, but modernity stresses openness to the point of having no values at all. Most Jews today need little Jewish encouragement for further experimentation. Our society entices us to the point of pimpery. Liberal Jews rather need help in setting proper limits to the use of their freedom. Their religion, surely, ought to be their best guide in determining them. Let us explore Judaism's approach to the great temptations, money, sex, and drink, by first investigating its attitude to extremist solutions.

Shall We Adopt a Judaism of Self-Denial?

While the world has known orgiastic religions, the more common spiritual tendency has been abstention. Often this is an ideal suggested only for those dedicating their lives to the religious quest. In Roman Catholicism and Buddhism, members of the priesthood and religious orders practice celibacy; in the orders, various groups take a vow of poverty, occasionally of very great stringency. In some religions, a prohibition may apply to the whole community. Thus Moslems may not drink alcoholic beverages.

The motive leading to abstention is not obscure. Money, sex, and drinking are so enticing, or people are so weak in dealing with them, that nothing less than total avoidance is safe. For our ultimate spiritual gain we should be happy to sacrifice some human pleasure. The rabbis did something similar when they spoke of "putting a fence around the Torah." They extended the limits of the forbidden to make certain we would not get close to transgression.

In some religions—we are best acquainted with the Christian examples—this leads on to the doctrine that, by increasing the hardships, one acquires greater merit before God. At the extreme, one inflicts special punishments upon oneself, thereby demonstrating how much one will bear for the love of God. In Christianity, the crucifixion serves as the model for the ascetic. Jesus' willingness to bear suffering for the love of God and for the sake of humankind sets the highest standard of Christian service. The record of the Christian hermits is perhaps the most astonishing manifestation of self-denial among Western religions.

What Is the Jewish Attitude toward Pleasure?

Judaism rejected the fully proscriptive way without sanctioning license. In tracing the subtle interplay of permission within limits, we must be careful not to emphasize one pole of its balanced position at the expense of the other. With that caution in mind, let us outline its positive attitude toward pleasure.

To begin with, the world God created was good. The urge-to-evil and the great tempters, being part of God's creation, therefore contain a measure of God's goodness. Some rabbis taught that the world as we know it could not long exist without them. A talmudic legend relates that once the rabbis captured the urge-to-evil and sought to kill "him." A prophet then admonished them that, should they do so, the world would revert to chaos. They therefore imprisoned the urge-to-evil and pondered what to do. After three days had gone by they discovered that there was not a single fresh egg in the whole Land of Israel. They knew then that they could not kill him but they did not want to free him unimpaired. So they let him go after putting out his eyes; and now, at least, Jews are no longer tempted to practice incest. (Yoma 69b)

Grateful for God's gifts, our people gave the great human joys a place in Jewish life, of which the use of wine provides the best instance. The Bible and Talmud do not ignore its potential evil. "Wine is a mocker, strong drink a brawler; none who reels from their effects is wise." (Prov. 20:1) "They stagger to and fro like drunkards and lose all their wisdom." (Ps. 107:27) R. Meir asserted that the tree from which Adam ate was actually a grapevine "for there is nothing which so easily causes one to lament as wine." (San. 70a-b) And we hear, "When wine enters, sense leaves; when wine enters, secrets come out." (Num. R. 10:8) This did not cause them to deny the benefits of wine. God is praised in Psalm 104, verse 15, among other things, for creating "wine which cheers one up, making one's face brighter than cosmetic oil can." The author of Ecclesiastes, notorious for complaining that all is vanity, waxes optimistic enough to declare, "A feast brings laughter, wine gladdens life, and money is an answer to everything." (10:19)

The rabbis decreed an obligatory cup of wine at every major Jewish religious celebration—and no less than four cups at the Passover *seder*. Unfermented grape juice may be used but, when there are no therapeutic reasons, Jews generally shun that alternative. The rabbis advocate drinking on such occasions because they believe the effects of wine will enhance our celebrating. R. Judah b. Bethyra said flatly, "There is no rejoicing without wine." (Pes. 109a) R. Bana'ah put it more strongly when teaching certain Gentiles who recorded his saying, in the name of "the elders of the Jews," as "the best of all medicines is wine; and only where there is no wine are medicines required." (B. B. 58b) In Eastern Europe it was common for people honored at a daily or *Shabbat* service to provide a bottle of whisky for the worshipers to share, and this tradition of providing a *Kiddush* is still found in some American synagogues.

Setting the Proper Priority for Pleasure

Our tradition took a positive attitude to money, sex, and drinking because it unequivocally subordinated them to higher values. In Judaism, pleasure is not life's goal and its pursuit is not a major Jewish activity. Perhaps our lawgivers and rabbis realized what philosophers have often commented upon, that nothing makes finding happiness more unlikely than pursuing it vigorously.

372 · LIBERAL JUDAISM

More convincingly, they simply looked at existence in a less self-centered way. They understood people to be intimately linked to God and other human beings. The meaning of our lives derives from this ultimate interdependence. As we fulfill our responsibilities to others and ourselves we carry out our obligations to God. The greatest pleasures come as a by-product of sanctifying life, the everyday and the exceptional times alike.

The libertarian notion of being responsible only to oneself has become common enough that a brief Jewish rejoinder is in order. For Judaism, to dismiss obligation to anyone other than oneself is the equivalent of idolatry. It denies God as our common creator; it arrogates to the self all rights to command. It flatly contradicts the "golden rule" for what one does for oneself one refuses to do for others, that is, to make them a focus of responsibility. Libertarianism predicates as the highest value the sort of independence the rabbis called the unsavory "ethic of Sodom."

The limits to the self's exclusive claim on us become clear when we consider the Jewish attitude to "charity." That English word comes from a root meaning love and implies something we ought to do when appropriately moved. *Tsedakah,* the parallel Hebrew term, means acting righteously. Jews are commanded to give *tsedakah,* to share their means with others whether they feel like it or not. The duty can be enjoined upon us precisely because we are not, ultimately, independent. R. Elazar of Bertota said, speaking of *tsedakah,* "Give Him [God] some of His, for you and yours are His, as King David said, 'For all things come from You and of Your own have we given to You'." (P. Av. 3:8) Similarly, the talmudic master Mar Zutra ruled that even a beggar who himself is supported by charity must give something to charity. (Git. 7b)

Jewish teaching and practice over the centuries set our involvement with money, sex, and drink within the context of our intimate ties with others. We have obligations to family, to community, to the Jewish people, to humankind, and to God as well as to self. In depression or elation to be sure, but even in our everyday moods, we are almost certain to be wrong when we determine a course of action with essentially our own benefit in mind. Jewish law prohibits suicide on this general ground.

The Jewish Rejection of Asceticism

The rabbis had little use for people who thought to magnify their holiness by voluntary self-denial. They realized that Jews already lived with many prohibitions. Interpreting R. Simlai's dictum that there are 613 commandments in the Written Torah, they calculated that 365 of these are proscriptive, with only 248 positive injunctions. R. Isaac put it bluntly, "Are not the things prohibited by the Torah enough for you so that you want to add other things for yourself? A vow of abstinence is like a prisoner's heavy iron collar. Taking a vow of abstinence is like meeting a troop of Roman soldiers with such a collar and voluntarily sticking one's own head into it—or like driving a sword into one's body." (Y., Ned. 10:1) R. Jose sounds the interdependent theme in ruling, "One is not permitted to afflict oneself with fasting lest one become unable to work and then dependent on the public, perhaps finding no mercy." Rav said that the basis of that ruling was the verse, "And man became a living soul," (Gen. 2:7) which may be read to say, "Keep alive the soul I gave you!" (Taan. 22b)

A charming deprecation of asceticism is derived from the Torah's law concerning Nazirites. Allowing for the human proclivity to carry things to extremes, the Torah provides a special status for people who wish, for a limited period or even a lifetime, to take on special vows of abstinence. (The distinguishing acts are not cutting one's hair—so Samson's infidelity—and not drinking wine. See Num. 6:1–21.) When the stated term of service was over, the Nazirite, among other things, had to bring a sin-offering to the Temple. This led a number of sages to declare that, by virtue of their vows, Nazirites are sinners. R. Elazar Berabi said a Nazirite is a sinner because, by abstention from wine, he sinned against himself. "And if one who afflicted himself only in respect of wine is called a sinner, how much the more so one who wishes to practice asceticism by abstaining from everything." (Ned. 10a)

The theme had immediate relevance to the rabbis. Apparently, after the Temple had been destroyed, there were Jews who, in mourning for the loss of the service commanded by the Torah, would not eat meat or drink wine, since these were used on the altar. R. Joshua tried to persuade them to desist from their fast but they demurred. He then pointed out that by their reasoning they would also not be entitled to fruit, bread, or water, all of which were utilized in various Temple services. He added, "Not to mourn at all is impossible, for God's judgment has come upon us; but to mourn overmuch is also not required of us, for a decree is not imposed upon the community which the majority of the community is unable to endure." (B. B. 60b)

Asceticism Leads out of Judaism: The Essenes

The discovery and publication of the Dead Sea texts have renewed interest in the Jewish sect Philo called the Essenes. Though scholars still debate the equivalence of the two movements, the Dead Sea sectarians resemble the descriptions of the Essenes in many respects. In his book *Every Good Man Is Free,* Philo speculates that the term Essenes is a corrupt Greek version of the word for holiness. He suggests the name "was given them because they had shown themselves especially devout in the service of God, not by offering sacrifices of animals but by resolving to sacrifice the mind. . . . The first thing about these people is that they live in villages and avoid the cities because of the iniquities which have become inveterate among city dwellers. . . . Some of them labor on the land and others pursue such crafts as promote peace. . . . They have not the slightest idea of commerce either wholesale or retail. . . ." They were also celibate and replenished their numbers by acquiring recruits. The Dead Sea sectarian documents indicate that their group scorned the religious authorities in Jerusalem and their ways of serving God.

The Essenes and some other groups of that period—Philo also describes a sect like them called the Therapeutae—represent a pronounced Jewish effort to make self-denial a major way of carrying out the Covenant. With increasing Roman intrusion into Judaean affairs, life became very difficult. Many scholars see the rise of these ascetic groups and of Christianity as similarly motivated by a strong need to turn from this world. The overwhelming majority of Jews rejected the way of withdrawal, asceticism, and faith in a redeeming savior. Instead, they made the rabbis' teaching about sanctifying the everyday the authoritative interpretation of the Covenant. As a result, subsequent Jewish history did not give rise to hermits, celibate clergy, monastic orders, or extremist sects which believed in self-punishment.

During the Middle Ages, Jews did adopt much of their Christian and Moslem neighbors' negative attitude toward the body. In the pietistic, *musar* literature of those centuries, we often hear overtones of a dualism which exaggerates grossly the attitudes found in the Talmud. Yet Jewish law set bounds even for pietists. Scholars were expected to make their living from trade, intercourse with one's wife was commanded, and the holy days required imbibing a certain measure of wine. The *Sefer Hasidim*, a twelfth- or thirteenth-century compilation, presents the counsels of a German Jewish group described as the most ascetical sect ever to surface within the Jewish community. A passage in it nonetheless admonishes us, "Those who constantly fast are not following a good way. Scribes, teachers, and workmen are altogether forbidden to inflict penance upon themselves. If God had any particular delight in much fasting, He would have commanded it to Israel. God only asked of them that they serve Him in humility."

Solomon Ganzfried (1804–1886) summed up the long Jewish legal tradition on abstinence in this paragraph adapted from his *Kitsur Shulchan Aruch,* his abridged and updated (1846) version of the famous late medieval Jewish code: "Perhaps a man will say, 'Since envy, voluptuousness, ambition, and the like destroy our lives, I will entirely refrain from them, even to an extreme,' with the result that he will not eat meat, drink wine, marry, live in a comfortable home but wear sackcloth and the like instead of respectable clothes. This is an improper path. Our sages ordered that a man should abstain only from those things which the Torah forbade us and should not vow abstinence from things which are permitted. They forbade one to torment oneself with fast days more than is required. Concerning such matters King Solomon [Eccles. 7:16] said, 'Be not righteous overmuch, neither show yourself overwise. Why should you destroy yourself?' "

The Jewish Way between Indulgence and Abstinence

Rabbinic literature copiously indicates how Jews may avoid the extremes of self-punishment and self-indulgence. Chiefly it does this through the law, which sets forth in detail how Jews ought to live. Thus, in regard to our sexuality we learn that, though a woman cannot initiate divorce proceedings, she may get a Jewish court to compel her husband to have intercourse with her or grant her a divorce. (Ket. 61b–62a) So, too, the rabbis discuss the limits of a period during which a husband, even for the sake of studying Torah, may sexually absent himself from his wife. And, in regard to our wealth, we are enjoined that, "when a poor Jew comes into our community, we must provide him from community funds with bread enough for daily sustenance. If he stays overnight, we must make available a place for him to sleep. If he stays over the Sabbath, we must give him three meals." (Shab. 118a)

Custom and community practice filled out the continually developing provisions of the law. Jews grew up observing how their people sanctified the great human desires. Money made possible a family, a home, sustenance, medical care, education, Jewish celebration, help to relatives and friends, charity, and community projects. Sex had its proper place in marriage and, though modesty was encouraged, there was little husband and wife wished to do together that the law flatly prohibited. While Jewish marriage law sought to promote procreation, it also encouraged intercourse after menopause out of a recognition of the intertwining of love and sexuality. A similar approach was taken to alcohol. Tots sipped wine after chanting a blessing, thereby connecting drinking with Divinity and family and community in a way that counteracted the danger inherent in spirits. Historic Judaism made the great temptations a means to Jewish holiness.

Modernity has troubled the Jewish community greatly because we have found it difficult to translate our centuries-old patterns into appropriate modern rules. We have had less problem utilizing the ethical instruction which filled out the law and provided the frame of value in which it operated. Much of the *agadah* of rabbinic literature remains immediately relevant. Thus, in a list of opinions concerning things which may be harmful to us, we are told, "There are eight things of which a little is good and much is bad: travel, intercourse, wealth, work, wine, sleep, spiced drinks, and medicine." (Git. 70a) And in the same collection, we are advised, "Eat to a third of your stomach's capacity and drink to a third but leave a third empty."

Community style had as much to do with imparting and enforcing a life of moderation as did direct rabbinic exhortation. Some things were simply not to be countenanced (though they occurred) and the phrase, "But a Jew doesn't do such things," once carried substantial weight. To give an extreme example, the Chasidim, for all their drinking, rarely had a problem with alcoholics. Their communities not only taught the steady use of alcohol but the limits of the intoxication which were acceptable. By contrast, modern Jews are rarely rooted in one neighborhood very long. When they do settle down, their contacts with their Jewish community often remain tenuous because of the contemporary emphasis on personal privacy. Just as American enticements to indulge have multiplied, Jewish community constraints have become decreasingly effective. Part of the recent turn to Jewish tradition, I am convinced, has come from our hope that it may provide a more secure anchorage for our values than we have found elsewhere in our present confused society.

Remembering the Religious Context

Much of the Jewish wisdom with regard to meeting temptation would seem self-evident if we could come to it as did believing Jews of a previous generation. They knew their lives were intimately tied up with God and what they chose to do would affect this, their most fundamental relationship. If a beggar stands at our door, we are advised, the Holy One stands at his side. (Lev. R. 34:9) Sensing God's presence in whatever we had to do, we would approach it differently than we generally do now.

The corollary of this traditional perspective is an exalted view of self. By contrast, much of our contemporary experimentation with new values, I sense, arises from our feeling that what we do and who we are doesn't really matter. This self-deprecation robs our acts of any significance and makes it possible for us to do or try anything. Judaism will have none of such moral abdication, whether stemming from lack of faith in God or in ourselves. For our religion, affirming God—in whatever modern sense*—means valuing human life and human choices most highly. We human beings are the one natural force which can, by choice, direct history. Each of us, for all that we are but one atom in the vast sea of humanity, is directly linked to God. We therefore carry an inalienable particle of cosmic significance with us and might give it creative power by every act we do.

Jewish tradition does occasionally sound some negative notes

*See Part Two, *The God We Affirm*, chapters 3 and 4.

to help us resist indulgence. We have already discussed its view of our susceptibility to the urge-to-evil and we could cite here its many teachings designed to counter human pride. Instead, let us consider its major caution to our willfulness, the threat of death and judgment. The rabbis often remind us how limited our lives are and therefore how foolish we are to risk them for fleeting pleasures. "When one comes into the world, the hands are clenched, as if to say, 'Everything is mine and I will take possession of it.' When one leaves this world, the hands are open, as if to say, 'I have acquired nothing from the world'." (Eccles. R. 5:14) We all experience something of this upon hearing of the death of a friend or attending a funeral. The rabbis point to a similar intuition in relating parallel stories about the Babylonian sages Mar b. Ravina and R. Ashi. During the wedding feasts of their sons, both sages, noting that the rabbis had become hilarious, seized a costly goblet and broke it before the guests, thus bringing some sobriety into the celebration. (Ber. 30b ff.) Our custom of breaking a glass at a wedding may stem from later generations seeking to emulate these teachers.

The ultimate religious guidance for facing temptation lies in seeking to be true to God. How would God "look" at what we now propose to do? A well-established Jewish practice can serve as our model. Jewish law requires us to say a blessing before we drink whisky (even as we are accustomed to do before we drink wine). For whisky, the blessing is the universal one for those pleasures for which no special texts have been designated, namely, ". . . *shehakol niheyeh bidevaro*"—"We bless You, *Adonai*, Ruler of the universe, by whose word all things came to be." So to speak, by our blessing we dedicate our drinking to God. Saying such a blessing before every drink will not prevent the urge-to-evil from finding ways to persuade us to get drunk. Foolproof protections against human willfulness cannot be devised. But saying the blessing with some meaning would put this choice— or any other—in its proper Jewish context and give us some hope of later being proud of what we did.

If we could similarly make our preoccupation with money or sex or any other urgent human drive an integral part of our living in Covenant, we might, with authentic Jewish pride, survive an era of unparalleled temptation.

A Word about the Jewish Legitimacy of Drugs

Symptomatic of our unique situation is the growing problem of taking drugs for pleasure. Never have they been so widely available or had such social prestige attached to them. Young people grow up taking for granted their contemporaries' or parents' utilization of drugs, despite its illegality. The classic dilemma of temptation now repeats itself. We are allured by the special delights which drugs bring, with the greatest pleasures apparently given by the most dangerous ones. Yet the depradations of addiction are well known and even the lesser risks are considerable. What attitude should a liberal Jew take toward this new temptation?

In my personal opinion, some things remain as clear and valid in this case as they were in the others we have discussed. Any activity which substantially destroys our capacity to exercise responsible freedom ought to be avoided. Addictive drugs, even psychologically addictive drugs, have no place in our lives—and I would hope that thoughtful physicians and friends would help people find ways to be weaned from overusing tranquilizers or from other chemical dependencies. My negative ethical bias is reinforced by the possibility of physical damage from the drugs and by the perils which arise from engaging in illegal activities. Were all that not sufficiently compelling, a concern with drugs generally indicates a poor sense of values. The drug taker's emphasis on feeling good usually is inordinate. The pursuit of pleasure should not be the goal of our existence; there is much far worthier of our ultimate concern. I can find only one possible exception to that blanket prohibition, marijuana.

The issue of marijuana cannot easily be settled, in part because the facts concerning it remain highly disputed. Its partisans suggest that marijuana, while not as harmless as drinking coffee, has been shown to be nowhere as damaging as most other drugs and perhaps even less so than alcohol or nicotine. It is not addictive, though it can become habit-forming. Its illegality may be more a matter of previous misinformation and fright rather than the rational conclusion of an objective effort to set responsible public policy. For all these reasons, marijuana has become part of the way of life for many Americans. One bit of Jewish data may be added to the positive argument. Hashish has apparently been utilized by some Jews in Moslem countries for many centuries. As far as I have been able to tell, no Sephardic sage banned or decried its use. It is also my impression that the recent openness of some young Jews to Jewish mysticism and their consequent increased levels of Jewish observance have been connected with their having .had the consciousness-expanding experience of smoking marijuana.

I have not yet been persuaded by the case for marijuana. The research on its effects is highly contradictory and I often sense that, on both sides, it is more ideological than objective. With so many substances having demonstrated their deleterious effects upon us any new one we are urged to ingest must definitely prove its innocence. The case for marijuana's safety remains to be made. I am also troubled by the suggestion that one of the significant civil rights causes of our time is the legalization of another form of intoxication. In many cases, the marijuana habit signals a withdrawal into the self against a healthy investment in the world. Perhaps I would be less negative to opening our community to marijuana if we could guide its use with something of our community attitudes and practices with regard to drinking. Yet for all their strength our defenses against alcoholism seem to be crumbling. Despite our Sephardic experience, we have almost nothing of equal weight to teach us how to contain the power of marijuana and harness it in the service of the Covenant.

But I cannot say flatly that there are no conditions under which I might see marijuana being used alongside alcohol as part of our Jewish community life. We cannot any longer easily say what personal acts can never be part of our Jewish practice. Our people has found a way to sanctify wealth, sexuality, and alcohol, though other faiths prohibited them. Our surest approach to all new temptation will be to live so rich a Jewish life that we will have a strong and stable context to help us determine what acts might yet legitimately become a part of it. The Gerer *Rebbe* spoke for our time as well as his when he said, "There will be many temptations of a most grave sort. He who has not prepared himself for them will be lost. For it is too late to prepare oneself to resist when temptation is actually at hand. Temptation comes as a test of what you are. It shows you what within you is dross and what is true metal."

·3·

DO OUR ETHICS CHANGE?

We must now consider a troubling consequence of our religious liberalism: Jewish ethics change even as all of Judaism has changed.* If what is morally right today may not be so some years from now, can we ever insist that some acts truly should or shouldn't be done? Could we ever overcome the temptation to avoid ethical decisions until we were certain of our ethical duty?

Jews have a special stake in the permanence of ethics. Several of our greatest modern Jewish thinkers—most notably Hermann Cohen and Leo Baeck—identified ethics as the essence of Judaism. By this they meant that it was the element which remained unchanged while everything else in Judaism was evolving. If now we hear that Jewish ethics also develops, we seem to lose the rock on which our shifting Jewish faith had found stability. And if our religion is in as great flux as is our morally troubled social order, of what particular ethical worth can it be?

These probing questions require thoughtful answers and we shall spend this chapter slowly finding them. We begin in our customary modern way by taking a look at some of the historical evidence. I would like us to study three instructive cases, though I confess that I included the first one because I hope you will find it intellectual fun. Analyzing them should prepare us to consider the subtle issue of permanence and change in our ethical outlook.

---

*See In Beginning, the introductory chapter to this volume entitled, "Eternal Truths in Changing Forms."

Case One: The Rebellious Son

At *Shabbat* morning services late in the summer you will hear the following astonishing passage read from the Torah: "If someone has a stubborn and rebellious son who will not listen to what his father and mother say though they punish him, let them take him to the elders of the city (at the city gate). Let them then declare, 'This son of ours is stubborn and rebellious. He will not listen to what we tell him. He is a glutton and a drunk.' Then the men of the city should stone the son until he is dead. That will get rid of this evil in the community. Moreover, other Jewish sons will hear about it and be afraid to act the same way." (Deut. 21:18–21)

That's hardly what we have in mind when we speak of the loving Jewish family! If we can transcend our modern sense of proper parent-child relationships for a moment and jump back far in time, perhaps we can understand the intent of this law. We must go back to a day when fathers had absolute power over their children. Thus the *patria potestas* of the Roman citizen originally gave the father the power of capital punishment over all the members of his household—and that in a relatively civilized society. The much older Deuteronomic law may well be a rejection of the father's unconditional rule as practiced among the primitive peoples of the ancient Near East.

From this perspective, note how this rule introduces "due process." Both the father and the mother must make a formal declaration to the court about their son's degeneracy. The participation of the mother is not only somewhat surprising in itself but may constitute a further restrictive amendment of the father's right. Though it is not explicitly stated, the court must then agree that there is substance to their charge, for they must lead the citizens in executing the sentence. Thus we may say that, though the Bible's provisions sound incredibly harsh to our ears, they represent an ethical advance over the rule of parental will in ancient times.

I am relieved to report that, as far as we can tell, this law was never followed in all the thousand-years-plus of biblical times. The law seems only a vestige of what may distantly once have been Hebrew practice. I would guess that it survived in the later law codes out of veneration for God, their supposed author.

The Rebellious Son in Jewish Tradition—and Today

The rabbis of the Talmud had their own way of saying practically the same thing. An early anonymous statement declares, "There never has been a 'stubborn and rebellious son' and there never will be. Why then was the law written? So that one may study it and receive reward." (San. 71a)

Obviously, the rabbis were as ethically outraged by the law as we are. Indeed, we owe much of our ethical sensitivity to the values they inculcated in our people. In this respect, we may say that our ethics has not changed for about 2,000 years.

But the rabbis carried on what we see as their ethical development of the biblical law in their own religious way. Believing God gave this law, they could not possibly abrogate it. It had to be of some value, in this case, as study material. They as good as ended its practicality by hedging it about with so many administrative restrictions—as they did with homicide—that it would be impossible for a court to carry them out. (San. 8:1–5) They then settled the matter for all time with their exceptional declaration that this was a purely theoretical statute.

Surely something had changed in the Jewish ethical perspective from the time when this law first entered the Jewish legal tradition to the time of the rabbis.

I suggested that this case might be fun not only because it shows how selective our reading of the Torah usually is but because we today can hardly resist extending its ethical implications by giving it a psychoanalytic interpretation.

Rationalists may be outraged by the thought, but even loving Jewish parents can have a fleeting but passionate desire to kill their children—the parental side of Freud's Oedipus complex. I would speculate that the Torah's authors, out of their religious and human sensitivity, were responding to this universal experience. To be faithful to their new vision of God, they created a constraining procedure for treatment of a rebellious son and they also told the story of the binding of Isaac. (Gen. 22) In these ways they made it powerfully clear that we Jews might not rationalize the killing of our children by saying, "God wants what is dearest to us." God does not want and the Jewish community will not approve our acting this way, no matter how urgent our impulses.

Oddly enough, these passages can now give us some psychic

comfort when we are troubled by our occasional murderous feelings toward our children. For thousands of years Jews have been part of a community that substituted complaining about them for abusing and killing them. I also consider it ethical progress for Freud to have taught us not to judge feelings in the ethical way we judge acts. Having "bad" *feelings* does not make us bad people, only bad *acts* do that. We are far more humane when we learn to accept such negative feelings in others and in ourselves as natural and not a perversion.

I mean all that most seriously and simultaneously consider it pleasant mental play. But now to a more substantial case.

Case Two: Lex Talionis, "An Eye for an Eye"

In three places the Torah records its standard that the punishment should equal the crime. The version in Exodus 21:23–25 is the longest, following verse 22 which states the penalty for causing a woman bystander to miscarry when two men fight. "But if other misfortune ensues, the penalty shall be life for life, eye for eye, tooth for tooth, hand for hand, foot for foot, burning for burning, bruise for bruise." Leviticus 24:19–20 deals with one guilty of maiming another. "As he has done so shall it be done unto him: fracture for fracture, eye for eye, tooth for tooth. The injury he inflicted on another shall be inflicted on him." The third occurrence is in Deuteronomy 19:19–21. It refers to the punishment to be given one who gives false testimony. It is exacted as a deterrence to others: ". . . You shall do to him as he schemed to do to his fellow. . . . Nor should you show pity: life for life, eye for eye, tooth for tooth, hand for hand, foot for foot."

These passages have been used again and again to justify anti-semitism. In the days when Jew-hatred stemmed from directly religious reasons, Christian polemicists regularly attacked Judaism as a mechanistic, legalistic parody of a true religion. From this caricature of Judaism it is but a small step to Shylock demanding his pound of flesh before the court while his opponent speaks of mercy. Even today, when anti-semitism has become essentially a secular political or social-psychological matter, the stereotype of the merciless, rule-bound Jew still makes itself felt. It therefore becomes difficult to approach these texts with academic objectivity. Fortunately, modern scholarship can provide us with a consensus concerning their meaning.

Tracing the Ethical Roots of the Law of Talion

We begin again by inquiring what these laws might have meant in the era in which they were promulgated. Clearly, some primitive peoples did not consider an equivalent blow adequate punishment for transgressors. Even today when people speak of "getting *even*," they mean something very different. They do not wish to do to others simply what was done to them but "to punish them" for their misdeed. That is, they want to do far more damage in return and thus exact "satisfaction"—but that is not justice but revenge.

An old poem of the Book of Genesis brings home the prevalence of our human desire for vengeance. Lamech was in the seventh generation after Adam. We are told that he boasted to his wives Adah and Zillah:

> I've killed a man for wounding me,
>   And a youngster for bruising me.
> If Cain had to be avenged sevenfold
>   Then Lamech will be avenged seventy-seven-
>   fold. (4:23–24)

To limit the Lamechs of the world to equal punishment—to demand that justice replace vengeance—would be ethical progress indeed.

Once again we must note that the Bible records no case where these laws were utilized or enforced. We cannot say that, like the law of the rebellious son, they were theoretical and not meant for actual practice. Surely cases of injury from fighting, maiming, and false witness actually occurred. But we are given no further data. Speculation must take over for the biblical period with results that will say more about our predilections than of what anyone actually knows.

An Eye for an Eye in the Talmud

Rabbinic law categorically ends corporal retaliation. It calls for monetary compensation in every case of injury except murder. (B. K. 8:1)

The talmudic discussion on this Mishnah text indicates the rabbis' consciousness of the change. "Why payment? Does not the Torah specify, 'Eye for eye'? Why not take this literally? Let this not enter your mind for we have a tradition . . . [based on the similarity of two phrases in the Torah] that just as in the case of harming an animal compensation is to be paid, so also in the case of harming a person compensation is to be paid." R. Dosthai b. Judah then proves the Torah text cannot be meant literally. "What will you say where the eye of one was big and the eye of the other little, for how can I in this case apply the principle of 'eye for eye'? . . . Indeed, how could capital punishment then be applied in the case of a dwarf killing a giant or a giant killing a dwarf?" A further *reductio ad absurdum* is given by R. Simeon b. Yohai who raises a similar question about a person with a fatal organic disease killing a healthy person. (B. K. 83b-84a)

The rabbis rule that in cases of personal harm a monetary payment is to be made equivalent to the value of the damage done. While no one can ever be precise about such an amount, the court is authorized to estimate what might be considered appropriate compensation. This ethical advance has become the basis for adjudicating similar issues in all civilized countries. But we have not yet learned how to take the next ethical step, devising sentences which are rehabilitative and not merely compensatory or deterrent.

Case Three: The Status of Women in Judaism

No issue is more deeply troubling to the modern Jewish conscience than the treatment of women in our society and in our religion. The special disabilities people face merely because they were born with female gender extend beyond our ability to specify them. How strange it now seems that until recently single women, even those with good jobs, could not get bank loans or that married women had to have their husbands sign their loan applications. Women seemed suited for a few, relatively marginal jobs but not ones with power or administrative control, even over large numbers of other women. Of course, there were some few exceptions to these rules but they were just that, exceptions.

Even worse, everyone "knew" that these arrangements were for the women's own good. They were too delicate for the rigors of higher education, business, government, or careers. They needed men to protect them from the realities of life and to provide the sheltered sort of existence where they could flourish.

Naturally, no one bothered to ask women what they wanted. They were expected to do what their menfolk said, for the men knew what was right.

Sensitized by feminism, we must say that Judaism also substantially denied women their rights to be fully self-determining. A case can be made for the *relative* humaneness of the Jewish tradition. When compared to other religions and cultures in similar periods, the status of the Jewish woman was higher and legally much more secure. She had an honored, stable, significant position in community and family life and a distinct if separate role in observing God's law.

Viewed as a human creation, Judaism's law concerning women reflects the universal prejudice of premodern mankind somewhat alleviated by the humane sensitivities of Jewish faith. But seen traditionally, as God's own dictates, Jewish law and custom concerning women are unacceptable to the modern conscience. Simply put, Judaism made women a different category of persons than men and this differentiation rationalized their subordination to men. Men set the terms under which women were to operate, the classic sign of discrimination—one Jews have no difficulty recognizing when Christians do the same thing to them.

We Must Continue to Change Our Old Jewish Ethics of Women

I do not wish to review the details of the many problems Jewish women must still face in fighting for equality in Judaism. But I must note that this imperative surely also applies to liberal Judaism despite its old commitment to women's rights (as expressed in family seating at services and equality of Jewish education). For instance, Reform Jews have ordained women as rabbis and invested them as cantors for some time—but some congregations still will not accept women clergy. Conservative Judaism nearly split apart over the issue of ordaining women. In all groups, the day seems far off when, for reasons of merit, a woman will serve as a senior rabbi with male assistants.

Surely our old religious attitudes toward women must be changed. The inequality and discrimination which seemed ethical, indeed laudatory to a previous generation, now must be seen as demeaning and inhuman. In this area we have an immediate agenda for our moral growth even as the various generations of the Bible and Talmud had theirs. We face many complex problems—intellectual, symbolic, and human—in implementing our new vision. Yet the difficulty of creating and teaching new patterns of female-male relationships must not itself become an excuse for evading action. The Bible authors and rabbis managed to overcome the laws of the rebellious son and an eye for an eye. So must we reform all that prevents the equality of women in Judaism and devise the new forms which will give it expression.

In these three instances, Jewish ethics has changed or is changing. We could adduce many others. How then shall we assess what remains permanent and what must develop in our Jewish ethical outlook?

The Fundamental Beliefs Which Ground Our Morality

Permit me, please, to introduce one word of technical jargon. It will make my task of explanation very much easier. Philosophers call the assumptions on which an ethics rests its "meta-ethics." I propose to identify some of the major beliefs about God and humankind which underlie our Jewish ethics. I suggest that it is these basic principles which remain relatively the same in our people's ethical point of view. I shall argue that though *applied* Jewish ethics may vary over time, particularly when new social challenges arise, the *meta-ethics* of Judaism has remained stable. (The same pattern of permanence and evolution is also found in other ethics.)

Let us begin by examining the way in which our belief in God will affect our ethics.*

If we believed that reality ultimately makes no sense or is only erratically meaningful, we could not have the Jewish ethics we know. Only when we are willing to stake our lives on our intuition that a standard of quality grounds all existence, will we demonstrate the high devotion characteristic of Jewish morality. Much of the ethical emptiness of our time, I am convinced, arises less from our ambiguity over specific decisions than from a pervasive suspicion that the world has no compelling standard of decency. Not believing easily becomes not caring, or not caring very much. Believing nothing does affect our ethics. Moral dedication no

*Further elaboration of these themes is found in Part Two, *The God We Affirm.*

longer commends itself self-evidently. With skepticism all-embracing, we will have no strong ethics without a firm meta-ethics.

The Inseparability of Jewish Monotheism and Ethics

Until the recent secularization of Judaism, the root of all Jewish ethics was belief in *Adonai,* the God of whom the Bible speaks. The fact is easily overlooked: *Adonai* is not exactly like every other sovereign, unitary God. The monotheism of many Asian faiths manifests itself in the final fusion of all opposites, including, somehow, good and evil. In other words, for Asian religions, ultimate reality no longer distinguishes between the moral and the immoral. *Adonai* is not that kind of one God. Rather our religious seers said that *Adonai* is ultimately good and holy, words which overlap considerably in the Bible.

The Jewish sense of responsibility flows from this primal intuition. Because *Adonai* is our standard and ideal, goodness and holiness become the primary concerns of Jewish character, not secondary or instrumental interests. We do not seek to transcend these qualities for a higher state in which they merge with their opposites. The Jewish passion for the ethical derives from this bedrock consciousness of the ground of our being. With any lesser view of the place of righteousness in reality I do not see that we can have anything like the imperative Jewish ethical style.

The moral corollaries which arise from this religious insight are relatively familiar. The unity of God implies that there is but one ethical standard for all people, in all places, and at all times—though, as we shall see, efforts to apply it in a given society are necessarily but approximations of it. Hebrew monotheism requires our ethics to have this universal reach, to expand our personal moral horizon beyond our self, or class, or race, or tribe.

Moreover, *Adonai* is not a withdrawn, uninvolved, solitary sovereign. The Bible teaches that the one God of all the universe is intimately concerned with people. For all our littleness, God "wants" us to do good. God "commands" the right and we are the one creature in the universe who "hears" that command and is free to respond to it positively. Ethics has a great immediacy and significance in Judaism because the one, good God relates to us, "asking" that we respond with our deeds. And our ethical responsibility is consequently activist, social, and directed toward building covenants with others.

Jewish Meta-Ethics: Our View of Humankind

If God were everything and people were but God's slaves or serfs, our resulting "ethics" would consist of mere instinct or habit. Human beings—all of them—have an extraordinary status among created things. They are fashioned God-like enough that they may be God's co-workers. They are co-creating the universe. They must therefore be treated with high regard. Ben Azzai (early second century c.e.) said that the most inclusive principle of the Torah was the statement, "When God created humankind, in the likeness of God He created them, male and female He created them." (Gen. 5:1–2)

All human beings have a direct relationship with God. None may claim to have displaced the rest of humankind from God's embracing concern. " 'Do you not belong to me as do the Ethiopians, O Israelites?' declares *Adonai*. 'Did I not bring Israel up out of Egypt and likewise the Philistines from Kaftor and the Arameans from Kir? Behold, the eyes of *Adonai* are on your sinful kingdom, to wipe it from the face of the earth—though I will not utterly destroy Jacob's household,' declares *Adonai*." (Amos 9:7–8)

It takes no special training or occult experience to understand one's ethical responsibilities. All people can know what God wants of them. Therefore study, as well as ritual and prayer, is a religious duty. But living with a touch of sanctity is the apex of Jewish duty. As R. Simeon b. Gamaliel said, "Not the study but the doing is critical." (P. Av. 1:17)

Life, therefore, has supreme value. R. Simeon b. Yehozadak reported that, by a majority vote, the rabbis ruled that when there is a legitimate threat to death one may violate every commandment of the Torah except three: those against murder, idolatry, and the forbidden sexual relationships. R. Ishmael's dissent is also recorded. He declared that one may even worship an idol if it is done in private. He gave as his reason the verse, "Keep My commandments and statutes, which if one does, one shall live by them." (Lev. 18:5) This implies, he said, "and not die by them." (San. 74a)

Knowing that there is a God, we should have hope as long as we live. Both R. Yohanan and R. Elazar are credited with the statement, "Even if a sharp sword rests on a man's neck he should not desist from prayer, for it is written [Job 13:15], 'Though God slay me, yet will I trust in Him'. " (Ber. 10a)

And, against much contemporary morality, classic Jewish ethics is emphatically social. People are not created isolates but as members of families, neighborhoods, and peoples. They therefore are enjoined, as Hillel put it, "Do not withdraw from the community." (P. Av. 2:5) In contrast to Ben Azzai, cited above, R. Akiba taught that the most inclusive principle of the Torah was Leviticus 19:18, "Love your neighbor as you love yourself." (Sifra 89a)

Applied Jewish Ethics: Our Inherited Rules and Counsels

On the whole, Jewish meta-ethics has not changed much over the centuries. The language and other symbolic forms we have used to draw closer to God have certainly varied.* So, too, have our ways of describing human nature and our responsibility. Nonetheless, we easily recognize ourselves as the heirs of the Talmud as against, say, the Bhagavad Gita or the Pali canon of Buddhism. And, for all our modernity, we share the religious faith of our Jewish forebears in much greater depth than we do that of the non-Jewish thinkers from whom we have learned a great deal.

Significant change comes into our ethical life as we move from ideals and general principles to rules of conduct or, the most specific ethical instruction, decisions in a given case. For all that, a word needs to be said in defense of old rules and decisions. To exaggerate, the old is not automatically wrong. Many ethical dicta of centuries ago still prick our consciences. Despite our radically different socioeconomic situation and our changed self-consciousness, our basic human nature and Jewish relationship to God have not greatly altered. Living under the same Covenant as did our forebears, we often understand and express it as they did.

My favorite story in this connection is that of Shmelke, the *rebbe* of Nikolsburg. When he was called to head the chasidic community in that town, he was told they had a special custom. They honored their new *rav* by having him inscribe in the community

*See Part Two, *The God We Affirm*, chapter 1, "How Can We Talk about God?"

chronicle a particular regulation for everyone thereafter to observe. Shmelke delayed doing so again and again, saying he
wanted to get to know the townspeople. Finally, they insisted that
he comply with their request. He thereupon went to the record
book and wrote in the ten commandments.

Most of us would gain considerable insight into our contemporary ethical responsibilities by studying the old Jewish formulations of our duties. The ten commandments remain an excellent
place to begin—though the first four, technically speaking, are
not ethical precepts. One might then expand one's introductory
curriculum by reading such biblical passage as Leviticus 19 or the
more diverse collection of statutes in Deuteronomy 22 through
25. If you are game for more, peruse an ethical section of any of
the later Jewish legal codes. Most are now translated into English,
for example, the Mishnah, Maimonides's *Mishneh Torah* and his
enumeration of the Torah's legendary 613 *mitsvot, The Book of
Commandments,* or, somewhat more problematical, Hyman Gol-
din's rendering of the *Kitsur Shulchan Aruch.*

Much of classic Jewish ethical teaching reveals a heavy-handed
emphasis upon divine reward and punishment. Such motivation
and the literalistic treatment of the Bible texts aside, what they
say about human relations is often remarkably apt. Here is a text
the rabbis ordained we mull over before beginning our daily
prayer: "These are the investments whose dividends one enjoys
in this life but whose capital remains for us in the life of the
world-to-come: honoring one's father and mother, acts of benev-
olence, early attendance at Jewish study, hospitality to strangers,
visiting the sick, dowering the bride, accompanying the dead to
the grave, devotion in prayer, and making peace between one
person and another. But the study of Torah is equal to them all."
(Shab. 127a) To which others have rejoined, study is equal to
them all only because it leads to doing them all.

The Least Permanent Ethics: Applying Ideals to a New Social Challenge

Yet we cannot deny the evidence of our study of the cases of
the rebellious son and an eye for an eye. What made ethical sense
in one setting may no longer apply in another. Surely we must
change traditional Jewish practice with regard to women. In large

part that ethical imperative, like others, results from our society opening up new human possibilities to us. Thus in the areas of genetic engineering or the aged we are asked for relatively unprecedented Jewish ethical responses. Often we cannot be certain how to respond. We can then seek such guidance as our tradition offers and strive to be true to our Jewish ideals as we seek an answer. We shall also gain much from hearing what thoughtful, learned people in our community are saying. But we have no simple, clear-cut way of ending all our perplexity. When it comes to applied ethics, liberals must be ready to learn and grow with each decision. I can, however, give you an example of this sort of ethical thinking. Let me present, if all too quickly, my way of dealing with the troubling problem of abortion.

The Mishnah says, "If a woman is having a difficult childbirth (and is in danger of dying), one cuts up the fetus within her womb and extracts it limb by limb. In this situation, her life takes precedence over that of the fetus. But, if the greater part of the child was already born, one may not touch it. We may not set aside one person's life for that of another." (Oh. 7:6) Traditional Jewish law grants an exceptional status to a fetus. It does not always consider it merely another part of the mother's body. Despite this regard, the law dictates that, when the mother's life is at stake and the child is not yet born, abortions are not only permissible but mandatory. This position brings even our Orthodox authorities into conflict with those rigorous Catholic and fundamentalist Protestant theoreticians who rule that abortions are almost never permitted.

Traditional Judaism may therefore be said to be permissive when a *therapeutic* abortion is mandated. But what happens when, as in our time, the word "therapeutic" begins to be stretched so as to mean whatever the mother considers essential to her well-being? What shall Jewish ethics say about a completely personalistic determination about aborting the fetus one carries?

Some guidance may be gained from seeing the struggle Jewish legal authorities have had with the various circumstances in which women have come to them seeking guidance. Thus, one widely but not universally accepted stream of Orthodox legal opinion holds that extreme mental anguish is the equivalent of a threat to life, hence permitting abortion in such a situation. However, the permission given is not very wide, for the ruling carefully delineates that the mother must exhibit presuicidal tendencies or the equivalent.

Let us make the question more difficult. Almost no Jewish authorities allow abortion when a woman has conceived as a result of rape or incest. So, too, the high medical probability that the fetus may be born badly deformed or suffering a highly damaging or fatal genetic disorder only most rarely brings a *halachist* to permit abortion. And, of course, should a pregnancy occur late in life, long after a woman believed she had fulfilled her duty to propagate, abortion is utterly forbidden.

Facing the Uncertain Ethical Decisions as a Liberal

These rulings—all made by men—seem to liberal Jews not to give sufficient credence to the mother (and the father) of the fetus. Except where her life is at stake, the mother's well-being is grossly subordinated to that of the fetus. That she must, if she is reasonably sound emotionally, bear her rapist's or close relative's child against her will seems a violation of her humanity. For that reason it is unethical. The same is true in the case of her genetically or chemically impaired offspring-to-be. And I do not think many devout and learned liberal Jews would reject the abortion of a fetus conceived by accident long after the time family formation had ceased.

The position I have outlined seems quite permissive—but further difficulties arise. Some people assert that the fetus should be considered part of the mother's body in the same way her fingernails or a cyst are, hence it should be as freely excised. To my Jewish sensibilities, that makes too little of life, even in the embryonic stage. Abortion as another form of contraception is not liberation. Rather, it dehumanizes the mother and the process of life-giving. Ethical people ought to be fighting to add whatever dignity we can to the possession of life. Thus, a *laissez-faire* attitude to abortion seems the wrong position to take.

Where, then, shall we draw the line of permissibility of abortion for concerned liberal Jews? I do not believe I or anyone can make a precise determination for you, though I hope you have found my ideas instructive. I have brought the issue to this point of high ambiguity to illustrate our ethical situation. Often, as we face specific choices, we must think as much as we can and, then, in our unresolved uncertainty, make a decision from the heart, recognizing that we are subject to the judgment of our Covenant community and our God. For Jews must not only be true to themselves but to the Jewish people and to their Divine Partner. True, I believe individual conscience needs to be given far more sway than classic Jewish law allowed it. But I also insist, against an older, individualistic liberalism, that to be a faithful Jew means to exercise one's conscience as part of our people's long-term, continuing relationship with God.

Many confusing questions like abortion bedevil us today. When exactly does death come, allowing us to remove an organ for transplantation? What portion of our limited charity funds should go to the world's underprivileged? How shall we make plain our conviction that nuclear weapons must never be used while recognizing that unilateral disarmament in our era would be humanly catastrophic?

But to one question I think we can give a definite and traditional answer. If we ask how we can make decisions moment-by-moment when we cannot know with certainty what is right, Hillel's epitome of Jewish ethics can guide us. He said, "If I am not concerned for myself, who will be? But if I am only concerned for myself, what good am I? And if not now, when?" (P. Av. 1:14)

·4·

WHAT ARE OUR DUTIES
TO HUMANITY?

Contemporary Jews take citizenship so much for granted that we can hardly imagine a time when it seemed an unattainable dream. In some American Jewish families European grandparents still tell tales of growing up amid pre-Nazi persecution. Sephardim from the rural areas of North Africa or the Near East may recount more recent experience with political discrimination. The record is a long one. In 313 C.E. Christianity became the official religion of the Roman Empire, and Jews, while tolerated, were relegated to the fringes of society. Islam began in the seventh century and, shortly thereafter, Moslems instituted the first formal pattern of segregating and degrading Jews. After the First Crusade (1096 C.E.), Christian countries intensified the maltreatment of Jews, including various forms of spiritual coercion and physical violence. Not until the eighteenth century did some people argue that Jews (and other exotic social aliens) might become full participants in the life of the nation. A revolutionary change in political theory made this possible. Since it still provides the context for modern Jewish life, it deserves careful consideration.

The religious character of the premodern state made Jewish participation impossible. Thus, in Saudi Arabia today, as in all unsecularized nations (Christian and Moslem), religion and the state are thoroughly intertwined. (Islam, being organized as a "nation," not as a church, engenders an even closer relationship than does Christianity.) In such countries, sharing an odd faith

396

prevents one from swearing the religious oaths by which all important agreements are made. An infidel then exists outside the law, technically, an "out-law." In some European areas special legal arrangements were created to legitimize Jewish residence, and educing them from medieval legal records is a major interest of contemporary Jewish historians.

Jews could be citizens only when religion and nationality were separated, that is, when the state became secular. Once faith had nothing to do with citizenship, Jews could be equals. After 1,500 years of segregation and oppression, secularization provided Jews with the opportunity to reach their present unparalleled level of security and well-being. As a result, liberal Jews have been passionately devoted to the separation of "church and state."

The Intellectual Challenge of Citizenship

Fifteen centuries of growing anti-semitism had prepared neither Jews nor Christians for western Europe's enfranchisement of the Jews. The experience in France illustrates the difficulties Jews later faced everywhere in being emancipated.

After a revolution fought for "liberty, equality, fraternity," the French should have had no questions about Jewish rights. The revolutionaries had broken the church's tie to the state because of its identification with the old order. Instead, they looked to reason as their social guide. They therefore should have quickly given French Jews full citizenship. Such logic overlooks the power of old usage and prejudice. In fact the new French Assembly debated for three years before deciding to enfranchise the Jews.

This initial determination did not end the matter. A decade later, when Napoleon came to power, Jewish rights still troubled French officials. In 1806 Napoleon issued an imperial decree calling for an Assembly of Jewish Notables (and later a "Sanhedrin") to provide a formal answer on behalf of French Jewry to a number of questions. A certain Count Mole submitted twelve inquiries to the assembly of which three are relevant to our inquiry: "(4) In the eyes of the Jews, are the French their brethren or their enemies? (5) In either case, what duties does Jewish law prescribe toward the French who are not of their faith? (6) Do those Jews who are born in France and who are treated as French citizens regard France as their native country? Do they feel themselves obligated to defend it, to obey its laws, and to submit to all regulations of its civil code?"

Hearing these questions, American Jews often respond with outrage. How dare they suggest that Jews consider their neighbors their enemies and are not loyal to their country! Our emotion in such matters betrays our anxieties over the Gentile's perceptions of us. No matter what extraordinary contributions we make to our society—further evidence of our insecurity—nothing washes away the prejudices of our fellow citizens, or, at least, some portion of them.

Perhaps this feeling can help us imagine, two centuries later, the attitudes Jews faced when they took their first exploratory steps outside the newly destroyed ghetto wall. They encountered a populace accustomed to think of Jews as misanthropists, haters of humankind, and lovers only of their co-religionists. Not the least difficulty Jews had in responding to this charge was its unconscious origin. The civilization which had despised Jews for fifteen centuries now projected its hatred on to its victim. Getting Gentiles to acknowledge their own prejudices before presuming to make judgments about Judaism has been a major Jewish battle ever since the Emancipation.

Fashioning a Jewish Philosophy of Non-Jews

On one level, the notables of the Jewish community had little difficulty giving an answer to Napoleon. They could base themselves on the long history of Jewish loyalty to regimes that had treated them fairly. They could also see that, if the ideals of the Revolution were carried out, undreamed of opportunities would open up for the French Jewry.

In their formal statement they outlined a position later adopted by the leadership of all Jewish communities who received freedom. Here are some critical sentences taken from their protocols: (To question 4) "When the Israelites formed a settled and independent nation, their law made it a rule for them to consider strangers as their brethren. . . . A religion whose fundamental maxims are such, a religion which makes a duty of loving the stranger, a religion which enforces the practice of social virtues, must surely require that its followers should consider their fellow citizens as brethren." (To question 5) "At the present time, when the Jews no longer form a separate people [in the literal sense] but enjoy the advantage of being incorporated within the great nation France—which privilege they consider a kind of political redemption—it is impossible that a Jew should treat a Frenchman not of his religion in any other manner than he would treat one of his Israelite brethren." (To question 6) "Jeremiah [chapter 29] exhorts the Jews to consider Babylon as their country even though they were to remain there only for seventy years. He tells them to till the ground, to build houses, to sow, and to plant." Most Jews took his injunction so to heart that only a few returned with Ezra to rebuild the Temple. "In the heart of Jews the love of country is a sentiment so natural, so powerful, and so consonant with their religious opinions that, visiting in England, a French Jew considers himself as among strangers, although he may be among Jews; and the case is the same with English Jews." The answer closes by reminding the emperor of the many Jews who have fought in his campaigns against Jews of other nations and the many scars they now proudly bear as a sign of their bravery.

Beyond Politics to Doctrine

Jewish scholars and thinkers later sought to clarify the Jewish religious bases on which these positions might authentically be taken. They could not simply cite the texts exhorting Jews to be good citizens for no prophet or rabbi had ever written on Jewish duty in a democracy. How could they have? There was no democratic, secular state in their time. For all the Jewish participation in the cultural life of Hellenistic Alexandria or Moslem Spain, the Jews there had not been political equals.

Not only were Jews outsiders until modern times but for much of that time they chose isolation. In the days of the Bible, only the Jews worshiped the one God. "The nations" practiced idolatry and lived by standards the Jews found spiritually repulsive. Participation in gentile affairs then would have meant the end of ethical monotheism. The Talmud largely reflects the same attitude. In later years the antipathy of Christianity and Islam to Judaism excluded the possibility of developing a guide to Jewish citizenship.

The Emancipation required Jewish thinkers to clarify a Jew's duties to the non-Jewish society. They did this by explicating traditional Judaism's positive attitude toward humankind and by gathering the sages' few comments on the topic. They fashioned these sources into so persuasive an outlook that most modern Jews accepted it. Let us sketch in some of their central ideas.

The Ethical Implications of the Creation Story

God did not begin the world with Jews. Instead, God creates humankind undifferentiated (except for having two genders) and establishes a covenant with it. The God of the Jews is first the God of all humanity and retains that status in all subsequent Jewish teaching. The Bible takes the ultimate worth of all people for granted; the prophets would not rail so against the nations if they did not believe that all human beings were God's covenant partners.

In the Talmud the rabbis carry forward the concept of one human family. Here is the Mishnah's statement of the exhortation given to witnesses before they testify in a capital case, "Therefore but a single man was created in the world to teach that, if anyone has caused a single soul to perish from Israel [some texts omit 'from Israel'], Scripture imputes it to him as if he had caused a whole world to perish. And he who saves a single Israelite [some texts omit 'Israelite'] soul, Scripture imputes it to him as if he had saved a whole world. Again, [but a single man was created] for the sake of peace among mankind. Now none can say to his fellow, 'My ancestor was greater than your ancestor'; and also that heretics should not say 'There are many ruling powers in heaven.' Again, [but a single man was created] to proclaim the greatness of the Holy One, blessed is He. For a man stamps out many coins with one seal and they are all identical but the king of kings of kings, the Holy One, blessed is He, has stamped every man with the seal of the first man, yet none of them is like his fellow. Therefore, every one must say, 'For my sake the world was created'." (San. 4:5)

Modern Jewish thinkers added their own interpretation to this theme. Few took the Torah's creation story literally for they accepted the evolutionary view of the origins of humankind. They nonetheless steadfastly affirmed the moral values of the creation myth.* They saw in its having God begin humankind with but one pair of people an early intuition of the truth that ethics is necessarily universal. Put symbolically, one Divine Parent meant that all human beings have familial obligations to one another. To limit one's ethical duties only to those of one's neighborhood or nation or religion was unethical. Human relations had to transcend all the old barriers or else no one could be truly human. By including Jews in the family of humankind, the European nations had shown the power of universal ethics to overcome prejudice. In what had happened to them, Jews could recognize the fulfillment of one of their oldest, most central ideals.

What Does the Law Enjoin Jews to Do?

This theory was bolstered by pointing to the provisions of Jewish law regarding duties to non-Jews. The Mishnah says, "For the sake of peace, impoverished idolaters are not prevented from gathering gleanings or forgotten sheaves or from the corner of the field though the Torah provides only that these be left for poor Jews." (Git. 5:8) In the Talmud, this is extended in terms of an anonymous teaching, "We support the poor among the idolaters along with the poor of Israel, and visit the sick among the idolaters along with the sick of Israel, and bury the poor among the idolaters along with dead of Israel, for the sake of peace." (Git. 61a) While there are some other halachic passages which deal with duties to Gentiles, the notion of *mipne darche shalom,* for the sake of peace, constitutes the central theme of the subsequent discussions of this issue in Jewish law.

Several features of the later legal material are noteworthy. Some halachic authorities are troubled by the prospect of allowing non-Jews to take Jewish agricultural produce (in the Land of Israel) or benefit from Jewish charity funds. Both the produce and the money as good as belong to the poor Jews for whom they were set aside. *Tsedakah* funds in particular are a community trust whose terms may not be violated. To use such money for heathens is tantamount to stealing from the Jewish poor. Though such arguments are raised, the authorities agree that needy Gen-

*See Part Three, *The Bible and Tradition*, chapter 3, "How True Is the Bible?"

tiles are not to be denied succor because of scruples about improper disbursement.

A similar indication of the weight attached to these laws may be found in the unexpected development they underwent. They specify that, when needy Gentiles come for help along with needy Jews, we assist them. But what if the gentile poor alone solicit our aid? The medieval authorities rule that they are still to be helped "for the sake of peace" (and once again they insist that such exclusive disbursement to Gentiles is not *de facto* robbery of the Jewish poor). Considering the treatment of Jews then, this ruling, for all its likely defensive motivation, shows exceptional commitment to the interdependence of humankind.

The Jew as God's Representative

A broader theological consideration reinforced the legal tradition. Quite commonly, the rabbis call the attention of Jews to the religious impression created by their acts. They want Jews to consider what non-Jews will think of the Jewish religion when they observe Jewish behavior. It will indicate to them the sort of God the Jews have. This conception of the public consequence of Jewish deeds is termed the doctrine of *kiddush hashem.* The rabbis demand that a Jew's acts should always "sanctify God's name" (in effect, God's reputation) among people.

At its extreme, *kiddush hashem* leads to martyrdom (and is the common Hebrew term for it). Then a Jew, who normally can do anything under extreme duress except commit murder, idolatry, or sexual offenses, refuses to do what is demanded and instead accepts death. Under the extraordinary circumstances of the Middle Ages, we even hear of Jewish communities where parents killed their families and then committed suicide for *kiddush hashem,* to sanctify God's name.

Jews have discouraged martyrdom as a means of gaining God's special favor; people punish themselves enough and history has been sufficiently cruel to Jews that our sages considered it a virtue to avoid unnecessary suffering. But, in its broader connotation, *kiddush hashem* was part of everyday Jewish life. There was little more one could say to condemn an act than to call it a *chilul hashem,* a profanation of God's name, thus the opposite of *kiddush hashem.* A well known use of *chilul hashem* applies directly to our topic. "Robbery from a Gentile is more heinous than robbery from a Jew because it also involves *chilul hashem.*" (Tos. San. 10:15) In Jewish conduct toward non-Jews no less than God's honor was at stake.

The positive ideal is portrayed in a legendary story about Simeon b. Shetah. He once bought an ass from an Arab. When his servants brought it home they found a costly jewel in its harness. Simeon at once ordered it returned on the grounds that he had intended to buy only the animal. This caused the Arab to proclaim, "Blessed be the God of the Jews who renders His people so scrupulous in their dealings with others." (Y., B.M. 2:5, 8c) This constitutes *kiddush hashem* at its highest.

These biblical and rabbinic traditions informed the Jewish ethos. No matter how oppressed Jews were they did not deny the basic unity of humankind. Two comments from recent centuries illustrate this even if we cannot say that their authors had Gentiles primarily in mind. Yaakov Yitzhak was the chasidic *rebbe* of Pzhysha. His identification with the Jewish people was so intense that he was known simply as the Yehudi, the Jew. He once inquired, "Why is the stork not *kosher?* After all, the Talmud says that its name, *chasidah,* the loving one, stems from its tender concern for mate and young. Why should such a bird be ritually unclean?" He then answered himself, "The stork is not *kosher* because it gives love only to its own." Something of the same universalism is found in the Yiddish maxim created by common folk, "You must love your neighbor—even when he plays a trombone."

The Liberals' New Sense of Jewish Priorities

The liberal Jews who had developed these sources into a full-scale doctrine of democratic responsibility added a startling emphasis to it. They argued that Judaism's general ethics—its "universalism," as they termed it—was its most important and hence unchanging element. Jewish rituals and customs had altered over the centuries, as historical study demonstrated. But, they insisted, the ethical essence of Judaism had remained constant. It had not always been expressed, as, for example, in the biblical laws of slavery. But, even then, it gradually made itself felt in the abolition or the modification of the inequitable pattern, as in the case of Jewish slaves. Modern thinkers, they asserted, have merely clarified an old Jewish trust. We must reject any Jewish tradition which clashes with it, such as segregating women at services. But we ought steadfastly maintain all our Jewish ethical teachings as well as those ritual practices which enlarge our moral sensitivity.*

Their program went even further. They contended that universal ethics, our duty to humankind, was the ultimate test of our Jewishness. Until then, most Jews had connected being a good Jew with punctilious observance of the commandments, particularly the rituals. The liberals now proclaimed that, in an emancipated community, how one acted toward one's fellow-human beings (now largely gentile) must be the standard of our Jewish virtue.

In this reordering of Jewish priorities, these thinkers considered themselves the heirs of the prophets. They enthusiastically cited those biblical texts criticizing trust in ritual as a compensation for moral failings. In the opening chapter of his book, Isaiah says God is weary of all the Jewish rites at the Temple and desires rather that the people change their ways.

> Put away your evil doings
> from before Me.
> Cease doing evil;
> learn to do good.
> Devote yourselves to justice;
> aid the wronged.
> Uphold the rights of the orphan;
> and defend the cause of the widow. (1:16–17)

Jeremiah (in chapter 7) denounces his countrymen for thinking that they can be unethical with impunity as long as the Temple is in their midst. They so misunderstand God's priorities, he announces, that God will now allow His Temple to be destroyed.

If we can transpose the prophetic messages from Israel and Judah to our own society, many of them remain uncannily apt. Consider this denunciation by Amos, the first prophet whose speeches were preserved:

> You turn justice into wormwood,
> and throw righteousness into the dirt. . . .

*On this theme, see the immediately preceding chapter, "Do Our Ethics Change?", as well as Part Two, *The God We Affirm*, chapters 3 and 4.

You hate critics who come to court,
and detest people whose plea is just.
You exploit the poor
and extort his wheat. . . .
I [God] note how many are your crimes
and how countless your sins.
You enemies of the righteous,
you takers of bribes,
You who subvert the judicial process
when the needy come to court.
Assuredly, it is so evil a time
that a prudent man will keep silent.
Seek good and not evil
that you may live!
Then *Adonai,* the God of hosts
may truly be with you. . . .
I loathe, I spurn your festivals,
I am not appeased by your solemn assemblies.
If you offer me burnt offerings or meal offerings,
I will not accept them.
I will pay no attention
to your fat peace offerings.
Spare me the sound of your hymns
and let me not hear the music of your psalteries.
But let justice well up like waters,
righteousness like an unfailing stream. (5:7–24)

The Political Implications of Prophetic Judaism

This identification of Jewish duty with universal ethics came to
be known as "Prophetic Judaism." For more than a century and
a half it spoke powerfully to Jews who modernized. Remembering
the discrimination which pressed down on their parents, Jews
leaving the ghetto and shtetl were euphoric that ostracism was
giving way to equal rights. In their physical well-being, their
personal security, their educational, cultural, and economic attainments, they saw the messianic power of inclusive ethics. They
had no difficulty imagining a day of universal peace, justice, and
compassion if all people would only live rationally. It seemed

self-evident that the ancient Jewish hope for humankind would best be fulfilled by pursuing universal goals, not parochial ones.

Despite their rhetoric, hindsight discloses that these liberals were almost certainly also motivated by an unconscious Jewish self-interest. They knew Jews were the scapegoat of Western society. If social frustrations rose, Jews would suffer. To remain secure Jews should do what they could to defuse social discontent before it became explosive. Social ethics was a preventive strategy as well as an ethical ideal. With belief and self-interest as motivations, Prophetic Judaism became a dynamic theme in modern Jewish life. Only the mutual reinforcement of these basic drives explains the record of extraordinarily disproportionate Jewish involvement in universal social causes over the past century or so.

Occasionally an additional unconscious impulse also added its special impetus, one strongly tainted by self-hate. When Jewish duty is essentially universal, one need not do acts which distinguish Jews from other people. Judaism as pure universalism can achieve assimilation without the stigma of rejecting one's heritage.

These motives all surfaced in the Jewish fascination with Marxism. Many Jews in Europe found various kinds of socialism the only realistic way of reaching the Messianic Age. They were convinced that only a complete reconstruction of the social order could eliminate the exploitation and oppression built into Western civilization. Unless ethics became politics suffering would continue.

With their acculturation, most American Jews spurned Marxist substitutes or supplements to Judaism. Instead they happily espoused a democratizing capitalism which gave them a steady accretion of social gains and personal freedom. What little was left of Jewish Marxism suffered irreparable damage from the actual behavior of Soviet communism and the more recently organized Marxist states. Instead of ethical paragons, they regularly showed themselves to be cynically political, humanly reprehensible, and continuingly anti-semitic.

Social Action, the Application of Prophetic Idealism

By the 1930s American Jewry felt sufficiently at home that modern Jewish ethics found a new outlet, liberal political activism. The federal government was now seen as an agent for social change. Remedying the Depression provided the initial impetus for government leadership. The ethical agenda soon expanded to include legislation outlawing discrimination and providing the underprivileged with effective opportunity. The fight against dictatorship overseas in World War II made it subsequently possible to insist on fully functioning democracy at home. The civil rights struggles of the 1960s and the bitter difference of American opinion over the Vietnam War brought these decades of ethical activism to a climax.

In these American struggles Jews were involved in numbers far beyond their proportion of the population. And the same was true of most local causes like good education, better mental health facilities, and more adequate care for the needy, handicapped, and aged. Institutionally, synagogue social action committees involved their congregations in general ethical causes while national Jewish organizations regularly passed resolutions taking a liberal stand on issues of social concern. In overwhelming numbers, American Jews had accepted civic responsibility as a major element in Jewish duty. Even disaffected Jews regularly chose the secularized path of Jewish duty, activist politics, as their surrogate for Judaism—often to find that a high proportion of their universalistic comrades were other marginal Jews.

When the Holocaust came to the forefront of Jewish consciousness in the early 1960s, it added a special Jewish incentive for participating in liberal politics. The demented Nazi program was carried out not by deranged savages but by ethically passive ordinary people. The silent German now became the model of what good people can do to create monstrous evil. If everyone had a duty to protest when inhumanities occurred, Jews surely had a special obligation to cry out. They had long been commanded, "Do not stand idly by your brother's blood." (Lev. 19:16) And they had just undergone the most awesome suffering in their history while humanity and not just the Germans stood by in silence. Joachim Prinz summed up the ethical Jewish devotion of this period when he said at the great 1963 civil rights march in Washington, "When I was the rabbi of the Jewish community in Berlin under the Hitler regime, I learned many things. The most important thing that I learned under those tragic circumstances was that bigotry and hatred are not the most urgent problem. The most urgent, most disgraceful, the most shameful, and the most tragic problem is silence."

How Shall We Live Out Our Jewish Ethics Today?

By the 1980s the almost total identification of Jewish ethics with the agenda of liberal politics had ended. Two major shifts in attitude had produced differing views about Jewish social responsibility.

The first of these arose out of disenchantment with government as a moral leader. In the sixties the automatic solution for major problems was the passage of a new law or the establishment of a new agency. Experience with this approach in employment, education, welfare, mental health, and other fields was mixed. We and our experts do not seem as competent as we once thought. The ills perpetrated by government programs, from creating dependency in the needy to building immobile bureaucracies, have not infrequently offset or overbalanced their successes.

The second change in Jewish attitudes came with the rise of an urgent sense of self-interest: If the Jewish community did not give primary attention to its own problems, its survival might be in doubt. One major reason for this new particularism was the perilous situation of the State of Israel. Without sustained, heavy American Jewish support, the Israelis would find it most difficult to maintain a viable country. Practically speaking, energies summoned in this commanding ethnic cause would not be available for universal social programs. More troublingly, universal and particular concerns could now directly clash. American Zionist leaders argued that the Israeli army depends upon American military supplies in an emergency and that a powerful United States is the only deterrent to further Soviet provocation in the Middle East. Hence they insisted that American Jews ought to support a strong United States military posture even if this meant cuts in the funding of human welfare programs.

The internal aspect of this new self-concern was the community's anxiety about its own future. The symptoms of its failing health were immediately evident: a high rate of intermarriage, a low rate of reproduction, static or declining institutional involvement, and widespread ignorance, apathy, and indifference. Externally, American culture no longer offered anything like salvation, and the increase in anti-semitic incidents and intergroup distance impelled Jews to search for their roots. A sizable minority of Jews began giving Judaism increased priority in their lives. Some particularists now demanded—in private, to be sure—that Jewish energies be exclusively devoted to Jewish causes. Others counseled a pragmatic strategy: participating in universal causes only as required to maintain our political alliances and keep us from bad repute. On the whole no new community consensus has appeared. The majority of Jews seems to accept neither a new particularism verging on self-isolation nor a universalism so devoted to humankind it ignores Jewish needs.

This ambivalent situation is unlikely soon to disappear. Contemporary liberal Judaism affirms both the universal God and the particular people Covenanted to God. We remain devotedly liberal because we personally are living testimony to the human benefits that come from actualizing universal ethics. As supreme beneficiaries of democracy, we have a special responsibility to be involved in the solution of its problems. We are also devoted Jews. The survival of our people must be one of our highest priorities. Whatever we can do for humankind must begin with our efforts to see that our own people flourishes. Yet our people's vision has always transcended its own well-being. Most Jewish generations could do little directly to contribute to this greater goal. Jews in democratic lands have an unparalleled Jewish opportunity to make our idealism felt in our nations and among humankind as a whole. We cannot say simply how Jews ought to face those social choices which seem to pit their loyalty to their people against that to humanity. Yet we know that we will not be true to the special situation in which God has placed us if we do not make the human issues of our age a major part of our Jewish duty.

·5·

A LIBERAL JEWISH
APPROACH TO RITUAL

I find that when I try talking to liberal Jews about the importance of ritual they often become quite uncomfortable. They do not mind some Hebrew and ceremonialism when at temple. Perhaps they include the lighting of *Shabbat* candles as part of their life-style. But that is about as far as they are willing to go personally, so their attitude in these discussions indicates.

I am not certain why my positive appeal for more ritual makes them anxious. Perhaps they fear that opening their lives in this way may soon lead to their being swamped with religious demands. Consider the traditional blessing before performing a major rite. We thank God "who has sanctified us by divine commandments and commanded us to. . . ." If we took these words literally—and did not choose to rebel—we would indeed have to undertake the entire repertoire of Jewish ceremonial.* Our first step, then, in talking together about ritual must be a quick reminder: liberal Jews emphasize personal freedom in Judaism.

We believe that religion is as much humankind's creation as God's inspiration. Most of our thinkers say that ethics is as close as we can come to what God "wants" of us. When it comes to ritual, they admit we are dealing largely with what people have wanted to do for God. In this view, ceremonial discloses more of human need and imagination than it does of God's commands. So when liberals use the classic words of Jewish blessing (trans-

*This topic is discussed in detail in Part Three, *The Bible and Tradition*, chapter 6, "Must We Observe All the Commandments and Traditions?"

lated above), *"asher kideshanu bemitsvotav vetsivanu le . . .,"* we are pausing to acknowledge God's part in our human religious creativity. The God-given authority of the commandments our Jewish forebears took literally has become figurative for us.

Understanding the essential humanity of Jewish ritual endows us with the right to decide which traditional acts we shall still do or not do. More excitingly, it empowers us to create the new rites needed to express better our present-day Jewishness. The strongly positive attitude to ritual I reflect in these pages is not intended to infringe on your personal freedom to choose for yourself. I am not writing to tell you what you *must* do but only to help you make your own informed, conscientious choice.

Untangling Our Rational and Emotional Motives

For many years liberal Judaism proclaimed itself to be a rational religion, though it included a strong esthetic component. Its thinkers spoke more often of the idea of God or the God-concept than directly of God. They also saw universal ethics as the primary way of living one's religion. Ritual therefore became a relatively unimportant part of their conception of Jewish obligation. If anything, their new sense of liberal freedom operated negatively in relation to Jewish tradition. Personal responsibility now meant they were now free *not* to do most of the classic Jewish rites.

Many liberal Jews today still contend that they are too rational to need a ritual component in their lives. I detect an emotional undertone in many such protestations. It comes out most clearly when one suggests that they use their liberal Jewish freedom to *take on* ritual practices as well as to dispense with them. Suggest, say, that perhaps we ought to rethink our old attitudes toward keeping *kosher* or to praying bareheaded and people who claim to be thoroughly rational can become quite heated. I find that quite appropriate for, as we shall see, rituals involve the affective as well as the cognitive aspects of being human.

Another factor needs to be considered. People who have grown up with a Judaism relatively empty of rite have an emotional stake in a restrained, coolly dignified, liberal pattern of practice. They may be embarrassed by not knowing the words or acts or songs involved in a richer Jewish ceremonial life. They may simply never have learned how to let themselves feel the special mood ritual seeks to create. At the extreme are those poor people who shudder at the possibility of doing an act which will clearly identify them as Jews. In such cases, the insistence on "rationality" is only a rationalization for their Jewish self-hate.

The more positive recent approach to ritual among liberal Jews stems largely from two causes: our changing perceptions of ourselves as human beings and as Jews.

For some time now, Western civilization has warped our personalities by stressing intellect to the neglect of our bodies and our passions. A more holistic view of the healthy self today includes an appreciation of our physical and emotional needs—hence ritual.

In these years, too, Jews have reclaimed our pride in our Jewishness so that we savor the special pleasures that accrue to us from our distinctiveness. Evading our Jewish identity seems unhealthy while living Jewishly adds a rootedness to our lives many other Americans desperately desire. And ritual helps us achieve that.

Once we acknowledge that we are less exclusively cerebral and more happily Jewish than we once may have thought, we can share in the new contemporary openness to ritual.

Humans Everywhere Have Their Rites

Anthropologists assure us that no human community anywhere has lived without ceremony. Let us begin our exploration of this topic by seeing what scholars tell us about secular rites. For our study specimen I propose to take one with which we are all familiar and still somewhat emotionally involved, namely, the birthday cake.

Our birthday celebrations seem incomplete without a special cake. Bringing it out is one of the highlights of the festivity. It should have candles on it as symbolic representations of our mounting years. Someone lights them in a place we cannot see. Often the lights are turned down. Then the cake appears to the sound of many "oohs" and "aahs." In deference to the dripping wax, many people do not sing the required "Happy Birthday" then. Instead a silence falls upon the room. We are supposed to make a wish, silently. And, preferably with one breath, we try to blow out the candles. When all are extinguished—even if more than one breath is required—everyone will cheer. Then, if not before, the singing of "Happy Birthday" takes place. If we are old enough, we get to cut the first piece and everyone will then want some of the cake.

Though this procedure varies in some clans and locales, it remains surprisingly constant across the American continent.

Some general features of a rite are immediately apparent. It occurs at a particularly significant moment which it then marks by special, symbolic acts. While we could do all this at any time, it would seem quite strange to do so: the acts take on unique power by being done just on this occasion. So, too, to omit them—here the cake and its ceremonials—is, somehow, not meeting the event properly. The rite also has an accustomed order. All the participants know it and participate in it. As a result we can become involved in what goes on with a certain freedom. We thus get a special pleasure from anticipating what is about to happen. Once the rite starts our mood changes, for its performance requires a special emotional tone—in this case to be joyous and playful. To hold back from the bubbling emotions of the company marks us as antisocial and as inhibitors of the general mood. We all hate a grouch at a celebration.

The Special "Logic" and "Meaning" of Personal Rites

The birthday cake seems a ritual for children—but do not count on that! Rather staid older folk suddenly turn warm and soft when a birthday cake appears for them, even if it is only a muffin with one candle in it. Surely that is because someone cares about them and their particular day. Memory also plays an important role. Since we were little, family and friends have done this for us. The many repetitions now add their pleasure to this moment. Our lives are summed up in such events. For an instant we are again closely linked with all those we have loved and who have loved us. And if they are not present for our celebration, we would like a "ritual" phone call.

This entire procedure makes no sense in terms of our usual way of looking at things. We may not like cake or avoid it as a matter of our diet. But, like a wedding, a birthday without a cake seems somewhat incomplete. So too, though we are usually careful about conserving energy, we are unlikely to object to lighting many candles which, as quickly as possible, will be blown out and thrown away. Some remnants of magic obviously function here. Everyone must have some of the birthday cake, even if only a taste. But the height of irrationality is reached in the blowing out of the candles. Ordinarily, we reject the efficacy of wishful thinking and would deny that extinguishing all the candles with one breath makes wishes come true. Yet we are unlikely not to make a wish and do our best to blow out the lights. If we do, we'll momentarily feel good and the cheers of the bystanders will extend our joy. Note too their silence as we approach the task. The wishing moment is filled with a certain anxiety, but, once we have safely passed through the trial, the tension relaxes and we cheer to indicate our great relief and happiness.

If, in a skeptical mood, you should challenge us as to why we do all this, I doubt that any of us could give what you would consider a rational reply. Perhaps the best we can say is that we like it and, despite its silliness, it doesn't hurt anyone except, perhaps, the dieters. But the truth is, the more we do it, the more we would like to have it done for us. And if you don't understand that, you have most sadly been emotionally deprived.

Peoples also Have Their Rites

Social groups have always been held together by their communal ties, which were largely religious. With the secularization of society few highly involving public ceremonials remain. The diminished American celebration of Independence Day is a good example of this process.

Some decades back everyone in the United States knew the major events which would mark July 4th. There would be speeches by public leaders to sizable crowds. The flag would be prominently displayed, the pledge of allegiance recited, and the national anthem sung, all with great seriousness and enthusiasm. These rites would usually be preceded by a parade down a major thoroughfare, complete with military groups or veterans marching to band music. Onlookers would gather to applaud and cheer. In smaller towns, communal picnics might be held, but almost everywhere families, friends, and organizations gathered to eat and play outdoors. By day, the sound of firecrackers would be heard and at night a splashy display of fireworks could be seen.

In recent years such celebrations have fallen off in numbers and in public interest. Students of these matters speculate that rites may be described as alive or ailing. And they can die, as seems to be happening to the once significant Labor Day parades and speech-making.

In the case of Independence Day, the urbanization of America made the older style of celebration difficult and a shift in belief robbed it of motivation. For two decades now, many Americans have grown cynical about their government and its leaders. The continuing revelation of venality in high places and the frequent sense of having been betrayed by our leaders have robbed many people of their old patriotism. We cannot now easily utilize the old, innocent forms of celebrating America's birthday.

For all that, Americans could not ignore the celebration of America's bicentennial in 1976. Crowds thronged to various special celebrations, including the traditional parades, speeches, and fireworks. And millions more shared in the festivities via television. Oddly enough, the highlight was not an old rite but one created for the occasion. A private citizen conceived the idea of having the world's remaining few great sailing ships rendezvous outside New York Harbor that day and parade up the Hudson River. Why that should so have excited the American imagination or tantalized a generation which had watched men land on the moon can only be conjectured. But the majestic movement of those great old ships "spoke" eloquently to people about the establishment and continuity of a great nation. Rites not only endure and die, they also can be created. In the case of the sailing ships, the rite took place, was greatly successful, and became history. On rare occasions such innovations take on a life of their own, as with Halloween trick-or-treat collections for UNICEF.

Religious Rituals: Humankind Reaching for the Holy

All of the features we have found in human ritual generally are also found in religion. Its distinguishing characteristics arise from religion's unique view of reality. Secular rites mark special moments. Religion does this as well, but, because of its transcendent view of things, it goes much further. It seeks to turn much of everyday life into special moments. It aims to have us share its seers' insight that every instant is a precious gift, not anything we could by right demand. It therefore provides us with rituals by which we may interrupt the apparent profanity of commonplace activity and, by reaching for the holy, sanctify our lives.

This transforming view of existence begins with individual lives. All religions have ceremonies to herald the great moments of the life-cycle: birth, maturation, marriage, death, and whatever else they value highly. Such rites can reach so deep into our souls that even skeptics often temporarily suspend their questioning and rejoice that, among the infinite possibilities of existence, this blessing has been vouchsafed them—or, in mourning, acknowledge that life has deeper meaning than what they normally have seen in it.

Religion also seeks to refresh our usual sense of time. This begins with each day. Is awakening in the morning not worth an instant of celebrating? Then we can say the *Modeh Ani,* "I acknowledge before You, O enduring ruler, that you have graciously restored my soul to me." Is having another meal not worth an expression of gratitude? Then we can pronounce the *Motsi* and give thanks to the ultimate source of our sustenance. And, of course, Judaism has been most successful in changing people's views of time by its notion of a Sabbath.

These rites and the many others which might punctuate our daily lives immediately connect us with our Jewish people. Our sages identified many moments when we should try to bring a touch of the sacred into our lives. They provided us with words to say on such occasions; in some cases, they described acts to do. Utilizing their Hebrew words links us with them, with all the Jewish generations before us, and with all those today who carry on the Covenant. If, as well, we share their sense of the Sacred, performing these rituals strengthens our dedication to Judaism's high ideals.

Jewish ceremonies celebrate our people's special moments as well. Through the ritual calendar, we today renew the critical experiences of ancient Israel's encounters with God: Exodus, Sinai, and wilderness trek. We also join with our community in celebrating the steady cycle of the seasons, on which we so depend, and the unvarying progression of the years which, with our Jewish vision, we take as occasions of high judgment, forgiveness, and reconciliation. In these communal rites, our personal time is infused with historic significance and metaphysical dignity.

Through Ritual We Approach God

The difference between religious and all other human rituals arises from religion's unique focus: its rites direct us to God. By words, acts, tunes, attitudes, silences, perhaps with the use of special or ordinary artifacts, we human beings pause and reach out to God. Through religious ritual we seek to transcend the ordinary and open ourselves up to the sacred dimension of reality, what Rudolf Otto termed "the numinous." We often use quite prosaic means—bread and wine, for example. Through earthly words or things, utilized in the special way we call ritual, we renew our relationship, even for an instant, with the Extraordinary.

Rituals are highly charged examples of religion's heavy reliance on symbols.* Everything we said previously about the nature of symbols applies to religious rituals as well. Here too we must avoid the great danger of taking the symbols literally. When we take them as anything more than a poetic effort to be self-transcending, we leap from the realm of religion to that of magic.

In many rituals the approach to God is quite direct. Jewish blessings—often themselves the ritual—begin, *"Baruch Atah Adonai . . ."*—"Blessed are You, *Adonai.* . . ." Our tradition directs each of us to turn to God often in gratitude and thanks. Thus, before we munch a carrot we are told to say, "Blessed are You, *Adonai,* Ruler of the universe, who creates the fruit of the ground." Through nine Hebrew words we relate another routine act of eating to the essential ground of all existence, the ultimate reality on which we base our lives.

In other cases the relation with God is indirect. We leave our home and our eyes fall on or our fingers reach out to our *mezuzah.* If we allow its significance to register, a quick consciousness of our Jewish identity dawns in us. We remember that our home has been built on Jewish values and that we ought now to apply them in the world. If we are more spiritually sensitive we may also recall the texts of the *mezuzah.* They not only proclaim God's unity—the same one God outside our home as in it—but the corollary duty to love God with all our heart, soul, and might. In that fleeting instant we are reminded of the standard of our lives and the Covenant partnership which endows us with inalienable personal dignity.

Pausing for a second before our *mezuzah* and letting all this sink

*See Part Two, *The God We Affirm,* chapter 1, "How Can We Talk about God?"

in will not necessarily keep us from behaving like scoundrels. Rituals have no magic power. They may not change us and they cannot coerce God. Doing them does not excuse abusing our freedom by doing evil, and they do not win us God's favor despite how badly we have behaved. But they can provide us with a means of trying to maintain a personal, Jewish contact with the Holy. In a world where so many other influences work to demean us, religious ritual must be considered a therapeutic necessity and a life-affirming activity.

The Many Layers of Meaning in a Rite

Religions have always centered more about rituals than philosophies. Rites are uniquely accessible. Almost everyone can perform or participate in simple ceremonies. Equally important, rituals convey a depth of meaning to whatever temperament people bring to them. "Living" rituals communicate so much that one can never exhaust their meaning. If anything, as each generation uses and reinterprets them, their message is renewed and strengthened. To explore the extraordinary communicative power of religious rituals, let us analyze a much criticized example, the Jewish wedding.

Rationally evaluated, a wedding ceremony seems rather superfluous today. If two people wish to pledge their lives to one another as to no other human being, hopefully until death, they require no more than a sincere covenant between them. Particularly now that couples often live with one another in serious devotion for extended periods, their transition to marriage hardly seems momentous enough to mark with great solemnity and festivity. Such rites, the argument goes, were appropriate in the days when two household united their fortunes by having the scion of the one take the young, virginal daughter of the other to bride. In our time the hoopla which normally accompanies a wedding easily becomes excessive to the point of being unethical.

From a Jewish perspective, all such rejections of the Jewish way of celebrating a wedding may contain some germ of truth but largely derive from a false because constricted view of the self. Liberal Judaism does not consider people isolates whose lives move in essential detachment from others. Rather, our selfhood is fulfilled in our relationships not only with spouse but also with family, friends, community, people, society, and God. We can be true to ourselves, therefore, only as we are involved with them. And that social, religious view of the self lies behind the Jewish wedding.

The Jewish Case for Celebrating Weddings Grandly

It takes no special religious talent to recognize that an ultimate commitment to another human being—or at least as ultimate as people can make—differs from a temporary one. Indeed, knowing that marriage changes relationships makes some people insist on remaining only at the level of temporary commitment. They do not wish to be "tied down." Perhaps some few people can turn continual choice into an ultimate, lifetime devotion. Most of us understand such true involvement best when challenged to make a specific decision. So people who have lived together will often recognize the benefit of a formal act of commitment when children become part of their relationship. The rite will publicly and solemnly signify the total responsibility the partners undertake toward each other and their potential offspring.

Taking the step into marriage is surely worth more note than a birthday, a graduation, a big raise, or a holiday. Being human and therefore celebrating creatures, we should mark this great transition with ample rite and festivity. Even if it is a second marriage, so significant an act demands a rich celebration.

Our personal lives, Judaism teaches, cannot be detached from family and folk. They have invested much of themselves in us. Were it not for them we would not be who we are. Facing life, we are grateful if we have them to ease our trials, enhance our joys, and bolster us in our ideals. How then can we leave them out of our wedding? Ten is the minimum traditional number of a group to represent the Jewish people. If we can afford it, emotionally as well as financially, we know we will want to share this event with the distant relatives and old neighbors, the present-day colleagues and trusted friends, all those who have seen us through to this time. Rejoicing with them is reliving our lives in the light of this happy hour. How much more it means to stand in their presence and rededicate ourselves to what all of us have hoped we might become.

With wine and ring and canopy and blessings the small community now reaches far beyond itself to unite with all the lengthy Jewish past and the diverse Jewish present. The littleness of one couple is projected against the people of Israel's millennial history of devotion. Our lives take on something of the inestimable worth of a folk which, despite the most diverse circumstances, has known supremely well how to sanctify the relations between husband and wife.

All this is linked to God through the prayers said aloud and all those that course through our hearts in the hush that falls as the ceremony begins. How did these two find each other? What joyous providence brought them and us to this beautiful moment? Who knows what awaits them? Thanks, then, to God for what has been given and earnest prayers for blessing in what is yet to be.

Must we then drink and dance and overeat? Is it not possible to avoid tedious aunts and embarrassing cousins? Why can't there be a wedding without someone's feelings being hurt? Isn't there a way to be as relaxed and casual about this unique event as we like to be in all the rest of our lives? Or, to take the other side, is there any reason why we should not be as formal and elegant about this supreme moment as we have always dreamed we one day might be?

I do not know the answer to these and many other detailed questions about weddings. I wish you luck when you are arranging one. I only urge you to bear in mind that, as Judaism sees it, not just two people but two families and communities of friends and the Jewish people and God all have their place in a Jewish wedding. And, as we liberal Jews see it, you should have your wedding in your own way, so that our Jewish rituals and customs fuse with your individual style to make a statement about love, family, community, people, and Reality fuller than any other you may ever again make in your life.

Our Many Reasons for Doing Rituals

Why do many liberal Jews want to perform rituals and now seek to do so more than ever before? Many suggestions have been offered.

Being human, we simply enjoy making moments special. Perhaps if we did nothing different to mark Friday night dinner it might still have a special tone because of family custom or an inherited menu. But if we light candles, the sense of the meal immediately changes. A blessing over them will set the unique sacred context of this meal. To then make *Kiddush* and say the *Motsi* will anchor this dinner in cosmic meanings carried on by an eternal people. If we also take the time to read "A woman of valor" (Prov. 31:10–31) and to bless our children, an incomparable family moment enters our week, regularly bringing us together as little else in our lives does.

Many of our rituals are a joy, particularly if one brings a modicum of Jewish know-how, self-respect, and enthusiasm to them. The *seder* is an almost irrefutable case in point. I say "almost" for many people forget that while we are commanded to be joyous and drink four cups of wine, we are absolutely not required to be grim or tedious about the proceedings. Simchat Torah and Purim can get positively dionysian in some synagogues. And Judaism also knows the quiet pleasures of the braided candle, the spice, and the final cup of wine when we make *Havdalah* at home to mark the end of *Shabbat*.

Many rites teach us lessons we need to know or be reminded of. We consider it a duty to go to a funeral and we pay our *shivah* call not only to help the bereaved—have you not often been surprised how much it has been appreciated—but also because of the deep sense of meaning we momentarily recapture then. So too we read the prayers at the service not only for what they say to God but for what they are simultaneously saying to us. Or we say the *Shehecheyanu* blessing over a joy which has come to us, for something apparently as trivial as a lovely new jacket or the season's first taste of honeydew. Then, for an instant, we remember how much we have to be grateful for.

The New Liberal Appreciation of Ritual's Value

In recent years most of us have tried to be less rigidly rationalistic than a previous generation of liberal Jews. We respond to many forms and levels of instruction. We enjoy many emotive and bodily modes of self-expression. So too, not having to turn religion mainly into ideas, we are far more open to ritual in our lives than they were.

I think it also fair to say that we probably enjoy our Jewishness more than they did; we certainly seem more comfortable doing demonstrably Jewish acts. This itself now constitutes a reason for some liberal Jews observing rites: we do them because other Jews do them and we want to be loyal members of our people.

I think the most practical instance of this concern for Jewish identification has been the return of the Hebrew language to Reform Jewish services. The rise in Hebrew literacy among Reform Jews hardly explains it. Most people still do not know what most of the Hebrew prayers say. Nonetheless, there is a widespread desire for considerable Hebrew in the service. We know it makes our worship "more Jewish" and, though we don't want linguistic overload, we enjoy having Hebrew that we don't fathom.

The same interest in identifying with the rest of the Jewish people has prompted what to some is the shocking turn of a minority of liberal Jews to keeping *kosher* (or some variety thereof) or wearing a *yarmulke* or *kipah* during prayer. We cannot scorn *kashrut* with a previous generation's rationalistic notion that a pure religion would have nothing to do with such physical concerns as eating. Coming from the mouths of a generation addicted to diets, new restaurants, and food talk, that would sound almost hypocritical. And American Reform Jews remain almost the only Jews in the world who have Jewish services with heads uncovered. Obviously, the more one wishes to associate oneself with the Jewish people the more traditional rituals one will want to employ.

The most surprising motive leading to greater observance has been the quiet rise of a new spirituality, or at least of a spiritual search, in the liberal community. Being less certain how far reason or technique will take us, we are open to other levels of consciousness than cognition. We seek to be sensitive to the realm of the spirit in a felt, personal way. Taken to an extreme, this has led Jews out of our community to cults of the most diverse forms. In a more organic religious development, Jews take up their traditional means to bring one in touch with God.

Permit me a somewhat shocking but nonetheless realistic example, the Jewish practice of reciting a blessing after excretion. (". . . Who created people with many ducts and hollows. You know full well that if one of these were to shut tight or stay open we could not survive and stand before You. We bless You, *Adonai,* healer of bodies and worker of wonders.") There is nothing mystical or ecstatic involved in saying such a blessing as one leaves the toilet. But Jews have had so embracing a sense of human holiness that they·have connected this animalistic act—one from which we tend to dissociate ourselves—with God. Long before the notions of psychosomatic illness and holistic health were formulated, Judaism knew that we must connect our spirituality with our bodies as well as with our minds. A classic Jewish spiritual life would not deny reality while seeking God. Learning to say the blessing after excretion—among other rituals—would surely extend our effort to bring a touch of the holy into our everyday lives.

The Personal Factor in Determining What to Do

Obviously, I do not think that, having made the transition to modernity, modern Jews any longer need a heavy diet of the rationalistic debunking of Jewish ritual. Rather, with Jews often "ritual-less" to the point of folk and spiritual sterility, I agree with the many leaders of liberal Judaism who have called on us to bring greater Jewish practice into our lives.

This position can easily be misunderstood. I am not saying that liberal Jews need to do everything the classic Jewish codes prescribed. Nor must they do what they choose to do in the exact manner dictated by Jewish law. This attitude, "If you don't do it the Orthodox way you might just as well not do it at all," is the antithesis of liberalism. For us creative adaptation is the chief sign of Judaism's vitality. Rituals, appealing largely to the affective side of us, will necessarily be chosen, in part, as a subjective judgment—and communities appear to have sensibilities as do individuals. Liberal Judaism will therefore always have a variety of practice among individuals and some difficulty in reaching community agreement for joint observances. From the liberal perspective, such pluralism is not only healthy but desirable; from it, particularly from the creative energy it releases, arise the new forms which keep Judaism alive.

We need to keep this subjective factor in mind when we seek to determine what rituals we will practice. Some simply appeal to us and I believe we need have no more justification for them than that. A problem arises when we are put off by observances. Then we must inquire whether they do not "work" for us or whether something in us prevents our religious growth. Thus, few liberal

Jews grew up saying grace after meals, the *"benchen."* Many have now become accustomed to it from attendance at camp, retreats, or, perhaps, congregational affairs. For others, getting the Hebrew words out with reasonable accuracy in time with the chant can be a considerable problem. Unfamiliarity makes them quite inhibited about this rite. Some, who are at ease with the *Motsi* because of the Protestant analogy, dislike chanting long Hebrew paragraphs after the meal. In all such cases I counsel that, unless a rite seems inherently unacceptable, you try it long enough to feel comfortable with it. Only then can you make a fair decision whether it can "work" for you.

There are some Jewish rituals which, by their nature, I could not observe or recommend to others to follow. A classic instance is the rite of *chalitsah.* A widow, childless by her husband, should by the Torah's law (Deut. 25:5–10) be married by his brother. By rabbinic edict, the practice is to avoid this by a formal ceremony of rejecting the widow. Before a court of five (men), the widow reads the relevant texts, draws off a ritual shoe from her former brother-in-law, and spits on the ground in front of him. For all its antiquity and present practice, this rite is ethically and esthetically ruled out of my Jewish practice. Whenever human dignity is significantly compromised or when the forms of a rite radically clash with modern ethical sensibilities, we must forgo it.

Ancient Rites in Reshaped, Modern Forms

Many apparently troublesome rituals can be recast so as to preserve and perhaps enhance their classic power. Thus, liberal Judaism began as a revolution to change the esthetics of the synagogue. The introduction of decorum, instrumental music, singing by mixed voices in modern styles and other such changes revitalized the older style of worship.

Not every experiment worked out. The decorum they sought so stressed a somber, unemotional tone that an instrument as unreliable as a *shofar* became an embarrassment at High Holy Day services. At first a cornet was substituted for it; some congregations preferred notes sounded on the organ. Then, with increasing traditionalism, a *shofar* fitted with a trumpet mouthpiece came into use. By now, many congregations prefer the risk of the squeaks and misses from an unadulterated *shofar* in the hope that they may possibly hear those blasts which unmistakenly signify Jewish High Holy Day services. In this case, the archaic reasserted its validity.

I do not think we liberal Jews yet know how many old observances our new mood might welcome into our Jewish practice. The endless numbers of *aliyot* in the traditional Torah reading do make the service tedious—particularly when the delays are extensive due to the private blessings said after each *aliyah.* At the same time, having men and women from the congregation read from the scroll proves not only rabbis ought to be learned Jews. And, loving all the Torah Scroll symbolizes, I am delighted these days to see it borne into the congregation in regal procession. Then, when the scroll passes by near me, I follow the old tradition of reaching out, lovingly touching my fingers to its mantle, and kissing them in lieu of it.

I also stand open to the new religious pleasures that will come to us from the rituals yet to be created. My favorite thus far is that consummate American Jewish creation, the end-of-service *Shabbat* kiss. By some unwritten yet universal law, everyone knows one ought to kiss one's spouse after the service has closed. In the days of separate seating for women and men, such an act was not possible; the more pious even thought it wrong ever to kiss one's spouse in public. But as decorum became less stiff and kissing became a communication rather than a climax, someone—we do not know who—reached over and planted the first *Shabbat* kiss. Others soon did it as well and an American Jewish custom was born. The rite is quite pleasant in itself and, if fully meant as a conclusion to our worship, an act of the deepest significance.

In sum, the more we see our humanity as multileveled and the more we wish to express ourselves as loyal and believing—or spiritually searching—Jews, the more ritual will be important to us. And, while no one should presume to tell you just which ceremonies are right for you, a common rule often applies here: The more you do, the more you find you can do.

·6·

FEELINGS VERSUS RULES:
THE CASE OF PRAYER

Our ambivalence to Mother's Day aptly epitomizes our difficulty in living either by law or spontaneity. Of course we love our mothers and feel indebted to them. We may even still have a growing relationship with them. We do not forget to say, from time to time, how much they mean to us, or even to do acts which make them light up with joy. But considering the depth of our feelings, disturbingly long gaps can elapse between our calls, visits, gifts, or I-love-you's. So Mother's Day arrives as an occasion of atonement. Or less weightily, it provides an opportunity for acting on our oft-announced intentions. Celebrating it gives motive, focus, and structure to our lagging wills. That is its justification.

But what a trial it can be! First, there's the problem of the present. Of course, you don't "have" to bring one but if you appear empty-handed she will be hurt. Then what shall it be? Not any lovely or expensive present will do. You must avoid her peeves, remember her inventory, and reflect her standards. All that accomplished, you must now plan the activities. At what distance may an extended phone call substitute for a visit? But, then, what will you chat about for more than a minute or two? If you do visit or she comes to your place, will it be to sit and talk, or go to a movie, or out to dinner? Just what will keep everyone happy?

The truth is that we often have a miserable time on Mother's Day. For all our good intentions, we simply cannot get our feel-

ings to perform on schedule. Our spontaneous re;
one another is so much more deeply satisfying. But ..
the right mood, the days may drag on into weeks or longe.
nothing may happen. The rules, at least, give us periodic remind-
ers of what we ought to be doing—even though we may not be
able to live up to their demands.

But the Doing Can Produce Feeling

William James was one of the authors of the psychological
dictum that emotions are better described in terms of acts rather
than as internal states. We validate James's notion whenever we
act out of pure discipline and a lovely feeling results. Visiting
hospitals or homes for the aged often works this way. Thinking
of the decrepitude we shall encounter and the smells we cannot
avoid may keep us from going. Once there, we have often discovered that, despite our discomfort, we are very glad we went. This
can easily be more than the cessation of guilt. We may find ourselves deeply moved by love given and returned, of being
affirmed ourselves in our reaching out to another. In such cases,
the doing brought the feeling; the performance validated the
rule.

Franz Rosenzweig had a somewhat similar theory of liberal
Jewish duty. Against Orthodoxy, he insisted that we cannot fairly
be asked to observe what, at our depths, we know we cannot
honestly do. But against the liberals he argued that this had
nothing to do with convenience or one's feelings. No such superficial reasons for determining one's practice could claim any
religious dignity.

Rosenzweig's Judaism was based upon his modern view of God
and the people of Israel's relationship to God. With the Covenant
the ultimate basis for his life, Rosenzweig had a demanding sense
of Jewish obligation as liberal theories go. He felt that, in principle, we ought to accept the whole of Jewish law as addressed to
us personally. Of course, we did not have to do what we truly
"could not" do but we should consider ourselves obligated by it
all. This causes us no difficulty when the commandment appeals
to us, like "Honor your father and your mother." But what about
those many Jewish rules which make little sense to us but are
clearly not "impossible"? Rosenzweig urged us to do them, for

only in the performance would we discover their validity. For him whatever personal sense of command we require did not come before the act but in its doing.

Rosenzweig carried this strong sense of duty a step further. He did not feel that laws we now rejected should be permanently eliminated from Jewish obligation. Once, when asked whether he put on *tefilin,* he capsulized his philosophy in the response, "Not yet."

Much of the recent turn back to Jewish observance has followed Rosenzweig's insight. When we perform ritual acts or other Jewish duties we once thought were not for us, we find that they fill a void in our lives and enrich us. And only by becoming familiar with them can we discover if they ought to be part of our repertory of observances.

Unfortunately the James-Rosenzweig observation does not work with any consistency. People try to be more observant and find it dull or oppressive. Much of that result may come from the ambivalence we bring with us. But even an informed, sensitive person can find a classic Orthodox or Reform service empty. And, considering the many minutiae of rabbinic rules, this experience was common and, thus, the spur to the reform of Jewish practice.

The Constant Tension between Consistency and Spontaneity

Wherever we turn in human relations, we shall not escape this dilemma: people need regularity but prefer what is fresh. Without a combination of the two we are doomed to boredom or flightiness. We cannot put the proper balance between them into a rule for that would put an end to spontaneity. The best we can do then is to analyze both values so as to see how we might keep them in proper tension in our lives.

I think we need not dwell too much on being true to ourselves. Much of this book has been taken up with our thinking for ourselves, and our culture strongly reinforces this notion. But a word should be said about the heavy weight we give to personal integrity. More than any previous generation, we make ourselves, at some distance from family, religion, or society, the source of our authority. To be an individual in the literal sense of the word means being unique, oneself, not someone in general. It implies not merely doing what everyone else does. Rules speak to a group standard, hence they can seem particularly burdensome to people concerned with their individuality.

Religious regulations are particularly troublesome in this regard. In social matters, some hypocrisy may be desirable. But petty lying or polite dissembling to smooth things over is not the same as deceiving God. Whatever mature view of God we shall work out would be infantile if it provided for our ability to lie to God. The great strength of liberal Judaism has been its abhorrence of hypocrisy and its insistence on personal integrity. You need do as a liberal Jew only what you conscientiously determine is right. This respect for individual autonomy has caused liberal Judaism many problems in setting group regulations and standards, but it has preferred the risks of anarchy to surrendering its concern for conscience.

Traditional Judaism, despite its desire for sincerity, and liberal Judaism, despite its respect for the individual, have given priority to acts over intention. Our people's root religious concern makes itself felt here. How one actually lives, not the thoughts one has or the feelings one gets, is its ultimate interest. Not all religions give deeds such preeminence but Judaism unequivocally does. And the intuition that God "cares" most about our deeds is responsible for the fabled Jewish activism and energy.

We can epitomize Judaism's strategy for dealing with the dilemma of fixity and freshness as seeking a realistic balance between the real and the ideal. Our sages would prefer that we always carry out our religious obligations with complete devotion, *kavanah*—and go so far as to esteem acting out of the love of God more than doing so out of "fear." But if, as often happens in the real world, we do not feel inspired, they demand that we do our prescribed duty anyway (though some rule we should then repeat the act, this time with proper intent). They do not trust spontaneity as a basis for ongoing existence. Rather, they have a strong sense of our ability to deceive ourselves and of the power of our Evil Urge. The Torah's rules (and techniques) are the best antidote they know to the human will-to-evil. And only through an objectively delineated, publicly disseminated body of law can the people of Israel corporately fulfill its historic responsibility to God.

Liberal Jews, for all their stress on freedom, have reasserted this traditional Jewish emphasis on duty. It begins with a simple question, if you care about being part of a Jewish family, or our people, or our relationship to God, what are you doing about it?

Liberal Jews of a prior generation had no difficulty being more specific. Though they had given up Orthodoxy's Oral Law, they were devoted to what they called the Moral Law. The term was not idly chosen. They did not speak of moral inclination or aspiration. For them ethics was a matter of duty, a requirement of Judaism. We may judge this a limited sort of Jewish discipline but it was one they accepted and acted on. Today, liberal Jews have a greatly enlarged horizon of Jewish responsibility. Whatever it encompasses, the need to act—and to do so as a community—will make its pressure felt against the high value given to individual decision.

Let us analyze the demand for action as it makes itself felt in a major traditional clash between regulation and intention, the requirement that we pray stated services regularly.

All Jews Must Pray for Themselves

Some Jews are surprised to discover that Jewish worship is thoroughly individualistic, that a rabbi or a cantor cannot do their praying for them. They seem to imagine our liturgy to be something like a Christian sacrament, in which a specially designated —ordained—person performs a rite in which God then participates actively.

Since the destruction of the Temple and the end of the priestly service, there is nothing like that in Judaism. All Jewish services depend on the individual Jews involved—so any person can lead them. A rabbi or cantor may add a certain expertise or flavor to the service, thus enabling the worshipers to pray better. But the responsibility for what transpires remains with each person in the congregation. A talmudic tale reflects this principle. Hanan the Hidden was the grandson of the great prayer-leader Honi the Circle-drawer. When the country needed rain, the rabbis would send the school children to him. They would grab his cloak and say, "Father, give us rain." But he would say, "Master of the universe, give us rain for the sake of those who do not know the difference between the Father who gives rain and a father who does not." (Taan. 23b)

Maimonides epitomized individual responsibility at services in these instructions: "Prayer without devotion is no prayer at all. . . . So, before starting to pray, a person ought to stop everything for a little while in order to get into a prayerful mood. Then one should pray quietly and with feeling, not like somebody who carries a burden and finally drops it, quite relieved. Even after prayer one ought to sit quietly for a few minutes and then go on one's way." (Mishneh Torah, Hil. Tef. 4:15–16) Centuries later this same individualism was reflected in an anecdote about Menachem Mendel, the chasidic *rebbe* of Rymanov. One Rosh Hashanah he came into the synagogue and seeing the many people there he called out, "You're a fine crowd of Jews but I can't carry you all on my back."

Obviously, the rabbis' desire that all commandments be done with *kavanah*, proper intention, applies with special force to prayer. In discussing why some rabbis in talmudic times could pray for rain and get it while others despite great learning could not, the text says simply, "The Merciful One desires the heart." (San. 106b) It is as good a summary of the essence of prayer as we have. Yet the very same rabbis ruled that there should be three sizable, substantive orders of service a day, morning, afternoon, and evening. For each of these they prescribed the structure and much of the content of the prayers. The Hebrew term for a prayer book is *siddur*, "the order." Abraham Heschel pointed out that rabbis called a regular performance *keva*. Proper Jewish prayer, he sought to remind modern Jews, needs to be a blending of *keva* and *kavanah*.

God Deserves and Our Community Requires Rules

The rabbis make rules for prayer because they believe it must be an ongoing ingredient of Jewish life. They have a simple reason for requiring regularity: God remains God and is not, so to speak, merely occasionally God. And that constant God is the most important reality in the universe. If so, we ought to stay in touch with God. Though we may feel we do not need God or we can get along without God, we should discipline ourselves to keep our relationship with God strong. Not because repeating certain hallowed words frequently can force God to fulfill our desires. As the Yiddish proverb points out, "If praying was reliable, they'd be hiring people to pray!" And it is certainly not because if we pray to God regularly we shall not have to take personal responsibility for our lives. Over two thousand years ago Ben Sirach properly described the Jewish mix of dependency on God and on self when he wrote:

> My son, do not be negligent when you are sick
> But pray to God, for He can heal
> . . . And see that a physician is near
> For the Lord has created him.
> Nor should he be far away, for one has need of him.
> There is a time your well-being depends on him
> And he too prays to God
> To guide him to bring relief
> And effect a cure and a restoration to health. (38:9, 12–14)

We should pray regularly because, of course, it is God's due as the Ruler of the universe. So, when the service proper begins, the leader says, "Praise *Adonai,* to whom our praise is due!" Whereupon the congregants announce their willingness to participate by responding, "Praised be *Adonai* to whom our praise is due now and forever!"

Practically, too, we ought to pray each day because we are all likely at some time or another to have great need of God. When that moment arrives and we crave intimacy with God, what will overcome the estrangement we have created between ourselves and God? Yet, in their agony, people who have steadily turned their backs on God often demand to know "Where is God?"

The Jewish prayer patterns transmit to us what generations of our people found valuable for regular communication with God. They have another function as well: they make community worship possible. Indeed, we may say that the Jewish service continually recreates the Covenant community.

We must now spend a moment on the other, the folk side of the Covenant.* Jewish prayer must begin with the individual Jewish soul but it cannot end there for we share our people's corporate, historic relationship with God. Classic Jewish worship speaks for this spiritual community, gathered to express and renew the Covenant. The rabbis set ten as the minimum number to represent our folk as a whole and constitute a quorum for a full worship service. The congregants are expected to pray not

*See Part One, *The Jewish People,* chapters 1 and 3.

merely for themselves alone but also for the Jewish people. Mendel, the chasidic *rebbe* of Kotsk, said, "When a man prays, even if he does so all alone in his house, he ought to unite his heart with the whole people of Israel. In every true Jewish service it is really the community that is praying." The oft-repeated "we" and "our" of the prayer book is not an editorial nicety. It stands for "Us, the people of Israel," assembled here in miniature. Pinhas, the chasidic *rebbe* of Koretz, insisted that "a prayer which is not spoken in the name of all Israel is no prayer at all!"

We must have regularity in Jewish prayer, then, for pragmatic reasons: the Jewish people needs to know when to gather and what to do together. Without rules, no community can long survive. And all of us know that if we want a group to continue we must sacrifice some of our personal predilections for its welfare.

What the Community Can Do for the Individual

Community discipline can so irk us that we forget how much the group helps us. Simply to let it impinge on our consciousness has ethical value. We generally come to services preoccupied with ourselves and our troubles. Linking ourselves to the community "we" puts our self-concern into proper context. In our own congregation, we can share the pains or joys of those with whom we are praying. A fervent "we" also unites us with oppressed Jews who cannot pray with our freedom; it links us with the State of Israel in its immediate peril or promise. And with a bit of imagination we unite with all those Jews who, for two millennia, have said these same words in awesomely varied circumstances. When one feels oneself part of this company, one sees oneself and one's prayers differently.

By coming together to pray, the community puts itself in a greater state of spiritual readiness than most of us are in on our own. We spend our days gaining and expending, plotting and executing. We work at exploiting opportunity. Prayer radically breaks our routine; it is an antidote to our compulsion for mastery. God "rules," not we. Hence, we need to stop our manipulative activity from time to time and humbly renew our sense of Ultimate Reality.

Our Jewish prayer practices help bridge our way from the profane to the transcendent. The synagogue has its own proper pace, its sound and its silence. They direct us to "Know before Whom we stand," as the customary ark wall motto says. (Ber. 28b) The music and chants are evocative. Even when we do not know what the words mean, the melodies lift us beyond ourselves (as when the *Kol Nidre* is sung). Listening to the cantor or singing with others can move us more than any words. The chasidic *rebbe* of Koretz, Pinhas, once commented, "It happens that a person may want to sing and cannot. Then another who can sing comes and joins him. Now the first is able to lift his voice too. That is the secret of the bond between one spirit and another." Something like that holds equally true for all the symbols of the synagogue: the ark, the tablets of the Covenant, the eternal light, and, mostly, of course, the Torah Scroll itself. Centuries of community devotion and creativity have crystallized in forms which can infuse us with their power.

Reaching Far Enough beyond Ourselves

The communal pattern also sets a tested ideal of prayer before us. Generations of Jews shaped these forms out of their religious experience. Religious geniuses created prayers and rites to help us reach out to God, and the usage of masses of ordinary Jews refined them into practices that might be expected even of the less than saintly.

Modernity has decreased our patience with prayer and altered our notion of the esthetics which enhance worship. Nonetheless, the fundamental Jewish mix of praise, thanks, and petition, of communal and personal prayer, of study and instruction, of quiet time and social time, of order with variation still strikes us as the proper way of refreshing the Covenant relationship. Saying these words, performing these rites, we may hope to rise to the spiritual level of their creators. Uri, the chasidic *rebbe* of Strelisk, said he was not downhearted that he could not compose psalms as King David did. For he had a talent that lifted him to levels like those of King David—he could recite psalms with *kavanah.*

Perhaps the most common personal objection to the Jewish service is its fulsome praise of God. God cannot be so egocentric as to "need" such adulation. To this traditionalists respond that no matter how much we praised God it would never be adequate. As the *Nishmat* prayer puts it "Though our mouths were filled with song as the sea and our tongues with joyous praise like the roaring waves . . . we should still be unable to thank You . . . for one thousandth, thousandth of the thousands of thousands and ten thousand instances of favors which You have done for our ancestors and us."

To my mind the piling up of praise of God has more to do with us than it has to do with God. We need little reminder of who we are and what is on our minds. We are bursting with self-consciousness. But prayer has to do with consciousness of an Other, of that Ultimate which is not ourselves, yet in terms of which we can best understand ourselves. Praise leads us beyond the confines of the ego to contact with the Holy. It helps us reach ever further toward the Sacred so we can properly appreciate Whose partners we are. Perhaps we can best think of praise as a liturgical "stretching exercise" for the self, better enabling it to touch its ultimate Source and Goal. The Baal Shem Tov, the founder of Chasidism, had something similar in mind when he wrote in his testament, "When one is on a low level of attachment to God, it is better that he pray from the prayer book. Then, when he reads the words before him and concentrates, he will be able to pray with more intention. But when he is already at a high level of attachment to God, it is better to close one's eyes so that even the act of seeing should not interfere with his attachment to God."

Standardizing worship for all Jews enabled our sages to fix a basic content to each service. There are four matters they believed we ought to review with God each day. The service proper begins with praising and thanking God for establishing and maintaining the beneficent order of nature. Second, we acknowledge again that God is one and that the only God of the universe made and keeps a Covenant with the people of Israel (as the Exodus showed). Third, our God regularly helps individuals. We gratefully confess God's help to us and now rely on it as we utter our daily petitions, the climactic one of which is for peace. And, fourth, having said what befits every Jew, we should now speak to God for ourselves. From *Barechu* to silent prayer, the service is a psychic journey directing our attention from the cosmos, to our people, to our communal requests, to our individual needs. I find this structure of worship fully compelling for a believing liberal Jew.

Accommodating Individual Needs Traditionally

Traditional Judaism also provided much place for private prayer. The Psalms were always treasured as a guide to personal meditation. Beyond that what individual Jews wanted to do about solitary worship was largely left to them and the records indicate that Judaism had a lively history of private spirituality. As we continue our discussion, we need to keep in mind that set regulations do not describe all of Jewish prayer. Indeed, there can be laws for praying because insofar as they do not meet one's personal needs one is encouraged to supplement them. The regulations fix a communal minimum; the aspiring soul will go far beyond them.

One makes the Jewish service one's own by the way one "says" it. The worshiper is not expected merely to run the rabbis' thoughts through one's head as if there were one correct interpretation of the prayers. As practitioners of *midrash,* the rabbis were fully conscious of the virtues of evocative, multileveled language. They composed their prayers in a similar highly charged style. Proper worship consists of taking up these imagistic phrases, filling them with personal meaning and directing them to God. Jewish prayer is this moment's directed commentary on these ancient, multivalent texts. An opera libretto provides a fine analogy. Before we can fully enjoy the opera, we need to know its text well enough to be able to respond to what is transpiring. Liturgy is not nearly so passive. At a service, we are the artists who use old words and perform inherited acts in our own way to achieve the ideals of Jewish worship.

The single most significant device the rabbis created for individualizing the stated service was the silent meditation which concludes the *Shmoneh Esreh,* the "Eighteen Benedictions," the central bloc of Jewish worship. The Talmud records some of the personal prayers various rabbis said at that point in the service. Our prayer book text there, "O God, keep my tongue from evil and my lips from speaking guile . . . ," is largely the private petition of Mar, the son of Ravina. (Ber. 17a) It is included in the *siddur* to help those whose own words have failed them. But one may say whatever one wishes to the God "before Whom one stands." Probably the greatest success of the modern reform of Jewish liturgy has been the revival of personal prayer then. For many worshipers, it is the highlight of the service.

Our sages also introduced variety into the liturgical pattern so as to relieve the boredom inherent in repetition. Some texts change from morning to afternoon to evening, others with the season, and more radically with Sabbaths, festivals, and High Holy Days. At some services we read from the Torah and on five occasions we read *Megillot,* short books from the Biblical Writings. Poetry is introduced for special occasions and changes in the music occur with every significant shift in worship. Alas, most modern Jews are far better equipped to pick up the subtle hints that appeal to the sophisticated theatergoer rather than those communicated by the synagogue service. In sum, we may say that traditional Jewish worship makes considerable provision for variation, though, by modern standards, it does so in a highly limited way.

Accommodating Individual Needs Today

The desire to involve the individual worshiper more actively strongly motivated the modernization of Judaism after the Emancipation. For people whose education, activities, and esthetic values were now largely determined by general society, the traditional service no longer was evocative and fulfilling. So the early liberals reworked its forms to make it culturally effective.

Two of the major changes the liberals introduced clearly illustrate their hope to make Jewish worship more meaningful. They translated much of the liturgy into the vernacular. This created a communal furor but made it possible for the worshipers to pray with understanding. Individual participation could now again aim at *kavanah,* rather than merely reciting the Hebrew texts, which had unfortunately become the accepted traditional norm.

They also aimed at greater participation by shortening the service. Previously, one of the few ways of changing the service had been to add new material. Few of these additions had been dropped over the centuries, making the Sabbath and festival services quite lengthy. The only remedy available was speeding up the saying of the prayers. Without considerable practice one could hardly complete the prayers much less say them with proper devotion.

The length of the service was also due to its required repetitions. First, the worshiper said the entire bloc of *Shmoneh Esreh* which was then repeated by the cantor. In the Temple in Jerusalem on Sabbaths and holidays, the daily offering was supplemented by an "additional," *musaf,* sacrifice. After the Temple was destroyed, the rabbis instituted a *musaf* service on these days as a memorial and a compensation. It consisted of another set of the *Shmoneh Esreh* prayers, with appropriate alterations recalling the Temple sacrifices. Once again, a public repetition followed the private recitation. Thus, some of the prayers were said four times.

The early Reform Jews omitted the *musaf* service from their prayer books. They had no wish to pray for the restoration of sacrifices. They also decided to say the *Shmoneh Esreh* only once, but to do so deliberately and with proper intention. In addition, they deleted many of the old poetic accretions to the service. The result was a service people did not feel compelled to race through and to which they could give full attention.

The same concern lay behind many other of the changes introduced into modern Jewish worship: arriving on time; praying in reasonable unison; maintaining decorum by not chatting or moving about during the service; the beautification of the synagogue; the introduction of modern musical styles; the printing of sequential, bilingual prayer books; the introduction of the sermon. All these innovations were designed to involve the modern Jew personally in the work of Jewish worship. Their success over the years is attested by the way they have been adopted or adapted by the groups who once decried them as un-Jewish.

The Reform movement furthered this strategy in a totally unprecedented way, by revising its prayer books about every thirty years. The current Reform *siddur, Gates of Prayer,* continued the pattern of including new prayers which speak to contemporary religious needs, like ones which recall the Holocaust and celebrate the State of Israel. It also includes much more Hebrew and traditional material than did previous Reform prayer books and is available in a binding which opens in the Hebraic fashion, from right to left—all in response to a generation seeking to express its Jewish identity. At the same time, because of the increasing variety of religious sensibility among liberals, *Gates of Prayer* includes ten different Sabbath eve and six different Sabbath morning services as well as an anthology of special readings. Thus a broader range of traditional and modern options are now available to Reform congregations.

Creative Services, the Test Case of Individualism

For all their concern with *kavanah,* liberals have not generally discarded the classic order and motifs of the Jewish service. Their liturgical stance is closer to the fixed rather than the open approach to regular worship. For example, they are not as free as is much of contemporary Protestant worship. In most churches the Sunday service is created afresh each week—but the form of the service and many of its motifs remain largely the same week-to-week. The least structured of all regular services is the Quaker meeting in which silence reigns and is broken only when the Inner Light moves someone to speak. Among liberal Jews, there has been considerable experience with creating services afresh through the practice of encouraging young people to write their own liturgies.

Creative services were introduced to our youth to overcome the irrelevance of which they complained when they attended the synagogue. Their success in enabling young people to pray, particularly in camp settings, has spurred rabbis to create similar services for their congregations. This process originated many of the new prayers included in *Gates of Prayer.*

Creative services move the soul by surprise. New language, even for old themes, different music, a fresh look at reality, a previously unheard poem or song, an uncommon instrument or arrangement, a familiar reading presented in a new context—these and other devices break through our jaded consciousness to move the heart. And when the service speaks to a special occasion, it can summon up what moves the congregation as no fixed and timeless liturgy could. On such occasions the new service reminds us of what we can easily forget: that true community worship is one of the greatest human accomplishments.

But the unique moment is fleeting. It passes and this day gives way to another, and another, and so on in the sameness which characterizes most of life. In that steady procession of time, religious people will still try to maintain contact with their God. Before long, spontaneity fails even the most creative of us. Seeking to reuse a creative service which once moved us greatly, we are regularly disappointed. Few things we write retain their ability to inspire us. Fewer still can bear a community's repetition week after week after week.

There is a further paradox concerning spontaneity. Even as we delight in what is fresh, so we often gain special pleasure from the familiar. When a melody to which we have become accustomed is replaced in the service, we can be quite put out. Hearing an old *Barechu* or *Mi Chamochah* can stir us deeply. We not only delight in surprise but in tradition. Creativity can move us out of our spiritual doldrums; tradition keeps us steadily on course. We cannot bear the burden of being continuously creative but all traditions know how flat their finest observances can become.

We cannot escape our human dilemma. We need rules to guide and spur us but we cannot be fully human unless our free spirits animate our relationships. Jews also know that their needs as individuals must be balanced by their relationship with God as part of the Jewish people. In prayer as in all the fixed structures of our religion, *keva,* regularity, rightly makes its claims upon us as does *kavanah,* inner devotion. We create our liberal Jewish way of life out of a judicious balance of the two.

·7·

BUILDING A JEWISH LIFE:
MARRIAGE AND A FAMILY

Growing up in Columbus, Ohio, I had a detailed sense of what I was supposed to do with my life. I was to get good grades at school, stay out of trouble, finish the university and perhaps a professional school, marry a nice Jewish girl, find a decent job, work hard at it, have children, raise them to be good Jews and decent people, and help out the Jewish and general communities as best I could. There was considerable anxiety in making the innumerable decisions that gave substance to that plan. But compared to people these days who, at eighteen, thirty-six, or sixty, are still trying to find themselves, I knew the grand plan of my life. And I did not expect to revise or radically remake it as the years went by. It was very largely given to me, and, in my own way, I had little difficulty accepting it.

My conformity in this regard does not mean that I merely aped what my father and mother had done in their lives. That would have made no sense. My parents were immigrants and I was a native born American. Being teenagers when they came here, they had already broken with their own parents' life-style, but economic and other pressures kept them from fully acculturating. My sister and I, it was quite clear, were expected to complete the process they had begun. Since we would have a higher education and naturalness about being Americans, our lives would obviously take a different path from theirs. They worried about the breach this might create between us but they never wavered in their desire that we enter fully into the life American Jews were beginning to develop.

The Contemporary American Commitment to Self-Determination

My parents exercised choice more and continuity less than did their parents. In my life the balance shifted even more in the direction of self-determination. But in the present generation "choosing one's life-style" has taken a quantum leap forward.

Many reasons have been given to explain this phenomenon. We are all very much more mobile. Neighborhood and community ties do not mean much, and education, opportunity, or the lure of nicer surroundings can prompt us to relocate. We also have much greater economic and social latitude. When money was tight people could not be very experimental and the behavior most neighborhoods would tolerate was severely limited. More important, we assume that we can readily improve on the accepted patterns of the good life. In the 1960s, Americans realized that they didn't have to dress, or groom themselves, or restrict their enjoyments, or kowtow to authority as they once had. Many of the older social conventions made little sense; some did harm or hid the damage they did from view.

Since those heady days alternative life-styles have become the reality of ordinary neighborhoods and the stuff of mass entertainment. Historians may insist that Americans at the end of the twentieth century are very much like their predecessors at its beginnings. But we operate with quite a different consciousness. They were happy to situate themselves within the patterns their society set before them. We are far more concerned to be true to ourselves.

The loss of social credibility pervades our lives. We have little confidence in government, religion, science, or any other institution. Experts in one field after another have proved themselves fallible. In the last analysis we know we must rely on our own good judgment. Besides it is we who have the final authority over our own lives. Why should we subordinate our standards to what some nameless "they" say is right? By determining for ourselves how we shall live we exercise the fullest responsibility of which we are capable. Our failures may then be more bitter for we ourselves chose the faulty path. But if we succeed we shall have fulfilled our inner freedom. In the truly self-actualized person a new human ideal has been born.

Like all great dreams, the project of choosing a life for oneself has brought many people much pain. Life is too complicated to be lived by constant innovation. We need considerable continuity in much of it in order to exercise intelligent choice in some of it. With much of our inherited social style now thrown into question, we cannot help occasionally feeling ill at ease. Grandparents are uncomfortable not knowing what to expect of their grandchildren; both sexes find it awkward that women do not know what initiatives they can now take with men. More disturbingly, not knowing what we ought to do can rob us of the ability to do anything. Confronting numberless intriguing but imperfect options, we often find we cannot choose any one of them. In the new age of freedom, indecision replaces guilt as the society's pervasive psychic malaise.

Judaism's Special Problem with Building One's Own Life

This time of social transition leaves many Americans uneasy. If we do adjust to the current mood, our new stability may not last for any length of time. Our cultural swings have been too sharp for us to have much confidence in the staying power of any course of action. We seem condemned to an unceasing flow of social change.

In this setting, the genius and limits of liberal Judaism stand out sharply. Valuing individual freedom, it is open to worthwhile additions to Judaism. But, by viewing our tradition critically, it may not have given uncertain, lazy, or weak Jews sufficient guidance as to their Jewish duty.

This failing of liberalism has been exacerbated by the newness of the American Jewish emancipation. My family story is typical of the vast East European migration at the turn of the twentieth century which provided the bulk of contemporary American Jewry. My grandparents remained, to their death, immersed in their European, premodern life-style. My parents were the first modern Jews in our family. My sister and I formed the first generation whose entire lives would be spent under the conditions of emancipation. In three generations American Jews moved out of one way of life and created another. The Jewries of Spain and Poland, to cite two outstanding precedents, seem to have taken centuries to create their unique ways of living as Jews.

We not only have had less time but greater challenges. God and Torah concern us less than people; science tells us more about the world than revelation. We moved from autocracy to democracy, from segregation to equal rights, from indigence to affluence. Unlike the structured social milieu in which liberal Judaism developed, there seem few social constraints these days to what supposedly decent people will do. We cannot count on accepted standards of social decorum to channel the use of our freedom.

We can take some hope from one unanticipated development. Some liberal Jews now acknowledge that American culture is not always wiser than Judaism. If anything, America now needs a revival of its religious traditions to remoralize society. Jews who share this understanding now seek stronger personal Jewish foundations. In a reversal of the self-hating flight from Judaism of a half century ago, their choice of a new life-style includes a desire to be "more Jewish."

I cannot give a rule as to how to choose and combine the best of our American and Jewish heritages. Their values clash too often to be easily resolved, and we do not have many models of the life we seek. Instead, I shall try to demonstrate how I think we ought to go about creating a worthy Jewish life. My example is building a modern Jewish marriage and family. This test case should provide good insight into the opportunities and difficulties we would find in other instances of determining a Jewish way of life for ourselves.

Continuity with Development in Jewish Marriage

Despite my previous stress on social discontinuity I begin by acknowledging that we do not undertake this effort totally afresh. Consider, for example, that idealized Jewish shtetl couple, Tevye and Golde, of *Fiddler on the Roof.* They recapitulated, with minor variations, the lives of their parents. But even their oldest, most compliant child was no longer willing to have her father determine whom she would marry. Each of the other daughters' choices moved progressively away from Tevye's Judaism.

In my family, my paternal grandparents married for love in Eastern Europe, whereupon my grandfather's rather well-to-do father disowned him. As young adults in the United States, my parents met, kept company, and decided to marry in a pattern roughly similar to what we know today. By now, the modern Jewish community has accepted marriage by choice rather than arrangement though, as we shall see, it has led to some new problems.

Despite the differences between American Jewish parents and children there is generally less cultural antagonism between them today than the post-immigrant generation felt toward its parents. No comparable bitterness now separates rebellious young adults from their families. Commonly they are only somewhat more radical about their parents' commitments. Observers often comment that the goals of young and old Jews are more alike than different.

In a more fundamental respect, the establishment of new forms of marital relationship has emerged slowly. Though founded on personal attraction, my grandparents' marriage was lived out essentially as a fulfillment of roles. My grandfather sought to fulfill the usual expectations of a good husband-father-Jewish man while my grandmother worked at the duties of the good wife-mother-Jewish woman. Migration barely changed the standards by which they judged themselves and each other.

This was still largely true of my parents, but their role expectations were modified by being part of the upper-middle class. They were changed more as their children moved away and my father retired. Slowly, hesitatingly, they began to make personal demands on one another.

Estelle and I began our marriage with a conscious commitment to develop a new sort of relationship. Each of us sought personal fulfillment through the life we would build together. It seemed like a highly personalistic conception of marriage. To our surprise, the decades since disclosed great gaps between the ideal and the unconscious role expectations we brought to one another. (The conflicts such differing standards can cause are delightfully illustrated by Tevye's query to Golde, "Do you love me?" She cannot comprehend his personal intent, so different is her view of marriage. She can only answer by reminding him how well she has performed her wifely duties.)

We have moved far beyond that stage today. Young people are highly sensitive to the difference between carrying out a role and fulfilling a relationship. They demand much more of themselves and others, with the result that marriage has become quite difficult for them. If women are equals, one cannot "naturally" expect that one's spouse will do or be this or that. We simply do not know how two people can grow with one another during our extended, many-phased lives. Establishing fully personalized Jewish marriages promises us great fulfillment—but we are only now seriously exploring the specifics of such relationships.

Some Central Jewish Marital Imperatives

What still seems relevant in Judaism's teaching about marriage?

The Bible and Talmud show unusual unanimity in their insistence on marriage. It is a prime consideration of the creation stories. "And *Adonai* God said, 'It is not good for a man to be alone. I will make an appropriate helper for him'." (Gen. 2:18) When God brings Eve to Adam, he recognizes her, as it were, as part of him. The text then continues, "Hence a man leaves his father and mother and clings to his wife so that they become one flesh." (Gen. 2:24) Some scholars surmise that marriage was so important to the early Hebrews that they framed their creation stories to account for its exceptional status. Eve is taken from Adam's flesh to explain why a man leaves his biological kin, with whom he truly shares "one flesh," and gives his relationship with his wife higher priority. (Of course, the Bible describes this in the ancient Semitic sexist fashion.)

The Bible authors do not detail the appropriate roles of the Jewish husband and wife, though we get some hints of this for the patriarchal period. Apparently, the social patterns were so unproblematic and unvarying that explicit directions were unnecessary. However, in two places in the Bible we can see the roots of our modern vision of marriage.

Little separates our feelings of love from the rhapsodic, erotic sentiments of the Song of Songs which begins:

Let him kiss me with the kisses of his mouth,
For your love is better than wine. (1:2)

In what follows, the mix of longing and ecstasy, of sexuality and concern, of sorrow and triumph testifies to the three-thousand-year continuity of the lovers' experience.

In the Book of Proverbs a poem extolls the exceptional wife.

She is praised primarily for her initiative and industry in tasks which extend far beyond care for her household. To be sure, she makes clothes for herself and for her family (even should it snow!) and she sees to it that her household and her servants are all properly fed. She also makes and sells garments and girdles, buys real estate, and plants a vineyard. She is charitable and of high character.

> Strength and dignity are her clothing
> and she looks confidently at the future.
> She opens her mouth with wisdom
> and the law of kindness is on her tongue.
> She looks well to the ways of her household
> and does not eat the bread of idleness. (31:25–27)

Appropriately, the rabbis decreed the reading of this poem at the *Shabbat* table as part of welcoming the Sabbath Queen.

The rabbis of the Talmud had no use for bachelors. Many a pungent comment reinforced their rule that all Jewish males must marry. R. Elazar said, "Any man who has no wife is not a proper man for the Torah says, 'Male and female created He them and [only then] called their name Adam, that is, man'." (Yev. 63a citing Gen. 5:2) R. Tanhum said in the name of R. Hanilai, "Any man who has no wife lives without joy, without blessing, and without goodness." The Palestinian sages added, "Without Torah and without protection." And Rava b. Ulla added, "And without peace." (Yev. 62b)

The rabbis were also realists. Though matchmakers might arrange things to two families' satisfaction, two individuals had to find a way to live together in peace. R. Akiba described the alternatives this way: "When a husband and wife are worthy, God's Presence dwells with them. [A play on the *yod* and the *heh*—God's name, in the short form—found in the similar Hebrew words for man and woman.] When they are not worthy, fire consumes them. [Without the *yod* and *heh*, both words read only *alef shin*, Hebrew for fire.]" (Sot. 17a) Rabbah bar Bar Hanah said in the name of R. Yohanan, "It is as difficult to make a good match as it was to divide the Reed Sea." (Sot. 2a) So, though the Bible makes only passing references to divorce, an entire tractate of the Talmud is devoted to it.

The rabbis realized there could be such things as bad marriages. Dissolving them so that the partners could find better ones was closer to the Jewish ideal of holiness than requiring an incompatible couple to live together in intimacy. Rabbinic law is remarkably lenient with regard to grounds for divorce. Its stringency comes from tight administrative procedures. Coupled with the community opprobrium, these kept the number of Jewish divorces low until recent years.

Accepting the Single Jew

It will not do, however, to give the impression that one must be married to be a good Jew. Rabbinic realism allows for exceptions even to very important laws. One early sage, Ben Azzai, refused to take a wife. He was forgiven his eccentricity since he insisted that he wanted to devote himself single-heartedly to the study of Torah.

Of course, we must remember that only men had the commandment to marry. In our time, the number of people who choose not to marry has risen sharply; and with the loss of matchmakers, the development of extended education, and years devoted to one's career, so has the number of young adults who want to marry but cannot find a suitable partner. Family for them will mean something different than it does for married Jews with offspring—and perhaps even than it does for those who are divorced or whose spouse has died. At the least their family consists of the parents and siblings and relatives with whom one always retains unique bonds. When our congregations and communities are properly caring, they become, in effect, part of our Jewish family. Single or married, rich or poor, old or young, in a village or a metropolis, there is always a way to build a Jewish life.

For all that, nothing that contemporary culture has created has displaced marriage as Judaism's preferred condition in which to work out one's destiny. No other state as fully and completely involves partnership. No other form of personal intimacy requires one to take on such complete responsibility. Because it is a unique fusion of love and demand, of understanding and judgment, of personal giving and receiving, nothing else can teach us so well the meaning of covenant. It is the situation where we are most thoroughly challenged to be a Jew and where, if we are blessed, we may personally exemplify what it means to be allied with God in holiness. All the human good which Judaism sees us gaining from marriage derives from this, its transcendental dimension.

If marriage remains that important then a special responsibility devolves upon Jews today to facilitate its occurrence. The loss of the *shadchan,* matchmaker, was not troublesome when small communities, extended families, and the university could be counted on to make our matches. Today, with cities increasingly impersonal, with privacy an increasing shell about people, and with personal standards ever more demanding, the absence of effective means for finding spouses is a major Jewish problem. The divorced, the widow or widower, as well as the seeking young adult have legitimate claims on our Jewish concern. We need to abet our community projects on behalf of singles through personal efforts at bringing together people who wish to marry.

Children as a Duty and a Blessing

Jewish tradition closely links marriage and procreation. Once again, the creation stories give us the clue. The first command given to Adam and Eve is, "Be fertile and multiply." (Gen 1:28) While the "woman of valor" of Proverbs 31 is not commended for being unusually fecund, she is, of course, expected to have offspring. Again and again, the biblical authors describe children as a blessing from God. By contrast, their accounts of barren women—most notably that of Hannah, the mother of Samuel (1 Sam. 1:1–2:11)—convey a poignancy we know well from our friends who are infertile.

The rabbinic commitment to the begetting of children is equally intense. R. Elazar ben Azariah said that not to bring children into the world is, so to speak, to impair God's image, for each human being is created in the divine likeness. (Gen. R. 34:14) They specified how many children we must have to fulfill the duty to procreate. Though the School of Shammai ruled that one must beget two sons, the law follows the School of Hillel which said one daughter and one son are the measure of carrying out the commandment. (Yev. 6:6) To this was added the injunction of R. Joshua that though one had married young one also ought to be married when old, and though one had children young one ought to continue to beget them when old. (Yev. 62b) A most telling indication of the rabbinic regard for children is their rule that after ten years of a childless marriage a man should take another wife. (Yev. 64a) But, when monogamy became Jewish law, the authorities did not enforce this ruling. Though they valued children, they also respected the desire of an infertile husband and wife to remain together without them.

Jewish parents usually manifest extraordinary concern for their children and overprotection rather than neglect has been their characteristic failing. Jewish literature regularly directs Jewish parents to discipline their children, perhaps because overindulgence goes back quite far in our history.

Children have a special function in the Jewish relationship with God. The Covenant is a historic matter. It stretches back to Mt. Sinai and beyond and will reach its completion only in the Messianic Age. Through our children our millennial purpose is carried on and transmitted. Without them the striving of all the Jewish ages would be frustrated. The human joy and suffering of Jewish parents with their children arise from this theological root.

The incomparable human virtue of serving as a parent should also be mentioned. Another human being is utterly dependent on our care and faithfulness. A boundless love is freely given us—how will we respond to it? A searching soul makes us its primary source of guidance about life—what are we ready to teach? There is no art as creative as helping an infant become a worthy human being, nor any test as demanding as having to let our children go their own free way. A good child is a great gift—and, for a Jew, all the vindication one's life ever needs.

Against this, some Jews have suggested that there are cogent reasons why people should not have children. Some are temperamentally unfit for it. Then too the world is threatened by overpopulation. Such arguments have not convinced the large masses of Jews. People who fear they cannot be good parents are far less likely to damage their offspring than those who claim they have no problems. The anxious are at least likely to seek therapy for themselves and their children. If temperament is but a cover word for selfishness or immaturity then such people ought indeed try to grow up somewhat before they start a family. Such people may be avoiding children because they do not wish to face their own failings. In an odd way, they reinforce the Jewish view that raising children is a major way to maturity.

The world population problem is quite real—but, though many supporters of Zero Population Growth seem to be Jewish, it has little directly to do with the Jewish people. The cold facts are that every Jewish community that modernized has had little or no natural population increase. That has been true of American Jewry for some decades. Modernized Jews have abandoned Hillel's dictum—and certainly the utter indeterminacy of R. Joshua! —in favor of having only as many children as they feel they can give proper personal attention. They enthusiastically adopted the practice of contraception despite the strictures of traditional Jewish law. In this matter, as in their vocational distribution and educational patterns, the Jews forecast a future American trend. In any case, greater infertility by some five million American Jews would hardly affect the world population statistics. A small reorientation of nations like India and China would radically alter our global situation. Besides, a case can easily be made for our having larger Jewish families. They would not only make up for the decline in marriage, but bring the Jewish population back to the level it was before the Holocaust.

The Jewish Home, Its Activities and Aura

The Jewish home of yesteryear gave much to its family that the modern home, for all our efforts, does not. Sentimentality aside, Judaism was always centered in the home and family life was therefore strongly influenced by religious faith and practice.

Consider the effect of classic Jewish ritual. An observant Jew begins each day with the rituals of awakening and the morning service, then eats meals prepared to be *kosher,* says blessings over them, enters and exits from the house by kissing the *mezuzah,* and devotes some of what "leisure" time there is to Jewish study. The weekly *Shabbat* routines are the climax of each week and set the other days in context. The special occasions and festivals are also marked by distinctive meals and rituals. In sum, Jewish observance ideally is an integral part of Jewish family existence and thus powerfully reinforces its bonds.

To most modern Jews, Jewish acts come almost as an intrusion on the family's accepted routine. A household may unhesitatingly call itself Jewish but its repertoire of regular Jewish activity no longer gives the family its values and direction. But our families need not live that way. The current interest in greater ritual stems from a recognition of the spiritual emptiness, even the sterility of the upbringing of the previous generation. We now acknowledge that a rich round of Jewish practice tends to cement family values. When synagogue activity and community life are perceived as organic extensions of one's home, they reenforce its positive effect on children and parents alike.

The spirit of the ideal Jewish family pervaded its specific activities. When traditional Jewish authors occasionally spoke of it, they invoked the term, *"shalom."* Their understanding of *shelom bayit* can only inadequately be translated as "a household at peace." That too easily sounds like a family which has momentarily stopped arguing. We catch something of its flavor of concern for others—particularly when we note the mitigation of its sexism —in this talmudic teaching: "R. Awira used to give the following exposition 'What is the meaning of the verse, "Well is it with the man that dealeth graciously, that ordereth his affairs rightfully"? A man should always eat and drink less than his means allow; clothe himself in accordance with means; and honor his wife and children more than his means allow. For they are dependent upon him and he is dependent upon "Him who spoke and the world came into being." ' " (Chul. 84b citing Ps. 112:5)

A similar tone is found in medieval Jewish ethical wills. Here is an early example, excerpted from the testament of Judah ibn Tibbon (1120–1190), the famous Hebrew translator of Arabic books. "My son, I command you to honor your wife to your utmost capacity. She is intelligent and modest, a daughter of a distinguished and educated family. She is a good housewife and mother, and no spendthrift. Her tastes are simple, whether in food or dress. Remember her assiduous attendance on you in your illness, though she had been brought up in elegance and luxury. Remember how she afterwards reared your son without man or woman to help her.

"If you would acquire my love, honor her with all your might. Do not exercise too strict an authority over her; our sages have expressly warned men against this. If you give orders or reprove her let your words be gentle. It is enough if your displeasure is visible in your look. Let it not be vented in actual rage.

"My son! Devote yourself to your children as I did to you. Be tender to them as I was tender; instruct them as I instructed you; keep them as I kept you; try to teach them Torah as I have tried. As I did unto you, do unto them!"

The values here encountered in a Sephardic document are echoed five centuries later in an Ashkenazic will of the late eighteenth century. Joel, the son of Abraham Shemariah, apparently a resident of Vilna, wrote his testament in 1773 and lived on until 1799. "In the first instance, your home must be the abode of quietude and happiness. No harsh word must be heard there, but over all must reign love, amity, modesty, and a spirit of gentleness and reverence. This spirit must not end with the home, however. In your dealings with the world you must allow neither money nor ambition to disturb you. Forego your rights, envy no man. For the main thing is peace, peace with the whole world. Show all men every possible respect, deal with them in the finest integrity and faithfulness. Habakuk summed up the whole Torah in one sentence [2:4], 'The righteous shall live by his faith'."

We cannot say to what extent Jewish family life exemplified these high standards through our long history. We do know that Jewish writers from Josephus's time on (first century C.E.) have not hesitated to compare to our advantage the quality of Jewish family life to that of other peoples. Despite a negative shift in contemporary data and much subjective uneasiness about the state of the Jewish family, many observers would argue that something of the same kind remains true today.

Adapting the Ideal to the New Personalism

Modernity is making its own contribution to the Jewish effort to fashion a family that lives in sacred covenant. Most notably, the contemporary ideal that every human being is a person of equal dignity is radically reshaping our notions of *shelom bayit*. If *shalom* truly implies fullness and completeness, then the Jewish family must now operate with a greater democracy and concern for the personal welfare of each of its members. As the sexism of our previous citations blatantly demonstrated this requires a view of Jewish women as fully equal partners in a marriage, not as subordinates to their husbands' needs and duties. For example, will there be bilateral decisions on matters the spouses consider critical—like the proper use of the family's capital—or will male dominance and female subterfuge merely reassert themselves in new forms?

A genuine commitment to new patterns of mutual respect will by no means end our problems. We have not yet had sufficient experience with egalitarian marriages to create readily available role models or even widely known patterns we might utilize for ourselves.

We are also confronted by the corruption of contemporary personalism into a narcissism that sees little virtue in becoming involved in close, lengthy, demanding relationships. We enter marriage these days expert in pursuing personal not joint ends. The crasser among us live by a consumer mentality. They judge marriage as if it were another service to be tried out to see if it fit into one's life-style.

A Jewish marriage begins with Hillel's insight, "If I am only for myself, what good am I?" The Jewish ideal arises from the partners' common commitment to the covenant between them. They envision their marriage as a uniquely valuable means of working out their individual destinies. R. Eliezer b. Jacob ruled, "A man must not marry a woman with the mental reservation that he may well divorce her." (Yev. 37b) Something of our modern plight was already visible among our European Yiddish speaking masses. They had a saying, "Oh yes, they are both madly in love —he with himself and she with herself."

Even if genuine mutuality can be attained, spouses still face the unsettling challenge of growing both as individuals and as a couple. Once rules and custom instructed us as to our duties and expectations. Now our means have expanded greatly and the opportunities society extends to us have multiplied even more unexpectedly. We do not recognize the selves we wish to be in the lives of our grandparents, often not even in those of our parents. Searching for our kind of marriage in this uncharted openness we can easily get lost, as the many failed marriages around us indicate.

We assume the risks of creating egalitarian marriages not because we underestimate their dangers but because we seek to be more fully human. For us that means equality in relationships and continued personal growth. A religion that perpetuates male dominance and refuses to face the dynamism of the self refutes its claims to believe in the dignity of each individual. Jews, for whom freedom and equality have proved so beneficial, should be among the first to recognize the sacred implications of the new personalism.

When Children Are also Persons

These difficulties seem almost small when compared to those involved in raising children with full respect for their personhood. Our spouse is an adult, capable of making a responsible choice and accepting its consequences. But a child must grow into freedom and its proper use.

The way is treacherous. To restrict liberty unnecessarily will retard the child's maturation. To give greater freedom than the child can reasonably handle damages the young psyche. If the parent cannot tolerate exercising power in some form, the child cannot learn limits and build a sturdy self. But heavy parental coercion robs our children of the ability to make decision for themselves and thus of genuine selfhood. How can we be the parents we aspire to be when no rules and few models adequately instruct us?

We may draw some consolation from recognizing that the struggle between the generations today is not entirely new. Young moderns have always demanded greater freedom while their parents insisted that they were not yet ready for it. There is one, awesome qualification to that observation. The horizons of freedom, for good and evil, are now almost unimaginably wide. Thus the young confront options ranging far beyond beer, lipstick, jitterbugging, and petting. Anyone who has seen young people burnt out by drugs or unraveled by vagabondage will know that the penalties one may have to pay today are appallingly high and often irreversible.

I am convinced that the helping professions constitute a secularized form of high Jewish ethical service for many Jews. They realize how Jewish a task it is to help people survive the traumas incurred in trying to become a person today. Our society is so permissive it is almost neutral morally, thus encouraging a heightened subjectivity. In this situation all our physical and psychological quirks eventually cause us to do unintended harm to ourselves and others. If, to liberals, responsibility begins with the self, then *teshuvah,* turning from sin, must for us first mean repair of the self. Therapy thus becomes a Jewish religious duty and for that reason I hope that the oft-noted Jewish propensity to seek it will expand and grow. We seek a goal that exposes us to many dangers. Along the way, we need all the help we can get.

Our one great positive response to our shaky social situation has been the creation of *chavurot,* the face-to-face associations of people seeking ways to live Jewishly with one another. With family generations geographically and psychologically distant from each other, the *chavurah* becomes our extended family—chosen, not given, voluntarily maintained, not required, capable of rational redirection, not hemmed in by hierarchy and history. In such groups the self creates its own larger family and so brings into being a new possibility for Jewish existence.

We cannot know now whether our generation will mold a personalistic Jewish way of living that future generations will commend. Regardless of the ultimate results, America's dynamism powerfully effects living as a Jew today. Confronted with unprecedented personal freedom we seek to sanctify it and thereby make our contribution to the long history of life in Covenant.

IN PARTING

JEWS WHO DO;
JEWS WHO DON'T

"**W**hen I considered all the ways people go astray and the evil it causes them, my heart was grieved for my species, humankind, the rational animals, and my soul was stirred because of our people, the children of Israel. I saw in this age of mine many believers whose belief was not pure and whose convictions were not sound. At the same time, many of the deniers of the faith boasted of their corruption and looked down on those who adhered to the truth although they themselves were in error. Furthermore, I saw, so to speak, men sunk in seas of doubt and overwhelmed by waves of confusion. Worse, there was no diver to bring them up from the depths and no swimmer who might take hold of their hands and carry them ashore. But God has granted me some knowledge by which I might come to their aid and has endowed me with some ability that I could put at their disposal for their benefit. Therefore, I thought it was my duty to help them and my obligation to direct them to the truth." Thus writes Saadya Gaon in the course of the introduction to his *Book of Beliefs and Opinions,* written about 930 C.E.

Little seems to have changed over a thousand plus years. Jewish idealists still lament the state of Jewish belief—and practice and learning and much else besides. Dirges about the prospects for American Judaism are so common that a positive word about our condition comes as something of a shock. I propose to end this book on a note of hope but not at the expense of sober realism. The simple truth is that the overwhelming majority of American

459

Jews neither believe in nor do much about the matters treated in this book. They consider someone who does a bit odd. Without giving another lengthy, lugubrious description of our failings, let me outline what makes our situation more troublesome than that of previous, unobservant, Jewish eras. Only a hope which can stand up to the hard realities we face is worth our thoughtful consideration.

The Special Sacrifices That Have Accompanied Acculturation

We begin with a critical paradox. American Jewry is now overwhelmingly native born and fully acculturated, sometimes for several generations. It benefits from an equality unknown to historic Jewries. But though our society celebrates pluralism it effectively works to diminish significant group differences.

For some generations the assimilation which resulted from the avid Jewish push to acculturate was made up by new waves of immigrants who were learned, observant, or ethnically committed. Such replenishment from abroad came to an end with the arrival of the post-World War II survivors. Today's immigrant Israelis and Russian Jews share our need for a significant Jewish way of life; they add to our problem of assimilation.

American Jews no longer live in neighborhoods so largely Jewish that sheer contact and peer pressure reinforce Jewish identity. No Diaspora Jewry has ever lived in such local dispersion, utterly exposing itself to non-Jewish influence. For us, community cannot be a geographic term. Rather it consists of the activities in which we voluntarily engage in order to maintain certain social ties.

As a consequence we have lost the old Jewish conception of an estimable Jew. Ritualistically, we still speak of learning and character as important to us. Practically, secular, not Jewish, scholarship awes us. We aspire to associate with those who have fame, power, and money rather than those known for their piety. For the first time in two millennia, the average Jew is not observant. In other periods sinners were social deviants; today that is true of those who seek to be faithful to tradition. Ironically, the ideals of classic Judaism must be defended against the disinterest of the average Jew.

These traumas stem from our widespread loss of belief. With modernization came the secularization of our world view. Emancipated Jews could no longer believe that their people was God's only chosen, that the Torah and its admonitions were God's own will, and that God's provident justice could be counted on to rule the intimate affairs of individuals and nations. They also rejected the liberal Jewish reinterpretation of these doctrines for they now had a better faith by which to live, Western culture. Not caring much about God, Torah, or Israel, they have done little about them. I am convinced that, until our Jewish belief becomes so strong that it overcomes our personal and social resistances to Jewish responsibility, things will not change much.

For a few years now, we have seen a small but definite turn to such liberal Jewish faith. Our society, which had become resolutely secular and unbelieving, demonstrated how amoral it could be without a Judeo-Christian underpinning. And the arts, sciences, and politics in which we had ultimate confidence have increasingly shown themselves empty of a commanding human vision. The loss of the new gods has enabled many Americans to find a new-old abiding wisdom in the traditional faiths they once scorned. It is possible again to be a believer; sophistication no longer implies principled agnosticism.

Caring Jews, those searching for a deep sense of what they can honestly believe and undertake, remain a tiny minority among us. And one with a strong sense of isolation. They not only find themselves distant from much in our society but from many activities our community terms "Jewish." Their special variety of Jewish loneliness is broken only by occasional contact with other Jews of similar uncommon commitment and by the personal assurance they gain as they manage to renew their faith. These devoted liberal Jews, I am convinced, are the great hope of American Jewry.

In Defense of a Certain Elitism

In one respect, our Jewish situation is similar to that of adherents of any high human ideal. Most people settle for very little. Even if they can envision some great good, they will not do much about it. Out of inertia, ennui, fear, disillusion, cynicism, self-destructiveness, or malevolence, they thwart their own ideals.

Were it not for a handful of determined visionaries, no significant progress would be made. Surely that is how we Jews have thought of ourselves among the nations.

Even within our own community, an elite, not the bulk of the people, kept the children of Israel faithful to their Covenant. The biblical evidence is unmistakable. The incomparable event of hearing God's own voice speak the Ten Commandments is quickly succeeded, the stories insist, by the ultimate apostasy, the worship of the golden calf. The rest of the biblical record tells again and again how the backsliding of the people was reversed by the dedication of the prophets and the few who followed them. Communities which were faithful to their Jewish responsibilities did arise in Jewish history. But, in most periods, we hear of constant tension between the spiritual leaders and the people at large. Isaiah once spoke of the "faithful remnant" God would save when God allowed their enemies to triumph over them. In modern reinterpretation we can say that the remnant of Jews who continue to care is the means by which the people and its ideals survive through history. And that remains true for us.

The Varieties of Jewish Existence

I see three sorts of Jews in our community. At our margin stands that large group who are indifferent to their Jewishness. They will not deny their origins but otherwise they ignore them. They are quite satisfied to be people, Americans. They would, of course, like to be good people but to do that they do not feel they need the aid of Judaism—and certainly not the disabilities which come from being Jewish! By quirk of history or providence, some of them or their children may yet turn and take up a positive Jewish existence. But looking at this sector of our community we can easily despair of our future.

We can partially offset this gloom by remembering that a half century ago the assimilators were the ascendant group among us. Today we can fairly say that they are only a small, if disturbing, fraction of our numbers.

Most indicatively, the pathological element among them has strikingly decreased. Once it was common to know Jewish liberals who fought for every minority but avoided Jewish activism as "parochial." They embraced humankind in all its diversity—except for the specific ethnic group from which they had obviously sprung. Unconsciously, they hated being Jews and so tried to dissociate themselves from everything Jewish. Self-hate has not disappeared from among us. It still sets peculiar limits to Jewish involvement and often prompts the judgment that some acts are "too Jewish." But it no longer appears among us with the threatening virulence which infected a pre-World War II generation dedicated to denying its ethnicity.

In recent decades the overwhelming majority of American Jews live in healthy self-acceptance. They are the second variety of Jewishness I see among us. Such Jews are proud of what their people has done and stood for, and they do not hesitate to share their Jewish joys with their non-Jewish neighbors. In an emergency they will give generously and publicly demonstrate in vast numbers. By contrast, their ordinary Jewish activity is sporadic, depending on their life phase, their friends, their mood, or an intricate inner calculus of reward, guilt, boredom, nostalgia, and the like. Their knowledge of Judaism comes largely from magazines, speakers, and trips; few read Jewish non-fiction, fewer still take adult education courses, and only a minute number ever get much beyond a round of introductory courses. They want to be Jews but, on the whole, strengthening their Judaism is low on their lengthy list of life priorities.

At its best, the Jewish middle creates loyalists and leadership. Many Jews care deeply about their people and make considerable personal efforts to see that it continues. Without such a solid bulk of devoted Jews we would not have much of a community at all. They continually produce individuals who give prodigious amounts of time and energy to mobilize the mass of Jews for various causes. Anyone who has ever seen the wealth of devotion and talent which such volunteers bring to a demanding project cannot but marvel. And the manner in which such leadership emerges year after year in the most varied places is a small wonder.

The glories of the Jewish middle are offset by its shortcomings, chiefly its uncertain and erratic motivation. Much of the best of our Jewish activity derives its energy from the glow of sentiment or the shock of emergency. Neither is an unworthy reason for Jewish duty but neither can be counted on for long. Memory fades and institutionalizing it only testifies to its loss of living power. Then too the trumpet cannot summon us to the barricades continually or we become deadened to its tones. Can we long go on living a Judaism centered on what happened or is happening to other Jews? If our community life is to flourish, Judaism must speak to our daily lives. Most of the Jewish middle refuses to make Judaism the ground of its personal existence. So our community compulsively continues to speak of Jewish duty in terms of what we must do for others.

We confront this issue most poignantly when we inquire about the sense Jews of the middle have about religious responsibility. Perhaps they observe a ritual or two each week and occasionally attend the synagogue. They also have a devotion to family and a high sense of human dignity in dealing with others. Compared to the emptiness of many modern lives, that is praiseworthy. But this level of concern will not make our religion come alive or long keep its community vital. The resources are there for possible great accomplishments—but the future is as likely to lead to somnolence and sterility.

By itself, the middle may enable Judaism to endure but, if that is to mean more than recognizable continuity, it must have leadership from outside. And that is what makes the role of the committed minority critical for our future.

The Need for a Liberal Jewish Elite

My hope for American Jewry is based on the recent spontaneous, grass roots rise of Jews who are deeply devoted to Judaism. Their commitment, for all its faltering experimentalism, has led to acts of learning, observance, ethics, and piety and these characterize it as a spiritual elite.

Dedicated Jews are most easily visible in European-style Orthodoxy. In that Jewish way one's clothes and hair and demeanor instantly announce one's divorce from society and distance from the rest of the Jewish community.

In modern Orthodoxy, the believing few are less withdrawn. They do prefer to cluster in communities—in recent years in suburban areas—which can give them institutional and neighborhood support.

The committed non-Orthodox Jews are not quickly spotted for

they continue to live much as they did before they started on their Jewish search. They are most easily seen in the *chavurot* where devotion has triumphed over time's erosion of the group's early excitement and idealism.

In greater number dedicated liberal Jews are to be found as isolated selves pursuing a lonely way amid their largely indifferent Jewish communities. But I know that they exist, that they are of all ages and stations, and that almost no community is without them. Wherever I have been and spoken of this phenomenon people are surprised that others know what they have privately experienced. And they are delighted to discover that there are numbers who share their Jewish dedication.

These liberal Jews want to be Jews for themselves. Of course, that also means for their children if they have any. But note the wording. In their case the usual motives for Jewish activity are reversed. Most of us practice some aspects of Judaism for the sake of our children—who quickly get the message that Judaism is not really for sophisticated adults. The newly concerned Jews are involved with Judaism primarily for their own spiritual welfare. They also hope it will become part of their children's lives as the next generation seeks to model itself after its parents.

A similar shift of values applies to the many other motives which power contemporary Jewish life. These Jews attend synagogue not because of the social contacts, or to keep up appearances, or the rabbi's personality, but because a believing Jew needs a community to pray and study with. They participate in Jewish community activity not because everyone expects it, or to maintain their social status, or because they enjoy power and prestige, but because they have a Jewish obligation to help other Jews.

I do not mean to imply that such devoted liberal Jews are our new "saints," filling every hour with ritual and study, or even that they follow a well-defined pattern of how to live a more significantly Jewish life. In my experience, they are as filled with doubts as with certainties. Like typical liberals, they are more at the beginning of a way than anywhere near its goal. What they importantly share is the will to make their Judaism the core of their existence and then let its influence flow out to all else that they do. In my theological language, they have linked their very selves to the Jewish people and its Covenant with God. They are fashioning the liberal Jewish elite which I hope will one day move the Jewish middle to greater Jewish dedication.

Consider the effect on a synagogue with a sizable minority of such Jews. At present, most synagogue decisions are made with one eye on the irascible minority who grumble that the congregation already makes too many demands and is "becoming Orthodox." The threat of their resignations is enough to make most boards of trustees timid about intensifying their congregation's Jewish activities. But what if there were also a sizable, vocal group participating in the synagogue's programs not for as little Judaism as they could manage but seeking better ways to serve their personal Jewish needs? Would they not require their board to stop thinking defensively about exercising leadership for Judaism, and, instead, to envision the synagogue's Jewish role in a more creative, activist fashion?

Think for a moment of the effect of such a group on the rabbi's role. As it is, with the bulk of congregational members ambivalent about their religion, the rabbi is forced to merchandise Judaism. Members must constantly be sold ideas or practices as "good for them." The rabbi must continually show through effective personal demonstration or programed event why they ought to keep coming back for more. The burden is overwhelming for the task is impossible. No wonder rabbis and congregations suffer so. But if the congregation contained a significant minority already committed to Judaism, Jews who shared the rabbi's faith in their own way and who were serious about their observance, the rabbi could stop apologizing for Judaism and be the teacher/model through whom it spoke for itself. I believe such a dedicated minority could become the critical mass by which the bulk of a congregation could be moved to greater Jewish dedication—and perhaps then the surrounding Jewish community as well. For that is how groups make progress.

And Where Are You in This Picture?

I have written this book because I would like to enlist you for the liberal Jewish elite. I am convinced the future of American Judaism is tied to the fate of its religious liberalism, so I have tried here to make its message clear. To be sure, I have dealt only with the intellectual side of being a devoted liberal Jew. There are many fine resources available to help you determine what you might now do. It is my hope that thinking more deeply about your Judaism will deepen your dedication and strengthen your resolve. If that only makes you a more steadfast member of the Jewish community, that is already a Jewish accomplishment. More helpful for the realization of our Jewish dreams would be your decision to make your Judaism the very core of your being. From there a blend of Jewish search and action would gradually flow into everything you do. If all of us who care this way and now cannot easily find one another would reach out to the others who feel for Judaism as deeply as we do, a new, effective religious force would be introduced into liberal Judaism. At the least, it would counterbalance the assimilation and inertia which, unopposed, debilitate our community life. But it might also lead our community in the creation of a vital American Jewish liberal spirituality. Such hopes are not grandiose for a people with our experience. Their realization depends upon the will of individuals; the Messianic Age begins with you.

AFTERWORD

Somewhere in the course of writing these pages I realized that I was engaged in fulfilling a childhood vow. Again and again in religious school and at services I had the sense that Judaism could not be as confused and incoherent as it was being presented to me. In exasperation I said to myself that if I could ever find out what it was all about I would try to explain it better than it had been explained to me.

With this volume I complete a trilogy in which, apparently, I have tried to make good on that promise. *Understanding Judaism* (UAHC) seeks to communicate to young teenagers the same Jewish ideas dealt with in this volume. *Choices in Modern Jewish Thought* (Behrman House) introduces college students to contemporary Jewish philosophy. And in *Liberal Judaism* I have tried to bridge the gap between the academic and lay levels of thinking about Judaism. I can now leave the task of clarification to others who will bring their special gifts to this unending, important task.

> R. Giddal said in the name of Rav, "Whence do we learn that an oath may be taken to fulfill a precept? From the verse (Psalm 119:106), 'I have sworn and confirmed it, to observe your righteous ordinances'." (Ned. 7b–8a)

To which I now add in thankfulness Psalm 119, verse 108:

נִדְבוֹת פִּי רְצֵה־נָא יְהוָה וּמִשְׁפָּטֶיךָ לַמְּדֵנִי

Accept, O *Adonai*, the free-will offerings of my mouth and continue to teach me Your ordinances.